BROKEN HARMONY

BROKEN HARMONY

SHAKESPEARE AND
THE POLITICS OF
MUSIC

JOSEPH M. ORTIZ

CORNELL UNIVERSITY PRESS
Ithaca and London

Copyright © 2011 by Cornell University

All rights reserved. Except for brief quotations in a review, this book, or parts thereof, must not be reproduced in any form without permission in writing from the publisher. For information, address Cornell University Press, Sage House, 512 East State Street, Ithaca, New York 14850.

First published 2011 by Cornell University Press

Printed in the United States of America

Library of Congress Cataloging-in-Publication Data
Ortiz, Joseph M., 1972–
  Broken harmony : Shakespeare and the politics of music / Joseph M. Ortiz.
    p. cm.
  Includes bibliographical references and index.
  ISBN 978-0-8014-4931-4 (cloth : alk. paper)
 1. Shakespeare, William, 1564–1616—Knowledge—Music. 2. Shakespeare, William, 1564–1616—Criticism and interpretation. 3. Music in literature. I. Title.
  PR3034.O78   2011
  822.3'3—dc22   2010035502

Cornell University Press strives to use environmentally responsible suppliers and materials to the fullest extent possible in the publishing of its books. Such materials include vegetable-based, low-VOC inks and acid-free papers that are recycled, totally chlorine-free, or partly composed of nonwood fibers. For further information, visit our website at www.cornellpress.cornell.edu.

Cloth printing   10 9 8 7 6 5 4 3 2 1

For my parents,
George and Martha Ortiz

For twenty-five centuries, Western knowledge has tried to look upon the world. It has failed to understand that the world is not for the beholding. It is for hearing. It is not legible, but audible.

—Jacques Attali, *Noise: The Political Economy of Music*

"Do you agree?" asked Margaret. "Do you think music is so different to pictures?"

"I—I should have thought so, kind of," he said.

"So should I. Now, my sister declares they're just the same. We have great arguments over it. She says I'm dense; I say she's sloppy." Getting under way, she cried: "Now, doesn't it seem absurd to you? What *is* the good of the arts if they're interchangeable? What *is* the good of the ear if it tells you the same as the eye?"

—E. M. Forster, *Howards End*

Contents

List of Illustrations   *xi*
Acknowledgments   *xiii*

    Introduction: Disciplining Music   1

1. *Titus Andronicus* and the Production of Musical Meaning   18

2. "Her speech is nothing": Mad Speech and the Female Musician   45

3. Teaching Music: The Rule of Allegory   77

4. Impolitic Noise: Resisting Orpheus from *Julius Caesar* to *The Tempest*   142

5. Shakespeare's Idolatry: Psalms and Hornpipes in *The Winter's Tale*   180

6. The Reforming of Reformation: Milton's *A Maske*   213

Selected Bibliography   *243*
Index   *257*

ILLUSTRATIONS

1. Henry Peacham, *Minerva Britanna* (1612) — 7
2. "The Temple of Music," Robert Fludd, *Utriusque cosmi… historia* (1617) — 95
3. Title page from Thomas Morley, *A Plaine and Easie Introduction to Practicall Musicke* (1597) — 108
4. "A table containing all the usuall proportions," from Thomas Morley, *A Plaine and Easie Introduction to Practicall Musicke* (1597) — 112
5. "A generall Table comprehending two parts in one," from William Bathe, *A Briefe Introduction to the Skill of Song* (1596) — 117
6. "Gladius musicus," from William Bathe, *A Briefe Introduction to the Skill of Song* (1596) — 118

❦ Acknowledgments

The ideas contained in this book have had a long and enjoyable history. At Yale my interests in Renaissance literature and music were guided and nurtured by Annabel Patterson, Heather James, Cyrus Hamlin, and Jeremy Lanni. Harold Bloom read and approved my earliest foray into the subject of music and Ovid in Shakespeare. At Princeton my many discussions with Michael Goldman, Nigel Smith, and Andrew Feldherr made the work of research both exhilarating and productive. Lawrence Danson was an ideal mentor, reading my work with the perfect blend of toughness and encouragement. Thomas P. Roche, whose wit and shrewdness is outstripped only by his kindness, remains to this day my inspiration as a teacher.

Many people gave useful comments and suggestions as I was writing this book. For their wisdom and encouragement I wish to thank Carolyn Abbate, Frederick Ahl, Oliver Arnold, Linda Phyllis Austern, Leonard Barkan, J. K. Barret, Brett de Bary, Jonathan Bate, Jeff Dolven, Ross Duffin, Leslie Dunn, Gabriel Egan, Alan Farmer, Wes Folkerth, Diana Fuss, Robert Gemmett, Genelle Gertz-Robinson, Wendy Heller, Gail Holst-Warhaft, Jean Howard, Claudia Johnson, David Scott Kastan, Paul Kelleher, Johanna Kramer, Albert Labriola, David Lindley, Kathleen Lynch, Richard McCoy, Earl Miner, Jessie Ann Owens, Anna Parkinson, Linda Levy Peck, Helen Petrovsky, Stephen Stallcup, Rachel Trubowitz, Jennifer Waldron, and Amanda Eubanks Winkler. I am especially grateful to William Kennedy and Bruce R. Smith, whose generous feedback during the later stages of this book improved it considerably.

A Hyde fellowship from Princeton University allowed me to spend a productive year conducting research at the British Library. A postdoctoral fellowship at Cornell University's Society for the Humanities was instrumental in honing my argument. A Dr. Nuala Gann Drescher Affirmative Action fellowship provided a timely leave during which I finished the book. The Folger Institute, on more than one occasion, generously supported my participation in its seminars; the Folger's ongoing commitment to bringing together musicologists, historians, and literary critics has made it a model of interdisciplinary support. Finally, a timely research grant from Safelight Security Advisors (Providence, Rhode Island) helped to make publication of this book possible.

At Cornell University Press, I have been fortunate to work with Peter Potter, who has been an enthusiastic editor, and with Susan Specter and Marie Flaherty-Jones, who have given much care to the final manuscript. Parts of this book have been previously published. A version of chapter 1 appeared as "Martyred Signs: *Titus Andronicus* and the Production of Musical Sympathy" in *Shakespeare* 1 (June 2005). A version of chapter 6 appeared as "'The Reforming of Reformation': Theatrical, Ovidian, and Musical Figuration in Milton's Maske" in *Milton Studies* 44, edited by Albert C. Labriola, copyright 2005. I am grateful for permission to reprint.

Finally, I wish to thank my parents, who gave me books and music as early as I can remember, and Paul S. Hinkle Jr., whose unflagging support and encouragement have meant more to me than either words or music can say.

BROKEN HARMONY

Introduction
Disciplining Music

Among Shakespeare's critics of music, few are as prescient as Portia in *The Merchant of Venice*. At the climax of the play's famous casket scene, as Bassanio is about to choose the casket that holds her portrait, Portia commands a musical performance while deftly deconstructing its effect on her audience:

> Let music sound while he doth make his choice.
> Then if he lose he makes a swanlike end,
> Fading in music. That the comparison
> May stand more proper, my eye shall be the stream
> And wat'ry deathbed for him. He may win,
> And what is music then? Then music is
> Even as the flourish when true subjects bow
> To a new-crownèd monarch.
>   (3.2.43–50)[1]

This is a remarkable moment, not least because it is one of the few instances in Shakespeare in which a description of music precedes a musical

---

1. All quotations of Shakespeare's works are from *The Norton Shakespeare,* ed. Stephen Greenblatt (New York: W. W. Norton, 1997).

performance instead of following it. At the same time, the passage seems to strike a note of insincerity, suggesting as it does that "swanlike" music and royal "flourishes" are indistinguishable. After all, we might ask, who but the most foolish listener would confuse the meaning of a lilting, melancholic song with that of a trumpet fanfare? The question is rhetorical—until we ask, why should a trumpet fanfare signify royalty? Or, what exactly makes a song melancholic? Which aspect of music is responsible for its emotional import? What are we doing when we use particular words—"swanlike," "fading," "lilting," "dying," "martial," "merry"—to describe music? When is music misunderstood? If dwelled on, these questions needle at our assumptions about music, just as they needle at the longer, more popular speech about music at the end of *The Merchant of Venice*. While there is no shortage of grand, unifying theories about music in the Renaissance that attempt to answer these questions, Portia instead chooses to point out music's promiscuous ability to sustain an infinite number of verbal meanings. *What is music then?* The question denies the possibility of musical meaning even as it calls for it. For all its apparent simplicity, Portia's speech puts forth the radical idea that music is *always* subject to the vagaries of its listeners, and that any legibility claimed for music ultimately derives from the context of its performance or from the discursive sense of its visual and verbal representations. Musical meaning, in this way, always comes from the outside.

This book aims to recover the multiplicity of ideas about music in Renaissance England, and to argue that Shakespeare is extremely skeptical about the claims to authority made on their behalf. To a modern set of ears that have been trained to hear music as inherently expressive, the early debates over music may seem strange or arcane. This sense of unfamiliarity is aided by the fact that the history of Western music has often been presented as a steady narrative of progression, either as a development from outmoded theories of cosmology to more enlightened ideas about rhetoric and acoustics, or as an evolution from labyrinthine polyphony to the expressive, emotionally nuanced forms of madrigal and opera.[2] Yet, as is often the case, the situation on the ground is much more complex. The older, scholastic theories about music continued to exert a powerful influence throughout the Renaissance, long after their scientific foundations had been debunked. One of the reasons for this is that mathematical and philosophical definitions of music are often a strong antidote to the nagging sense that music is unintelligible,

---

2. One of the most straightforward expositions of this version of the history of music also identifies it as expressly English. See Wilfrid Mellers, *Harmonious Meeting: A Study of the Relationship between English Music, Poetry and Theatre, c. 1600–1900* (London: Dobson Books, 1965).

especially in the face of evidence that music can accommodate an infinite number of meanings. In this respect, the hybridity of musical writing in Renaissance England does not reflect confusion over scientific facts so much as it constitutes an emphatic challenge to the radical promiscuity of musical experience. At the heart of this conflict is a deeply rooted concern over language's ability to translate sensuous experience and render it meaningful. Shakespeare's plays, with unusual frequency, exploit the gap between the *logos* of meaningful language and the *materia* of musical sound, and in doing so they frame the early modern debates over music as an ideological contest between textual and sensuous authorities. In his most skeptical moments, Shakespeare seems to suggest that music is nothing like a language.

The idea that Shakespeare drives a wedge between music and language has rarely been fashionable. When Richmond Noble commented in 1923 on the "absolute dramatic propriety" of music in Shakespeare's plays, he set the tone for generations of later critics who found it perfectly reasonable that Shakespeare would put music in the service of drama and poetry, not the other way around.[3] From this point of view, music is always cooperative and Shakespearean drama is exemplary because it deftly uses music to enhance the text of the play: Gertrude tells us that Ophelia is mad, and the wilting music that the audience hears a few lines later makes us think (or feel) that Ophelia is indeed mad. Somewhat differently, in what has become the most frequently cited work on English Renaissance music and poetry, John Hollander proposed that Shakespeare developed original ideas about music, worthy of inclusion in the history of Renaissance musical thought.[4] Here as well, the experience of musical sound was considered extraneous: Shakespeare's ideas about music were to be found in the plays' poetry, not in their musical performances, which could largely be explained away in terms of theatrical convention. Poetic language, not the stage, was ideally suited to work out and articulate the complex set of issues and questions raised by theorists of music. Although there has been groundbreaking work on the cultural effects of sound in Renaissance England, most notably in books by Bruce Smith in 1999 and Wes Folkerth in 2002, Shakespeare criticism has been slow to relinquish a conventional, literary approach to music.[5] Even a work like Ross Duffin's impressive *Shakespeare's Songbook,* which meticulously attempts to

---

3. Richmond Noble, *Shakespeare's Use of Song* (Oxford: Oxford University Press, 1923), 14.
4. See John Hollander, *The Untuning of the Sky: Ideas of Music in English Poetry 1500–1700* (1961; repr., Princeton, NJ: Princeton University Press, 1993). References are to the 1993 edition.
5. Bruce R. Smith, *The Acoustic World of Early Modern England: Attending to the O-Factor* (Chicago: University of Chicago Press, 1999), and Wes Folkerth, *The Sound of Shakespeare* (London: Routledge, 2002). A work that brilliantly unsettles assumptions about the relationship between music, sound, and

reconstruct what Shakespeare's audiences might have actually heard, gives a nod in its opening paragraph to the idea that "the relation between poetry and music is as old as poetry itself."[6]

Part of the reason that music's kinship with poetry has so often been taken for granted is that Renaissance poets themselves had a tendency to overstate the point. When George Puttenham begins his *Arte of English Poesie* with the claim that poetry "may be termed a musical speech or utterance," he puts forth a definition of music that is repeated several times over the course of the treatise, and which becomes a commonplace in almost every manual of poetry in the period.[7] Yet even poets have their biases. Puttenham's decision to treat music as though it were a form of rhetoric may partly stem from his belief that poetry can—and should—be learned through a systematic process. Likewise, when the poet and composer Thomas Campion writes that "what Epigrams are in Poetrie, the same are Ayres in musicke," he may be alluding to his efforts (which he describes elsewhere) to apply prosodic theory to musical composition. Or he may be attempting to raise his musical status by aligning it with classical authorities, as he explicitly does a few sentences later: "Ayres have both their Art and pleasure, and I will conclude of them as the Poet did in his censure, of *Catullus* the Lyricke, and *Vergil* the Heroicke writer."[8] For all his deftness with analogies, even Campion knows that a musical effect in poetry is not the same thing as music. This is not to say that composers were not influenced by developments in poetry, and vice versa. There have been many fine studies of the generic interaction between music and poetry in Renaissance England, but this book does not aim to be one of them.[9] Rather, I am interested in the rhetorical, textual, and theatrical methods by which music is made to *seem* like language (or, in some cases,

---

language, although in a different period, is Bruce W. Holsinger, *Music, Body, and Desire in Medieval Culture* (Stanford: Stanford University Press, 2001).

6. Ross W. Duffin, *Shakespeare's Songbook* (New York: W. W. Norton, 2004), 11. The quotation is from the book's foreword by Stephen Orgel.

7. George Puttenham, *The Art of English Poesy* (1589), ed. Frank Whigham and Wayne A. Rebhorn (Ithaca, NY: Cornell University Press, 2007), 98.

8. Thomas Campion, *A Booke of Ayres* (1601). Cited in Thomas Campion, *A New Way of Making Fowre Parts in Counterpoint*, ed. Christopher R. Wilson (Aldershot, UK: Ashgate, 2003), 1.

9. See Henry Tompkins Kirby-Smith, *The Celestial Twins: Poetry and Music through the Ages* (Amherst: University of Massachusetts Press, 2000); Diane McColley, *Poetry and Music in Seventeenth-Century England* (Cambridge: Cambridge University Press, 1997); Louise Schleiner, *The Living Lyre in English Verse from Elizabeth through the Restoration* (Columbia: University of Missouri Press, 1984); Elise Bickford Jorgens, *The Well-Tun'd Word: Musical Interpretations of English Poetry, 1597–1651* (Minneapolis: University of Minnesota Press, 1982); James Anderson Winn, *Unsuspected Eloquence: A History of the Relations between Poetry and Music* (New Haven, CT: Yale University Press, 1981), 122–93; John Stevens, *Music and Poetry in the Early Tudor Court* (Cambridge: Cambridge University Press, 1979); Bruce Pattison, *Music and Poetry of the English Renaissance* (London: Methuen, 1948).

seem alien from it), and the cultural and political work performed by such acts of translation. Part of the reason for this interest is the fact that Shakespeare and Milton, the two writers explored in this book, are themselves less inclined to accept unconditionally the premise that music can be translated into words. Ever conscious of the generic effects of their work, Shakespeare and Milton are keenly interested in the ideological or religious motives that underpin theories of art, including music. Shakespeare, in particular, instead of aspiring to a "concent" model of art in which dramatic unity is the terminus ad quem, repeatedly stages contradictory versions of music that highlight its resistance to verbal and visual forms. In doing so, he exposes a fault line in the conventional interpretations of music, which early modern writers are increasingly at pains to cover up.

In the following pages I document the ways in which Shakespeare denaturalizes his culture's presumptions about music, both in the text of the plays and in their musical performances, and I will argue that the plays reveal connections between theories of music and specific ideological ends. In this respect, the word "politics" in my book's title has a double sense. First, the discursive and textual methods that are applied to music in order to make it yield particular meanings constitute a recognizable system of interpretation that is continually in need of authorization and legitimization. This is a "politics of interpretation" that is enforced both by texts and individuals and that is observable whenever a particular idea is felt to be orthodox or unorthodox.[10] Second, arguments about music often demarcate political and cultural standpoints, particularly in the case of institutions whose power is invested in linguistic and textual systems. This idea that theories of music are driven by ideology may seem odd given the commonplace nature of musical definitions in the Renaissance, many of which are echoed in Shakespeare's plays. However, a sign of power is often its ability to work undetected. Hence, the "true subject" imagined by Shakespeare's Portia may be expressing her deeply felt sense of loyalty when she bows before the monarch, or she may be acting carefully to avoid recrimination from an untested, "new-crowned" leader. In a similar way, the trumpet flourish that accompanies the same event may be recognized as a natural sign of royal authority, but this understanding is just as likely to be the product of convention, education, or—depending on how broadly one considers the term—coercion. An effective politics of government sometimes requires not looking too deeply into the hearts of its

---

10. See Lydia Goehr, "'Music has no meaning to speak of': On the Politics of Musical Interpretation," in *The Interpretation of Music: Philosophical Essays*, ed. Michael Krausz, 177–90 (Oxford: Clarendon, 1993).

subjects. And a stable politics of music may require not attending too deeply to what listeners actually *hear*.

Two examples will serve as a preliminary illustration of the way in which political ends can instruct a model of musical interpretation. The first is from Henry Peacham's *Minerva Brittana* (1612), in which England's conquest of Ireland is figured through the image of an Orphic harp (figure 1). The text below the emblem reads as follows:

> While I lay bathed in my native blood,
> And yeelded nought save harsh, & hellish soundes:
> And save from Heaven, I had no hope of good,
> Thou pittiedst (Dread Soveraigne) my woundes,
> Repair'dst my ruine, and with Ivorie key,
> Didst tune my stringes, that slackt or broken lay.
>
> Now since I breathed by thy Roiall hand,
> And found my concord, by so smooth a tuch,
> I give the world abroade to understand,
> Ne're was the musick of old Orpheus such,
> As that I make, by meane (Deare Lord) of thee,
> From discord drawne, to sweetest unitie.[11]

The dedication at the top of the page is addressed to King James, and the imagined speaker of the emblem text is Ireland herself (*Hibernica respublica*). Thus, as an allegory for royal power, the narrative meaning of the emblem is straightforward: the monarch, in the person of James, transforms the violence of civil strife in Ireland into political harmony. Because the scene of rebellion is so devastating, the peace that ensues (whether voluntary or not) is interpreted as a sign of James's unique status in history: "Ne're was the musick of old Orpheus such." The emblem makes convenient use of the image of the harp, which is both the national symbol for Ireland and a symbol of musical concord.

Less obvious is the way in which Peacham's emblem negotiates the distinction between musical sound and an allegorical, visual conception of music. The first three lines of the text evoke a sense of intense corporeal and acoustic experience: the "native blood" and the "harsh and hellish

---

11. Henry Peacham, *Minerva Britanna* (1612), in *English Emblem Books,* ed. John Horden (Yorkshire: Scolar Press, 1969), 5:45.

FIGURE 1. "Poenitentia," from Henry Peacham, *Minerva Britanna* (1612). By permission of the Folger Shakespeare Library.

soundes" are both produced and experienced by the poem's speaker. While these phrases admit a symbolic reading, their direct indexing to somatic experience reminds the reader that political rebellion can be literally noisy and that its effects can (and will) be felt on the body. In the next several lines, however, the experience of actual sound is displaced by a model of music that is more metaphorical and that makes heavy use of verbal puns. For example, the "stringes" that the king "tunes" at line 6 at first suggest harp strings, but the implied, more relevant meaning is "heartstrings," as a metonymy for the Irish political subject who is brought back under the protective arm of English rule. The other terms in the poem— "key," "slackt," "broken," "concord," "meane," "discord," "sweet," "unitie"—have specific meanings for musical composition, but their practical sense has little bearing on the emblem's political meaning. They call for an allegorical reading, not an acoustic one. In this respect, Peacham's emblem instructs its audience on two points. First, James orders the political state in a way that resembles musical consonance. Second, for musical "consonance" to be understood correctly, it must be read through the metaphors of its verbal description rather than simply heard or recalled in the ear. To become embroiled in the experience of musical sound, the emblem suggests, is to return to the noisy, bloody battlefield, where individual desires run amok until they are struck down ("tuned") by an uncompromising sovereign.

In effect, the emblem teaches its reader to read the image of the harp *as* an image, as well as a representation of Jacobean power. Once educated, the reader might then notice that the harp has exactly ten strings, corresponding neatly to the Pythagorean decad with its relevant musical symbolism. In this way the emblem employs the conventional rhetoric of Renaissance *musica speculativa,* the large body of writing that seeks to explain music's place in the cosmos and that dominates most academic writing about music through the seventeenth century. Peacham's emblem shares with speculative music many of its rhetorical strategies, such as the appeal to literal puns, the repeated emphasis on unity, the idealization of a kind of music that has never been heard before, and the subtle displacement of actual sound. It is this last tactic—the suppression of sound—that I will draw special attention to in chapter 3, but it is useful here as a reminder of the stakes involved in distinguishing performed music from music in poetry. When the subject of music in literature is brought up, the question is often asked: Are we talking about "actual" music or musical metaphors? By answering this question definitively from the outset, we overlook the rhetorical advantage gained by eliding the difference between the two. In fact, a careful bait-and-switch game between musical sound and visual allegory can often help illustrate a philosophical or political point, while making that point seem grounded in the real, observable workings of the physical world. The sight of music shapes our listening.

My second example also reflects the desire to ground music in the natural and visible world, but it does not sidestep the experience of sound. In *The Feminine Monarchie* (1609), one of the most imaginative pieces of natural philosophy to come out of Renaissance England, Charles Butler transcribes the sound of a beehive as a musical composition. Using systems of musical notation and solmization (the practice of using syllables to denote the notes of the scale) that were only recently becoming standardized, Butler carefully categorizes the various sounds made by bees and associates them with particular activities and meanings:

> When the prime swarm is gon... the next Prince, when shee perceiveth a competent number to bee fledg and reddy, beginneth to tune, in hir treble voice, a moornful and begging note, as if shee did pray hir

Queene-mother to let them goe. Unto which voice, if the Queene vouchsafe to reply, tuning hir *Base* to the yung Princes *Treble*... then doth shee consent.... And as the Queenes voice is a grant, so hir silence is a flat denyall; the Proverb heere hath noe place: (*Qui tacet consentire videtur.*) For without this Consent there is noe Consent.

This song being conteined within the compass of an *Eighth* (from *C-sol-fa-ut* to *C-sol-fa*) the Prince composeth hir part within the fowr upper Cliefs (*G, A, B, & C*) usually in triple mode, beginning with an od Minim in *G-sol-re-ut,* and tuning the rest of hir notes, whereof the first is a *Semibrief,* in *A-la-mi-re.* Sometime shee taketh a higher key, sounding the od *Minim* in *A-la-mi-re,* and the rest in *B-fa-b-mi.* Sometime, specially toward their coming forth, shee riseth yet higher, to *C-sol-fa,* holding the time of three or fowr *Semibriefs,* more or les. Nou and then shee beginneth in duple time, som two or three *Semibriefs,* but always endeth with *Minims* of the triple Mode.

The passage, which continues at length, is a remarkable display of technical specificity. Not only do the bees observe the voice structure of three- and four-part compositions (base, treble, mean); they also correctly hit on the various notes of the scale (C-sol-fa-ut) and observe regular time signatures and note values (semibreve, minim). Butler goes so far as to plot the various sounds made by the bees on a musical staff, and, lest anyone doubt that he intends this to be understood as actual music, in the later editions of the treatise he adds a *melissomelos:* a complete, four-part bees' madrigal that incorporates the figures and rhythms of his earlier transcriptions.[12]

For all his inventiveness, Butler is not a musical hack. In his *Principles of Musik* (1636), a painstakingly researched compendium of rules governing musical theory and composition, he shows himself to be extremely well versed in both speculative and practical music. Butler's peculiarity lies in the extreme lengths to which he goes to establish a natural foundation for musicological principles. The Western diatonic scale of seven notes, to which Butler devotes the entire second chapter of his *Principles,* is given an apiarian etymology in *The Feminine Monarchie.* Other music theorists had asserted the naturalness of the diatonic scale, and other philosophers had compared the buzzing of bees

---

12. Charles Butler, *The Feminine Monarchie; or, A Treatise concerning bees and the due ordering of them* (London, 1609). The quotation is taken from the 1634 edition. The musical context of Butler's treatise is discussed at length in Linda Phyllis Austern, "Nature, Culture, Myth, and the Musician in Early Modern England," *Journal of the American Musicological Society* 51 (1998): 1–47. See also James Pruett, "Charles Butler—Musician, Grammarian, Apiarist," *Musical Quarterly* 49 (1963): 498–509.

to music, but Butler proves the case with unusual specificity. His queen bee does not merely emit a sound *like* a musical tone: she sings G-sol-re-ut. Accordingly, sounds that do not correspond to a specific note are implied to be rude and meaningless noise, ready to be discarded by a human musician who can tell the difference. Equally important, Butler's treatise asserts the idea that music *can* be transcribed, that it can be fully realized and preserved in a printed text. By identifying the music of bees and representing it on a musical staff, he gives a scientific demonstration of the point, stated explicitly in his *Principles*, that music is a form of writing.[13]

Other early modern writers had used the music of bees to paint a picture of the ideal political state, in which monarchs, senators, aldermen, soldiers, and sentries each carry out their assigned tasks in concert with the appropriate music.[14] To the extent that Butler's treatise does not pursue this line of thought, it is not "political" in the narrow sense. It is, however, ideological. The idea that music is meaningful—and fully capable of being translated into text—was not accepted by everyone, including many Reformist writers, who characterized certain types of music as meaningless noise comparable to the bleating of animals. Butler's ability to find music in the animal world thus constitutes a direct challenge to contemporary attacks on music. At the same time, his obsession with systems of notation gives evidence of his belief that written language is fully capable of ordering and making sense of the natural world. Twenty-five years after *The Feminine Monarchie,* Butler published his *English Grammar* (1634), in which he developed an intricate system of phonetic spelling that attempted to document fully the sound of the English language. Seen from this perspective, sensuous experience is not to be rejected, but transcribed. And music, far from being meaningless sound, is very much like a language.

Throughout this book I will adduce similar examples that throw into relief the ideological and cultural presumptions behind theories of music. Doing so will often require looking beyond the canonical works of music theory and composition that frequently serve as the introduction to histories of Renaissance musical thought. Thus, in addition to treatises on bees, I look at emblem books, poetry manuals, Reformist attacks on the theater, personal accounts of theatergoing, handbooks on practical music, and classical mythographies for evidence of the rich heterogeneity of ideas about music in

---

13. Charles Butler, *The Principles of Musik in Singing and Setting* (London, 1636), Preface, sig. ¶¶r.
14. See, for example, Edward Topsell, *The Historie of Serpents* (London, 1608), 68–69, discussed in Austern, "Nature, Culture, Myth."

early modern England. What this book will seldom do is look at particular musical compositions for the purpose of performing a musicological analysis of them. The idea, for example, that discovering the original musical setting for a ballad in *As You Like It* may yield important clues to the play's meaning may seem intuitive, but only because we live in a musical culture weaned (if sometimes indirectly) on Wagnerian opera and Beethoven symphonies, in which the difference between a leap of a minor third and a leap of a major third can sometimes mean the difference between redemption and the end of the world. Early modern listeners did not, on the whole, share this expectation of music.[15] Thus, rather than approach music in Shakespeare's plays as a code to be deciphered, I examine the ideological implications of musical codes themselves. This critical sensitivity to practices of musical interpretation is one that the plays demonstrate with unusual regularity, and it often reveals itself in the question that Shakespeare's characters find themselves asking over and over again: "What does this music *mean*?"

This last question provides the starting point for chapter 1, which addresses the radical promiscuity of musical meaning in early modern England. While Renaissance theorists of poetry often sought to align music and language, Reformists tended to stress music's incoherence. Shakespeare's *Titus Andronicus* speaks to both sides of the debate by constructing a system of musical signs for the theater, while exposing the arbitrariness of this system. Chapter 2 continues the exploration of music's promiscuity, focusing on the convergence between attacks on music and early modern representations of women. Renaissance writers frequently associated music and women as producers of unintelligible sound, and this anxiety drives the attempt to transform music and women into "speaking pictures." *Hamlet* and *The Rape of Lucrece* document the suppression of musical sound and the female voice, an aesthetic move that becomes a hallmark of Romantic versions of Shakespeare. If early modern Protestantism tends to stress music's meaninglessness, then Neoplatonic theory presents itself as an antidote to music's apparent inscrutability. Accordingly, in chapters 3 and 4 I analyze the tendency to allegorize music, noting the common ground occupied by Ovidian mythography and *musica speculativa*. Shakespeare frequently links the moralized Ovid and Renaissance *musica speculativa* in the plays in order to shed light on their

---

15. This is not to say that composers did not occasionally develop rhythmic or harmonic figures that became associated with particular moods or scenarios. For example, in her study of seventeenth-century stage music, Amanda Eubanks Winkler shows how a common set of musical figures came to be associated with madness and melancholy. See *O Let Us Howle Some Heavy Note: Music for Witches, the Melancholic, and the Mad on the Seventeenth-Century English Stage* (Bloomington: Indiana University Press, 2006).

shared political and ideological interests, although he also demonstrates the power of performed sound to disrupt Neoplatonic, moralizing representations of music. Finally, in the two closing chapters I explore the debates over music in the context of the seventeenth-century discourse of idolatry. The associations between music, magic, and superstitious belief reach a high pitch in Jacobean England, prompting ingenious defenses of music and theatricality in *The Winter's Tale* and Milton's *A Maske*.

The proximity of Ovidian allusion to musical rhetoric in the plays reveals a perhaps unexpected aspect of Shakespeare's representation of the politics of music. With unusual regularity, Shakespeare turns to Ovid when he scrutinizes assumptions about music, and Ovidian poetry often provides the imaginative key to Shakespeare's reorganization of the relationship between music and language. (Indeed, one of the earlier drafts of this book included Ovid in its title.) There are several reasons why Ovid would have been an attractive source for Shakespeare's exploration of musical meaning. First, Ovidian poetry, like music, is at the center of many Renaissance debates over the validity of certain kinds of knowledge. As I mentioned above, the political and religious pressures that drive the allegorization of music in the Renaissance, thus curbing its sensuous appeal, also drive allegorizations of Ovid. For Shakespeare, music and Ovid uniquely challenge the authority of moralizing interpretations because they draw attention to their material and sensuous effects, independent of their representation in texts. Music resists language in ways that visual art does not, just as Ovid resists moralization in ways that Virgil does not. Shakespeare's foregrounding of music's sonorous texture and Ovidian polysemy can thus be seen as a strong challenge to ideological attempts to establish the primacy of textual knowledge. Second, and more important, Ovidian metamorphosis often has much to do with voice—or, more accurately, with the *loss* of voice. Several of Ovid's tragic figures—Philomela, Io, Niobe, Orpheus, Actaeon, Echo, Hecuba—experience transformation in the *Metamorphoses* as a crisis of enunciation, and all of them are evoked at crucial moments in Shakespeare's plays as examples of music's uneasy relationship to language and noise. This is an aspect of the works that criticism has rarely identified, much less theorized. While much scholarship in the last twenty-five years has established the centrality of Ovid to a dizzying number of Shakespearean topics, from humanism to poetic subjectivity to imperialism, it remains for this book to demonstrate the significance of Ovid for Shakespeare's musical thought.[16] If the theater

---

16. Two of the best examples of the extent of Shakespeare's Ovidianism are Lynn Enterline's *The Rhetoric of the Body from Ovid to Shakespeare* (Cambridge: Cambridge University Press, 2000) and

provided Shakespeare with an ideal laboratory to test conventional assumptions about music, then the *Metamorphoses* was surely his favorite theory book through which to articulate his findings.

Because the convergence of music and Ovid will be a common refrain in this book, a brief example at the outset will be worthwhile. In act 4 of *A Midsummer Night's Dream,* Hippolyta speaks for only the second time in the play, in a passage that is routinely cut from performance:

> I was with Hercules and Cadmus once
> When in a wood of Crete they bayed the bear
> With hounds of Sparta. Never did I hear
> Such gallant chiding; for besides the groves,
> The skies, the fountains, every region near
> Seemed all one mutual cry. I never heard
> So musical a discord, such sweet thunder.
> (4.1.109–15)

Here, Hippolyta's speech begins as a narrative account of what has happened ("I was") and ends as a statement of what almost never happens ("never did I hear," "I never heard"). As a description of music, Hippolyta's narrative ultimately breaks down into a series of contradictions and oxymora that confound musical terminology itself ("gallant chiding," "so musical a discord," "sweet thunder"), as if to suggest the idea of something that cannot be represented in language. In this respect, her words attest to language's inability to comprehend fully the memory of her previous experience, or even the experience of that experience. Thus, despite the extraordinary poetic appeal of Hippolyta's speech (would anyone deny that it "sounds" beautiful?), it gives us the almost certain impression that *we* are not hearing what she is hearing.

As an example of Ovidian allusion, Hippolyta's speech is not especially subtle. This is one of the few moments in the play in which Shakespeare gives his audience a glimpse of Theseus's "past life" in Ovid's poetry and Thomas North's Plutarch, where he is most famous as a chronic deserter of women.[17] In this respect, Hippolyta's fleeting allusion to Hercules and Crete

---

Heather James's *Shakespeare's Troy: Drama, Politics, and the Translation of Empire* (Cambridge: Cambridge University Press, 1997). The indispensable works on Shakespeare's Ovid remain Jonathan Bate's *Shakespeare and Ovid* (Oxford: Oxford University Press, 1993) and Leonard Barkan's *The Gods Made Flesh: Metamorphosis and the Pursuit of Paganism* (London: Yale University Press, 1986).

17. Both Ovid and North describe Theseus's exploits with Hercules, his disastrous affair with Ariadne in Crete, and Hercules' gift of Hippolyta (Antiopa) to Theseus. In his edition of the play,

calls to mind a version of Theseus that is starkly at odds with his role as the play's defender of marriage.[18] More important, by playing fast and loose with definitions of music, Hippolyta returns to the Ovidian scene of linguistic failure, which more than once in the *Metamorphoses* is exemplified by the sound of barking dogs. By calling the loud peals of hunting dogs "musical," Hippolyta inverts the idea of music as universal order and reminds us, as Ovid does, that the experience of music is fundamentally an acoustic event, dependent on the materiality of physical sound. This raises a number of difficult questions about the nature of music. For example, does the muffled sound of an orchestra heard from outside the concert hall count as music? Are the noisy echoes of a trumpet playing in a New York City subway station "musical"? Such questions are not intended to belie the metaphoricity of Hippolyta's speech: she is not saying that barking dogs and church polyphony actually *sound* the same to her (even if some of Shakespeare's fellow Londoners occasionally did). Nonetheless, her speech promotes the idea that the pleasure afforded by barking hounds, like the pleasure afforded by certain tonal intervals or harmonic progressions, is a supremely subjective and personal event. In this light, to call something "musical" is always to invite the charge of metaphor, if not outright repudiation. Hippolyta's words are proof of the fact that, centuries before a parent ever yelled at his or her teenage child for blasting Pearl Jam, the distinction between music and noise was hardly settled. Her speech is a manifesto for "hearing green," as Bruce Smith has put it—for listening to music as a purely sonorous event, independent of its legible, formal, or quantifiable aspects.[19]

Yet the impulse to quantify music is hard to shake. Arguing for the superiority of *his* hounds, Theseus appeals to a principle of intonation that portrays music as measurable and precise:

My hounds are bred out of the Spartan kind,
So flewed, so sanded; and their heads are hung
With ears that sweep away the morning dew,

Harold F. Brooks notes that some editors mistakenly read Hippolyta's "bayed the bear" as a reference to the Calydonian boar hunt, which Ovid has Theseus playing a part in, in book 8 of the *Metamorphoses. A Midsummer Night's Dream,* ed. Harold F. Brooks (London: Methuen, 1979).

18. Louis Montrose's reading of the play, which argues that Shakespeare's intertextuality undermines the play's propping up of patriarchy, is instructive here. See *The Purpose of Playing: Shakespeare and the Cultural Politics of the Elizabethan Theatre* (Chicago: University of Chicago Press, 1996), 109–205.

19. Bruce Smith, "Hearing Green," in *Reading the Early Modern Passions,* ed. Gail Kern Paster, Katherine Rowe, and Mary Floyd-Wilson, 147–68 (Philadelphia: University of Pennsylvania Press, 2004).

Crook-kneed, and dewlapped like Thessalian bulls,
Slow in pursuit, but matched in mouth like bells,
Each under each. A cry more tuneable
Was never holla'd to nor cheered with horn
In Crete, in Sparta, nor in Thessaly.
Judge when you hear.

(4.1.116–24)

Theseus's remark to Hippolyta to "judge" with her own ears indicates his confidence in his dogs and in the perceptibility of musical sound. (It is also a gentle command to refine her hearing in accordance with his.) Although Theseus misses the point of Hippolyta's speech—she does not really care about the pedigrees of hunting dogs—his response represents music as an ordered, intelligible signifying system. Hence, when Theseus uses the term "music" itself, its physical and metaphorical meanings are almost impossible to distinguish: "My love shall hear the music of my hounds.... We will, fair Queen, up to the mountain's top,/And mark the musical confusion/Of hounds and echo in conjunction" (103–8). Just as the cadences of his last two lines echo the sound he is describing ("confusion... conjunction"), Theseus implies that music is an aspect of poetry, capable of being represented and ordered in language. Like Butler's bees, the natural world according to Theseus needs only a human auditor who can discriminate between its musical and nonmusical sounds. The vantage point that he chooses for himself and Hippolyta—"up to the mountain's top"—indicates his tendency to abstract music and to observe it from afar, as well as his confidence in language's ontological elevation over music. Music, thus understood, becomes a sign of Theseus's authority: it is "the music of *my* hounds," he tells Hippolyta, that you will listen to from now on.[20]

Together, Hippolyta and Theseus offer two starkly different ways of listening to music, as well as two different ways of thinking about Shakespearean drama. On the one hand, music as a promiscuous form of sound is always dangerously close to noise, subject to the varying imaginations of its listeners. On the other hand, music's ability to function as a code makes it an appealing representation of reality itself, opaque only to those who are unable to appreciate or understand it. Criticism of Shakespeare has tended to favor the

---

20. This is Harley Granville-Barker's reading of the play, which, although regarded now as conservative, is instructive for the way in which it identifies Theseus with Shakespeare and makes Theseus the guarantor of the play's "tonal" integrity. See Harley Granville-Barker, *More Prefaces to Shakespeare,* ed. Edward M. Moore (Princeton, NJ: Princeton University Press, 1974), 6:112–25.

latter approach, either by reconstructing early systems of musical symbolism, or by attempting to reconstruct as much as possible early performances, as though sitting in one of Shakespeare's original audiences would answer many, if not all, questions about music's function in the plays.[21] While I do not want to downplay the important contribution these reconstructions make to our understanding of the Renaissance theater, I want to point out the ways in which Shakespeare insistently denaturalizes the habits of listening that these readings often presume—indeed, the ways in which Shakespeare often alienates his audience from their own habits of musical hearing, frustrating the impulse to quantify music and turn it into a sign.

In a 2004 article in the *New York Times,* the music critic and composer Edward Rothstein asks his reader to imagine hearing two musical works in a locked, utterly empty room: a Beethoven symphony and an Indian raga. The situation would clearly be going against the grain of modern educational approaches to music, he admits, since "to understand music, we have been taught, that room has to be unlocked, the windows opened and the world fully engaged." However, he notes, times change: "The appeal of a more abstract way of thinking about music may be growing. There is a search for timeless laws and principles . . . a renewed interest in the relationship between music and mathematics."[22] A recent stroll of mine through the science section of a local bookstore seemed to corroborate Rothstein's point. *Music and Mathematics: From Pythagoras to Fractals, This Is Your Brain on Music, The Math behind the Music, Musimathics*—the array of titles on display seemed to imply that Pythagoras may have been on the right track after all. While it is not my task to adjudicate the merits of this new musical research against other approaches to music, such as those in the humanities, the proliferation of books

---

21. Although the history of musical studies of Shakespeare is too long to list here, the following are exemplary. Edward W. Naylor, *Shakespeare and Music* (London: J. M. Dent, 1896; rev. 1931); Edward J. Dent, "Shakespeare and Music," in *A Companion to Shakespeare Studies,* ed. Harley Granville-Barker and G. B. Harrison, 137–62 (New York: Macmillan, 1934); J. S. Manifold, *The Music in English Drama from Shakespeare to Purcell* (London: Rockliff, 1956); John H. Long, *Shakespeare's Use of Music: The Final Comedies* (Gainesville: University of Florida Press, 1961); Gretchen Ludke Finney, *Musical Backgrounds for English Literature: 1580–1650* (New Brunswick, NJ: Rutgers University Press, 1962); F. W. Sternfeld, *Music in Shakespearean Tragedy* (London: Routledge, 1963). Since the 1990s scholarship has taken a more critical approach to musical symbolism, although the impulse to decode music is still strong. See, for example, Pierre Iselin, "Music and Difference: Elizabethan Stage Music and Its Reception," in *French Essays on Shakespeare and His Contemporaries,* ed. Jean-Marie Maguin and Michèle Willems, 96–113 (Newark: University of Delaware Press, 1995). For an overview of ideas about music and musical practice in the Renaissance, along with many readings of musical moments in the plays, see David Lindley, *Shakespeare and Music* (London: Thomson, 1996). This is a welcome addition to the field and indispensable for future work on the topic.

22. Edward Rothstein, "Deciphering the Grammar of Mind, Music and Math," *New York Times,* June 19, 2004.

on music and mathematics—and the fact that it is considered "news"—reminds us of the unstable place that music has historically held among the various disciplines. In the last twenty years the field of musicology itself, as Susan McClary has famously documented, has seen a radical, and not painless, shift from formalist studies to approaches to music that take into account gender and culture studies.[23] These disciplinary pangs do not represent mere philosophical differences but changing attitudes about what counts as authoritative forms of intellectual inquiry. Shakespeare's plays and poems, as I will show, inscribe a similar struggle between competing forms of authority in Renaissance England, and they fully participate in its development. To define music, we learn, is to mark the boundaries of knowledge itself.

---

23. Susan McClary, *Feminine Endings: Music, Gender, and Sexuality* (Minneapolis: University of Minnesota Press, 1991), 5–31.

Chapter 1

Titus Andronicus and the Production of Musical Meaning

> Such a lively song (now by this light)
> Yet never hearde I such another note.
> It was (thought me) so pleasant and so plaine,
> *Orphæus* harpe, was never halfe so sweete,
> *Tereu, Tereu,* and thus she gan to plaine,
> Most piteously, which made my hart to greeve.
>
> —George Gascoigne, *The Complaint of Philomene*

The debate over the meaning of music in the Renaissance begins not with bees, but with birds. Martin Luther, in commending music's ability to make nature comprehensible, cites birdsong as the best example of music that praises its divine Creator: "Music is still more wonderful in living things, especially birds, so that David, most musical of all kings and minstrel of God, in deepest wonder and spiritual exultation praised the astounding art and ease of the song of birds when he said in Psalm 104, 'By them the birds of the heaven have their habitation; they sing among the branches.'"[1] In a very different context, Gascoigne's *Complaint of Philomene* (1576) prefaces its adaptation of Ovid's Philomela with a fantastic meeting between the poem's speaker and the nightingale, whose musical warble ("Tereu") inspires great sympathy despite the speaker's ignorance of its verbal sense. In this way, the episode attests to music's supposed ability to evoke true sympathy in the absence of language. At the same time, in invoking the familiar trope of the nightingale as poetic eloquence, Gascoigne necessarily effaces the focus of Ovid's story, which reads more as a map of communicative *failures*. As Lynn Enterline has shown, Ovid's version of the

---

1. Martin Luther, *Symphoniae jucundae* (1538), trans. Ulrich S. Leupold, in *Luther's Works,* vol. 53 (Philadelphia: Fortress Press, 1965), cited in Piero Weiss and Richard Taruskin, *Music in the Western World: A History in Documents* (New York: Schirmer, 1984), 101.

TITUS ANDRONICUS AND THE PRODUCTION OF MUSICAL MEANING

myth—which ends abruptly at the moment of Philomela's transformation, thus cutting off the possibility of musical sublimation—demonstrates the utter "unspeakability" of the mutilated female, who can replicate the scene of sexual violence but not translate the experience of its horror.[2] Thus the attempt to find meaning in birdsong, whether by Luther or Gascoigne, requires turning a deaf ear to the alienating effect of nonverbal sound—an effect that Ovid is so fond of re-creating.

In this chapter, I argue that Shakespeare's *Titus Andronicus* returns to Ovid's Philomela in order to explore the possibility of meaning in music. Like Gascoigne, whose poem the play frequently echoes, Shakespeare evokes music as a privileged model of nonverbal communication. Unlike *The Complaint of Philomene,* however, *Titus* raises serious doubts about music's ability to impart understanding—or, more generally, to mean anything at all. Through the figure of Lavinia, *Titus* confronts the problem of a resonant body that must translate itself into language, all the while implying that music, like the mutilated woman, is in a constant state of dismemberment and inarticulateness. Against this radical "deconstruction" of music, the play offers the familiar rhetoric of *musica speculativa* as an antidote to meaningless. Yet Shakespeare denies this rhetoric any real persuasive power, at once by juxtaposing it with the overwhelming theatrical effect of Lavinia's bleeding body, but also by evoking several Ovidian models of voicelessness that undermine any sense of communal understanding. The Ovidian figures of Io, Actaeon, and Hecuba, memorable for their speechlessness in the *Metamorphoses,* might suggest possible ways of reading Lavinia after her mutilation, but Shakespeare reminds us that it is the utter untranslatability of their sound in Ovid's poem that marks their distance from the reader and reveals the poet's limits of representation. Thus, by producing a second Hecuba onstage, Shakespeare forecloses on a "sympathetic" reading of Lavinia in favor of highlighting the "noisiness" of her grotesque, hyperphysicalized body.[3] Counterintuitive as it may seem, music in *Titus* ultimately does not reveal itself as a compensatory voice for someone who has lost both hands and tongue; instead, it embodies the radical promiscuity that erupts when one's meaning is determined by another.

Reading *Titus* as a meditation on music's promiscuity—or, more unconventionally, as a kind of musical performance itself—allows us to reexamine

---

2. Lynn Enterline, *The Rhetoric of the Body from Ovid to Shakespeare* (Cambridge: Cambridge University Press, 2000), 5.
3. See Katherine A. Rowe, "Dismembering and Forgetting in *Titus Andronicus,*" *Shakespeare Quarterly* 45 (1994): 279–303. Similar to my argument that music's acoustic quality often intrudes on its conventional meanings in this play, Rowe notes how actual, physical hands in the play "obtrude their self-referential and figurative qualities, even (perhaps especially) when least appropriate" (285).

the signifying and affective economy of Shakespeare's theater. In order to produce intelligible meaning and "move" its audience, the theater relies on and validates a number of adjoining systems of aural and visual signification. In this respect, Susan McClary's observation that meaning in music is "kept afloat only because communities of people...agree collectively that [its] signs serve as valid currency" accurately describes how Shakespeare's stage participates in the construction of musical meaning even as it depends on a communally sanctioned system of musical signs to propel its own narrative.[4] (A trumpet flourish denoting the monarch is a paradigmatic example.) At the same time, Shakespeare's propensity to expose the seams of this system via Ovidian voicelessness puts him in dialogue with early modern critiques of music. In the next section, I discuss briefly the Renaissance debates over music's affective power, in order to show that Shakespeare's skepticism about musical sympathy has its historical analogue not in the massive corpus of Renaissance poetics, where the idea of aesthetic unity prevails, but in a strand of Reformist polemic that strongly suspects music's independence from language. The rest of the chapter addresses Shakespeare's deployment of music in *Titus,* showing how the play stages a series of increasingly ingenious and desperate acts of interpretation. In each case, the play reveals a nagging suspicion that will haunt the appearance of music in almost every Shakespearean play that follows: the suspicion that music is, in its most fundamental form, meaningless.[5]

"Whoryshe armonye": Musical Meaning in Early Modern England

In *The Praise of Music* (1586), John Case begins his chapter on music's "suavitie" by asserting that "poetrie...is but a part of Musicke, as *Plutarch* doth testifie."[6] Although the remark is conventional, Case's assertion of music's likeness to poetry is itself a consciously crafted defense against contemporary

---

4. Susan McClary, *Feminine Endings: Music, Gender, and Sexuality* (Minneapolis: University of Minnesota Press, 1991), 21.

5. The question of whether music is meaningful outside of its own formal structures has been the subject of vigorous debate among philosophers in the last thirty years. See Jenefer Robinson, *Deeper Than Reason: Emotion and Its Role in Literature, Music, and Art* (Oxford: Oxford University Press, 2005); Stephen Davies, *Musical Meaning and Expression* (Ithaca, NY: Cornell University Press, 1994); Peter Kivy, *The Corded Shell: Reflections on Musical Expression* (Princeton, NJ: Princeton University Press, 1980).

6. John Case, *The Praise of Musicke* (London, 1586), 37.

attacks on music's sensuous illegibility. The problem of musical signification had already been raised in Stephen Gosson's antitheatrical tract, *The Schoole of Abuse* (1579). After explaining the "right use of ancient Poetry," Gosson argues that music should be

> used in battaile, not to tickle the eare, but too teach every souldier when to strike and when to stay, when to flye, and when to followe.... Homer with his Musicke cured the sick Souldiers in the Grecians campe, and purged every mans Tent of the Plague. Thinke you that those miracles coulde bee wrought with playing of Daunces, Dumpes, Pavins, Galiardes, Measures Fancyes, or new streynes: They never came wher this grewe, nor knew what it ment.[7]

Gosson's reference to Homer likely pertains to the Greek theory of musical modes, by which certain tonal structures are said to correspond to specific psychological temperaments (for example, Mixolydian and sadness). In this scheme, music always *means* something. At its best, Gosson implies, music functions as suasive, instinctual language that is capable of being fully articulate and precise: *when* to strike, *when* to stay, *when* to fly. Yet the sheer proliferation of musical forms in Gosson's England throws this simple system of signification into chaos. The fact that Gosson's negative examples are mostly dance forms points his argument that music's semiotic capabilities have been subsumed by its bodily manifestations. As a result, English music has become as "meaningless" to its modern audience as it would be baffling to its classical predecessors ("they never came wher this grewe, nor knew what it ment").

Gosson's critique of English music is typical of much antitheatrical writing in its premise of a golden age, when the forms of music were simple and finite. Even so, Gosson's presentation of classical sources implies that music was always susceptible to innovation (and hence, degradation). Even the seven-stringed harp, which for other writers might represent the seven notes of the Pythagorean diapason, is shown by Gosson to be a distortion of an older, superior model: "He that compareth our instruments, with those that were used in ancient times, shall see them agree like Dogges & Cattes, and meete as jump as Germans lippes. Terpandrus and Olimpus used instruments of 7.strings. And Plutarch is of opinion that the instruments of 3.strings, which were used before their time, passed al that have followed

---

7. Stephen Gosson, *The Schoole of Abuse* (1579), ed. Arthur Freeman (New York: Garland, 1973), 4A4v–5A4r.

since."[8] Gosson's subsequent example makes it clear that music's embodiment in physical materials is largely responsible for this tendency toward innovation: it is Phrynis's "curiosity" about his fiddle that inspires him to add more strings, thus creating more possibilities for musical sound. The history of musical embodiment is thus for Gosson necessarily a history of decline, culminating in the grotesque vision of Musick's actual body: "To shew the abuses of these unthrifty scholers that despise the good rules of their ancient masters & run to the shop of their owne devises, defacing olde stampes, forging newe Printes, and coining strange precepts, Phaerecrates a Comicall Poet, bringeth in Musicke and Justice upon the stage: Musicke with her clothes tottered, her fleshe torne, her face deformed, her whole bodie mangled and dismembred."[9] Phillip Stubbes, whose attack on music copies faithfully entire portions of Gosson's tract, likewise represents music's abuses as a problem of materiality: "Their is no ship, so balanced with massie matter, as [musicians'] heads are fraught with all kind of bawdie songs, filthie ballads, and scurvie rymes, serving for every purpose, and for every Cumpanie."[10] For Stubbes, as with Gosson, the "massieness" of music is a sign of its adversarial relationship to *logos,* represented by the emptying out of musicians' heads. Paradoxically, then, the physicality of music makes it more difficult to contain, not less, since music's ability to proliferate ad infinitum threatens to overrun all attempts to preserve its ancient legibility.

Gosson's criticism of music is not entirely coherent, in part because he adopts wholeheartedly the practice of cramming several classical examples within a few pages. For example, his allusion to the story of Chiron "quenching" Achilles' fury with music would seem to suggest that music's abuses stem from its willful misuse rather than from an inherent deficiency. Nonetheless, Gosson's handling of his subject betrays a nagging suspicion that music is fundamentally independent of language. Hence, in a passage where Gosson permits himself amplification, the comparison of new and ancient music turns into a choleric diatribe against the strangeness of musical notation itself:

Were the Argives & Pythagoras nowe alive, & saw how many frets, how many stringes, how many stops, how many keyes, how many cliffes, howe many moodes, how many flats, how many sharps, how many

---

8. Ibid., Bv.
9. Ibid., B2r–B2v.
10. Phillip Stubbes, *The Anatomie of Abuses* (1583), ed. Arthur Freeman (New York: Garland, 1973), 3O3r.

rules, how many spaces, how many noates, how many restes, how many querks, how many corners, what chopping, what changing, what tossing, what turning, what wresting & wringing is among our Musitions, I beleve verily, that they would cry out with the country man: *Heu quod tam pingui macer est mihi taurus in arno.* Alas here is fat feeding, & leane beasts.[11]

Here, Gosson's language about music races with music's multiplicity of sound and is defeated. At the heart of such an attack is not so much a distaste for complex notation as the sense that music naturally exceeds its textual representation. In this way, Gosson depicts an inimical relationship between music and language simply by representing music *as* language. It is this sense of music's extratextual proclivities that ultimately leads Gosson to reject musical performance altogether: "Pythagoras bequeathes them a Clookebagge, and condemnes them for fooles, that judge Musicke by sounde and eare. If you will bee good Scholers, and profite well in the Arte of Musicke, shutte your fidels in their cases, and looke up to heaven."[12] Gosson finally decides that only the philosophical study of *musica speculativa,* which restricts music to cosmology and mathematics, yields "profitable" understanding.

Gosson's treatise exemplifies the Reformist anxiety over music's nonverbal commerce with the passions.[13] Calvin, for example, testifies to the idea that music "has a secret and almost incredible power to arouse hearts in one way or another."[14] Cornelius Agrippa, in a passage in *De incertitudine et vanitate scientarium* (1526) often cited by Reformist writers, also adduces music's ability to move its listeners, though with negative consequences: "Now a daies the unleeful libertie of Musicke, is so muche used in Churches, that together with the Canon of the Masse, very filthie songes have like tunes in the Organs, and the Divine Service is songe by lascivious Musitians hired for a greate stipende, not for the understandinge of the hearers, but for the stirringe up of the minde."[15] Accordingly, proponents of Reformist theology, even when

---

11. Gosson, *Schoole of Abuse,* B2r. The Latin phrase is from Virgil's third *Eclogue.*
12. Ibid., 5A4r.
13. On Reformist attitudes toward music in early modern England, see Peter LeHuray, *Music and the Reformation in England, 1549–1660* (Cambridge: Cambridge University Press, 1978); Hyun-Ah Kim, *Humanism and the Reform of Sacred Music in Early Modern England* (Aldershot, UK: Ashgate, 2008); Diane McColley, *Poetry and Music in Seventeenth-Century England* (Cambridge: Cambridge University Press, 1997), 53–93; P. S. Scholes, *The Puritans and Music* (New York: Russell and Russell, 1962).
14. Calvin, "Addition to the *Epistle,*" cited in Charles Garside Jr., *The Origins of Calvin's Theology of Music: 1536–1543* (Philadelphia: American Philosophical Society, 1979), 22.
15. Henry Cornelius Agrippa, *Of the Vanitie and Uncertaintie of Artes and Sciences,* ed. Catherine M. Dunn, trans. James Sanford (Northridge: California State University Press, 1974), 68.

they acknowledge music's ability to inspire godly devotion, firmly distinguish between music's nonverbal qualities and its textual accompaniment. Elizabeth I's injunction on the performance of music in church, which incorporates Lutheran and Calvinist ideas on the subject, establishes a strict hierarchy between music's "melody" and the "sentence" of its attendant text:

> That there be a modest and distinct song so used in all parts of the common prayers in the church, that the same may be as plainly understanded, as if it were read without singing; and yet nevertheless for the comforting of such that delight in music, it may be permitted, that... there may be sung an hymn, or such like song to the praise of Almighty God, in the best sort of melody and music that may be conveniently devised, having respect that the sentence of the hymn may be understanded and perceived.[16]

The fear that music will obscure its intended meaning, implied by Elizabeth and raised to a hysterical pitch by Gosson, is a constant refrain in the early modern critiques of polyphony, which is typically condemned for having too many voices—quite literally, too many musical parts that constitute its complex, intricate harmony. The popular Edwardian preacher Thomas Becon, in one of his religious pamphlets, argues that the innovations in church music amount to nothing more than "a confused noyse of voyces," leading to a general charge against all music:

> In the tyme of Paule there was no singing, but saying onely. Singing was with greate difficultye receaved of them of the latter tyme: and yet such singing, as was none other thing, than a distincte and playne pronunciation.... But nowe what other thing doth the common people heare, than *voyces signifying nothing*? And such for the moste part is the pronunciation, that not so much as the wordes or voyces are heard: *only the sound* beateth the eares.[17]

Sanford's translation, which was first printed in 1569 and again in 1575, actually mistranslates the grammar of Agrippa's sentence, making the affective power of music appear more suspect. A more accurate translation might read: "Not for the understanding of the hearers, *nor* for the raising of the spirit, but for the incitement of lasciviousness" (*non ad audientium intelligentiam, non ad spiritus elevationem, sed ad fornicariam pruriginem*). Agrippa, *Opera* (Hildesheim: Verlag, 1970), 2:49.

16. *Documentary Annals of the Reformed Church of England*, ed. Edward Cardwell (Oxford: Oxford University Press, 1844), 1:229.

17. Thomas Becon, *The Reliques of Rome* (London, 1563), 122r, my emphases. Much of Becon's characterization of music in this passage derives from Erasmus. See Kim, *Humanism and the Reform of Sacred Music*, 97–104.

There is an implicit paradox here, in that music lacks meaning precisely because it voices too many meanings at the same time. As with Gosson's prescription that music signify "when to strike and when to stay," Becon implies that music that fails to signify is simply empty sound. Again and again in the Reformist critiques, the question of music's legitimacy turns on whether it can accommodate a univocal, verbal meaning. Becon, this time translating Agrippa, writes that complex music "may justly seme not to be a noyse made of men, but rather a bleating of brute beastes, while the children ney discant as it were a sort of coltes: others bellowe a tenoure as it were a companye of oxen: other barke a counterpoynt as it were a number of dogges."[18] The comparison of human music with the braying and bellowing of beasts here is typical, attesting to the idea that musical "noyse" is incomprehensible. In another pamphlet, Becon describes singing in church as "bleating" not only because it can be harmonically complex but because, more generally, "outward melody is vain and transitory, and passeth away and cometh to nought."[19] Seen from this view, the problem is not how to distinguish between "good" and "bad" music, or between secular and church music, but how to manage an activity that is inherently opposed to language. Heinrich Bullinger's description of church singing, for example, characterizes the relationship between music and language as an endless tug-of-war: "There is hearde a long sounde, quavered and streyned to and fro, backwarde and forewarde, whereof a man cannot understand one worde."[20] The image of bodily torture suggested by Bullinger is explicitly realized by Edward Hake in his defense of metrical psalms: "I have not meant to defende...the prophanyng of Gods divine service by Musicke (as in tyme of Popery) namely by over curious, yea, and as I may say over tragicall dismembring not onely of wordes but of letters and sillables in the holy Psalmes and Anthemes appointed to the praysing of God."[21] Hake's description of polyphony as a "dismembring" force echoes Gosson's presentation of Musicke in the *Schoole of Abuse,* published the same year. And although, like Gosson, Hake admits the acceptability of a plainer musical style, what resonates most strongly in his passage is music's imagined

---

18. Becon, *Reliques of Rome,* 120r–121v.
19. Thomas Becon, *The Jewel of Joy* (1553), in *The Catechism of Thomas Becon,* ed. John Ayre (Cambridge: Cambridge University Press, 1844), 430.
20. Heinrich Bullinger, *Fiftie Godlie and Learned Sermons* (1577), trans. H. I., in *The Decades of Henry Bullinger,* ed. Thomas Harding (Cambridge: Cambridge University Press, 1849–52), 935. For a discussion of Bullinger's influence on English Reformers, see McColley, *Poetry and Music,* 82–83.
21. *The Psalmes of David in English Meter, with Notes of Foure Partes Set unto Them by Gulielmo [William] Damon* (1579), cited in Morrison Comegys Boyd, *Elizabethan Music and Musical Criticism,* 2nd ed. (Philadelphia: University of Pennsylvania Press, 1962), 22–23.

ability to split the components of language itself, "not onely of wordes but of letters and sillables."

The focus on music's antipathy to language should not be overstated. Many of music's detractors, Gosson included, marshal an arsenal of charges in defense of their position. Still, the notion that music's meaningfulness is a real concern in Reformist thought is corroborated by the early modern defenses of music, which frequently cite music's expressiveness as evidence of its moral integrity. Richard Hooker, defending both instrumental and vocal music, ascribes music's appeal to "an admirable facilitie which musique hath to *express and represent* to the minde more inwardlie then any other sensible meane... the turnes and varieties of all passions whereunto the minde is subject: *yea so to imitate them.*"[22] Here, music's seemingly infinite variety stems not from an inherent wantonness but from the copiousness of its subject (the passions), which it "represents" with remarkable facility. Likewise, John Case responds to Gosson's comments about variety and dismemberment seriously, arguing that variety in music actually constitutes its wholeness and fitness for human representation: "For string hath beene added to string, part unto part, precept unto precept, one thing to an other so long til at length no one thing so much as variety hath made musick a perfit & uniform body."[23] Arthur Lake, attempting to assuage both sides of the debate, makes a similar case in a passage that appears to respond to Becon's distinction between the heart's prayerful voice and musical sound: "Though the instrument be the *Mouth*, yet the Musitian is the Heart, he causeth the tune of the voice to sound, and addeth the Dittie to the Tune."[24] One of the most forceful proponents of music's expressiveness is Sir Thomas Browne, who rejects altogether Gosson's distinction between ancient and "vulgar" music:

> Whatever is harmonically composed delights in harmony.... Even that vulgar and Taverne Musicke, which makes one man merry, another mad, strikes in mee a deepe fit of devotion, and a profound contemplation of the first Composer; there is something in it of Divinity more than the eare discovers. It is an Hieroglyphicall and shadowed lesson of the whole world, and [the] Creatures of God, such a melody

---

22. Richard Hooker, *Of the Lawes of Ecclesiastical Polity*, ed. Georges Edelen, vol. 2 of *The Folger Library Edition of the Works of Richard Hooker*, ed. W. Speed Hill (Cambridge, MA: Belknap, 1977), 151, my emphases.

23. Case, *Praise of Musicke*, 11.

24. Arthur Lake, *Sermons with Some Religious and Divine Meditations* (London, 1629), 197, cited in McColley, *Poetry and Music*, 88.

to the eare, as the whole world well understood, would afford the understanding.[25]

Browne's liberal endorsement of "Taverne music," with its suggestive pun on the polyphonic composer John Taverner, may be playful. Yet his defense shows that Reformist attacks on polyphony were not understood only within the context of a specific church debate, even at the height of Puritan revolution: the claim that even "vulgar" music is a "hieroglyphicall lesson" argues that Reformers have misunderstood the language of music altogether.

In the debate over music's expressiveness, John Case's use of Plutarch to define music as "poetrie" is a direct volley to Gosson's imitation of *De Musica* (originally thought to be written by Plutarch) in his portrait of a dismembered Musicke. Moreover, in wrestling over the correct understanding of music's classical image, Case and Gosson demonstrate how the debate over music could be mapped figuratively onto an argument about a woman's chastity. In fact, Reformist critiques of music frequently adapt the image of the whorish woman to stress music's indiscriminate relationship to language. For example, Becon, again translating Agrippa on the subject of music that fails to instruct, transforms Agrippa's gender-neutral "incitement to fornication" (*prurigo ad fornicariam*) to "whoryshe armonye."[26] Stubbes advises his reader that "if you would have your daughter whoorish, bawdie, and uncleane, and a filthie speaker, and such like, bring her up in musick and daunting."[27] Likewise, Joseph Swetnam yokes together music's affective power and the duplicitous nature of female speech, which he sets against the clear, meaningful language of men: women, he says, "have Sirens songs to allure thee, and Xerxes cunning to inchaunt thee, they beare two tongues in one mouth like Judas, and two heartes in one breast like Magus, the one full of smiles and the other full of frownes, and all to deceive the simple and plain meaning men."[28] By the time of William Prynne's notorious *Histriomastix* (1633), the association of elaborate music with female promiscuity is a polemical commonplace: "Chromaticall harmonies are to be left to impudent malapartnesse in wine, to whorish musicke crowned with flowers." Elaborating further, Prynne writes: "What a miserable Spectacle is it to chaste and wel-mannered eyes, to see a woman, not to follow her needle or distaffe, but to sing to a

---

25. Sir Thomas Browne, *Religio medici* (1642), vol. 1 of *The Works of Sir Thomas Browne,* ed. Geoffrey Keynes (Chicago: University of Chicago Press, 1964), 84.
26. Becon, *Reliques of Rome,* 121v.
27. Stubbes, *Anatomie of Abuses,* 3O3r–3O3v.
28. Joseph Swetnam, *The Araignment of Lewde, Idle, Froward and Unconstant Women* (London, 1615), B2v–B3r.

Lute? not to be knowne by her owne husband, but to be often viewed by others as a publike whore."[29]

The Reformist association of music with whorishness does not merely exemplify what Jean Howard has called "traces of the historically specific social struggles and dislocations manifesting themselves as attacks on the theater."[30] In other words, polemical attacks on music in early modern England are not merely disguised representations of social anxieties about women. Rather, ideas about music's promiscuity intersect with attitudes toward women in a very real way: just as polyphonic music "signifies nothing" because it proliferates too many voices, a promiscuous woman (as the tracts imagine her) does not point to a single, masculine authority. She does not signify. I will address the conflation of musical and female promiscuity more fully in chapter 2; for now, Howard's reading of the Reformist tracts in terms of gender and social struggles teaches us the important lesson that the attacks on music, despite their excessive reliance on classical and medieval citations, do constitute a serious argument in the early modern debates over music. Indeed, it may be precisely the nature of Reformist polemic, with its infamous habit of loading multiple sources and readings onto a single figure, that makes it uniquely capable of demonstrating the radical promiscuity of a phenomenon that cannot—as musical sound without words always cannot—speak for itself. It remained for Shakespeare's theater, with its access to different media, to deliver the affective experience of anxiety that can arise when a musical performance "says" more than it should.

Musical Alphabets

Titus Andronicus is not generally considered one of Shakespeare's musical plays. In his exhaustive account of the play's critical reception, G. Harold Metz notes that "in comparison to other Shakespearean plays, especially the comedies, there is indeed only a little music of any kind in *Titus Andronicus*."[31] However, there are more musical stage directions in *Titus* than in most of Shakespeare's other plays, including (depending on the version employed) a

---

29. William Prynne, *Histriomastix: The Players Scourge or Actors Tragedie* (1633), ed. Arthur Freeman (New York: Garland, 1974), 275, 277.

30. Jean E. Howard, *The Stage and Social Struggle in Early Modern England* (London: Routledge, 1991), 6. Although Howard is primarily discussing attacks on the stage in this passage, her general argument presumably extends to the tracts' critiques of music as well.

31. G. Harold Metz, *Shakespeare's Earliest Tragedy: Studies in "Titus Andronicus"* (Madison, NJ: Fairleigh Dickinson University Press, 1996), 255.

TITUS ANDRONICUS AND THE PRODUCTION OF MUSICAL MEANING

large number of flourishes, trumpet calls, hunting horns, oboes, and drumbeats. More importantly, *Titus* self-consciously stages music's potential as a means of theatrical signification: at several moments in the play, the dramatic plot relies on music to narrate specific events, and the process by which music assumes this narrative function is made explicit. For example, after a trumpet flourish in act 5, Lucius says that "the trumpets show the Emperor is at hand" (5.3.16). In act 4, Demetrius asks, "Why do the Emperor's trumpets flourish thus?" and is answered by Chiron, "Belike for joy the Emperor hath a son" (4.2.49–50). And again, in act 1, Lucius prepares his audience (and Shakespeare's) to interpret the trumpet flourishes that sound two lines later: "Remaineth naught but to inter our brethren/And with loud 'larums welcome them to Rome" (1.1.146–47). Passages such as these raise the issue of music's meaning at the same time that they secure it. In each case, music is tied to a specific dramatic event and is imagined as narrating that event: the trumpet flourishes tell us *when* the bodies of the dead Andronici are received in Rome. *Titus* thus participates in the establishment and evolution of musical, theatrical conventions—in a sense, creating a musical alphabet for the early modern theater—even as it makes the seams of those conventions apparent. In a work obsessively concerned with systems of communication, Shakespeare's foregrounding of the associative process by which an audience responds to music sets up a parallel lens through which to view the play's exploration of sympathy and expression.

There are certainly references to music in *Titus* that function merely as common Renaissance trope, where actual music is neither heard nor imagined as narrative, as in Aaron's comment that "should the Empress know/This discord's ground, the music would not please" (2.1.69–70). More often, however, Shakespeare outlines the process by which words about music give meaning to, and even compete with, music's sound. For example, during the illicit meeting between Tamora and Aaron early in the play, Shakespeare presents two examples of music that is arbitrarily attached to a specific context:

> And whilst the babbling echo mocks the hounds,
> Replying shrilly to the well-tuned horns,
> As if a double hunt were heard at once,
> Let us sit down and mark their yellowing noise,
> ....
> We may, each wreathèd in the other's arms,
> Our pastimes done, possess a golden slumber
> Whiles hounds and horns and sweet melodious birds

Be unto us as is a nurse's song
Of lullaby to bring her babe asleep.
                              (2.3.17–29)

The hounds, by mistaking the "babbling echo" for their masters' horn calls, erroneously attribute a specific meaning to the music that reaches their ears. These dogs are excellent examples of Gosson's ideal music auditor, since they hear music only as verbal command ("when to strike and when to stay"). Tamora, by contrast, separates the music that she hears from its context, enabling her to load the music (already thrown into confusion by its doubling) with her own additional meaning. By severing music from its intended meaning, Tamora performs consciously what the "babbling echo" does accidentally, thus revealing music's nearly infinite ability to accommodate multiple meanings. Shakespeare suggests that listeners who accept music as having an authoritative meaning may run the risk of being "mocked" (in our modern sense of the word) with the emperor's hounds.

Shakespeare's Tamora can exploit music's promiscuity for her own purposes because she recognizes it as an acoustic, physical event. This knowledge informs her analogy of the eagle in act 4, when she persuades Saturninus not to fear Lucius:

The eagle suffers little birds to sing,
And is not careful what they mean thereby,
Knowing that with the shadow of his wings
He can at pleasure stint their melody.
                              (4.4.82–85)

Tamora's imagined eagle does not care what birdsong might "mean," if it means anything at all. For Tamora, music is first and foremost a phenomenon of physical sound, of pulsating throats, resonating beaks, and beating wings that can be crushed at will. Indeed, her reception of music as acoustic event acts as a defense against an undesirable meaning: in act 2, in language that prefigures the eagle analogy, Tamora rejects Lavinia's pleas for pity by saying, "I know not what it means. Away with her!" (2.3.157). Tamora effaces the "meaning" of Lavinia's words, which might remind her of her own previous plea for mercy, by stifling their actual sound: "I will not hear her speak" (137). Ultimately, through her sons Chiron and Demetrius as proxies, Tamora literally focuses on the site of sound's production—Lavinia's tongue—and disables it.

The gap between music and meaning that Tamora exploits throughout the play is given topological form by Shakespeare in the dark forest in act 2, the same forest that disperses the sound of hounds and hunting horns. It is also the place where articulate speech ("tongues") cannot be heard or produced: "The Emperor's court is like the house of Fame,/The palace full of tongues, of eyes and ears,/The woods are ruthless, dreadful, deaf, and dull" (2.1.127–29). Shakespeare localizes and intensifies this image of the "deaf" forest (which here also means "deafening") a hundred lines later, in Tamora's description of the pit:

> And when they showed me this abhorrèd pit,
> They told me here at dead time of the night
> A thousand fiends, a thousand hissing snakes,
> Ten thousand swelling toads, as many urchins
> Would make such fearful and confusèd cries
> As any mortal body hearing it
> Should straight fall mad or else die suddenly.
> (2.3.98–104)

Heather James describes this pit as a semiotic vacuum that "substitutes, inverts, confuses, appropriates, swallows up, and engenders meanings."[32] At its extreme, the pit is the site where sounds are stripped of meaning entirely: the "fearful and confused cries" Tamora describes suggest chaotic sound that has been radically detached from its origin and rendered illegible. Moreover, through its capacity to "swallow up" both men and meanings, the pit replicates the early modern association between musical promiscuity and female voraciousness. In this way, Shakespeare associates the pit, the play's locus of unintelligible sound, with the topological figure of a monstrous, indiscriminate woman.[33]

With the entrance of the mutilated Lavinia in act 2, Shakespeare transfers the semiotics of the pit to an actual female body. Lavinia arrives onstage, "*her hands cut off and her tongue cut out, and ravished,*" and hears the following taunts from her rapists:

> DEMETRIUS. So, now go tell, an if thy tongue can speak,
>   Who 'twas that cut thy tongue and ravished thee.
> CHIRON. Write down thy mind, bewray thy meaning so,
>   An if thy stumps will let thee play the scribe.
> (2.4.1–4)

---

32. Heather James, *Shakespeare's Troy: Drama, Politics, and the Translation of Empire* (Cambridge: Cambridge University Press, 1997), 64.

33. The pit has often been read as a metaphor for the female genitalia in a particularly monstrous form. See Jonathan Bate, ed., *Titus Andronicus* (London: Routledge, 1995), 7–10.

Here, Demetrius and Chiron echo and reverse Justice's response to the mangled figure of Musick in Gosson's *Schoole of Abuse* ("Justice... questioneth with her howe shee came in that plight"),[34] exulting in rather than lamenting Lavinia's inability to name them or "bewray [her] meaning." At this precise moment, Shakespeare inserts one of his cruelest puns, immediately followed in the First Folio by one of the play's most ambiguous musical stage directions:

CHIRON. An 'twere my cause I should go hang myself.
DEMETRIUS. If thou hadst hands to help thee knit the cord.
    Exeunt
    Wind horns.

(2.4.9–10)

Demetrius's boast that Lavinia cannot "knit the cord" to hang herself punningly suggests that she cannot knit a "chord," or make formal, harmonious music. (There is also the suggestion of "con-cord," or musical harmony.) Moreover, the fact of Shakespeare's punning itself negatively sums up Lavinia's predicament at this moment: puns engender meaning by playing on a word's sound, which is something Lavinia can no longer do. In this context, the stage direction that immediately follows Demetrius's remark, "*wind horns,*" is profoundly unsettling. The conspicuous harmony of horns at this moment seems to mock Lavinia, left standing alone on the stage, for her inability to produce either meaning or harmony from the normal instruments of sound. The sound of the horns should *mean* the approach of hunters (who, incidentally, never appear), but its accidental convergence with Demetrius's "cord/chord" and Lavinia's speechless presence prompts Shakespeare's audience to associate backward—to "read" this music outside of its conventional context and apply it, rather grotesquely, to a character who has lost her ability to speak.[35]

The remainder of the play charts an attempt to reconstitute a system of meaningful signs from Lavinia's dismembered body and, by extension, to

---

34. Gosson, *Schoole of Abuse,* B2v.
35. There is another possible reading of the horn call, which also suggests a gap between music and language. In classical antiquity, wind instruments were often negatively distinguished from string instruments for their inability to produce words (i.e., a wind musician could not sing while playing). Therefore, the winding horn may signify Lavinia's new status as an instrument that can "blow" but not speak. See Bruce R. Smith, "The Contest of Apollo and Marsyas: Ideas about Music in the Middle Ages," in *By Things Seen: Reference and Recognition in Medieval Thought,* ed. David L. Jeffrey, 81–107 (Ottawa: University of Ottawa Press, 1979).

establish a visual-aural rhetoric for Shakespeare's theater. Titus's reaction to the mutilated Lavinia provides the locus classicus for such attempts to transform body into text:

> I can interpret all her martyred signs.
> She says she drinks no other drink but tears,
> Brewed with her sorrow, mashed upon her cheeks.
> Speechless complainer, I will learn thy thought.
> In thy dumb action will I be as perfect
> As begging hermits in their holy prayers.
> Thou shalt not sigh, nor hold thy stumps to heaven,
> Nor wink, nor nod, nor kneel, nor make a sign,
> But I of these will wrest an alphabet,
> And by still practice learn to know thy meaning.
> (3.2.36–45)

Each of the actions Titus identifies as part of his new alphabet (sighing, gesturing, winking, nodding, kneeling) corresponds to a different part of Lavinia's body, effectively creating a "language of the body" through which Lavinia becomes legible. Within this system of interpretation, Titus's pun on "hands" a few lines earlier— "O, handle not the theme, to talk of hands" (29)—is not merely bad decorum, as is often remarked; it also rehearses a hermeneutic process by which the resonant body is translated. As the play progresses, however, the "still practice" through which Titus says he will "learn to know" Lavinia's meaning becomes almost indistinguishable from the practice of *making* meaning—and of interpreting music. Titus's eccentric response to the buzzing fly, in particular, echoes both Tamora's statements about musical sound and his own alphabetization of Lavinia: "Poor harmless fly,/That with his pretty buzzing melody/ Came here to make us merry—and thou hast killed him!" (3.2.63–65). Once heard as melody, Titus's buzzing fly is apprehensible by the same interpretive processes that inscribe meaning on music. In other words, early modern descriptions of music provide a lexicon through which Titus's fly, and Lavinia's dismembered body, can be understood as expressive. Indeed, music's ability to admit any number of verbal contexts partly explains the repeated associations between Lavinia and music made by her interpreters:

> O, that delightful engine of her thoughts,
> That blabbed them with such pleasing eloquence,

Is torn from forth that pretty hollow cage
Where, like a sweet melodious bird, it sung
Sweet varied notes, enchanting every ear.
(3.1.82–86)

Here, Marcus's description of Lavinia resembles Titus's musical description of the buzzing fly, reinforcing the idea that Lavinia's voice, once imagined as music, enables interpretation.[36]

This conception of music's legibility—that a voiceless character can be imagined as meaningful when placed in a musical context—suggests a new reading of Marcus's speech at the end of act 2. Some critics emphasize the indecorousness of Marcus's "elaborate poetic language" in this speech as an accompaniment to "the physical image of Lavinia's mutilated body." Others argue that Marcus's poetic conceits reveal his attempt to articulate, and thus come to terms with, the "unspeakable."[37] These two stances differ sharply over whether Marcus's speech is a disturbing aestheticization of the very real violence done to Lavinia, or whether the affective distance between Marcus's words and Lavinia's body actually records that violence on a dramatic level. What has not received significant attention, however, is Marcus's consistent recourse to *musical* conceits, which imaginatively structure his lament.[38] A closer reading of these musical themes suggests an alternative way of conceiving the aesthetic problems posed by Marcus's speech, allowing us to sidestep the polarizing arguments for and against aestheticization.

Marcus's speech moves from Philomela to Orpheus, via a series of conventional musical metaphors:

Fair Philomela, why she but lost her tongue
And in a tedious sampler sewed her mind.
But, lovely niece, that mean is cut from thee.
A craftier Tereus, cousin, hast thou met,
And he hath cut those pretty fingers off
That could have better sewed than Philomel.
O, had the monster seen those lily hands

---

36. In Renaissance redactions of the Ovidian myth, "blabbed" is a frequent characterization of the sound made by Philomela *after* her metamorphosis (as in Gascoigne's *Complainte*). Thus its conjunction here with "eloquence" may be ironic.

37. See Bate, *Titus Andronicus,* 9. "Unspeakable" is from D. J. Palmer's description of Lavinia's plight, which Bate quotes at length in his introduction to the play.

38. Jonathan Bate, however, comments on the fusion of Philomel and Orpheus in the play. See *Shakespeare and Ovid* (Oxford: Oxford University Press, 1993), 76–77, 111–13.

Tremble like aspen leaves upon a lute
And make the silken strings delight to kiss them,
He would not then have touched them for his life.
Or had he heard the heavenly harmony
Which that sweet tongue hath made,
He would have dropped his knife and fell asleep,
As Cerberus at the Thracian poet's feet.

(2.4.38–51)

Marcus's Ovidian allusions chart a progression from a figure who has lost her voice to one whose musical voice (at least in Ovid's version) lives on after the death of its master. In this way, Marcus imaginatively resuscitates Lavinia's voice by recalling a famous dismembered body (*diversa membra*) that produces music.[39] Moreover, Marcus's poetic description of Lavinia's "lily hands" and "sweet tongue," which he subsequently associates with Orpheus's performances, promulgates a fantasy of music that is richly significative. The "heavenly harmony" that he associates with Lavinia's "sweet tongue" evokes conventional representations of music as emblematic of a cosmic or mathematical order, while his description of Lavinia's Orphic lute playing corresponds unproblematically to an allegorical tradition in which music is read as signifying higher, divine precepts. What is being mourned, then, in Marcus's speech is not music as sound, but music that is consistently meaningful. Marcus's comment a few lines earlier, "O that I knew thy heart" (34), should signal to us that his lament turns on a problem of knowing—of deriving meaning from a body that can no longer avail itself of spoken or sung language.

In sanctioning the use of music, Luther is compelled to commend the expressive qualities of the human voice, in its capacity to produce words as well as nonverbal sounds:

> How can the voice, at the direction of the will, sound forth so powerfully and vehemently that it cannot only be heard by everyone over a wide area, but also be understood? Philosophers for all their labor cannot find the explanation; and baffled, they end in perplexity; for none of them has yet been able to define or demonstrate the original components of the human voice, its sibilation and (as it were) its alphabet, e.g., in the case of laughter—to say nothing of weeping.[40]

---

39. Ovid, *Metamorphoses,* trans. Frank Justice Miller (Cambridge, MA: Harvard University Press, 1984), 11.50. All quotations and translations of the *Metamorphoses* are from this edition unless otherwise noted.

40. Luther, in Weiss and Taruskin, *Music in the Western World,* 102.

Luther's comments, strikingly echoed in Titus's claim that he "will wrest an alphabet" from Lavinia's sighs and tears, argue that expressiveness wins after all, with or without words. In *Titus,* Marcus similarly attempts to assert Lavinia's meaningfulness by exalting the power of her sounds, directing his audience's attention (however unsuccessfully) away from the grotesque physicality of Lavinia's wounds toward a vision of "heavenly harmony." His questions— "Shall I speak for thee? Shall I say 'tis so?" (2.4.33) — register both the desire to make Lavinia articulate and the ventriloquism that will be involved in restoring, or creating, Lavinia's "voice." *This is the condition of music.* Music, because of its uncontrollable promiscuity in relation to language, requires a violent act of "translation," most often in the form of an intensely regulated system of codification or theory, in order to be perceived as meaningful. Thus, the sense of depersonalization that Marcus's speech evokes for some readers stems from the way it voices a compensatory fantasy against Lavinia's speechlessness. At the same time, Marcus's speech does not ritualize or articulate the "unspeakable" so much as it denies unspeakability. By fantasizing an articulate Lavinia who "speaks" without tongue or hands, Marcus appropriates music's "alphabet"—the conventional, although by no means universal, conceits and sleights of hand by which actual music is imagined to be articulate—for his voiceless niece, paving the way for the more general alphabetization of Lavinia that follows.

Ovid and Sympathy

In developing a language through which to understand his daughter, Titus repeatedly alludes to the doctrine of sympathy to validate his efforts. In Renaissance England, "sympathy" denotes a correspondence of feeling between people, objects, or astral bodies. Musical sympathy, the physically observable concord between musical instruments (as when a vibrating string causes another tuned to the same pitch to vibrate) was seen as an especially concrete example of this phenomenon—not simply an analogy for it. Although descriptions of musical sympathy could be used as a "rich source of metaphors for representing other hidden phenomena which could neither be seen nor easily put into words," musical sympathy was taken as evidence that a very real, mutual influence regularly occurred, even if it was not always perceptible.[41] In this respect, when Titus claims that he can

---

41. Penelope Gouk, *Music, Science and Natural Magic in Seventeenth-Century England* (New Haven, CT: Yale University Press, 1999), 268.

interpret Lavinia, he uses language that evokes the idea of sympathy in its broadest sense:

> Mark, Marcus, mark. I understand her signs.
> Had she a tongue to speak, now would she say
> That to her brother which I said to thee.
> His napkin with his true tears all bewet
> Can do no service on her sorrowful cheeks.
> O, what a sympathy of woe is this—
> As far from help as limbo is from bliss.
>
> (3.1.143–49)

Titus's remark that he experiences a "sympathy of woe" appropriates a commonplace of Renaissance musical philosophy, while implying that such communication is possible in the first place. To the extent that this notion of sympathy suggests a musical event (made more apparent by the jarring sound of Titus's rhyming couplet), the play's critique of musical interpretation might render any sympathizing impulse suspect. Yet, as I will show in this section, Shakespeare relies more heavily on a strategic use of Ovidian *figurae* in the second half of the play to problematize Titus's assertion that he can truly "sympathize" (in the early modern sense of the word) with Lavinia. The Ovidian tales to which the play gestures present numerous examples of ineffectual voicelessness, and the play's ironic treatment of Orphic eloquence (itself an Ovidian theme) opens up a space in which Shakespeare can critique his own theatrical persuasiveness.

In act 4, Shakespeare introduces an actual copy of Ovid's *Metamorphoses* on stage as a prosthetic for Lavinia's absent tongue:

> TITUS. Lucius, what book is that she tosseth so?
> YOUNG LUCIUS. Grandsire, 'tis Ovid's *Metamorphoses*.
>   My mother gave it me.
> MARCUS. For love of her that's gone,
>   Perhaps, she culled it from among the rest.
> TITUS. Soft, so busily she turns the leaves.
>   Help her. What would she find? Lavinia, shall I read?
>   This is the tragic tale of Philomel,
>   And treats of Tereus' treason and his rape,
>   And rape, I fear, was root of thy annoy.
>
> (4.1.41–49)

A few lines later, Lavinia completes the story outlined by Ovid's tale of Philomel by following the pattern of another Ovidian rape victim. Like Io, who draws her name in the ground for her father to read, Lavinia inscribes the names of her rapists in the ground: "*Stuprum*—Chiron—Demetrius" (77). To the extent that Lavinia and Titus use Ovid to "read" their situation, the *Metamorphoses* becomes a vital part of the alphabet that makes Lavinia intelligible, thus functioning as a bridge to true sympathy. At the same time, the actual presence of Ovid's book onstage raises subtle questions about the reliability of this ingenious mode of communication. Marcus's seemingly inappropriate response ("For love of her that's gone,/ Perhaps she culled it from among the rest") reveals that there are other possible narratives enabled by the Ovidian context. Thus, just as Titus physically "helps" Lavinia turn the page to Ovid's Philomel, Lavinia's interlocutors direct our attention away from other Ovidian stories of voicelessness that might also comment on her situation.

The attempt to communicate effectively is itself a frequent subject of the *Metamorphoses*. Several figures in Ovid's poem demonstrate remarkable verbal or musical power (Orpheus, Mercury, Ulysses, Tereus, Polyxena), while others overcome, at least partially, the loss of voice (Philomela, Io, Echo). Yet there are many other figures in Ovid's poem who fail altogether to communicate or persuade when physical voice is lost or suppressed (Daphne, Actaeon, Orpheus, Itys, Boreas). In many of these instances, Ovid represents the crisis of communication as a violent confrontation with nonverbal sound. For example, when Io tries to complain after being transformed into a cow, she is startled by the sound of her own altered voice: "And when she attempted to voice her complaints, she only mooed. She would start with fear at the sound, and was filled with terror at her own voice" (*conatoque queri mugitus edidit ore/pertimuitque sonos propriaque exterrita voce est,* 1.637–38). Similarly, after Actaeon is transformed into a stag, he tries to utter the same words that Io's writing inspires in her father (*me miserum*), but he can only groan. The sound that Actaeon makes is so strange that it defies categorization: "He groans and makes a sound which, though not human, is still one no deer could utter" (*gemit ille sonumque,/etsi non hominis, quem non tamen edere possit/cervus,* 3.237–39). Neither human nor animal, Actaeon's *sonus* not only fails to signify who he is; it cannot signify *what* he is.

Shakespeare alludes to the myth of Actaeon twice in *Titus Andronicus,* each time suggesting its appropriateness to Lavinia. In act 2, Bassianus and Lavinia inadvertently intrude on Tamora and Aaron in the forest:

BASSIANUS. Who have we here? Rome's royal empress
    Unfurnished of her well-beseeming troop?

> Or is it Dian, habited like her
> Who hath abandonèd her holy groves
> To see the general hunting in this forest?
> TAMORA. Saucy controller of my private steps,
> Had I the power that some say Dian had,
> Thy temples should be planted presently
> With horns, as was Actaeon's, and the hounds
> Should drive upon thy new-transformèd limbs,
> Unmannerly intruder as thou art!
> (2.2.55–65)

Although Tamora directs her threat to Bassianus, it is Lavinia who will be "new-transformed" by the next scene and lose her ability to speak. Later, in act 4, precisely when the *Metamorphoses* appears onstage, Lavinia assumes an Actaeon-like pose: "Why lifts she up her arms in sequence thus?" (4.1.37). In Ovid's poem, Actaeon raises his arms (or what would have been his arms) toward his dogs as a last effort to communicate: "And now on the ground with bended knees, like one who is pleading, he raises to them his silent face, just as he does his own arms" (*et genibus pronis supplex similisque roganti/circumfert tacitos tamquam sua bracchia vultus,* 3.240–41, my translation). Actaeon's dogs, of course, do not recognize the gesture, and the implicit conflation of Actaeon with Lavinia raises doubts about the legibility of *her* raised arms. Although Marcus offers a convincing reading of Lavinia's gesture, he himself cannot be sure: "I think she means that there were more than one/ Confederate in the fact. Ay, more there was,/ *Or else* to heaven she heaves them for revenge" (4.1.38–40, my emphasis). Unlike Ovid, who can narrate directly from Actaeon's perspective to reveal the gulf between sound and meaning, Shakespeare can only suggest a failure of communication by presenting Lavinia as a second Actaeon.

The effectiveness of the Ovidian voice (or of substitutes for voice) in the *Metamorphoses* is often gauged by a character's ability to "move" his or her audience. Philomela, using a figure of speech that occurs frequently in the *Metamorphoses,* vows to "move the conscious stones" to outrage over Tereus's rape (*conscia saxa movebo,* 6.547). Orpheus "moves" the strings of his lyre as he moves the Stygian spirits to pity him (*talia dicentem nervosque ad verba moventem/exsangues flebant animae,* 10.40–41). Conversely, Orpheus is killed by the bacchantes when he cannot "move" them with his voice (*in illo tempore primum/ inrita dicentem nec quicquam voce moventem,* 11.39–40), and thus cannot move the actual stones being thrown at him. Ovid repeatedly connects the ability to evoke pity in one's audience to the ability to "move" physical objects (strings, tongues, stones), eliding—as Ovid so often does—the metaphorical meaning of the word with its literal one. In this respect, the Ovidian sense of *movere*—denoting the affective response of an audience *and* the physical act of moving things—corresponds to the effects of sympathy as they were often characterized in Renaissance writings on natural philosophy.

Just as Ovid ironically literalizes Orpheus's ability to "move" things with his music, Shakespeare ironizes (though more cynically) the early modern notion of sympathy by casting Titus as a failed Orpheus who unsuccessfully attempts to "move" stones with his voice:

> Why, 'tis no matter, man. If they did hear,
> They would not mark me; if they did mark,
> They would not pity me; yet plead I must.
> Therefore I tell my sorrows to the stones,
> ....
> When I do weep they humbly at my feet
> Receive my tears and *seem to weep with me,*
> And were they but attirèd in grave weeds
> Rome could afford no tribunes like to these.
> A stone is soft as wax, tribunes more hard than stones.
> A stone is silent and offendeth not,
> And tribunes with their tongues doom men to death.
>
> (3.1.33–46, my emphasis)

Titus's confusion of the literal and metaphorical senses of "move," a word implied but not stated in his speech (stones are "soft" enough to be moved physically, tribunes are too "hard" to be moved emotionally), invokes the doctrine of sympathy in a way that appears ridiculous. Lucius tells Titus that he "lament[s] in vain...and...recount[s] [his] sorrows to a stone" (27–29), suggesting that sympathy, the phenomenon by which persons and objects can influence each other without words, is merely an empty conceit in the universe of the play.

Shakespeare critiques the doctrine of sympathy more subtly in his allusion to Ovid's Hecuba in act 4, when Lucius's boy explains his fear of Lavinia:

> For I have heard my grandsire say full oft
> Extremity of griefs would make men mad,
> And I have read that Hecuba of Troy
> Ran mad for sorrow. That made me to fear.
>
> (4.1.18–21)

Ovid's Hecuba first appears in book 13 of the *Metamorphoses* as someone more famous for her fearful sound than for her pitiable history: "The poor wife of Priam after all else lost her human form and with strange barking affrighted the alien air" (*Priameia coniunx/perdidit infelix hominis post omnia formam/externasque novo latratu terruit auras,* 13.404–6). A hundred lines later, following Ovid's account of Polyxena (whose noble speech "moves" her captors to sympathize with her), Hecuba delivers a long speech on the sacrifice of Polyxena, only to discover the corpse of her youngest son, Polydorus. At this moment, Hecuba is speechless; Ovid compares her sudden silence to that of a stone (*duroque simillima saxo,* 540). After quietly plotting the death of Polymestor, her son's killer, Hecuba incurs a shower of stones literally moved against her by the angry Thracians, in sharp contrast to her earlier scene of verbal eloquence: "The Thracians, incensed by their king's disaster, began to set upon the Trojan with shafts and stones" (*clade sui Thracum gens inritata tyranni/Troada telorum lapidumque incessere iactu/coepit,* 565–67). In a grotesque vision of orality, Hecuba bites at the stones, and "though her jaws were set for words, barked when she tried to speak" (*rictuque in verba parato latravit, conata loqui,* 568–69). Ovid ends the tale by circumscribing the raucous sound of Hecuba's howling with the more general account of her "sad fortune," which "moves" the Trojans and Grecians, and the gods themselves, to pity (*illius fortuna deos quoque moverat omnes,* 573). The fact that Hecuba's audience is moved to sympathy by the *narrative* of her tragedy rather than her sound is all the more striking given the episode's placement in book 13, which begins with Ulysses' eloquent speech on the arms of Achilles. Through Hecuba's strange barking, Ovid refers his reader to an instance of voicelessness that cannot be recuperated, even though it can be heard. By pointing to Ovid's Hecuba at a crucial moment in *Titus,* Shakespeare suggests a similar reading of Lavinia that undercuts any sense of true sympathy or expressiveness. Like the sound that Hecuba makes after her transformation, Lavinia's speechless body—on its own—imparts only fear.

Lucius's fear of Lavinia as a second Hecuba reflects the anxiety that nonverbal sound, like music, might really mean nothing. By reminding his audience of the frightening, alienating aspect of Hecuba in Ovid's poem, Shakespeare points out the irony that Hecuba was often used as an exemplum of sympathy in Renaissance rhetorical handbooks.[42] Moreover, Shakespeare's use of Ovid and music in *Titus* ultimately demonstrates the limits of rhetorical representation itself: when extreme grief is represented in the

---

42. Bate, *Shakespeare and Ovid,* 20, 198.

most copious way possible, it is the *gap* between experience and expression that becomes apparent, and alienation, rather than sympathy, becomes the defining effect. This notion of self-defeating sound is suggested most poignantly in Titus's description of Lavinia as a "map of woe," a passage which grotesquely alludes to both the musical and metamorphic aspects of the tale of Philomela:

> Thou map of woe, that thus dost talk in signs,
> When thy poor heart beats with outrageous beating
> Thou canst not strike it thus to make it still!
> Wound it with sighing, girl; kill it with groans,
> Or get some little knife between thy teeth
> And just against thy heart make thou a hole.
> (3.2.12–17)

This vision of Lavinia recalls the fabled nightingale, who leans its breast against a thorn to produce music, while the image of Lavinia's irrepressibly "beating" heart is a perversion of the more popular notion (favored by Gascoigne) of music as a language of the passions. As an instrument that sighs and blows through its wounds (its pierced "hole"), Lavinia's body suggests a kind of music that, instead of producing expressive sound, can only replicate the original rape and mutilation.

In response to the specter of perpetual violence and meaninglessness, the last lines of the play attempt to recuperate a legibility which the Ovidian subtext has eroded. Lucius professes that his "scars can witness, dumb although they are" (5.3.113), articulating a fantasy that the "dumb" body unproblematically signifies. A few lines later, Lucius, speaking to his son, evokes the memory of Titus's storytelling *as* music: "Many a time he danced thee on his knee,/Sung thee asleep, his loving breast thy pillow./Many a story hath he told to thee" (161–63). Like Orphic music, Titus's music (in Lucius's mind) speaks even after death, its meaning guaranteed by patrilineal succession. By contrast, Tamora's body (in many ways the original site of musical anarchy) is purposefully denied any meaningful music:

> As for that ravenous tiger, Tamora,
> No funeral rite nor man in mourning weed,
> No mournful bell shall ring her burial;
> But throw her forth to beasts and birds to prey.

> Her life was beastly and devoid of pity,
> And being dead, let birds on her take pity.
> (5.3.194–99)

Lucius's disposal of Tamora's body symbolically banishes meaningless sound from Rome. The birds that for Luther and Gascoigne were signs of music's innate expressiveness are at the end of *Titus* the producers of inhuman, unsympathetic noise. "Pity," the last word in Shakespeare's play, marks a symbolic boundary between Rome and the surrounding wilderness, as well as a boundary between expressive music ("mournful bells") and inarticulate music (birdsong). Yet Shakespeare suggests that even this last boundary may only be imagined: at the least, it requires not only the banishment of Tamora's body but also of Lavinia's, which Titus does finally render readable—by killing her and making her a second Virginia. *Titus* leaves its audience with the knowledge that although Lavinia is "speechless," she is nonetheless a sounding body that sobs, sighs, groans, and resonates through the theater, irreducible to the "alphabet" that Titus imposes on her. And ultimately, as with music, only the forceful silencing of this excessive resonance can end its proliferation—and thus evacuation—of meaning.

The emphasis placed on language's inability to control music's meaning is all the more striking in a play so obsessed with formal rhetoric. In *Titus*, Shakespeare uses Ovid and music to demonstrate, as he does in many other ways, the limits of rhetorical representation. Ironically, the desire to articulate human experience in language sets off a virtuosic display of words that ultimately follows an alien logic of its own. Lawrence Danson's comments on the alienating effect produced by the failure of rhetoric in the play are instructive:

> What is it, after all, that disturbs us about the rhetorical showpieces? Is it not that, in them, the sheer prominence of language breaks the expected bonds between words and world until we feel that the former has gained mastery over the latter? Mad-speech is, similarly, a language that has lost its connections with objective reality, words without referents in the shared world of the sane. The art of rhetoric, which can be the index of man's reason, can also, when it grows to a surfeit, be the token of madness.[43]

---

43. Lawrence Danson, *Tragic Alphabet: Shakespeare's Drama of Language* (New Haven, CT: Yale University Press, 1974), 16.

In the next chapter, I show how Shakespeare uses music in *Hamlet* to explore further the gap between experience and language, this time making madness itself the index of language's failure to apprehend theatrical and sonorous experience. To the extent that it exists outside of its representation in language, musical sound is *always* "mad-speech." This observation, both an indictment and a commendation, profoundly informs Shakespeare's representation of music in the plays that follow.

CHAPTER 2

"Her speech is nothing"
Mad Speech and the Female Musician

> Frailty, thy name is woman—
> A little month, or ere those shoes were old
> With which she follow'd my poor father's body,
> Like Niobe, all tears....
>
> For Hecuba!
> What's Hecuba to him, or he to her,
> That he should weep for her?
>
> —*Hamlet*

Among Shakespeare's works, *Hamlet* is not a particularly Ovidian play.[1] Still, the allusions to Niobe and Hecuba in *Hamlet* point to powerful models of female grief, famous for their ability to evoke sympathy. Moreover, for both Niobe and Hecuba, grief is speechless. Ovid's Niobe is transformed into a marble statue whose only signs of mourning are the streams of water that flow continually from her face, while Hecuba is transformed into a barking dog. In the *Metamorphoses*, Ovid draws connections between the two women by emphasizing their rhetorical virtuosity (both Niobe and Hecuba have long "set speeches") and the ultimate "stoniness" of their grief. In fact, when Ovid recounts Hecuba's reaction to the death of her son, he alludes to Niobe by describing Hecuba, now bereft of speech, as a hard stone (*duroque simillima saxo,* 13.540). In both cases, extreme grief transforms the speechful woman into a silent emblem.

Ovid's distinction between speech and emblem bears directly on Shakespeare's representation of mourning in *Hamlet* and *The Rape of Lucrece*. Mourning his father, Hamlet berates himself for being able to do nothing but speak: "[I] must, like a whore, unpack my heart with words/And fall a-cursing like a

---

1. One of the few studies that addresses Ovid's relevance to the play is Yves Peyré, "Niobe and the Nemean Lion: Reading *Hamlet* in the Light of Ovid's *Metamorphoses*," in *Shakespeare's Ovid*, ed. A. B. Taylor, 126–34 (Cambridge: Cambridge University Press, 2000).

very drab,/A scullion!" (2.2.563–65). Likewise, after being raped by Tarquin, Lucrece decries the ineffectiveness of her verbal complaint: "Out, idle words, servants to shallow fools,/Unprofitable sounds, weak arbitrators!" (1016–17). Hamlet's and Lucrece's disparagement of verbal mourning prompts them to craft visual demonstrations of the crimes committed against them: Hamlet's staging of *The Murder of Gonzago* and Lucrece's staging of her own bleeding body. For Hamlet, the recourse to theater stems from his desire for speech that is intensely audible and physical: imagining himself as the Player, Hamlet fantasizes that he will "drown the stage with tears,/And cleave the general ear with horrid speech" (2.2.539–40). Here, Hamlet imagines a type of sound that is masculine and penetrative, in stark contrast to the feminine, "whorish" speech that he brands as excessive and ineffectual. It is this fear of the vacuity of the female voice, which Ovid sets against the stony image, that drives Hamlet toward an embrace of the visual. After witnessing a theatrical representation of Hecuba herself, Hamlet professes a desire for a performance that will "amaze indeed/The very faculties of eyes and ears" (2.2.542–43). As *Hamlet* makes clear, this spectacular model of language is in constant need of iteration, since speech is always subject to its reception as purely material sound. By accusing himself of "whorish" speech, Hamlet squarely locates the idea of language's empty sonority—as we have seen writers like Gosson and Prynne do—in the female body.

In this chapter I argue that Shakespeare's use of music problematizes the models of feminine vocality and masculine visuality that Hamlet and Lucrece cite as their parameters for action. As in *Titus Andronicus,* Shakespeare foregrounds the promiscuity of musical meaning, but in ways that specifically identify this promiscuity with the female voice. In this respect, he rehearses a strand of early modern Reformist and misogynistic rhetoric that represents music's meaninglessness and women's unruliness as equivalent.[2] Shakespeare is well aware of the negative association of music and women, but he is also critical of positive representations of music that ennoble the female musician

---

2. In a series of influential essays, Linda Phyllis Austern has traced the myriad ways in which music and femininity are associated in early modern England. See "'Sing againe Syren': The Female Musician and Sexual Enchantment in Elizabethan Life and Literature," *Renaissance Quarterly* 42 (1989): 420–48; "'Alluring the auditorie to effeminacie': Music and the Idea of the Feminine in Early Modern England," *Music and Letters* 74 (1993): 343–54; "Music and the English Renaissance Controversy over Women," in *Cecilia Reclaimed: Feminist Perspectives on Gender and Music,* ed. Susan C. Cook and Judy S. Tsou (Urbana: University of Illinois Press, 1994): 52–69; "'My mother musicke': Music and Early Modern Fantasies of Embodiment," in *Maternal Measures: Figuring Caregiving in the Early Modern Period,* ed. Naomi J. Miller and Naomi Yavneh (Aldershot, UK: Ashgate, 2001); "The Siren, the Muse, and the God of Love: Music and Gender in Seventeenth-Century English Emblem Books," *Journal of Musicological Research* 18 (1999): 95–138.

at the risk of pictorializing her. The alignment of music and the female voice is in fact a double-edged sword. On the one hand, the perception of music's inarticulateness and sensual immediacy gives a singing Ophelia (and occasionally Hamlet) the effect of speaking outside of logocentric, male discourse, effectively opening up, in Lynn Enterline's words, "unexpected possibilities for the representation of subjectivity and of sexual difference."[3] On the other hand, as I will show, when music is represented in language, it becomes almost indistinguishable from simple metaphor. When this happens, musical language fuels a visual aesthetic that transforms the mourning female subject into a "speaking picture." Music's discursive promiscuity—its susceptibility to endless interpretation—makes it vulnerable to colonization by the image, making the loud, singing woman almost indistinguishable from the silent, "stony" figure whose meaning is controlled by others.

My discussion of music and the female voice in *Hamlet* necessarily centers on Ophelia, the play's most prominent musician and, for more than two centuries now, Shakespeare's most popular icon of grief. As Elaine Showalter points out in her essay on female madness in *Hamlet,* "Though she is neglected in criticism, Ophelia is probably the most frequently illustrated and cited of Shakespeare's heroines."[4] This visual legacy of Ophelia stands at odds with her role as the play's most musical character. In this way, the cultural reception of Ophelia replays an impulse *within* the play that attempts "to emblematize her, to turn her into a 'speaking picture' which, being visual rather than aural, can more easily be read."[5] For example, when Ophelia goes

---

3. Lynn Enterline, *The Rhetoric of the Body from Ovid to Shakespeare* (Cambridge: Cambridge University Press, 2000), 160. Enterline's book, which has influenced the present chapter, persuasively shows how Ovidian fictions of the voice and Petrarchan notions of subjectivity profoundly inflect Shakespeare's representation of female subjectivity in *The Rape of Lucrece.* However, unlike Enterline, I do not see music primarily as an analogue for poetic language, as her remarks on the "language of music" suggest (187–96). See also Leslie C. Dunn, "The Lady Sings in Welsh: Women's Song as Marginal Discourse on the Shakespearean Stage," in *Place and Displacement in the Renaissance,* ed. Alvin Vos, 51–67 (Binghamton, NY: SUNY Press, 1995), and Heather Dubrow, *The Challenges of Orpheus: Lyric Poetry and Early Modern England* (Baltimore: Johns Hopkins University Press, 2007), 215-27.

4. Elaine Showalter, "Representing Ophelia: Women, Madness, and the Responsibilities of Feminist Criticism," in *Shakespeare and the Question of Theory,* ed. Patricia Parker and Geoffrey Hartman (New York: Methuen, 1985), 78. On the visual and aural representation of Ophelia in the dramatic tradition, see also Bridget Gellert Lyons, "The Iconography of Ophelia," *English Literary History* 44 (1977): 60–74; Sandra K. Fischer, "Hearing Ophelia: Gender and Tragic Discourse in *Hamlet,*" *Renaissance and Reformation/Renaissance et Reforme* 26 (1990): 1–11; and David Leverenz, "The Woman in *Hamlet:* An Interpersonal View," in *Representing Shakespeare: New Psychoanalytic Essays,* ed. Murray M. Schwartz and Coppélia Kahn, 110-28 (Baltimore: Johns Hopkins University Press, 1980).

5. Leslie C. Dunn, "Ophelia's Songs in *Hamlet:* Music, Madness, and the Feminine," in *Embodied Voices: Representing Female Vocality in Western Culture,* ed. Leslie C. Dunn and Nancy A. Jones, (Cambridge: Cambridge University Press, 1994), 63.

mad, Claudius quickly mutes her speech by framing her as "poor Ophelia/Divided from herself and her fair judgement,/Without the which we are pictures or mere beasts" (4.5.80–82). Likewise Horatio describes the way in which Ophelia's strange speech is translated by her listeners into a system of visual signs:

> Her speech is nothing,
> Yet the unshapèd use of it doth move
> The hearers to collection. They aim at it,
> And botch the words up fit to their own thoughts,
> Which, as her winks and nods and gestures yield them,
> Indeed would make one think there might be thought,
> Though nothing sure, yet much unhappily.
>
> (4.5.7–13)

The emphasis on "winks and nods and gestures" here recalls the willful interpretation of Lavinia's body in *Titus Andronicus*. My point is that, by giving Ophelia a conspicuously large number of songs (more than any other character in the tragedies), Shakespeare sets up Ophelia for such acts of interpretation. And although criticism of the play has been slow to pick up on it, Shakespeare portrays these acts *as* interpretation, demonstrating the ease with which early modern critiques of music's illegibility could be applied to women in general.

For Showalter, any modern critical discussion of Ophelia is inextricable from the history of her critical and aesthetic reception. I believe this is especially the case with music, and accordingly I begin this chapter by exploring nineteenth-century representations of Ophelia, in part because they reveal to us modern assumptions about music and madness, but also because they throw into relief the play's conflation of music and female speech. In her groundbreaking study on femininity in music, Susan McClary shows that ideas about madness in the nineteenth century are organized around female sexuality and that these associations inform contemporary representations of music.[6] Romantic formulations of musical subjectivity routinely draw on narratives of madness, typically feminized, in order to describe a kind of musical experience that is beyond rational speech and that is felt to signify

---

6. Susan McClary, *Feminine Endings: Music, Gender and Sexuality* (Minneapolis: University of Minnesota Press, 1991), 80–111. McClary cites in particular the work on feminine madness done by Elaine Showalter in *The Female Malady: Women, Madness, and English Culture, 1830–1980* (New York: Pantheon Books, 1985).

true interiority.[7] Thus, not surprisingly, musical paradigms regularly appear in the Romantic accounts of Ophelia, which treat her music—when they mention it at all—as a palimpsest for their own stories of sublime experience. By "sublime," I generally mean the experience of the infinite and the transcendent in art or nature, which Romantic writers often associated with irrationality and ineffability—in Kirk Pillow's words, "that unpresentable Beyond that gives the lie to the totalizing claims of rational cognition."[8] The Romantic association of sublimity and irrationality exerts a powerful influence on nineteenth-century interpretations of Shakespeare's Ophelia, who simultaneously loses her rational voice and lapses into song. Likewise, the emphasis placed by Romantic writers on the ineffability of the sublime, especially in discussions of music, logically leads critics of Ophelia to treat her songs as if they lacked words. It is in this musical context, I suggest, that the critical tradition that identifies Ophelia as the "pathetic" center of *Hamlet* takes its distinctive shape. Romantic representations of Ophelia, both in print and on the stage, reinforce cultural associations between music, female madness, and sublimity.

Consideration of the Romantic Ophelia yields many critical dividends. First, the Romantic version has had remarkable staying power, especially in studies of music in Shakespeare. By scrutinizing Romantic claims about music, we can begin to historicize assumptions about music that have preempted a more nuanced analysis of female expressiveness in *Hamlet*. Second, Romantic criticism of Ophelia shows, with remarkable clarity, how music can be transformed into a visual object.[9] In the last twenty years critics noting the inadequate study of music in *Hamlet* have drawn attention to the competition between visual and musical modes in the play, often citing Laertes'

---

7. For a discussion on how the celebration of subjectivity in music became the structuring paradigm for its interpretation in the nineteenth century, see Jacques Barzun, *The Use and Abuse of Art* (Princeton, NJ: Princeton University Press, 1974) and Michael P. Steinberg, *Listening to Reason: Culture, Subjectivity, and Nineteenth-Century Music* (Princeton, NJ: Princeton University Press, 2004), 1–22.

8. Kirk Pillow, *Sublime Understanding: Aesthetic Reflection in Kant and Hegel* (Cambridge, MA: MIT Press, 2000), 5–6. The history of the idea of the sublime is, of course, long and complex. For example, Edmund Burke, in contrast to early English theorists of sublimity, sharply opposed the sublime with the beautiful. Other Romantic writers, including many discussed in this chapter, were less inclined to find sublimity and beauty incompatible. For general accounts of the idea of the sublime, see Samuel H. Monk, *The Sublime: A Study of Critical Theories in XVIII-Century England* (Ann Arbor: University of Michigan Press, 1960) and Thomas Weiskel, *The Romantic Sublime* (Baltimore: Johns Hopkins University Press, 1976).

9. Richard Leppert also shows how musical meaning has historically been shaped by its representation in visual modes, although he reads this phenomenon in a more positivist vein than I do. See *The Sight of Sound: Music, Representation, and the History of the Body* (Berkeley: University of California Press, 1993).

description of Ophelia—"a document in madness"—as representative of an impulse in the play to prefer visual signs to aural ones.[10] I suggest that a particular, Romantic conception of musical sublimity has helped diffuse the strangeness of Laertes' phrase, which conspicuously attaches the visual image of the "document" (with its Renaissance connotations of "emblem") to an instance of female "madness" that is perceived by Shakespeare's audience primarily through the noisy rendition of ballads and songs. Thus, almost without knowing it, modern criticism of Ophelia has from the start been tipped by contemporary musical discourse to regard as unremarkable Laertes' clunky attempt to emblematize his sister. By drawing on the rhetoric of musical sublimity, Coleridge, Hazlitt, and other commentators of the play were able to mute Ophelia's singing voice more effectively than Claudius ever dreamed of.

Yet this is not the whole story, and in the rest of the chapter's section on *Hamlet* I show how Shakespeare generates several musical contexts that strain against the emblematizing narratives of madness so willingly lapped up by Laertes and his Romantic descendants. Shakespeare's choice of songs, in particular, encourages his audience to associate freely, imagining other Ophelias than the "pretty" one prescribed by Claudius. In the chapter's last section, I consider Shakespeare's Lucrece, who also confronts the problem of translating unspeakable grief into effective expression. Like Lavinia and Ophelia, Lucrece is repeatedly associated with music, with the difference that it is Lucrece herself who makes the association. Lucrece is aware of the fact that her voice, like music, can accrue different and conflicting meanings, and that this promiscuity of sound may encourage rather than diffuse the "suspicion which the world might bear her" (1321). Moreover, just as Shakespeare uses different Ovidian models to refract Lavinia's voice in *Titus Andronicus,* Lucrece herself turns to Ovid in her search for a suitable means of expression, alternately considering Orpheus, Philomela, and Hecuba as possible figures for the female voice in crisis. "Poor instrument without a sound," Lucrece says to a painted image of Hecuba, reversing Ovid's *Metamorphoses,* which casts Hecuba as someone who can ultimately produce *only* sound. Lucrece's rewriting of Ovid's Hecuba reinscribes the two options available to the female subject: silent emblem or senseless noise. Unlike Lavinia and Ophelia, however, Lucrece is allowed to weigh and consider different models of self-representation: Philomela or Hecuba, voice or body, music or sound. It is this last grouping—music or sound—that most vividly illustrates the pitfalls of

---

10. See, for example, Dunn, "Ophelia's Songs," 50–51.

subjective expression for Lucrece, since music detached from sound is always subject to interpretation from the outside. As in *Hamlet,* Lucrece's ability to speak as subject, outside of the male-controlled discourses of sexuality and madness, hinges precisely on whether her voice is heard as music—with its susceptibility to metaphor and visual image—or as a noisy, bodily sound that "speaks across the crushing plot."[11]

Reading Ophelia

In Charles Wingate's book on Shakespearean heroines, published in 1895, the chapter on Ophelia begins, dramatically, with the following account:

> An Ophelia actually mad, chanting her pathetic song, and uttering her sad words, with all the realism of genuine insanity!
>
> It was a weird sight, and one that chilled the blood of the spectators, as they gazed in silence upon the uncanny scene.
>
> They all recognized the actress, and realized the situation. Poor Susan Mountfort, the former bright actress of Lincoln's Inn Fields, in her insanity had escaped from her custodian, and... had made straight for the playhouse. There, with all the cunning of an insane person, the woman had hidden for a time behind the wings, while her former associates carried on the play of "Hamlet." But just at the moment the Ophelia of the evening was to enter for the mad scene, Susan Mountfort, seizing her by the arm to push her back from the entrance, sprang forward in her place, and with wild eyes and wavering motion rushed upon the stage uttering the words:—
>
> "They bore him barefaced to the bier;
> Hey no nonny, nonny hey nonny."
>
> For a moment the spectators were amazed. As they began to realize the situation, a murmur ran through the house; and then came the strained silence of wonderment and perplexity.[12]

---

11. Carolyn Abbate, *Unsung Voices: Opera and Musical Narrative in the Nineteenth Century* (Princeton, NJ: Princeton University Press, 1991), ix. Abbate's book, though it does not address Romantic constructions of Shakespeare, brilliantly demonstrates how the female voice in Romantic opera can problematize assumptions about music's narrativity. Her work offers a lucid, insightful account of the way in which Romantic ideas about music continue to shape contemporary discourse about music.

12. Charles E. L. Wingate, *Shakespeare's Heroines on the Stage* (New York: Crowell, 1895), 283–84.

This passage, although it recounts a performance of *Hamlet* that took place in 1720, is remarkable for what it suggests about a nineteenth-century audience's reception of Ophelia. The narrator's seductive, gothic style of writing highlights those aspects of the historical account that he deemed most likely to appeal to his own, Victorian audience: "an Ophelia *actually* mad," "her *pathetic* song," "the *uncanny* scene," "the strained silence of *wonderment* and perplexity" (my emphases). Here, Wingate refashions the historical episode of Susan Mountfort into an early example of the Romantic object of wonderment or strangeness. Moreover, the appeal to wonderment that drives Wingate's narrative operates largely through an aesthetics of vision ("a weird sight," "they gazed in silence"), evidencing Showalter's claim that in the nineteenth century the mode of representation for Ophelia is primarily visual: "While the Augustans represent Ophelia as music, the romantics transform her into an *objet d'art*."[13]

However, while the mode of reception encouraged by Wingate prescribes that one look at Ophelia, the anecdote implicitly suggests that the theatrical Ophelia has an aural dimension as well. The initial reaction to Mountfort's Ophelia in Wingate's account is a sudden, chilled silence. The second reaction, which follows almost immediately, is an unintelligible "murmur" that runs through the theater as the audience realizes it is watching a genuine performance of madness. Next, a second, more powerful silence falls over the crowd: "the strained silence of wonderment and perplexity." Finally, amid the audience's alternating sounds and silences, the genuinely mad actress bursts onto the scene uttering snatches of ballad fragments and musical nonsense words ("Hey no nonny, nonny hey nonny"). The fact that Ophelia's verbal speeches are left out of Wingate's account suggests a connection between the authenticity of her madness and her performance of music. Thus, insofar as Wingate describes the ideal experience of *Hamlet* in the theater (as he implies), the tradition that gives representations of Ophelia their iconographic status in the nineteenth century is balanced by, and partly responsible for, a carefully controlled mode of listening. In other words, the visual representation of Ophelia is most effective when her music is heard *as* madness.

---

13. Showalter, "Representing Ophelia," 83–84. This aspect of nineteenth-century *Hamlet* criticism is vividly preserved on the cover of the latest reprint of A. C. Bradley's *Shakespearean Tragedy*, ed. John Russell Brown (1904; repr., New York: St. Martin's, 1992). The cover illustration reproduces John Everett Millais' well-known *Ophelia,* which Showalter cites as exemplary of the visual, Romantic Ophelia. In addition, Bradley's commentary on Ophelia does not address her music, except for an incidental, dismissive footnote on the "incurability" of critics who pay attention to her bawdy songs.

Nonetheless, the aural representation of madness that is recognized the moment an actress takes the stage seldom transfers to the written accounts of Ophelia in the nineteenth century. When William Hazlitt writes in 1817 that Shakespeare's Ophelia "is a character almost too exquisitely touching to be dwelt upon," he is not addressing the acoustic experience of Ophelia's songs. Hazlitt, who prefers that Shakespeare's plays be read rather than staged (*Hamlet* in particular), rejects the musical aspects of Ophelia's character in the play in favor of a purely verbal, poetic conception:

We do not like to see our author's plays acted, and least of all, *Hamlet*....[Hamlet] is, as it were, wrapped up in his reflections, and only thinks aloud. There should therefore be no attempt to impress what he says upon others by a studied exaggeration of emphasis or manner; no talking at his hearers. There should be as much of the gentleman and scholar as possible infused into the part, and as little of the actor.[14]

Not surprisingly, Hazlitt's discussion of Ophelia draws extensively on the poetic descriptions of her in the play (especially Gertrude's eulogistic passage at the end of act 4), never specifically mentioning her performed songs.

In positing a poetic Ophelia who is the supreme object of "pathos" and whose effects on the audience are too "exquisite" to be described in words, Hazlitt is echoing, perhaps unintentionally, contemporary views on absolute music. "Absolute music," in the context of nineteenth-century musical thought, generally refers to instrumental music that is not tied to any particular text or program.[15] It does not claim to "represent" anything. While some critics such as Eduard Hanslick argued that the subject of absolute music is its own musical form, others felt that it was precisely the nonrepresentational quality of absolute music that allowed it to intimate the divine, more so even than poetry or painting. In Daniel Chua's words (which, as we will see, resonate strongly with Romantic descriptions of Ophelia), absolute music was often "equated with Spirit, something too ethereal to have a history and too transcendent to be soiled by the muck of contextualisation."[16] Indeed, as

---

14. William Hazlitt, *Characters of Shakespeare's Plays* (1916; repr., London: Oxford University Press, 1966), 87–88.

15. The term "absolute music" does not have a stable meaning in the nineteenth century (the actual phrase was coined in 1846 by Richard Wagner). In current music history criticism, the term is generally discussed in the context of the historical debate about music's essential nature, particularly as the debate developed in the nineteenth century. The indispensable work on the subject is Carl Dahlhaus, *The Idea of Absolute Music,* trans. Roger Lustig (Chicago: University of Chicago Press, 1989).

16. Daniel K. L. Chua, *Absolute Music and the Construction of Meaning* (Cambridge: Cambridge University Press, 1999), 4.

CHAPTER 2

consideration of a number of nineteenth-century writings on music suggests, Hazlitt's representation of Ophelia, along with several other Romantic readings of *Hamlet,* draws on precisely those contemporary writings on aesthetics that represent music as irrational, sublime, beyond the reach of language, and intimating the absolute or infinite.

There are several reasons why the discourse on absolute music would have presented itself as a natural starting point for constructing the Romantic Ophelia. As the character who is given nearly all of the songs in *Hamlet,* Ophelia is unequivocally the musical center of the play (in fact, in the eighteenth century, the role had periodically been performed by a female singer rather than an actress).[17] Moreover, as music criticism in the nineteenth century moved away from valuations of moral character and sensibility toward an idealized view of the affections and of art for its own sake, Romantic ideas about music became well suited to interpretations of Ophelia as a figure of pathos. Equally important, as McClary has shown, musical philosophies and practices in the nineteenth century had developed a normative, culturally recognizable set of theoretical and formal procedures for representing and containing female madness in the theater. Romantic notions of subjectivity in music often depended on narratives of madness (usually female) to describe an experience beyond the limits of rational speech that could be recognized as true subjectivity.[18] In this respect, Romantic writing on music drew on and fostered a cultural association between women, music, and madness that could easily be imposed on Shakespeare's Ophelia. Nineteenth-century depictions of Ophelia, taking their cue from the contemporary discourse on music, followed suit and prompted audiences to hear her music *as* pathetic subjectivity. These practices not only allowed audiences to read and interpret a singing Ophelia; they also provided a rigid conceptual frame that could control the theatrical and acoustic excessiveness of the musical madwoman.[19] In assessing the impact of musical philosophy and practice on the Romantic reception of Ophelia, it is important to note that this discourse did not aim

---

17. Showalter, "Representing Ophelia," 83. Showalter notes that the practice of assigning Ophelia to a singer declined in the nineteenth century, unsurprisingly, as the importance of her visual appearance grew and an elaborate iconography for Ophelia developed. At the same time, even with the increased emphasis on visual representation, a successful Ophelia was still required to have a "melodious voice" (Wingate, *Shakespeare's Heroines,* 298, 308).

18. McClary, *Feminine Endings,* 80–111.

19. For a discussion on how madness in the nineteenth century is variously conceived as spectacular entertainment and threatening excess, see Michel Foucault, *Madness and Civilization: A History of Insanity in the Age of Reason,* trans. Richard Howard (New York: Vintage Books, 1988), and Klaus Doerner, *Madmen and the Bourgeoisie: A Social History of Insanity and Psychiatry,* trans. Joachim Neugroschel and Jean Steinberg (Oxford: Basil Blackwell, 1981).

to do away with music's actual sound, as Hazlitt wants to do with Ophelia's. Rather, these practices attempted to restrict significantly the meaning of that sound, especially when it was voiced by women.

The music-aesthetic paradigm, as Carl Dahlhaus has called it, that begins to take hold in Europe at the beginning of the nineteenth century typically starts out by clearing a theoretical space for itself, while simultaneously (and usually unreflectively) attributing the existence of this space to the musical phenomenon alone. True music, the new paradigm claims, is fundamentally "detached from the affections and feelings of the real world, [and] forms a 'separate world for itself.'"[20] This appropriation of a "separate world" for music was easily applied to Ophelia's character in act 4, which Claudius describes as a state of being "divided from herself and her fair judgment" (4.5.85). Nineteenth-century critics of Ophelia aestheticized her distractedness in act 4 as a manifestation of "golden-age" infantilism, perfectly embodied by what they termed "the complete innocence of the most ill-fated of all Shakespeare's heroines."[21] In this way, the Romantic reading of Ophelia typically begins by cordoning her off from the sordid politics of the Elsinore court. For the burgeoning philosophy of absolute music, one of the principal aims of theorizing a conceptual space outside of "the affections and feelings of the real world" was to posit a kind of experience not apprehensible by the written or spoken word. Thus, when E. T. A. Hoffmann writes in 1810 that "music reveals to man...a world in which he leaves behind all feelings circumscribed by intellect in order to embrace the inexpressible," he inaugurates an enduring tradition of aesthetic criticism that valorizes music precisely for its supposed inarticulateness.[22] Music, in this scheme, is truly beyond language. Quiet contemplation and an intensity of feeling, rather than analytical thought, are the necessary qualities for perceiving music's underlying beauty. In a similar way, Romantic readers of Shakespeare frequently authorize a reception of Ophelia that depends on feeling rather than speaking. In his commentary on the play, Edward Strachey removes Ophelia—and women in general—from critical discourse itself: "There is more to be felt than to be said, in the study of Ophelia's character, just because she is a creation of

---

20. Dahlhaus, *Absolute Music,* 7. The phrase in single quotes is from Wilhelm Heinrich Wackenroder, *Werke und Briefe.*

21. Charles Hiatt, *Ellen Terry and Her Impersonations* (London: Bell, 1898), 113.

22. E. T. A. Hoffmann, "Review of Beethoven's Fifth Symphony," in *E. T. A. Hoffmann's Musical Writings,* trans. Martyn Clarke, ed. David Charlton (Cambridge: Cambridge University Press, 1989), 236. On the influence of this essay on later Romantic thought, see Peter Schnaus, *E. T. A. Hoffmann als Beethoven-Rezensent der allgemeinen musikalischen Zeitung* (Munich: Musikverlag Katzbichler, 1977) and Robin Wallace, *Beethoven's Critics* (Cambridge: Cambridge University Press, 1986).

such perfectly feminine proportions."[23] Here, Strachey demonstrates how a theory of sublime beauty, consonant with the aesthetic theory of absolute music, could flow seamlessly and imperceptibly into the establishment of a purely visual aesthetic.

The Romantic exaltation of music's ineffability, its status as a "language beyond language" that cannot be apprehended by rational thought, partly explains why even music that includes a vocal text (such as a sixteenth-century folk song) could be treated as though it existed outside of language. A clear sign of the triumph of this perspective in the nineteenth century is the fact that the verbal aspects of music were generally denoted as "extramusical," thus institutionalizing a rejection of Rousseau's argument that true music is tied to language. As Dahlhaus has noted, "Without their perceiving it, the position [that proponents of Rousseau's theory of music] held had already been yielded terminologically. Whoever considers the text of a song or an opera to be 'extramusical' has appropriated [the theory of music as nonlinguistic], whether willingly or unwillingly." Dahlhaus goes on to remark that the exaltation of music's ineffability was itself influenced by the "poetic conceit of unspeakability," as put forth in poetic works like Moritz's *Andreas Hartknopf* (1785) and Jean Paul's *Hesperus* (1795); yet, even in these texts, the conceit of unspeakability is already described in terms of music.[24] For Romantic critics of Shakespeare, this idea of music enables the "de-verbalizing" of Ophelia's songs and exalts her music as the unmediated expression of "nature," as in Anna Jameson's commentary on Ophelia in *Shakespeare's Heroines* (1833): "That in her madness she should exchange her bashful silence for empty babbling, her sweet maidenly demeanour for the impatient restlessness that spurns at straws, and say and sing precisely what she never would or could have uttered *had she been in possession of her reason,* is so far from being an impropriety, that it is an additional stroke of nature."[25] For Jameson, Ophelia's sung words are not significant as language; instead, they signal a complete evacuation of linguistic meaning. Ophelia's "empty babbling" makes her the embodiment of an aesthetic ideal, just as music, unfettered by words, attains the status of "pure essentiality."[26] As in Strachey's commentary, the occlusion

---

23. Edward Strachey, *Shakespeare's Hamlet* (London, 1848), 84.
24. Dahlhaus, *Absolute Music,* 37, 60–63. Dahlhaus is referring here specifically to the thesis of Eduard Hanslick, who, in arguing that the essence of music is pure, nonverbal form, drew a sharp distinction between "musical" and "extramusical" forces, with the verbal text (whether as it appears in song, opera, or program notes) always falling under the latter.
25. Anna Jameson, *Shakespeare's Heroines: Characteristics of Women Moral, Poetical and Historical* (1833), 2nd ed. (1913; repr., London: G. Bell, 1978), 147, my emphasis.
26. This is Weisse's term. See Christian Hermann Weisse, *System der Ästhetik als Wissenschaft von der Idee der Schönheit* (1830), cited in Dahlhaus, *Absolute Music,* 100.

of verbal sense in Ophelia's music permits Jameson to slide from a discussion of music to a purely visual mode: "What an affecting, what an astonishing picture of a mind utterly, hopelessly wrecked!"[27]

Often in Romantic aesthetics, the elevation of the irrational in music leads inevitably toward a notion of the sublime. This was hardly the case for music in the eighteenth century, when the sublime was frequently linked to the "functional" and the "moral."[28] For late Romantic critics, it is precisely music's ability to *escape* the mundaneness and materiality of worldly judgment and experience that allows it to tap into absolute inwardness and achieve sublimity. This attitude toward music does much to explain Jameson's characterization of Ophelia's music as intimating both an inward, "true" Ophelia *and* a sense of timeless, universal nature. Jameson's representation of Ophelia's "sad, sweet music, which comes floating by us on the wings of night and silence, and which we rather feel than hear" creates the impression of an intensely private emotion that is never spoken, but it also suggests the transgressive experience of discovering one of nature's most fundamental secrets: "The love of Ophelia, which she never once confesses, is like a secret which we have stolen from her, and which ought to die upon our hearts as upon her own." Moreover, according to Jameson, the experience of watching and hearing Ophelia allows an audience to glimpse the "wondrous" nature of Shakespeare without realizing it: Ophelia's effect is "so profound in its pathos, that, as Hazlitt observes, it takes us back to the old ballads; we forget that, in its perfect artlessness, it is the supreme and consummate triumph of art."[29] Hazlitt's and Jameson's reference to "old ballads," though it could describe the actual ballads that Shakespeare includes in the play, pertain in this context to a figurative conception of music—music that "we rather feel than hear." The elision of actual, heard music in the reading of Ophelia has a basis in the Romantic idea that sublime music escapes, along with language, the entire world of the senses. From this perspective, "pure" music is distinct from the actual music that one apprehends with the ears. The theologian Johann Karl Friedrich Triest's comments on C. P. E. Bach's symphonies are typical of much Romantic writing on music in this regard: "Pure music is no mere shell for applied music, or abstraction from it.... It had no need to contort itself prosaically, or at best rhetorically as a mere game for the senses

---

27. Jameson, *Shakespeare's Heroines*, 146.
28. For example, Johann Georg Sulzer writes in 1771–74 that instrumental music is the medium best suited for expressing the sublime, but only insofar as it retains an indisputable, moral meaning. *Selected Writings of Johann Georg Sulzer and Heinrich Christoph Koch,* ed. Nancy K. Baker and Thomas Christensen (Cambridge: Cambridge University Press, 1995), 68.
29. Jameson, *Shakespeare's Heroines*, 134–35.

58   CHAPTER 2

or the intellect, but instead had the capacity to raise itself up to the level of poetry, which is the more pure, the less it is dragged down into the realm of common perception by words."[30] In other words, pure music is poetry, freed of both words and sound.

Of course, the Romantic tendency to metaphorize Ophelia's musical performances did not merely reflect a philosophical attachment to the idea of musical sublimity. There was a more immediate and urgent cause. Romantic readers of *Hamlet* were often embarrassed by the bawdiness and sensuality of Ophelia's songs, such as "Tomorrow Is Saint Valentine's Day." That this discomfort over the songs' actual content was widespread is evidenced by the fact that nearly all of the major nineteenth-century commentaries on Ophelia include an unambiguous (and usually very brief) rejection of the songs' relevance to the interpretation of character.[31] In this respect, the discourse of absolute music, with its habitual downplaying of music's worldly referents, provided a convenient theoretical model through which to reframe Ophelia's music as nonsensual. For example, Helena Faucit's (Lady Martin's) *Shakespeare's Female Characters* (1885) contains and sanctifies Ophelia's songs by relegating them to an innocent, irretrievable past:

> One can see the lonely child, lonely from choice, with no playmates of her kind, wandering by the streams, plucking flowers, making wreaths and coronals, learning the names of all the wild flowers in glade and dingle, having many favourites, listening with eager ears when amused or lulled to sleep at night by the country songs, whose words (in true country fashion, not too refined) come back again vividly to her memory, with the fitting melodies, only, as such things strangely but surely do, when her wits have flown.[32]

Here, Faucit weaves together elements from Gertrude's speech in act 4 with conventional notions of music's mythic, pastoral past to paint a picture of an Ophelia who lightly carries the "not too refined" words of the songs, insensible to their meaning. In Faucit's extrapolation, the "liberal shepherds" of

---

30. Johann Karl Friedrich Triest, "Remarks on the Development of the Art of Music in Germany in the Eighteenth Century," trans. Susan Gillespie, in *Haydn and His World*, ed. Elaine Sisman (Princeton, NJ: Princeton University Press, 1997), 346.

31. See Bradley, *Shakespearean Tragedy*, 140n; Jameson, *Shakespeare's Heroines*, 147; Strachey, *Shakespeare's Hamlet*, 85; J. W. von Goethe, *Wilhelm Meister's Apprenticeship* (1796), in *The Romantics on Shakespeare*, ed. Jonathan Bate (London: Penguin, 1992), 307; [Lord Byron and Percy Bysshe Shelley], "Byron and Shelley on the Character of Hamlet" (1829), unsigned dialogue, in *ibid.*, 348.

32. Helena Faucit, *On Some of Shakespeare's Female Characters* (Edinburgh: Blackwood, 1885), 9.

Gertrude's speech become the sublimated, disembodied singers often found in nineteenth-century music criticism. The pastoral setting that Faucit uses to frame Ophelia's songs is overtly idyllic, and any sexual content in the songs is carefully contained by the fantasy of "country fashion."[33] When Faucit finally does come to the scene of Ophelia's musical performance in Shakespeare's play, she transforms Ophelia's singing into an operatic scene of wrenching pathos: "[Ophelia's] forcing her way into the presence of the queen... clamouring for her will, and with her winks, nods, and gestures, 'strewing dangerous conjectures in ill-breeding minds,' tells with a terrible emphasis how all is changed, and how her reason, too, has become 'like sweet bells jangled, out of tune and harsh.'"[34] Here, Faucit appropriates Ophelia's own reaction to Hamlet's madness in act 3: "Now see that noble and most sovereign reason/Like sweet bells jangled out of tune and harsh" (3.1.156–57). Thus, Ophelia's musical metaphor is used against her, framing her musical performance as nothing other than genuine madness. By creating a poetic narrative of innocence and subsequent madness that sublimates Ophelia's musical eruptions, Faucit follows the approach taken by Samuel Coleridge, who is particularly adept at dispelling the sexual dimension of Ophelia's music. Without ever directly referring to the songs, Coleridge describes Ophelia's singing as "the guileless floating on the surface of her pure imagination of the cautions so lately expressed, and the fears not too delicately avowed, by her father and brother, concerning the dangers to which her honour lay exposed.... Thought, affliction, passion, murder itself—she turns to favour and prettiness."[35] Coleridge's remarks, which use Laertes' words as his own, imply that the appropriate critical approach to Ophelia is one that treats her as a sister and—more importantly—treats her music as a "pretty" picture.

Of course, different contexts yield different stories. While nineteenth-century models of art work hard to mystify and sublimate the sensuous physicality of a singing Ophelia, consideration of early modern practices of music composition and performance may yield a less totalizing view of a singing woman. To be sure, *Hamlet* evokes the most misogynistic writings about music and women in early modern England, but in giving Ophelia a large number of songs in act 4, it also presents a performative opportunity to challenge the reductive paradigms represented as fact in these writings.

---

33. See, however, Mary Cowden Clarke, *The Girlhood of Shakespeare's Heroines* (New York, 1852), in which Ophelia's early years are not at all idyllic.

34. Faucit, *Shakespeare's Female Characters*, 25–26.

35. Samuel Coleridge, *Literary Remains* (1836–39), in Bate, *Romantics on Shakespeare,* 321.

CHAPTER 2

Modern criticism of Shakespeare's Ophelia, drawing on historical and musicological contexts for sixteenth-century music, comes to different conclusions about the effect of Ophelia's music. F. W. Sternfeld, citing Castiglione's prescriptions for noble female behavior in *The Book of the Courtier,* emphasizes the indecorous, disturbing effect of Ophelia in act 4, characterizing her musical performance as a "betrayal of her nobility." Amanda Winkler, on the other hand, citing the popularity of mad scenes in seventeenth-century English drama, notes the potential attractiveness of a singing Ophelia, her music being "the aural equivalent of the flowers Ophelia adorns herself with before she drowns."[36] I believe that both readings speak to the ambiguous (and therefore unsettling) effect that Ophelia's presence has on her onstage and offstage audiences. The range of interpretation offered by a singing Ophelia also gives much latitude to the performer, who can make her either charming or disconcerting. (In my own Shakespeare classes, I often show Jean Simmons's and Helena Bonham Carter's performances side by side to demonstrate this.) As Winkler points out, some of this ambiguity is a function of the songs themselves: the setting for "How Should I Your True Love Know," for example, which follows a traditional English ballad style, "in its simplicity... gives the performer freedom of interpretation."[37] While the particular songs chosen by Shakespeare leave much up to performance, their ambiguity in the context of the scene also permits an audience's presumptions about music and women to play freely in producing an interpretation. In other words, by prompting his audience to form an idea of Ophelia based on her music, Shakespeare compels them to put their ideological cards on the table.

Much of Ophelia's music plays well into the hands of listeners who, like some sixteenth-century commentators, associate music and women with intemperate sensuous pleasure. For example, in one of the possible musical settings for Ophelia's second song, "Tomorrow Is Saint Valentine's Day," the melody is particularly brisk and rollicking—in contrast to Ophelia's first song, "How Should I Your True Love Know," whose sixteenth-century musical analogues are all accompanied by a relatively slow, plaintive melody. In "Saint Valentine's Day," through a rising melodic interval, the musical emphasis falls on "then up he rose" and "let in the maid," encouraging the listener to dwell on the incipient bawdiness of these phrases as well as

---

36. F. W. Sternfeld, *Music in Shakespearean Tragedy* (London: Routledge, 1963), 54–55, and Amanda Eubanks Winkler, *O Let Us Howle Some Heavy Note: Music for Witches, the Melancholic, and the Mad on the Seventeenth-Century English Stage* (Bloomington: Indiana University Press, 2006), 86.

37. Winkler, *O Let Us Howle,* 88.

pushing the singer to mimic vocally the sexual act by raising the pitch of her voice and creating a melodic tension that demands resolution.[38] Similarly, the lover's defection at the end of the song is lightened by a similar rising melodic line, suggesting that the lover's sexual enjoyment has been the song's predominant theme. Whether or not this setting resembles the one used in original productions of the play, it provides a good illustration of the way in which Ophelia's music *in performance* may emphasize precisely those aspects of her character that nineteenth-century critics attempted to ignore. Early twentieth-century critics who, in contrast to the Romantics, paid more attention to the affective aspects of Ophelia's songs, identified a discernible difference between an Ophelia who is read and an Ophelia who is heard, even if they approached the subject with some delicacy: "Her songs of love have a tinge of the forbidden."[39]

Even the Romantic conception of a pathetic, lovesick Ophelia can be partially constructed by comparing some of her songs to their contemporary analogues. For example, in attempting to explain the origin of Ophelia's madness, some critics have cited the songs as evidence of her grief over Hamlet's abandonment or her shock at Polonius's death.[40] In choosing one explanation over the other, these readings downplay the songs' discomfiting conflation of sexual desire with a sense of guilt about a parent's death—a conflation even more explicit in the analogues. For example, Ophelia's first song in act 4, "How Should I Your True Love Know," is generally read as touching on Ophelia's love for Hamlet, despite the references to a white shroud "larded

---

38. This is the setting suggested by Sternfeld, *Music in Shakespearean Tragedy*, 63. Ross Duffin suggests a similar (though slightly less rollicking) setting based on the same tune. *Shakespeare's Songbook* (New York: W. W. Norton, 2004), 407–8. Peter J. Seng, however, argues that the evidence that this tune was the actual one used in the original production of *Hamlet* is tenuous at best. *The Vocal Songs in the Plays of Shakespeare* (Cambridge, MA: Harvard University Press, 1967), 146. Certainly, there has been no reliable evidence to support the idea that the same musical settings for songs in the plays were generally maintained from production to production, or even from performance to performance. Rather, what I believe is relevant about Sternfeld's and Duffin's suggested settings is their representation of a *tradition* of English Renaissance song composition that, generally speaking, directly affected the inclusion of music in Shakespearean and other contemporary plays. In other words, by noticing the relatively general aspects of the possible settings for the songs (e.g., plaintive vs. brisk), one can identify certain qualities of sixteenth-century compositions that can suggest a possible range of performances.

39. Joseph T. McCullen Jr., "The Functions of Songs Aroused by Madness in Elizabethan Drama," in *A Tribute to George Coffin Taylor: Studies and Essays, Chiefly Elizabethan, by His Students and Friends*, ed. Arnold Williams, 185–96 (Chapel Hill: University of North Carolina Press, 1952). See also J. Max Patrick, "The Problem of Ophelia," in *Studies in Shakespeare*, ed. Arthur D. Matthews and Clark M. Emery, 139–44 (Coral Gables, FL: University of Miami Press, 1953).

40. For an account of the debate over Ophelia's madness, see Carroll Camden, "On Ophelia's Madness," *Shakespeare Quarterly* 15 (1964): 247–55.

with sweet flowers" (4.5.37). One sixteenth-century analogue, which shares a line with Ophelia's first song, also relates the theme of romantic disappointment, but it associates it with the death of an aging parent:

> I have loued her all my youth
> but now am old as you see
> loue liketh not the ffalling ffruite
> nor the whithered tree
> for loue is like a carlesse child.[41]

Although Ophelia's references to "true-love showers" suggest Hamlet, the latent theme of childish fickleness in the analogue evokes a context that speaks to the possibility of Ophelia's guilt over her father's death. Taken together, the representation of death and feminine sexuality, suggested by the double symbolism of burial flowers, paints a psychological narrative in which Polonius's death releases guilt-ridden fantasies of sexual profligacy for Ophelia.[42] The conjunction of the death of a man and female, sexual power is suggested by another analogue, also found in the Percy Folio, in which the song's female speaker relates a scenario in which her sexual allurement and subsequent rejection of a man results in his death.[43] Seen through this vocal tradition, Ophelia's contamination of funereal ballads with bawdy folk songs can be imagined as reflecting a model of filial love contaminated by sexuality. In this respect, her madness appears as a female version of Hamlet's fantasy of maternal sexuality, as articulated by Janet Adelman: "The idealized father's absence releases the threat of maternal sexuality, in effect subjecting the son to her annihilating power. But the dream-logic of this plot-conjunction is also reversible; if the father's death leads to the mother's sexualized body, the mother's sexualized body . . . leads to the father's death."[44] In Ophelia's case, the sexualized female body that causes the father's death is her own. Indeed, if we try to give coherence to Ophelia's music by contextualizing it within its contemporary musical tradition, as Peter Seng does in his source work on the songs, it is possible to create a narrative of female sexual guilt that stems from paternal proscription: "The heroine of the song is far from being the Ophelia

---

41. Seng, *Vocal Songs,* 137–38. The ballad that Seng compares here is "As Ye Came from the Holy Land of Walsingham."

42. See Showalter, "Representing Ophelia," who notes that Ophelia's flowers "suggest the discordant double images of female sexuality as both innocent blossoming and whorish contamination; she is the 'green girl' of pastoral, the virginal 'Rose of May' and the sexually explicit madwoman who, in giving away her wild flowers and herbs, is symbolically deflowering herself" (81).

43. Seng, *Vocal Songs,* 139.

44. Janet Adelman, *Suffocating Mothers: Fantasies of Maternal Origin in Shakespeare's Plays* (New York: Routledge, 1992), 18.

that Hamlet knew; rather she is the Ophelia that Polonius and Laertes, without real cause, had feared their daughter and sister might become."[45]

To be sure, these kinds of sense making presume that the meaning of Renaissance songs is determined by their texts, the paradigms associated with their melodic or harmonic conventions, or a combination of both. Each of these pieces of "evidence" is a context that can be used to curb the promiscuity of musical sound—to normalize its effect in performance. As some contexts fall out of critical favor, other ones emerge as valid. For one nineteenth-century English audience, the biographical story of Susan Mountfort (believed to have actually gone mad) was an especially persuasive context for understanding Ophelia's musical utterances. Shakespeare seems to have realized that the combination of music and femininity provided an especially rich site for competing contexts, since the inherent voicelessness of music and the imposed voicelessness of women offer manifold opportunities for acts of ventriloquism. If, as Linda Phyllis Austern has pointed out, women in early modern England provided "a cultural and political construct on to which men could project their own desires," then music only amplified the possibilities for projection.[46]

And yet, the compulsion to inscribe male fantasies on women is a subject of the play itself. One of the play's ironies is the fact that Gertrude provides what has become the most enduring sublimation of Ophelia's madness and music. In her account of Ophelia's death at the end of act 4, a tour de force of purple poetry, Gertrude gives a textbook demonstration of the way in which verbal descriptions of music can transform sound into image:

> There is a willow grows aslant a brook
> That shows his hoar leaves in the glassy stream.
> Therewith fantastic garlands did she make
> Of crow-flowers, nettles, daisies, and long purples,
> That liberal shepherds give a grosser name,
> But our cold maids do dead men's fingers call them.
> There on the pendent boughs her crownet weeds
> Clamb'ring to hang, an envious sliver broke,
> When down the weedy trophies and herself
> Fell in the weeping brook. Her clothes spread wide,
> And mermaid-like a while they bore her up;
> Which time she chanted snatches of old tunes,

---

45. Seng, *Vocal Songs,* 148.
46. Austern, "'Alluring the auditorie,'" 345. Austern here is citing an argument made by Virginia Mason Vaughan about *Troilus and Cressida.*

> As one incapable of her own distress,
> Or like a creature native and endued
> Unto that element. But long it could not be
> Till that her garments, heavy with their drink,
> Pulled the poor wretch from her melodious lay
> To muddy death.
>
> (4.7.137–54)

Here, the physical sound of Ophelia's singing voice disappears under the weight of its metaphorization. The conspicuous loudness of Ophelia's earlier songs is muted by a revisionist history that refers to them as "old tunes," a phrase that neatly places the songs in a distant, rustic environment. Similarly, Gertrude's speech hints at Ophelia's sexuality in a way that assimilates it into a pastoral scene ("long purples/That liberal shepherds give a grosser name"). In this case, "naturalization" is neutralization, and pastoral language cooperates with metaphorical descriptions of music to render the mad Ophelia poetically and visually—and harmlessly—pleasing. Insofar as Gertrude's speech is the inspiration for all subsequent literary descriptions of Ophelia, it institutionalizes an early modern practice of musical representation, all the while obscuring the difference between a sounding woman who "gives tongue" too much and a female image whose sound is muted by a narrative of pathos and wonderment.[47]

This is not to say that the play and its literary history efface all traces of Ophelia's sound. The presence of a sounding, theatrical Ophelia who resists the authorized readings of herself as pathos and pictorial beauty is briefly and unexpectedly glimpsed in A. C. Bradley's *Shakespearean Tragedy* (1904), a work that incorporates many nineteenth-century views in its interpretation of *Hamlet*. Typical of Bradley's style, critical bumps in the road are conveniently swept into the footnotes, which at first glance appear to be mere digressions. This is especially the case in Bradley's commentary on Ophelia. Emphasizing the aesthetic appeal of Ophelia's madness, he relegates to a footnote a possible qualification to his claim that Ophelia's expression of grief is "never the agonized cry of fear or horror which makes madness dreadful or shocking":

> I have heard an actress in this part utter such a cry as is described above, but there is absolutely nothing in the text to justify her rendering. Even

---

47. The phrase is borrowed from F. T. Prince, who uses it to describe Shakespeare's Lucrece, who "loses our sympathy exactly in proportion to the extent she gives tongue." See Shakespeare, *The Poems*, ed. F. T. Prince (London: Methuen, 1969), xxvi.

the exclamation 'O, ho!' found in the Quartos at IV.v.33, but omitted in the Folios and by almost all modern editors, coming as it does after the stanza, 'He is dead and gone, lady,' evidently expresses grief, not terror.[48]

What is most striking here is not its textual contradiction (only a few pages earlier Bradley vehemently defends a passage in *Hamlet* that is present in the Second Quarto but missing in the First Quarto and First Folio) but the way in which Bradley simultaneously evokes and dispels the problem of an overly sonorous Ophelia who challenges the Romantic attempt to reduce her to pictures. Here, a theatrical Ophelia who cries out loudly and who emphasizes the nonverbal aspects of her role ("O, ho!") disrupts the critical reading of an innocent, pathetic heroine. By treating Ophelia's music as poetry rather than performed sound, Bradley betrays the anxiety that musical sound is independent of verbal and textual systems of meaning. Thus Bradley's remark that there is "absolutely nothing *in the text* to justify" the sonorous exuberance of an actress playing Ophelia is on the mark, though not in the manner he intends.[49] By demonstrating how Ophelia's sound is moved to the margins—literally, in this case—of her critical history, Bradley shows how the translation of music into poetry and image is not merely an aesthetic whim or a rejection of medieval cosmography. These discursive practices, observable in early modern musical writing, are crucial in reining in music's promiscuity and making it legible. In turn, these same discursive practices have enabled a reading of Ophelia that has been remarkable for its durability well into the twentieth century and beyond, solidifying Ophelia as the figure par excellence of romantic pathos and female madness in Shakespearean drama.

"Weak words": Lucrece and the Musical Subject

In *Titus Andronicus* and *Hamlet,* Shakespeare demonstrates how the female voice, like music, is vulnerable to the politics of context. In this regard, Horatio's comment that Ophelia's listeners "botch the words up fit to their own

---

48. Bradley, *Shakespearean Tragedy*, 139.
49. In another footnote, Bradley suggests that Ophelia's singing is promiscuous in a literal sense as well: "There are critics who, after all the help given them...still shake their heads over Ophelia's song, 'Tomorrow is Saint Valentine's Day.' Probably they are incurable." (*Shakespearean Tragedy*, 140n). This is the only reference Bradley makes to Ophelia's actual music.

thoughts" points to a more general practice of meaning making that takes advantage of female silence and musical promiscuity. Instead of responding to this promiscuity by presenting an authoritative view of music in his works, Shakespeare makes interpretation itself the focus of attention. *The Rape of Lucrece* dwells on this slipperiness of musical meaning. Both the poem's speaker and Lucrece herself obsess over the ways in which Lucrece's voice and body, like music, are susceptible to interpretation. And again, Shakespeare amplifies the promiscuity of music and female voice by recourse to Ovid, offering for review a number of Ovidian analogues for Lucrece who straddle the boundary between music and meaningless sound (Orpheus, Philomela, Hecuba). As Lucrece becomes aware of the porosity of her own voice—the idea that she cannot control the meanings that will accrue to her "publishing" of Tarquin's rape—she comes to the realization that an aesthetics of vision can subsume both vocal and musical utterance, especially when authorized by men. In this sense, Lucrece confronts the possibility of becoming a visual objet d'art for posterity—a worry that, given the several paintings of Lucrece in Renaissance Europe, is well-founded. *The Rape of Lucrece* provides another powerful demonstration of the stakes involved in the bait-and-switch game that is often played out in the representation of music, image, and the female voice.

At the beginning of *The Rape of Lucrece,* sexual purity is imagined as part of a world in which meaning is always stable. Early on, Lucrece's chastity coincides with her ability to read people and events as clear texts: "For unstained thoughts do seldom dream on evil./Birds never limed no secret bushes fear" (87–88). In turn, the poem represents Lucrece at this stage as absolutely readable. As she listens to Tarquin's account of Collatine's martial victories, Lucrece's silent bodily gestures are clear expressions of her feelings: "Her joy with heaved-up hand she doth express,/And wordless so greets heaven for his success" (111–12). Unlike Ophelia's mad gestures, whose meaning changes according to the whims of her audience, Lucrece's "heaved-up hand" admits only a single meaning. With the arrival of Tarquin, however, Shakespeare compares Lucrece's tranquil mode of interpretation to an act of *mis*reading:

> But she that never coped with stranger eyes
> Could pick no meaning from their parling looks,
> Nor read the subtle shining secrecies
> Writ in the glassy margins of such books.
> She touched no unknown baits nor feared no hooks,
>   Nor could she moralize his wanton sight
>   More than his eyes were opened to the light.
>   (99–105)

Here, Lucrece is like the naive, untrained reader who, caught up in a poem's fiction, fails to understand, or "moralize," the true, allegorical meaning underneath. At the same time, Shakespeare's reference to marginalia ("glassy margins") is part of a larger pattern of metaphors of enclosure in the poem that typically represent Lucrece as the surrounded object: "the lightless fire/Which...lurks to aspire/And girdle with embracing flames the waist/Of Collatine's fair love" (5–7), and "This silent war of lilies and of roses/...In their pure ranks his traitor eye encloses" (71–73). In this way the poem repeatedly represents Lucrece as something to be read, as a text to be framed and glossed.[50] Thus, while Tarquin's rape exposes as inadequate Lucrece's belief in visual signs, it also demonstrates Lucrece's inability to control the meaning of her voice and body. When Lucrece heaves her hands a second time in the poem, she finds that they inspire a different meaning from what she intends: "To thee, to thee, my heaved-up hands appeal,/Not to seducing lust, thy rash relier" (638–39). Tarquin's response— "my uncontrollèd tide/Turns not, but swells the higher by this let" (645–46)—plays on the early modern meanings of "let," which can mean either "prevent" or "allow," and demonstrates the ease with which he shapes her responses to his own will.[51] As a hermeneutic event, Tarquin's rape portrays Lucrece as a text that can be endlessly interpreted: Lucrece, originally "published" by Collatine as a figure of chastity, is reinterpreted, or "moralized," by Tarquin as a willing sexual partner.

Tarquin's ability to interpret Lucrece at will points to the discursive promiscuity of visual signs, especially when they originate in the female body. Even more than visual signs, however, the poem emphasizes the instability of meaning in sound. For example, before the rape, Shakespeare describes a number of sounds that signify future events, but whose intended meanings are lost on the poem's characters:

Now stole upon the time the dead of night
When heavy sleep had closed up mortal eyes.
No comfortable star did lend his light,
No noise but owls' and wolves' death-boding cries
(162–65)

---

50. Tarquin also describes Lucrece as a text, when he compares his rape to defacing a text: "And die, unhallowed thoughts, before you *blot*/With your uncleanness that which is divine" (192–93; emphasis added). Shakespeare uses the term "blot" in a similar sense at line 948. On the idea that Lucrece imagines her own body as a text, see Enterline, *Rhetoric of the Body*, 153–54.

51. Joel Fineman makes a similar point, arguing that ambiguous signification in the poem turns Lucrece's "no" into "yes." See "Shakespeare's Will: The Temporality of Rape," in *The Subjectivity Effect in Western Literary Tradition* (Cambridge, MA: MIT Press, 1991), 165–221.

> The threshold grates the door to have him heard,
>> Night-wand'ring weasels shriek to see him there.
> They fright him, yet he still pursues his fear.
>
>> (306–8)

Tarquin reacts with "fright" to the grating doors and shrieking weasels, but he does not understand their conventional, emblematic meanings: "He in the worst sense consters their denial./The doors, the wind, the glove that did delay him/He takes for accidental things of trial" (324–26). As with Lucrece's body, Tarquin loads these signs with a meaning that encourages rather than warns against sexual action. Echoing Tamora in *Titus Andronicus*, and again playing on the different meanings of "let," Tarquin interprets the sound of birds as music conducive to his passion:

> 'So, so,' quoth he, 'these lets attend the time,
> Like little frosts that sometime threat the spring
> To add a more rejoicing to the prime,
> And give the sneapèd birds more cause to sing.'
>
>> (330–33)

The point is not that Tarquin simply misreads the sounds of owls and birds but that he contextualizes them within a biased system of meaning that favors his own campaign, in effect enacting the same kind of moralization that early modern marginalia often performs on its text.

Tarquin's habit of conferring the "worst" meaning on the various sounds in the poem is reflected and dilated in his response to Lucrece. As many readers of the poem have rightly noted, Tarquin's rape of Lucrece is tantamount to his attempt to control her voice: "Till with her own white fleece her voice controlled/Entombs her outcry in her lips' sweet fold" (678–79). Here, Tarquin's muffling of Lucrece not only dampens her actual sound; it also reduces her voice to nonverbal noise, capable of being aestheticized. Tarquin's rape is enacted through a series of interpretative acts in which the sound of Lucrece's voice is detached from its intended meaning and eroticized, much in the same way that he earlier interprets the sound of owls and birds as encouraging musical signs. At this point in the poem, Lucrece becomes fodder for poetry itself: "The wolf hath seized his prey, the poor lamb cries" (677). Enterline reads this scene as Shakespeare's construction of Lucrece as "both the Petrarchan object of praise and another Philomela."[52]

---

52. Enterline, *Rhetoric of the Body,* 154. See also Coppélia Kahn, "The Rape in Shakespeare's *Lucrece,*" *Shakespeare Studies* 9 (1976): 45–72, and Nancy Vickers, "'The blazon of sweet beauty's

Yet Tarquin is complicit in this Petrarchan project, and his eroticization of Lucrece's cries normalizes the aestheticization of Philomela's mangled body in the *Metamorphoses,* making her "clamorous" sound a cooling repository for male sexual relief: "He pens her piteous clamours in her head,/ Cooling his hot face in the chastest tears" (681–82). His violent contextualization of Lucrece's cries reiterates the point, made in *Hamlet,* that the female voice, like music, provides fertile ground for the inscription of male desire. The idea that Tarquin can bend both music and Lucrece's voice to his will is made explicit earlier in the poem, when Tarquin threatens to make Lucrece herself the subject of a musical performance:

So thy surviving husband shall remain
The scornful mark of every open eye,
Thy kinsmen hang their heads at this disdain,
Thy issue blurred with nameless bastardy,
And thou, the author of their obloquy,
    Shalt have thy trespass cited up in rhymes
    And sung by children in succeeding times.
              (519–25)

Here, Tarquin conflates the female body, with its inability to signify paternity ("thy issue blurred"), with music that is subject to the perspectives of the persons who are transmitting it ("rhymes...sung by children"). Her kinsmen's "obloquy," contaminated by Tarquin's rape and false account, would lead to an even more radical proliferation of meaning when transposed to music sung by children. Moreover, the violence of Tarquin's warning is such that it threatens to feminize Collatine himself, making him a voyeuristic object ("the scornful mark of every open eye"), as well as a subject for music.

Shakespeare explores the idea of music's uncertain effects through the rest of the poem, by recourse to a select group of Ovidian figures of speechlessness. Tarquin's reference to future "rhymes" may thus be read as a negative version of Ovid's remark at the end of the *Metamorphoses* that he will live immortally on the mouths of people (*ore legar populi...vivam,* 15.878–79). Along the same lines, the poem's narrator represents Lucrece's response to Tarquin's threat as the windy utterances ("pitchy vapours," 550) of a failed Orpheus: "So his unhallowed haste her words delays,/ And moody Pluto winks while Orpheus plays" (552–53). Here, the comparison

---

best': Shakespeare's *Lucrece,"* in Parker and Hartman, *Shakespeare and the Question of Theory,* 95–115.

with Orpheus functions as a testament of Lucrece's power of verbal eloquence, a mode of rhetoric that is distinguished by its nonverbal, physical qualities:

> Her modest eloquence with sighs is mixed,
> Which to her oratory adds more grace.
> She puts the period often from his place,
>   And midst the sentence so her accent breaks
>   That twice she doth begin ere once she speaks.
> 					(563–67)

Less noticed in Lucrece's Orphic utterance is the way in which Shakespeare points to music as a *nonverbal,* acoustic phenomenon.[53] In this respect, the poem follows Ovid's account of Orpheus in the *Metamorphoses,* which also draws attention to music's physical nature. Attacked by the Ciconian women, Orpheus demonstrates his ability to deflect stones with his music: "Another threw a stone, which, even as it flew through the air, was overcome by the sweet sound of voice and lyre, and fell at his feet as if 't would ask forgiveness for its mad attempt" (*alterius telum lapis est, qui missus in ipso/ aere concentu victus vocisque lyraeque est/ ac veluti supplex pro tam furialibus ausis/ ante pedes iacuit,* 11.10–13). Yet while it can move physical objects, Orpheus's music depends on a physical act of listening, and for this reason the louder music of the bacchantes eventually renders Orpheus's music powerless: "And all their weapons would have been harmless under the spell of song; but the huge uproar of the Berecyntian flutes, mixed with discordant horns, the drums, and the breast-beatings and howlings of the Bacchanals, drowned the lyre's sound" (*cunctaque tela forent cantu mollita, sed ingens/ clamor et infracto Berecyntia tibia cornu/ tympanaque et plausus et Bacchei ululatus/ obstrepuere sono citharae,* 11.15–18). Just as Orpheus's music cannot transcend the physicality of its production, Lucrece's eloquence fails against Tarquin's physical ability to stifle her voice. Moreover, while her Orphic rhetoric gives her speech a musical "grace," the bodily aspects of rhetoric (sighs, tears, beating heart) are construed by Tarquin as an impetus to lust: "His ear her prayers admit, but his

---

53. The Renaissance characterization of eloquence as Orphic song has a long tradition. See Sean Keilen, *Vulgar Eloquence: On the Renaissance Invention of English Literature* (New Haven, CT: Yale University Press, 2006). Enterline reads this stanza as an *un*musical moment, arguing that "such failures of phrasing...disrupt Lucrece's musical and verbal discourse" (*Rhetoric of the Body,* 173). However, grammatical fluency is not the same as musical effect. Shakespeare more often points out music's independence of its verbal sense, and his use of "grace" in this passage suggests that music's extratextual qualities are precisely what make it persuasive.

heart granteth/ No penetrable entrance to her plaining./ Tears harden lust, though marble wear with raining" (558–60). Quite literally, Lucrece's Orphic music fans the flames of Tarquin's desire.

The dubious efficacy of music as a model for the female voice is apparent after the rape, when Lucrece's task is to publicize the rape rather than persuade against it. At this point in the poem, Lucrece resembles Ovid's Philomela, who also attempts to publish an event that Ovid describes as *nefas* (literally, something that is indescribable).[54] In a passage that both echoes and alludes to Philomela, Lucrece announces that she too will cast aside shame and proclaim her rape by Tarquin:

'My tongue shall utter all; mine eyes, like sluices,
   As from a mountain spring that feeds a dale
   Shall gush pure streams to purge my impure tale.'

By this, lamenting Philomel had ended
The well-tuned warble of her nightly sorrow.
(1076–80)

The description of Lucrece as a "lamenting Philomel" who "warbles" evokes an uneasy identification between two Ovidian figures: the unmutilated Philomela who will speak her rape (*loquar*) and the metamorphosed nightingale whose power of expression lacks speech. The doubleness of this allusion registers the double sense of "lament," which can suggest either a verbal complaint or the affective quality of a plaintive melody. A similar ambiguity is suggested by "warble," which in early modern writing is sometimes used to describe poetic eloquence; more often, however, "warbling" denotes a poetic or musical performance that is enchanting in its physical sonority, regardless of its verbal sense.[55] In this way, Shakespeare's language makes tenuous the distinction between Lucrece's *speaking* voice and its mellifluous, aesthetically appealing *sound*. In other words, by framing Lucrece's "wordy" complaint as a musical performance, the poem demonstrates the way—familiar to us from the literary history of *Hamlet*—in which musically compelling speech

---

54. Enterline, *Rhetoric of the Body,* 3. On this reading of *nefas* in Ovid, see also Elissa Marder, "Disarticulated Voices: Feminism and Philomela," *Hypatia* 7 (1992): 158, and William S. Anderson, *Ovid's Metamorphoses, Books 6–10* (Norman: University of Oklahoma Press, 1972), 227–28.

55. The sense of "warble" as specifically nonverbal music or sound is especially popular in Renaissance attacks on polyphony and the theater. The different meanings of "warble" are taken up more fully in chapter 6.

can be transformed into an aesthetic object. Lucrece's verbal loss is the narrator's poetic gain.

The shift from verbal complaint to wordless music is registered a few lines later by Lucrece herself, again with reference to Ovid's Philomela:

> Come, Philomel, that sing'st of ravishment,
> Make thy sad grove in my dishevelled hair.
> As the dank earth weeps at thy languishment,
> So I at each sad strain will strain a tear,
> And with deep groans the diapason bear;
>   For burden-wise I'll hum on Tarquin still,
>   While thou on Tereus descants better skill.
>   (1128–34)

In this imagined duet with the nightingale, Lucrece blurs the relationship between music and its verbal meanings. "Burden" denotes a musical and verbal refrain, generally sung by the lowest voice, that repeats the song's main theme. Thus, by singing the "diapason" and the "burden," Lucrece assigns to herself the lower voice, which carries the "sense" of the song, while the nightingale will draw out and embellish the syllables of individual words in the "descant."[56] By making "Tarquin" her musical burden, Lucrece follows the example of Gascoigne's nightingale in *The Complainte of Phylomene*, who names her attacker by singing "Tereu" over and over again. However, Lucrece's remark that she will "hum" the burden implies a nonverbal kind of music, in effect blurring the difference between her voice and birdsong. This ambiguity helps create a "subjectivity effect" in the musical sound of the nightingale—a sense of sympathy between Lucrece and the nightingale—but at the risk of calling attention to the purely sonorous aspects of her own lament. Moreover, Lucrece's address demonstrates the arbitrariness and self-interestedness of musical interpretation; her representation of birdsong a few lines earlier makes the scene of musical sympathy seem like a solipsistic response rather than an inspired reading of natural sounds:

> 'You mocking birds,' quoth she, 'your tunes entomb
> Within your hollow-swelling feathered breasts,

---

56. This is the primary meaning that Thomas Morley ascribes to "descant," although he acknowledges that the term is flexible: "The name of Descant is usurped of the musitions in divers significations: sometime they take it for the whole harmony of many voyces: others sometime for one of the voyces or partes... last of all, they take it for singing a part extempore upon a playnesong, in which sence we commonly use it." *A Plaine and Easie Introduction to Practicall Musicke* (1597), facsimile reprint (Amsterdam: Da Capo, 1969), 70.

And in my hearing be you mute and dumb;
My restless discord loves no stops nor rests;
A woeful hostess brooks not merry guests.
 Relish your nimble notes to pleasing ears;
 Distress likes dumps when time is kept with tears.'
(1121–27)

Lucrece's identification with Philomela founds itself on a fantasy of musical meaning in which birdsong is heard as expressive, much in the same way that Tarquin fantasizes a meaning for birdsong when he attempts to find encouragement for the rape in the natural soundscape around him.

Lucrece's apostrophe to Philomela reveals both the advantages and disadvantages of representing her voice as music. Music's inexpressibility in words makes it a tempting vehicle for the untranslatable aspects of Lucrece's experience, the "more...than one hath the power to tell" (1288). At the same time, insofar as Lucrece's use of musical examples recalls Tarquin's and the narrator's formal strategies, it raises the idea that a musical reading of the female voice may actually preempt the intended meaning of that voice. Lucrece's recourse to formal music, marked by her reference to technical terms, puts into play a network of visual images that aestheticizes the musical subject:

'And whiles against a thorn thou bear'st thy part
To keep thy sharp woes waking, wretched I,
To imitate thee well, against my heart
Will fix a sharp knife to affright mine eye.'
(1135–38)

Here, Lucrece's musical identification with Philomela turns into a *visual* identification, in which the image of the "sharp knife" against Lucrece's heart suggests both the scene of rape and the image of the nightingale, who sings as a result of being pierced. This slide from music to visual icon is registered again a few lines later, in the language the narrator uses to describe Lucrece's voice as music:

This plot of death when sadly she had laid,
And wiped the brinish pearl from her bright eyes,
With untuned tongue she hoarsely calls her maid,
....
 Poor Lucrece' cheeks unto her maid seem so
 As winter meads when sun doth melt their snow.
(1212–18)

CHAPTER 2

Here, the musical representation of Lucrece's voice ("sadly she had laid," "with untuned tongue") gives way to a familiar set of visual, Petrarchan metaphors for the female body ("brinish pearl from her bright eyes," "cheeks...as winter meads"), demonstrating how the metaphoricity of musical language smooths its transition to the poetics of the blazon.

For Lucrece, the fear of becoming a visual icon is very real, since with iconicity comes the threat of an infinite number of narratives beyond her control: "That dying fear through all her body spread;/And who cannot abuse a body dead?" (1266–67). The anxiety over the discursive promiscuity of her dead body compels Lucrece to weigh the various effects of verbal, visual, and musical expression, most notably in her famous apostrophe to Hecuba on the tapestry of Troy. At first, the narrator describes the tapestry as a masterpiece of representation, capable of recording and producing aural experience:

> About him were a press of gaping faces
> Which seemed to swallow up his sound advice,
> All jointly list'ning, but with several graces,
> As if some mermaid did their ears entice.
> (1408–11)

Shakespeare's pun on "sound" here registers the translation of Nestor's spoken words into a visual representation of Nestor as sage. Likewise, the remark that the Greek soldiers look as though they would take up their swords "but for loss of Nestor's golden words" (1420) teases us with the idea that Nestor's persuasive speech is *somewhere there* on the tapestry. By contrast, Lucrece's address to Hecuba calls attention to the painter's inability to produce sound:

> On this sad shadow Lucrece spends her eyes,
> And shapes her sorrow to the beldame's woes,
> Who nothing wants to answer her but cries
> And bitter words to ban her cruel foes.
> The painter was no god to lend her those,
>   And therefore Lucrece swears he did her wrong
>   To give her so much grief, and not a tongue.
> (1457–63)

Lucrece's rebuke of the painter does not accuse him of failing to make the tapestry significative: the painting of Hecuba shows "a face where all distress is stelled" (1444). What the figure of Hecuba "wants," according to Lucrece, are "cries" and "bitter words" that have an impact on actual ears, independent of the discursive sense provided by a rhetorical speech or a visual program. As Lucrece attempts to transform Hecuba into a "speaking picture"— "She lends them words, and she their looks doth borrow" (1498)—her imagined identification with the painted Hecuba suggests to her that she is in danger of becoming merely another rhetorical exemplum. Lucrece's encounter with the tapestry enables her to make an important distinction between legible forms of art and a type of physical sound that cannot be reduced to a visual or textual representation of itself. For it is sound, Lucrece comes to realize, that the visualized figure of a mourning woman—and the musical instrument represented *as* image—crucially lacks: "Poor instrument... without a sound" (1464).

In attempting to recuperate a "soundful" Hecuba, Lucrece does not point to the Renaissance figure of sympathy found in emblem books. Instead, she seems to recall Ovid's Hecuba, whose transformation in the *Metamorphoses* is described in terms of sound: "The poor wife of Priam after all else lost her human form and with strange barking affrighted the alien air" (*Priameia coniunx / perdidit infelix hominis post omnia formam / externasque novo latratu terruit auras,* 13.404–6). Hecuba's strange barking (mentioned twice in the *Metamorphoses*), though it cannot be understood or translated, is loudly heard. It is this aspect of Ovid's Hecuba, I believe, that inflects Lucrece's statement that she will "tune [Hecuba's] woes with my lamenting tongue" (1465). This is the first time in the poem that "tongue" refers both to Lucrece's voice and a musical instrument, and it is arguably the first time that it registers both metaphorical and literal meanings: the metaphor for an effective, spoken voice and a physical instrument of sound.[57] Lucrece suggests that an adequate complaint must not only mean; it must physically ramify. The rest of the stanza reiterates Lucrece's desire for a truly performative utterance, by which she can "rail on Pyrrhus," "with [her] tears quench Troy," and "with [her] knife scratch out the angry eyes / Of all the Greeks" (1467–70).

By yoking together the idea of a musical lament with her own tongue and body, Lucrece, like Tamora in *Titus Andronicus,* returns to the site of music's production, anterior to its interpretation. In this respect, Lucrece endorses a mode of expression that she describes as musical ("I'll tune thy woes") but that she grounds in physical, bodily production. From the moment Lucrece sees the painted Hecuba, the word "tongue" appears seven times in three hundred lines, more often than in any other stretch in the poem, and only less

---

57. For a discussion on the tension between the metaphorical and physical meanings of words in the poem, see Katharine Eisaman Maus, "Taking Tropes Seriously: Language and Violence in Shakespeare's *Rape of Lucrece,*" *Shakespeare Quarterly* 37 (1986): 66–82.

frequently in the same section than "blood." The proliferation of references to "tongue" and "blood" prepares us for the poem's last image: Lucrece's "bleeding body," which Brutus swears to "show...thorough Rome,/And so to publish Tarquin's foul offence" (1851–52). The fact that Lucrece's body bleeds continually, even after the poem ends, works against her transformation into a static visual image, in contrast to Ovid's Niobe, whose continual stream of tears marks her monumentalization. Rather, it is Lucrece's audience, particularly Collatine, who is transformed into an image of stony, inarticulate grief: he "begins to talk; but through his lips do throng/Weak words, so thick come in his poor heart's aid/That no man could distinguish what he said" (1783–85). Her perpetually escaping blood acts as a voice that continues to speak beyond the bounds of the poem, making Tarquin, and not Lucrece, the poem's last image.

Lucrece's perpetually bleeding body is, of course, a fantasy, possible only because it exists in a narrative poem. Still, by refusing to pictorialize and sublimate Lucrece at the end of *The Rape of Lucrece,* Shakespeare accords her a very different end from the one he gives to Ophelia. The extent to which the violated female body, when it lacks the performative nature given by Lucrece, is susceptible to male inscription and interpretation is demonstrated by Thomas Peend's Ovidian allegory, *The Pleasant Fable of Hermaphroditus and Salmacis* (1565), which represents all women as texts in need of moralization. Peend locates the sexual promiscuity of women's bodies, figured as "the world/where all temptations be," as part of a more general deceptiveness of woman's "pleasaunt shape" and "subtle" mind, which can lead men to "fylthy sinne" if not correctly read and understood.[58] In the next chapter, I trace a similar impulse to "moralize" music in early modern England. Just as Peend sees in moralization an antidote to female sensuality, early modern writing on music often uses allegory as a powerful tool with which to constrain music's promiscuity. Insofar as Shakespeare's *Hamlet* and *The Rape of Lucrece* illuminate the attempt to turn music into an image, they teach us that the particularities of musical representation are both crucial and constitutive of its politics.

---

58. Thomas Peend, *The Pleasant Fable of Hermaphroditus and Salmacis* (1565), cited in R. W. Maslen, "Myths Exploited: The *Metamorphoses* of Ovid in Early Elizabethan England," in Taylor, *Shakespeare's Ovid,* 22–24.

Chapter 3

Teaching Music
The Rule of Allegory

> Meaning is an instrument used to exert force on the world as we find it, imposing on the intolerable, chaotic otherness of nature a hierarchical order in which objects will appear to have inherent "meanings."... Anything that appears to escape or to resist the project of meaning—passion, body, irony—is interpreted as a further extension of meaning. The rift that slashes through the center of the field of allegorical expression, opening into chaos, cannot be shown for what it is except by the poets who have the courage, at brief moments, to do so.
>
> —Gordon Teskey, *Allegory and Violence*

Few music lessons, real or fictional, go as badly as Hortensio's attempt to teach Katherine the lute in *The Taming of the Shrew*. The lesson, which happens offstage, is presented as a smaller version of the larger campaign in the play to tame Katherine and make her conform to prescribed models of feminine behavior: Baptista's question to Hortensio—"Canst not break her to the lute?" (2.1.145)—calls to mind the breaking of horses, an image frequently used in the play as a metaphor for Katherine's subjection in marriage. In Hortensio's account of his spectacular failure, Katherine shows herself to be supremely capable of bending both musical terminology and musical instruments to her will:

> she hath broke the lute to me.
> I did but tell her she mistook her frets,
> And bowed her hand to teach her fingering,
> When, with a most impatient devilish spirit,
> "Frets, call you these?" quoth she, "I'll fume with them,"
> And with that word she struck me on the head,
> And through the instrument my pate made way,
> And there I stood amazèd for a while,

> As on a pillory, looking through the lute,
> While she did call me rascal, fiddler,
> And twangling jack, with twenty such vile terms,
> As had she studied to misuse me so.
>
> (146–57)

The idea that Katherine is a poor candidate for the lute—"Iron may hold with her, but never lutes" (144)—is particularly fitting in light of Renaissance iconographies of music. As Linda Phyllis Austern has shown, images of women playing the lute appeared frequently in Renaissance representations of music as a "sweetly nurturing woman" ideally suited for matrimony and motherhood.[1] At the same time, by attempting to teach the lute, Hortensio requires Katherine to subject her body to his control—literally, to let him "bow" her fingers and place them on the correct places on the lute's fingerboard. In this way, Katherine's refusal to play the lute correctly both symbolizes and constitutes her resistance to traditional feminine role-playing.

Shakespeare does not, however, present Katherine's rejection of Hortensio's teaching simply as a chaotic rebellion against gender norms. Katherine's response appears to Hortensio as though she "had studied" to undermine him, suggesting that she has pedagogical resources of her own. Taken together, Katherine's willful interpretation of musical terms ("frets"), her contribution of "twenty such vile terms" of her own, and her inspired use of the lute as a pillory form a counterlesson to Hortensio's utterly conventional approach to music teaching. If we take the implications of this counterlesson seriously, then Katherine's noisy, unorthodox approach to music makes apparent the slipperiness of musical terminology, as well as the fact that music is a physically embodied activity. From this perspective, all music is—as the title of this book implies—"broken" music, insofar as it cannot shed its arbitrary relationship to language and the materiality of its sound. This is a lesson that Hortensio, finding himself on the wrong end of the schoolmaster's rod, learns at considerable expense.

In this chapter I examine pedagogical approaches to music in Renaissance England, paying special attention to the ways in which academic writing about music in the period systematically attempts to cordon off the physical, acoustic aspects of music from the serious discussion of its nature and effects. While this ritual displacement of musical sound is most apparent in the

---

1. Linda Phyllis Austern, "'My Mother Musicke': Music and Early Modern Fantasies of Embodiment," in *Maternal Measures: Figuring Caregiving in the Early Modern Period,* ed. Naomi J. Miller and Naomi Yavneh (Aldershot, UK: Ashgate, 2001), 240.

large body of writing on *musica speculativa* (the philosophical study of music's place in the universe), a similar method of representation also pervades early modern texts geared toward the instruction of musical performance. (It may be no coincidence, for instance, that Hortensio tries to teach Katherine the lute, since lute instruction books were among the earliest music instruction manuals printed in English.) In nearly all of the canonical writings on *musica speculativa,* the rejection of musical sound is a well-rehearsed pedagogical move, having been institutionalized in Boethius's early sixth-century treatise, *De institutione musica*. In this work, which Calvin Bower has called "the unique source for the thorough mathematical underpinning of Western musical theory," the proper study of music follows its division into three parts: performed music (*musica instrumentalis*), the music of the body and soul (*musica humana*), and the cosmological harmony of the spheres (*musica mundana*).[2] According to Boethius, only these last two, *musica humana* and *musica mundana,* are the proper object of musical study, and the true understanding of them is generally restricted to philosophers and theorists: "But those of the class which is dependent upon instruments and who spend their entire effort there—such as kitharists and those who prove their skill on the organ and other musical instruments—are excluded from comprehension of musical knowledge, since, as was said, they act as slaves."[3] Such dismissals of musical performance and acoustic experience are typical of medieval *musica speculativa,* and yet the ideology that subtends them persisted long after the cosmological precepts associated with Boethian harmony had been discredited. In other words, although the original scientific context of *musica speculativa* waned, its explanatory power did not.[4]

The displacement of musical sound so endemic to the teaching of music in the Renaissance could be reinforced in a number of ways. Visual representations of music, such as the frontispiece for Praetorius's *Syntagma musicum* (1615), imply the relative importance of *musica mundana* by visibly placing it above instrumental music. Other rhetorical and textual strategies, such as the etymological analysis of musical terms and the use of geometric diagrams to illustrate musical precepts, all bolster the idea that music is a philological or mathematical phenomenon rather than an acoustic one, and they all appear

---

2. Boethius, *Fundamentals of Music,* trans. Calvin M. Bower, ed. Claude V. Palisca (New Haven, CT: Yale University Press, 1989), xx.

3. Ibid., 51.

4. This is not to say that music ceased to be the object of serious scientific study. On the contrary, the study of music was central to many of the theoretical and experimental developments in natural philosophy in the seventeenth century. See Penelope Gouk, *Music, Science and Natural Magic in Seventeenth-Century England* (New Haven, CT: Yale University Press, 1999).

CHAPTER 3

regularly in early modern treatises on music. One of the most effective methods for skirting the problem of musical sound—and the one that is the main focus of this chapter—is the use of allegorical rhetoric to define and explain music's power over its listeners. In particular, the textual representation of music in the Renaissance in many ways resembles the moralizing interpretations often attached to classical poetry—most especially Ovid's *Metamorphoses*, which was still being subjected to allegorical interpretation as late as the seventeenth century.[5] As the following pages will show, the same rhetorical and textual strategies that were used to curb the moral promiscuity of the Ovidian text were also used to undermine the importance of musical sound.

Why would allegory have been such an appealing method for the teaching of music? What political, cultural, or religious interests did it serve? While the answers to these questions are as numerous as the forms of Renaissance allegory themselves, Richard DuRocher's description of the moralizing tradition of the *Metamorphoses* offers a useful starting point for thinking about the ideological work performed by allegorical interpretation:

> Essentially, medieval interpreters treated the poem as an appealing if suspect fiction that could be expounded in support of Christian theology and morality.... What underlies such comments is a concern to accommodate the *Metamorphoses* to an established order, or in Hulse's term, an ideology external to it. Given this concern, the allegorists largely neglected or even contradicted internal evidence, for example, poetic forms and their effects, verbal and structural parallels, surface meaning, and emotional coloring.[6]

Here, the formal aspects of Ovid's poem—its "poetic forms and their effects"—are distinguished from the "external" Christian theology that is presented by the allegorists as the poem's true meaning. Implicit in this formulation is the idea that the immediate experience of reading poetry is

---

5. The popularity of allegorical readings of Ovid in the Renaissance is still a matter of historical debate, although most critics now acknowledge the persistence of Ovidian allegory through the seventeenth century. See Laurence Lerner, "Ovid and the Elizabethans," in *Ovid Renewed: Ovidian Influences on Literature and Art from the Middle Ages to the Twentieth Century*, ed. Charles Martindale, 121–35 (Cambridge: Cambridge University Press, 1988); Clark Hulse, *Metamorphic Verse: The Elizabethan Minor Epic* (Princeton, NJ: Princeton University Press, 1981); D. C. Allen, *Mysteriously Meant: The Rediscovery of Pagan Symbolism and Allegorical Interpretation in the Renaissance* (Baltimore: Johns Hopkins University Press, 1970); Douglas Bush, *Mythology and the Renaissance Tradition in English Poetry* (New York: Norton, 1963).

6. Richard DuRocher, *Milton and Ovid* (Ithaca, NY: Cornell University Press, 1985), 21–22.

irrelevant when weighed against its hidden meaning, which is invariably articulated and policed by a stable set of canonical texts. In other words, allegory distinguishes between sensuous, subjective experience and textual authority. Peter Lavinius, whose commentary on the *Metamorphoses* was widely read in the sixteenth century, makes explicit the polarizing nature of allegory by portraying poetry as a material, fibrous "veil," in contrast to the biblical text: "Under a fictive veil, various themes from sacred scriptures are hidden by means of the allegorical sense" (*fabuloso…velamenta, variae sacrarum scriptorarum allegorico sensi teguntur historiae*).[7] Renaissance music theory makes a similar move when it uses allegorical rhetoric to abstract music away from its own sound, representing music as an inaudible, universal harmony that can best be apprehended through speculative or mathematical discourse. Put simply, allegory makes music *legible,* in the fullest sense of the word. In this respect, the allegorizations of music and Ovid are not simply analogous pedagogical practices in the Renaissance; they are both exponents of an ideology that seeks to affirm human knowledge as universal, definite, and—most importantly—manifested in written language. As such, these practices form a strong arm in the establishment of textual authority in early modern Europe.[8]

In the next section I consider some of the well-known versions of Ovid's *Metamorphoses* in Renaissance England, noting the rhetorical and textual strategies they use to promote allegorical interpretation. In particular, I refer to the *Ovide Moralisé,* Bersuire's *Metamorphosis,* as well as Golding's and Sandys's translations of the *Metamorphoses,* all of which construct Ovid's poem as a "fictive veil" overlaying a secret, Christian meaning. I then trace a similar rhetoric in writing about music, focusing on two English writers who come relatively late to the field of Renaissance music theory, Robert Fludd and John Taverner. Although medieval cosmology loses force as an explanatory context for music in the sixteenth century, the examples of Fludd and Taverner show that the allegorizing approach of conventional *musica speculativa* is well and alive throughout the seventeenth century, especially when music's legibility is at stake. I want to suggest that it is the *interpretive* power of allegory that explains its unexpected appearance in practical musical texts,

---

7. Peter Lavinius, *P. Ovidii Nasonis poete ingeniosissimi Metamorphoseos libri XV* (1527), cited and translated in DuRocher, *Milton and Ovid,* 21–22.

8. On the general idea that textual modes of knowledge achieve dominance over aural ones in early modern Europe, see Walter J. Ong, *Orality and Literacy: The Technologizing of the Word* (London: Routledge, 1988).

which, although usually distinguished from speculative works, often borrow their strategies. Accordingly, the chapter next considers two of the earliest English works on practical music, by Thomas Morley and William Bathe, to show the ways in which *musica speculativa* could influence the teaching of musical composition and performance—a topic that has received short shrift in both music history and literary criticism.

The final section of this chapter addresses Shakespeare's representation of musical learning, noting how the plays repeatedly evoke the allegorizing bent of early modern music education. In *Love's Labour's Lost, Twelfth Night, The Taming of the Shrew,* and *As You Like It,* Shakespeare stages "scenes of instruction" (to borrow Jeff Dolven's phrase), and in each case he ties the teaching of music to the moralization of Ovidian poetry. In this way, Shakespeare recognizes the shared interests of *musica speculativa* and Ovidian allegory. Moreover, in *The Taming of the Shrew* and *As You Like It,* Shakespeare conspicuously presents as the target of Renaissance educational practices a remarkable set of female figures who generally turn out to be "poor" students of music: Katherine, Bianca, and Rosalind. Although not all of these women respond to their musical instructors with lute-breaking fervor, they all demonstrate the limitations of orthodox methods of musical pedagogy. Thus, as in *Titus Andronicus* and *Hamlet,* women are once again made to bear responsibility for the failure to make music meaningful and coherent, though in a more direct way. In the comedies discussed in this chapter, taming music's promiscuity is literally tantamount to taming women's voices. Moreover, in these plays, Shakespeare allows his female figures to speak, if only very briefly, against the universalizing strictures of Renaissance *musica speculativa* and the institutions invested in its durability. Like Chaucer's Wife of Bath, who famously prefers "experience" to the "auctoritee" of canonical texts, Shakespeare's female characters bring to our attention the experience of musical sound as an acoustic, subjective event. In doing so, they remind us what it is like to *hear* music—an experience that Renaissance music theory would often have us forget.

"This same dark Philosophie": Ovid's *Metamorphoses* and Renaissance Allegory

The teaching of Renaissance *musica speculativa* typically begins where Ovid's *Metamorphoses* ends: with the story of Pythagoras. The consistency with which medieval and Renaissance histories of music return to Pythagoras attests to the remarkable ability of the myth to comprehend and render intelligible a subject as unwieldy and controversial as music. It is not surprising, then, that the figure of Pythagoras looms large over the first full English translation of the *Metamorphoses*, which corrals Ovid's endlessly digressive poem to a single, unwavering theme. In the epistle to Leicester in his translation of the *Metamorphoses* (1567), Arthur Golding writes:

> For whatsoever hath bene writ of aunctient tyme in greeke
> By sundry men dispersedly, and in the latin eeke,
> Of this same dark Philosophie of turned shapes, the same
> Hath Ovid into one whole masse in this booke brought in frame.
> Fowre kynd of things in this his worke the Poet dooth conteyne.
> That nothing under heaven dooth ay in stedfast state remayne.
> And next that nothing perisheth: but that eche substance takes
> Another shape than that it had. Of theis twoo points he makes
> The proof by shewing through his woorke the wonderfull exchaunge
> Of Goddes, men, beasts, and elements, too sundry shapes right straunge.
> ("The Epistle," 5–14)[9]

Although Golding does not explicitly mention Pythagoras here, his description of Ovid's poem closely paraphrases Pythagoras's speech at the end of the *Metamorphoses*: "All things doo chaunge. But nothing sure dooth perish," and a few lines later, "The soule is ay the selfsame thing it was, and yit astray/It fleeteth intoo sundry shapes" (Golding, 15.183, 191–92). Ovid represents Pythagoras as unique among humankind for his ability to apprehend mentally the secret, divine truths of nature. Golding's translation emphasizes this aspect of Pythagoras in terms that evoke allegorical reading: Pythagoras is able to see "the things which nature dooth too fleshly eyes denye" and "what soever other thing is hid from common sence" (15.71, 80). By framing Ovid's poem in terms of a mystical Pythagoras, Golding sanctions an allegorical mode of interpretation that posits a divinely inspired meaning underneath the poem's "fictive veil." Hence the prominence Golding gives to Pythagoras in the epistle to Leicester—over forty lines, far more than to any other figure. Through Pythagoras, Golding finds a hermeneutic theory with which to anchor his allegorical treatment of Ovid's poem.

The trope of a hidden truth that evades the "common sence" regularly appears in medieval and Renaissance moralizations of classical mythology. This supposition of "veiled" meanings (*fabulosa velamenta*) in classical poetry

---

9. Arthur Golding, *Shakespeare's Ovid Being Arthur Golding's Translation of the Metamorphoses*, ed. W. H. D. Rouse (London: Centaur, 1961). All quotations of Golding are from this edition.

is an important rhetorical move in Renaissance allegory, since it legitimizes the allegorical project as an excavation of Christian truth. For example, in his preface to the *Metamorphosis Ovidiana moraliter* (1509), Pierre Bersuire argues that classical poets either were unknowingly inspired by the Holy Spirit or deliberately hid Christian truths in their works.[10] Similar claims are made in the anonymous *Ovide moralisè*, Peter Lavinius's commentaries on the *Metamorphoses,* and George Sandys's translation of the *Metamorphoses,* which ascribes to classical poetry the store of "Natures secrets": "Phoebus Apollo (sacred Poesy)/Thus taught: for in these ancient Fables lie/The mysteries of all Philosophie."[11] While this idea of hidden truth justifies the large-scale allegorization of Ovid, it also raises the question of whether plain, straightforward language is preferable to allegory. For this reason, early modern writers offer many explanations for the necessity of allegory's mysteriousness. In *The Arte of Rhetorique* (1553), Thomas Wilson writes that classical fables, particularly Ovid, acted as a veil for politically dangerous commentaries: "The Poetes were wise men, and wished in harte the redresse of thinges, the whiche when for feare they durst not openly rebuke, thei didde in coloures paynte theim oute, and tolde menne by shadowes what they shoulde do in good south."[12] Golding offers a similar explanation in his *Metamorphoses*: "For under feyned names of Goddes it was the Poets guyse,/The vice and faultes of all estates too taunt in covert wyse" ("Preface to the Reader," 83–84). A more common explanation for the secretive nature of classical poetry is given by George Sandys in the preface to his translation of the *Metamorphoses*:

> I have attempted (with what successe I submit to the Reader) to collect out of sundrie Authors the Philosophicall sense of these fables of *Ovid,* if I may call them his, when most of them are more antient then any extant Author, or perhaps then Letters themselves; before which, as they expressed their Conceptions in Hieroglyphickes, so did they their Philosophie and Divinitie under Fables and Parables: a way not un-trod by the sacred Pen-men; as by the prudent Law-givers, in their reducing of the old World to civilitie, leaving behind a deeper impression, then can be made by the liveless precepts of Philosophie.[13]

---

10. DuRocher, *Milton and Ovid,* 21.

11. George Sandys, *Ovid's Metamorphosis Englished, Mythologized, and Represented in Figures* (1632), ed. Karl K. Hulley and Stanley T. Vandersall (Lincoln: University of Nebraska Press, 1970), 2.

12. Thomas Wilson, *The Arte of Rhetorique* (1553), ed. Thomas J. Derrick (New York: Garland, 1982), 388.

13. Sandys, *Ovid's Metamorphosis Englished,* 8.

For Sandys, allegory's veil is a sensuous cover that operates almost unconsciously, thereby leaving a "deeper impression" on the reader's mind. While this mysterious veil was conducive to the refinement of ancient civilizations, Sandys argues, in the present day it is the reader's responsibility to lift away the veil and find the valuable kernel of meaning within. Similarly, Golding in his epistle to Leicester:

> If Poets then with leesings and with fables shadowed so
> The certeine truth, what letteth us too plucke those visers fro
> Their doings, and too bring ageine the darkened truth too lyght,
> That all men may behold thereof the cleerenesse shining bryght?
> ("Epistle," 537–40)

Despite Golding's assertion that truth in poetry is a "cleerenesse shining bryght," he implies that the senses, including sight, are weak receptors for moral or philosophical truth. While acknowledging the "pleasure" that Ovid's "varietie and straungeness" affords ("Epistle," 545), Golding strongly warns against a reading of the Ovidian text grounded in sensuous perception:

> And if they happening for to meete with any wanton woord
> Or matter lewd, according as the person dooth avoord
> In whom the evill is describde, doo feele their myndes therby
> Provokte too vyce and wantonnesse, (as nature commonly
> Is prone to evill) let them thus imagin in their mynd.
> Behold, by sent of reason and by perfect sight I fynd
> A Panther heere, whose peinted cote with yellow spots like gold
> And pleasant smell allure myne eyes and senses too behold.
> But well I know his face is grim and feerce, which he dooth hyde
> To this intent, that whyle I thus stand gazing on his hyde,
> He may devour mee unbewares....
> (547–57)

Here, "intent" denotes the underlying meaning of Ovidian poetry, which Golding repeatedly sets in opposition to the surface appeal of the fable: "For sure theis fables are not put in wryghting to *thentent*/ Too further or allure too vyce" (561–62, my emphasis). According to Golding, a reader unaided by reason risks falling prey to the sensuous qualities of the poem and risks becoming an Ovidian victim of metamorphosis herself: in Golding's words, such a reader is no different "from beasts, but rather bee/ Much woorse than beasts, bicause they doo abace theyr owne degree" (61–62). The anonymous author of *The Fable of Ovid Treting of Narcissus* (1560) makes a similar connection between sensuous reading and Ovidian metamorphosis: the reader who gets caught up in the sensuous aspects of the poem is, like Narcissus, fatally embroiled in the surfaces of things and ignorant of the gifts which nature gave him "whyth good intente."[14] Such characterizations of the reader complicate the idea that English translations of the *Metamorphoses,* because they do not include the copious marginalia of medieval editions, leave "the reader free to enjoy his Ovid if (and as) he wished."[15] While the textual presentation of Ovid in these translations suggests a different reading experience from the medieval editions, it is clear that writers like Golding intend the reader to *internalize* the allegorizing impulse—to read the poem for moral and philosophical meaning rather than for narrative and sensuous pleasure.

As I suggested above, the degradation of sensuous reading in the moralizations of Ovid is somewhat at odds with their frequent recourse to a rhetoric of vision. For example, while the allegorists may discourage the enjoyment of Andromeda's beautiful nakedness, which Ovid elaborates in playful detail, they nonetheless appeal to a visual, iconological system of correspondences through which Andromeda is identified as the human soul, Perseus as Christ, and so on.[16] In the "Epistle," Golding repeatedly draws on visual models in order to establish the allegorical significance of Ovid's characters: Daphne is a "myrror of virginitie" (68), Narcissus is "of scornfulnesse and pryde a myrror cleere" (105), Theseus's deeds are "a glasse / How princes sonnes and noblemen their youthfull yeeres should passe" (155–56), and Julius Caesar is a "blazing starre" signifying virtue's fame and immortality (292).[17] This emphasis on visuality, which invites an emblematic reading of Ovid's poem, is typical of allegorical writing, and it is often reinforced by the texts themselves: frontispieces, illustrations, and elaborate glosses encourage the allegori-

---

14. *The Fable of Ovid Treting of Narcissus* (London, 1560), B.

15. Laurence Lerner, "Ovid and the Elizabethans," 122.

16. The early modern allegorization of Ovid's Perseus is discussed at length in Daniel Javitch, "Rescuing Ovid from the Allegorizers," *Comparative Literature* 30 (1978): 97–107. Javitch brilliantly shows how the moralizations of the tale systematically ignore the sensuous and stylistic aspects of Ovid's poetry, while incorporating illustrations in the texts that reinforce the conventional, moral interpretation. For example, in several illustrated editions of Ovid, such as the *Metamorphose figurée* of 1567, Perseus is shown riding the winged horse Pegasus, a detail not in Ovid but described and interpreted at length in the medieval allegories.

17. Raphael Lyne also notes how Golding's translation suggests an allegorical, specifically Christian, significance. See his "Golding's Englished *Metamorphoses,*" *Translation and Literature* 5 (1996): 183–200. For a somewhat different reading of the effects of these figures in Golding's translation, see Liz Oakley-Brown, "Translating the Subject: Ovid's *Metamorphoses* in England 1560–67," in *Translation and Nation: Towards a Cultural Politics of Englishness,* ed. Roger Ellis and Liz Oakley-Brown, 48–84 (Clevedon, UK: Multilingual Matters, 2001).

cal interpretation of Ovid's poem by visualizing it, such as an illustration of Mars in knightly garb in a fifteenth-century edition of the *Ovide moralisé*, or an illustration of Jupiter wearing a bishop's hat in Raphael Regius's edition of the *Metamorphoses*. In the latter case, the illustration of Jupiter occupies the center of the page while Ovid's lines are literally relegated to the margins. Likewise, the copious annotations that typically surround Ovid's poem in medieval and Renaissance editions suggest visually what the allegorists imply: namely, that the Ovidian text is secondary to its "intended" meaning. Allegory's dependence on visual models is explicitly explained by Sandys, whose *Metamorphoses* was originally published with elaborate illustrations:

> And for thy farther delight I have contracted the substance of every Booke into as many Figures... since *there is betweene Poetry and Picture so great a congruitie;* the one called by Simonides a speaking Picture, and the other a silent Poesie: Both Daughters of the Imagination, both busied in the imitation of Nature, or transcending it for the better with equall liberty: the one being borne in the beginning of the World; and the other soone after, as appears by the Hieroglyphicall Figures on the Acgyptian Obelisques, which were long before the invention of Letters: the one feasting the Eare, and the other the Eye, the noblest of the sences, by which the Understanding is onely informed, and the mind sincerely delighted.[18]

Here, Sandys's description of Egyptian hieroglyphics as "speaking pictures" recalls his comparison of hieroglyphics and allegorical fables a few paragraphs earlier. The appeal to the Horatian dictum that poetry is like a picture (*ut pictura poesis*) suggests that visual signs, although they require a skilled interpreter, are uniquely suited for conveying allegorical meaning. By describing vision as "the noblest of the sences," as opposed to the barbaric "feasting [of] the Eare," Sandys links it to reason, thus making it capable of apprehending the moral and philosophical knowledge signified by Ovidian poetry.[19]

---

18. Sandys, *Ovid's "Metamorphosis" Englished,* 9, my emphasis.
19. See DuRocher, *Milton and Ovid,* 20–29. Lee T. Pearcy argues for the nonallegorical quality of Sandys's *Metamorphoses,* although his definition of allegory is much more restrictive than mine. See *The Mediated Muse: English Translations of Ovid, 1560–1700* (Hamden, CT: Archon, 1984), 37–70. On Sandys's debt to the allegorical tradition of Ovid, see Liz Oakley-Brown, *Ovid and the Cultural Politics of Translation in Early Modern England* (Aldershot, UK: Ashgate, 2006), 72–93; Deborah Rubin, *Ovid's Metamorphoses Englished: George Sandys as Translator and Mythographer* (New York: Garland, 1985); Richard Beale Davis, *George Sandys: Poet Adventurer* (New York: Columbia University Press, 1955). For an interesting, nuanced discussion of Sandys's transformation of the Ovidian voice, see

Sandys's translation of the *Metamorphoses* demonstrates the staying power of allegorical rhetoric in the seventeenth century, even after the conventional allegorical interpretations had fallen out of favor. In other words, while the medieval, Christian reading of Ovid's *Metamorphoses* waned over the course of the sixteenth century, often replaced by readings based on moral and natural philosophy, the rhetorical and textual strategies of medieval allegory continued to shape the interpretation of Ovid. In the next section, I will show that these strategies also profoundly shape the representation of music in academic writing on *musica speculativa*. The rhetoric of hidden meaning and the degradation of nonvisual modes of understanding, both endemic to early modern allegory, provide a powerful way of dealing with the illegibility of musical sound. The fundamental lesson of the allegorized Ovid—that one must go beneath the surface of sense experience to apprehend truth—was well suited to writers wishing to hash out their theories of music on the printed page. In this respect, it is particularly fitting that Golding ends his "Preface to the Reader" by comparing the reader's task with Ulysses' resistance to the music of the mermaids. Having described Ulysses in the epistle to Leicester as the poem's "image of discretion, wit, and great advisedness" (249), Golding's "Preface" suggests that the reader of Ovid's poem may also need to stop up her ears in order to avoid the poem's sensuous allure. As we will see, this injunction to close the ears appears again and again, with varying degrees of subtlety, in Renaissance teaching about music.

Divinae particula aurae: Musica speculativa and the Universal Harmony

The study of *musica speculativa* in Renaissance Europe is by no means a *concors discordia:* the diversity of theories about the nature of music does not yield a coherent, unified narrative for later writers to draw on. As Claude Palisca has demonstrated in his copious study on Renaissance musical thought, Neoplatonic ideas about musical harmony constantly vie with more "earthly," Aristotelian notions about the effects of musical sound.[20] Yet despite the lack of consensus, the figure of Pythagoras and the fabled account of his discovery of

---

Gina Bloom, *Voice in Motion: Staging Gender, Shaping Sound in Early Modern England* (Philadelphia: University of Pennsylvania Press, 2007), 160–85.

20. Claude Palisca, *Humanism in Italian Renaissance Musical Thought* (New Haven, CT: Yale University Press, 1985). For an example of an anti-Pythagorean approach to music (founded on Aristotelian theory) in the Renaissance, see Palisca's discussion of Lodovico Fogliano on pp. 20–22.

harmony are remarkably pervasive in the musical treatises of the period. The Pythagorean notion of universal harmony is given special prominence in Boethius's influential *De institutione musica,* and this approach is in turn followed by Franchino Gaffurio and Gioseffo Zarlino, two of the most widely read music theorists in the sixteenth century.[21] Even for early modern writers who deny the idea of the music of the spheres, Pythagoras's discovery of harmony functions as a useful, recognizable example in discussions of musical consonance.[22] The situation is even more pronounced in England, where almost every treatise on speculative music in the sixteenth century draws attention to the story of Pythagoras. In this way, just as the iconographic figure of Pythagoras becomes a staple in frontispieces of musical treatises, the story of Pythagoras's discovery of music becomes emblematic of *musica speculativa* itself. Moreover, the prominence of Pythagoras in these works underscores the allegorizing bent of Renaissance *musica speculativa*, which employs many of the same rhetorical strategies as the moralizations of Ovid. As in the case of Ovid, the impulse to allegorize music is driven ideologically by a desire to establish the authority of textual discourse, which in the case of music is always especially in danger of being subverted by the subjective experience of sound. The unique story of Pythagoras, which privileges contemplation over hearing, thus makes him a fitting figure for the policing of musical meaning.[23]

Macrobius's *Commentary on the Dream of Scipio* (ca. 395–410 AD) provides one of the most comprehensive and most frequently cited accounts of Pythagoras's discovery of music, which is worth citing at length:

> Now it is well known that in the heavens nothing happens by chance or at random, and that all things above proceed in orderly fashion according to divine law. Therefore it is unquestionably right to assume that harmonious sounds come forth from the rotation of the heavenly

---

21. See ibid., 166–81.

22. See, for example, the rejection of Pythagorean cosmic harmony by Johannes Tinctoris in *The Art of Counterpoint* (1477), trans. Albert Seay (Rome: American Institute of Musicology, 1961). On the prominence of Pythagorean theory in Renaissance England, see Gretchen Ludke Finney, *Musical Backgrounds for English Literature: 1580–1650* (New Brunswick, NJ: Rutgers University Press, 1962), 1–20; S. K. Heninger, *Touches of Sweet Harmony: Pythagorean Cosmology and Renaissance Poetics* (San Marino, CA: Huntington Library, 1974).

23. In this respect, my reading of *musica speculativa* problematizes Gordon Teskey's claim that "the music of the spheres is the clearest imaginative expression of what would become, after Descartes, the doctrine of universal subjectivity." See his *Allegory and Violence* (Ithaca, NY: Cornell University Press, 1996), 166. While I disagree with Teskey's particular claim about music, his characterization of Renaissance allegory is wonderfully illuminating on the discursive practices I am tracing in this chapter.

spheres, for sound has to come from motion, and Reason, which is present in the divine, is responsible for the sounds being melodious.

Pythagoras was the first of all Greeks to lay hold of this truth. He realized that the sounds coming forth from the spheres were regulated by divine Reason, which is always present in the sky, but he had difficulty in determining the underlying cause and in finding ways by which he might discover it. When he was weary of his long investigation of a problem so fundamental and yet so recondite, a chance occurrence presented him with what his deep thinking had overlooked.

He happened to pass the open shop of some blacksmiths who were beating a hot iron with hammers. The sound of the hammers striking in alternate and regular succession fell upon his ears with the higher note so attuned to the lower that each time the same musical interval returned, and always striking a concord. Here, Pythagoras, seeing that his opportunity had been presented to him, ascertained with his eyes and hands what he had been searching for in his mind. He approached the smiths and stood over their work, carefully heeding the sounds that came forth from the blows of each. Thinking that the difference might be ascribed to the strength of the smiths he requested them to change hammers. Hereupon the difference in tones did not stay with the men but followed the hammers. Then he turned his whole attention to the study of their weights, and when he had recorded the difference in the weight of each, he had other hammers heavier or lighter than these made. Blows from these produced sounds that were not at all like those of the original hammers, and besides they did not harmonize. He then concluded that harmony of tones was produced according to a proportion of the weights, and made 'a record of all the numerical relations of the various weights producing harmony.... After discovering this great secret, Pythagoras chose the numbers from which consonant chords might be produced so that when stringed instruments had been adjusted with regard to these numbers, certain ones might be pitched to the tonics and others to the other consonant notes, numerically harmonious.[24]

Macrobius's description of Pythagoras exercises many of the rhetorical strategies of Renaissance allegory: the claim of universality, the supposition of hidden knowledge, and an emphasis on visual modes of reception. More

---

24. Macrobius, *Commentary on the Dream of Scipio,* trans. William Harris Stahl (New York: Columbia University Press, 1990), 187–88.

importantly, the story of Pythagoras provides a useful method for managing the problem of musical sound. By positing an original, utopian scene of musical hearing that is then immediately translated into mathematics, the story authorizes mathematics and philosophy as the proper domain of musical study, independent of acoustic experience.[25] By contrast, the irrelevance of musical sound is implied by the belief, often stressed in the narrative accounts, that Pythagoras was the only person in the history of the world who could hear the music of the spheres.

The Pythagorean context for music was reinforced in a number of ways, beyond the well-known story of the anvils. Descriptions of musical proportion and harmony in Renaissance musical texts are frequently accompanied by illustrations of Pythagoras deriving the proportions from an array of anvils—as well as various strings, weights, and, in one anachronistic case, water goblets. The title page of the 1518 edition of Gaffurio's *De harmonia musicorum* depicts the author lecturing on music to a group of attentive, young students.[26] Several details in the illustration suggest a Pythagorean model of instruction: behind the instructor is an array of organ pipes whose lengths are clearly numbered; an hourglass and compass (representing measurement and geometry) are prominently shown next to the instructor; and the instructor is lecturing from a large book that occupies the center of the illustration. The only sound represented in the illustration is that which emanates from the instructor's mouth: a voice scroll containing the Pythagorean dictum *Harmonia est discordia concors* ("Harmony is a concord of discords"). Taken together, the message of the illustration is clear: music is appropriately learned at the foot of a teacher well versed in mathematics and geometry—or, in the marketing subtext of the illustration, from an authoritative *text* produced by such an instructor. That the theoretical bent of Pythagorean music teaching was well-known may be gauged by Thomas Lodge's derisive quip about Pythagoras in his reply to Gosson's *Schoole of Abuse:* "*Pithagoras* you say alowes not that musik is decerned by eares, but hee wisheth us to ascend unto the sky & marke that harmony. Surely thys is but one doctors opinion (yet I dis-

---

25. This does not mean that aural experience is absent in *musica speculativa*. For an interesting discussion on the occasional prominence that Boethius gives to the "judgement of the ears" in his *De musica* (albeit in contradiction to the rest of the treatise), see Klaus-Jürgen Sachs, "Boethius and the Judgement of the Ears: A Hidden Challenge in Medieval and Renaissance Music Theory," in *The Second Sense: Studies in Hearing and Musical Judgement from Antiquity to the Seventeenth Century,* ed. Charles Burnett, Michael Fend, and Penelope Gouk, 169–98 (London: Warburg Institute, 1991).

26. The woodcut illustration is reproduced in Franchinus Gaffurius, *De harmonia musicorum instrumentorum opus,* trans. Clement A. Miller ([Rome]: American Institute of Musicology, 1977). The woodcut is itself an adaptation of a more lavish illustration from the manuscript version of Gaffurio's treatise. See Palisca, *Humanism,* 162.

like not of it) but to speake my conscience my thinkes musike best pleaseth me when I heare it, for otherwise the catter walling of Cats, were it not for harmonie, should more delight mine eies then the tunable voyces of men."[27] Whether or not Lodge knows the centrality of Pythagoras in the history of music ("but one doctors opinion"), he clearly understands that, in the case of music, Pythagorean teaching gives little value to the judgment of the ear.

The separation of rational thought and physical sound, exemplified by Pythagoras, becomes an organizing principle of *musica speculativa,* and it inflects the representation of music even after Pythagorean and Ptolemeic cosmology is invalidated. Thus the idea that *musica speculativa* functions only as "decorative metaphor" in the seventeenth century needs to be revised in light of the fact that its rhetorical strategies continue to shape musical thought in the period, not least in England.[28] Robert Fludd, who gives Pythagoreanism a central place in his musical theory, demonstrates the persistence of *musica speculativa* in seventeenth-century England, and his writings reveal the usefulness of allegory for representing music as a *textual* object of study. In his *Utriusque cosmi...historia* (1617–20), Fludd explicitly ties the allegorical interpretation of classical poetry to his own speculative theory of music:

> If we examine carefully the fables of the poets, we will find prodigious secrets in them. Why should Pan (by whom is signified Universal Nature) have made his pipe of seven syringes or reeds, by which hue [sic] evoked a sweet harmony, if not because the intellectual spirit which moves the heavens makes a corresponding music in these inferior parts? For by the composition out of seven pipes is meant the assembly of seven planetary spheres, with their wondrous harmony in Heaven and Earth, i.e. wherever that universal nature extends. Similarly, we may seek the reason why Mercury gave Apollo the lyre, and Apollo in turn gave Mercury the caduceus staff. If we examine all things succinctly in this way, we will find that it is no more outside nature's power that a wise man should cause to move by his music (*harmonia*) the essentializing (*essentificam*) substance of the aethereal heaven concealed in lower

---

27. Thomas Lodge, *A Reply to Gosson's "Schoole of Abuse"* (ca. 1579), ed. Arthur Freeman (New York: Garland, 1973), 29.

28. The phrase is John Hollander's, in *The Untuning of the Sky: Ideas of Music in English Poetry 1500–1700* (1961; repr., Princeton, NJ: Princeton University Press, 1993), 19. In the last few years critics have begun to challenge the notion that seventeenth-century music theory is divorced from earlier, speculative approaches. See, for example, Linda Phyllis Austern, "'Tis nature's voice': Music, Natural Philosophy and the Hidden World in Seventeenth-Century England," in *Music Theory and Natural Order from the Renaissance to the Early Twentieth Century,* ed. Suzannah Clark and Alexander Rehding, 30–67 (Cambridge: Cambridge University Press, 2001).

bodies, than that the soul situated in an animal should urge its body hither or thither at will.[29]

For Fludd, the supposition of hidden truth normally established by Renaissance allegory allows him to connect a grand model of universal harmony with the effects of music on individual listeners. Allegorizing music in this way, Fludd reconciles the usually opposed musical styles of Pan and Apollo: by subjecting the number of reeds in Pan's pipe to allegorical interpretation, Fludd is able to read Pan's music, usually associated with subjective listening and excessive sound, as a sign of "Universal Nature."

Fludd does not exclude the consideration of sound from his treatise, but his adherence to Platonist theory enables him to interpret musical sound as pointing to something that *cannot* be directly observed. For example, he uses the familiar example of musical sympathy to prove the existence of an "aethereal nature" that permeates the universe: "Place two lutes on the same table, and put a straw on the string of one of them. If you sound the string of the other which is in unison with the string carrying the straw, the string holding the straw will forthwith vibrate and move and throw off the straw with a sudden motion. From this we can learn the marvelous relationship of one creature to another by virtue of this harmony."[30] At the time of Fludd's writing, acoustic experiments were being carried out in many places in England,[31] yet Fludd's approach is such that he is able to incorporate this "scientific" evidence into an allegorical framework. Fludd again shows his indebtedness to Renaissance allegory in his extraordinary "Temple of Music," a masterpiece of illustration that takes allegory's method of visual emblematization to a dazzling extreme (figure 2). Nearly every detail of this impressive picture is meant to denote some aspect of speculative or practical music, from the gamut inscribed on the right side of the front wall, to the series of eight steps in the upper archways denoting the diatonic scale, to the scene of Pythagoras hearing the beating hammers, appropriately situated at the building's "foundation." The ingeniousness of Fludd's design can be gleaned from his explanation of a single section of the image: "The spirals of the big tower on the left denote the movement of air caused by sound or voice; the double gates below, which are surrounded by six musical instruments, denote the ears through which alone sound may gain access to the

---

29. Cited in Joscelyn Godwin, *Music, Mysticism and Magic: A Sourcebook* (London: Routledge, 1986), 145–46.
30. Cited in ibid, 145.
31. See Gouk, *Music, Science and Natural Magic*.

temple."[32] Fludd's temple is not simply a decorative showpiece; it attests to his belief that sound can be ordered and represented as a visual icon. In this respect, his decision to include the temple in the part of the treatise devoted to *musica practica* (the study of musical composition and performance) is somewhat less surprising. Moreover, Fludd's illustration represents with remarkable clarity his belief that all of the branches of human and divine knowledge are inextricably bound up together. Like the medieval allegorists, who argued that all of the secrets of the universe were hidden in Virgil's *Aeneid,* Fludd represents music as a compendium of all fields of knowledge. This principle underscores Fludd's illustration of the "World-Monochord" in the same work, in which the fields of geometry, cosmology, and music are superimposed and visually controlled by the hand of God. Here, as in the "Temple of Music," Fludd uses musical and astrological symbols to suggest a storehouse of hidden knowledge, even going so far as to make musical notation look like ancient runes—effectively making manifest the "hieroglyphicall figures" that Sandys had said encapsulated the true meaning of classical poetry.

For all his ingeniousness and showmanship, Fludd is not the philosophical aberration he is sometimes accused of being. In his own lifetime, Fludd was sharply criticized by Johannes Kepler and Marin Mersenne, who characterized his theories as "mere poetry and oratorical imagery."[33] Fludd's rampant Rosicrucianism has not endeared him much better to modern critics, who sometimes cast him as a superstitious romantic, not to be taken seriously.[34] However, even Kepler and Mersenne themselves borrowed heavily from the tradition of *musica speculativa* (in both his *Mysterium cosmographicum* and *Harmonices mundi,* Kepler relates musical harmony to the movement of the planets), and theorists like Athanasius Kircher also constructed elaborate visual models in an attempt to explain music's nature.[35] The study of Platonism was well and alive in English universities in the seventeenth-century, despite its

---

32. This is Peter J. Ammann's paraphrased translation of Fludd's text. "The Musical Theory and Philosophy of Robert Fludd," *Journal of the Warburg and Courtauld Institutes* 30 (1967): 205.

33. Ibid., 216.

34. See, for example, Morrison Comegys Boyd, *Elizabethan Music and Musical Criticism* (Philadelphia: University of Pennsylvania Press, 1962), 225. On the significance of Fludd's work and its place in seventeenth-century philosophical thought, see William H. Huffman, *Robert Fludd and the End of the Renaissance* (London: Routledge, 1988); Kathi Meyer-Baer, *Music of the Spheres and the Dance of Death: Studies in Musical Iconology* (New York: Da Capo, 1984), 191–202; Joscelyn Godwin, *Robert Fludd, Hermetic Philosopher and Surveyor of Two Worlds* (Boulder, CO: Shambhala, 1979); Ammann, "Musical Theory," 198–227.

35. Godwin, *Music, Mysticism and Magic,* 148–161. On Mersenne's theory of music, see Dean T. Mace, "Marin Mersenne on Language and Music," *Journal of Music Theory* 14 (1970): 2–34.

FIGURE 2. "The Temple of Music," from Robert Fludd, *Utriusque cosmi...historia* (1617). By permission of the Music Division, The New York Public Library for the Performing Arts, Astor, Lenox, and Tilden Foundations.

seemingly archaic outlook.[36] In this respect, Fludd's approach to music is fully representative of the enduring impulse to teach music through visual and textual modes—as the texts and diagrams produced by writers from Boethius to Isaac Newton show.

In stark contrast to Fludd's work, John Taverner's Gresham College music lectures, delivered sometime around 1610, do not present themselves as pioneers in the field of *musica speculativa*. However, Taverner's teaching of music is unique because of the remarkable transparency with which it employs allegorical rhetoric to negotiate the relationship between musical sounds and his own speculative project, so that the stock strategies of *musica speculativa* are made glaringly prominent. Part of this transparency may derive from the fact that Taverner had just come to occupy an academic position that had been historically associated with the performance of music. Beginning in 1597, when the chair of music at Gresham was established, the position of music professor had been held by John Bull, whose doctoral degree in music from Cambridge may have initially qualified him to the post but who was in fact extremely active as an organist and composer during his Gresham tenure.[37] With the appointment of Taverner (not to be confused with the sixteenth-century English composer of the same name) in 1610, however, the same post began to be associated more with music philosophy and less with musical practice. As Penelope Gouk has pointed out, Bull was the last professional musician to be formally appointed to the chair, the post going afterward "to a series of individuals who held the Master of Arts degree, and mostly possessed or were acquiring higher qualifications in medicine."[38] By the time William Petty acceded to the post in 1650, the distance between the professorship and the teaching of practical music was stated explicitly, as is evident from Petty's own proposal for Gresham College (and which may have been in part the basis for his hiring):

> The Professor of Musick need not so much to teach his Auditors actually to play or make melody as to explain the grounds thereof, to teach Men to know the differences and distances of Tones, the Nature of Concords and Discords, the Nature of Sounds and sounding bodies,

---

36. Mordechai Feingold, "The Occult Tradition in the English Universities of the Renaissance: A Reassessment," in *Occult and Scientific Mentalities in the Renaissance,* ed. Brian Vickers, 73–94 (Cambridge: Cambridge University Press, 1984).

37. Gouk, *Music, Science and Natural Magic,* 37–38. On John Bull's musical career, see H. R. Hoppe, "John Bull in the Archduke Albert's Service," *Music and Letters* 35 (1954): 114–15; Wilfrid Mellers, "John Bull and English Keyboard Music," *Music Quarterly* 40 (1954): 548–71.

38. Gouk, *Music, Science and Natural Magic,* 37.

the Reasons of the fabric and figure of all Musical Instruments. Not omitting enquiries after the Means to better hearing answerable to what hath been happily done for the advantage of sight.[39]

Petty's proposal articulates a clear preference for *musica speculativa* and natural philosophy over the performance and composition of actual music, a movement that had already been initiated when Bull resigned from the post in 1607.[40] In this respect, Taverner's Gresham lectures offer a unique vantage point for exploring the relationship between *musica speculativa* and practical music, since they were delivered at the precise time that musical performance and composition were beginning to be devalued by the Gresham faculty.

The awkward transition from Bull to subsequent professors of music at Gresham may partly explain Taverner's frequent heavy-handedness in his representation of music. After all, Taverner would have been lecturing to an audience that was accustomed to a distinguished composer and instrumentalist at the podium. As if in response to this expectation, Taverner is quick to establish that the appropriate study of music is grounded in history and philology, and the beginning of his first lecture posits the study of music as a an etymological problem:

Those which search out the Pedigree of wordes, hunting after the subtilties of Etymologies, would needs perswade us that out of the very fashion & composition of the name may bee gathered the true propriety of each thing: Generally in all wordes to attempt this extraction, might perhaps seeme too nice a curiosity, worthy to bee put amongst the number of those thinges, which Seneca calls "grave trifles." Yet in many wee see that the reason of the name & the condition of the thinge

---

39. Charles Webster, *The Great Instauration: Science, Medicine and Reform, 1626–1660* (London: Duckworth, 1975), 550n26, cited in Gouk, *Music, Science and Natural Magic,* 37–38. Gouk notes that the proposal was probably written in 1649, the year before Petty began the music professorship. On Petty's Gresham music lectures, see "Several Music Lectures" in *The Petty Papers: Some Unpublished Writings of Sir William Petty edited from the Bowood Papers,* ed. Marquis of Lansdowne, (London, 1927), 2:260–61.

40. Gouk, on the other hand, suggests that the approach to music at Gresham was more coherent than it seems, explaining that "the kind of person we might now think suitable for such a role (i.e. a professional composer) did not normally possess the kind of academic background [i.e., university degree] which was thought necessary for such a post" (*Music, Science and Natural Magic,* 37). However, Gouk seems to belie her own evidence that other comparable London institutions regularly employed teachers of practical music. Moreover, although Bull held a doctorate from Cambridge, the difference between his academic qualifications and those of the other faculty was apparent from the start, since he was given a special dispensation from the queen to deliver his lectures in English only, rather than in English and Latin. See John Ward, *Lives of the Professors of Gresham College* (London, 1740).

doe soe fitly & fully accord, that one would sometimes willingly yeild to their opinion, which held that names were first given to thinges att happe hazard, but rather upon good and mature Deliberation.[41]

From the start, Taverner forecloses on the possibility of a gap between word and music by arguing that the true essence of things resides in the "very fashion and composition of the name." This assumption of an absolute concordance between "the reason of the name" and "the condition of the thinge" leads to a somewhat tautological explanation of music, in which the experience of sound serves as a convenient, but inessential, intermediary: "This word Musicke sounds so like that of the muses, that it were hard to say whether borrowed their name from other [sic]." For Taverner, the name "Musicke" may sound like the thing itself, but more important is the fact that it sounds like the name of the Muses, which enables Taverner to pursue the subject along the lines of a classical literary history.[42] Indeed, although the lectures on music would have been delivered orally to a listening audience, Taverner presents his subject as something to be seen or read: "As they which goe to see some goodly temple, or curious peice of building, first stand & behold the frontispice, looke up to the top, Diligently beholding all that is without, before they goe into the inner roomes, soe also wee, before wee come to the more proper & intrinsicall matters belonging to this Art, examine a little the title itt selfe." Here, Taverner's depiction of music as a "goodly temple," a "curious peice of building," and a "frontispice" (lecture 1a) anticipates Fludd's "Temple of Music," which served as the frontispiece to his book's section on music. In this way, Taverner verbally describes as image what Fludd, as we have seen, represents fully translated *as* image.

Taverner's etymological approach to music is not unusual for an academic setting. In *The Praise of Musicke* (1586), John Case includes a long explanation of the history of music's name, which he treats as a subject for allegory: "Exception may bee taken against these things as fables and fantasies of the Poetes: yet if we drawe the vaile aside, and looke neerer into that, which nowe wee doe but glimpse at, what else is ment but that Musike is and ought to

---

41. John Taverner, lecture 1a, Gresham College Music Lectures, 1610, Sloane Manuscript 2329, British Library, London. Each reference to the manuscript is cited according to the numbered lecture in which it appears. For the sake of legibility, I have provided the full word where an abbreviation appears (e.g., "propriety" for "ppriety").

42. Taverner states, for example, that "others going yet farther, fetch the name of muse & musicke from the Hebrewe word Majem, which signifies water, because, as some would have itt, Musicke was first found out in imitation of some bubling rivers pleasant noyse" (ibid.).

be accounted *donum & inuentum deorum.*"[43] Like Case, whom he seems to be imitating, Taverner also locates the meaning of music underneath a "fictive veil" created by ancient, mysterious poets: "Heereupon perhaps the Poets feigned such great familiarity & correspondencie, betweeene the muses & the Nymphes of the waters, from the Hebrew musar, which signifies to meditate." Likewise, quoting the French poet DuBartas, Taverner joins the study of music with mathematics by virtue of their shared mysteriousness: "Long time safe keeping for their after kin/A thousand learned mysteries therein" (lecture 1a). Here, Taverner's references to "feigning Poets" and "learned mysteries" explicitly evoke the Renaissance moralizations of classical poetry (his habit of referring to DuBartas is only one of many signs of his indebtedness to the moralizing tradition). Throughout the Gresham lectures, Taverner draws heavily on the allegorists' rhetoric of secrecy, partly in order to justify his method of teaching music through an unending parade of classical and philosophical citations, rather than following the more mathematical and astrological approach of other Renaissance writers on music. In this way, the myth of a pure, watery music understood and ciphered by ancient poets orients the study of music as an examination of *texts.* For Taverner, the allegorical explanation of music—which becomes indistinguishable from its etymology—crucially helps structure his analysis of music as a philological problem.

As in nearly all of the medieval and Renaissance treatises on *musica speculativa,* Taverner's principal myth for music is the story of Pythagoras, which he gives a central place in the first Gresham lecture. However, Taverner is careful about the fact that Pythagoras is a pagan writer, and he accordingly adopts a line of defense well-known to the Renaissance allegorists:

> You may observe, howe cunningly this most ingenious Poet hath joined together both those fables or histories (you may call them as you please) of Pythag. & Mercurie, before mentioned, & made them serve his purpose; neither is itt to bee accounted wrong or injustice in him, seeing St. Augustines counsaile wills us to gather out of the writings of prophane authors, that soe taking the good & true from those unjust owners, wee might reduce them to their proper & primary use.

The practice of extracting what is "good & true" from classical authors and placing them within a Christian framework is endemic to the medieval

---

43. John Case, *The Praise of Musicke* (London, 1586), 5.

and Renaissance moralizations of classical poetry, and Taverner employs it to privilege Pythagorean cosmology. Following the same allegorical impulse, Taverner incorporates a more problematic author, Ovid: "Orpheus whoe having found out musicke, by the benefitt of that inchanting harmony, soe refined & charmed the rude & savage manners of men, that hee first brought them to a more civill kind of life, *which is the morall of the tale,* howe hee with his harpe tamed tygres & lions & made trees & stones to followe him" (my emphasis).[44] The conscious effort to distance himself from the Ovidian tale, by explicitly calling attention to its "morall," suggests Taverner's awareness (shared with Ovid's moralizers) of the particular dangers that Ovid poses to a Christian project. The fact that Taverner does not refer to Ovid by name when citing episodes from the *Metamorphoses* may suggest this awareness, particularly since he is scrupulous about naming other classical authors—in Ovid's case he simply refers to ambiguous "others" or "they." Moreover, after the allusion to Orpheus, Taverner dwells on the problem of classical authors when he comes to his next Ovidian allusion, the story of Deucalion and Pyrrha:

> I see noe reason, why the Gre. might not translate [music's] invention of Jubal to their Pythagoras, as well as they have taken many other thinges out of the history of the Bible, & thrust them among their impious fables, under other names devised by themselves. Soe they call their kinge of Gods, Jove, stealing the name from the true God of Gods Jehovah: And soe they report of Deucalion, that he was onely saved in the flood when others perished, making mention allso of a dove (as you may reede in a tract of Plutarch's whether water or land creatures bee the wiser or subtiler) which was sent out of Deucalion's shipp, (say they) to spy whether there were yet any firme land or noe, which relation out of question they stole out of the history of Noah & his arke. (lecture 1a)

By now Taverner has strayed far from his original subject. His need to place the study of music within a carefully controlled context—one which unequivocally ascribes authority to scripture—leads him to reproduce one of the most frequently used examples cited by Renaissance moralizers of Ovid: the reading

---

44. There are, of course, other Renaissance sources for the story of Orpheus, most notably Virgil. However, Ovid's version, arguably the most popular in Renaissance England, bears the strongest resemblance to Taverner's description. Cf. Golding: "Now whyle the *Thracian* Poet with this song delyghts the mynds/Of savage beastes, & drawes both stones and trees ageynst their kynds" (11.1–2).

of Deucalion as Noah. Taverner's clumsy style of writing, however, makes the arbitrariness and willfulness of this method of interpretation glaringly obvious, inadvertently revealing the seams of the critical tradition on which he banks his theory of music.

As in much Renaissance writing on *musica speculativa,* Taverner's allegorizing treatment of Pythagoras functions as an important prop to the idea that music is to be read rather than heard. And again, in his retelling of the canonical story of Pythagoras, Taverner enacts the textualization of music with a transparency that is not always present in his source texts:

> Boetius, as allso Divers others, ascribe [music] to Pythagoras: Whoe by chance passing by a Smithes forge, on a suddaine their hammers saluted his eares with soe orderly a noyse, that him seemed hee heard some though rudely, yet truely agreeing sounds. Whereupon imagining with him-selfe, that hee had nowe found an opportunity *of confirming that by sense, which before hee had in his mind conceived,* hee comes to the smithes & curiously observes their manner.... Then began hee to cast about & to examine the weight of the hammers, the difference of which having attained unto, hee makes experience of the same conclusion upon certain stringes made of shipps gutts.... When nowe on these hee found the harmony, which his observation in the hammers before had promised... hee suted those sounds with numbers awnswerable unto them. (lecture 1a, my emphasis)

Here, Pythagoras's theory of music begins as an idea "in his mind conceived," which only later becomes manifest in the sound of the smiths' hammers. The idea of a Pythagoras who hears conceptual music as actual sound accords with the belief, not mentioned in Taverner's lectures, that Pythagoras alone could hear the music of the spheres. Moreover, Taverner's version reveals why the idea of Pythagoras's privileged hearing is so useful: at a unique moment in the history of music, Pythagoras was able to hear "true" music as actual sound, which he then translated to diagrams and numbers ("att length hee suted those sounds with numbers awnswerable unto them"). From that point on, his followers apprehend true music not by hearing it, but by examining the numerical proportions that Pythagoras left behind. Thus, as Stephen Gosson prescribes, scholars of music "profit" by putting away their instruments and looking down at the speculative texts that record music's nature. In this way, Taverner's recourse to Pythagoras implies a preference for textual history that he is not at pains to disguise: "I have somewhat the longer insisted on this storie of Pythagoras, both because itt is the most received opinion amongst our writers & allsoe because itt is the very foundation whereon the whole frame of musicke relieth" (lecture 1a). By attributing "the whole frame of musicke" to Pythagoras, Taverner does not mean that Pythagoras invented music; he reserves this for the sons of Adam. Rather, Taverner implies that the *discipline* of music rests on the story of Pythagoras, which represents music in a way that insulates it from the messiness of physical sound. Similarly, the figure of Pythagoras legitimizes Taverner's own project, which, in its attempt to assert the authority of *musica speculativa,* distinguishes itself from the performative virtuosity of Taverner's better-known predecessor at Gresham.

Taverner's Gresham lectures demonstrate how the suppression of musical sound was an institutional concern, not merely a philosophical problem. In his second lecture, Taverner makes an explicit claim for the importance of *musica speculativa* over a "methodicall" approach to teaching music, and it is difficult not to hear in this claim a challenge to Bull himself:

> Amongest those which have undertaken the handling of any Art, you may observe a diverse course of delivery, some following one, some another, which may bee all reduced to these two maine wayes. The one historicall, the other methodicall.... Yet in mine opinion, itt were to bee wished, that more had laboured in that historicall search, which if they had done, they might have added much to their owne glory & our knowledge. For allthough one bee throughly & perfectly instructed in the precepts & theorems of an Art, yet if hee be ignorant, to what use those inventions did serve, & howe they were applied, I doubt whether ever hee shall bee able by his owne industry onely to attaine to the true & genuine use of the Art... for as that methodicall kind of tractation, which consisteth alltogether in precepts, is the ready way to come to the speculative knowledge of the Art, soe that those precepts beeing in themselves obscure & harsh, may bee the better understood. (lecture 2)

Although Taverner briefly distinguishes his "historicall" approach from "the speculative knowledge" of music, he argues that both are indispensable for "the true & genuine use" of music. In this respect, Taverner establishes a precedent for Petty's later, more sweeping prescription that the Gresham professor of music "need not so much to teach his Auditors actually to play or make melody as to explain the grounds thereof." Taverner promises that he will eventually "come to the methodicall handling of this Art" after treating its history, but he never does. Still, whether or not Taverner's emphasis on the historical and speculative aspects of music is intended to cover up his own deficiencies, the tradition of *musica speculativa* provides him with a well-established rhetoric with which to transform the study of music from a performative or mathematical problem to a philological one. Like the Renaissance allegorizations of Ovid, Taverner's strategy is to overwhelm his subject with historical, literary, and etymological context, in order to draw attention away from the aspects of music that do not neatly fit his bookish research. In this way, Taverner demonstrates that the allegorization of music could operate not only on the level of texts themselves but from the podium as well.

Musica Practica and the Representation of Sound

Taverner's separation of "precepts" and "invention" reinscribes the boundary between *musica speculativa* and *musica practica* that still structures the disciplinary approach to music and cultural studies in the early modern period—what Cristle Collins Judd has described as a "tacit agreement" between musicologists and other scholars to keep separate theoretical works and music books, and not to encroach on each other's archival domain.[45] However, as I hope to show in this section, the idea that musical theorists and musical composers operate in separate conceptual or disciplinary spheres in the Renaissance cannot be sustained. For one thing, *musica speculativa* appears in one form or another in nearly every work on musical instruction produced in Renaissance Europe. Gaffurio's *Practica musicae* (1496), for example, which contains much of the earliest printed versions of polyphonic music, relates much of its arguments about counterpoint and notation to material found in more speculative works, including his own *Theorica musicae* (1492).[46] Likewise, Thomas Robinson's *Schoole of Musicke* (1603), which is directed at teaching the correct method of fingering on the lute, introduces its subject by firmly establishing the importance of understanding music's speculative nature: "A Musition that would bee excellent...must read the scriptures, for it is the fountaine of all knowledge, & it teacheth the divine harmonie of the soule of man: for Musicke is none other then a perfect harmonie, whose divinitie is seene in the perfectnesse of his proportions, as, his unison sheweth the unitie, from

---

45. Cristle Collins Judd, *Reading Renaissance Music Theory: Hearing with the Eyes* (Cambridge: Cambridge University Press, 2000), 5. Judd's study is a wonderful example of scholarship that attempts to complicate this conventional distinction; her work pays careful attention to the textual and visual aspects of Renaissance music theory, noting the influence of speculative and humanist works in structuring the representation of musical examples.

46. See ibid., 17–30.

whence all other, (concords, discords, consonancies, or others whatsoever) springeth."[47]

In some cases, the deference to *musica speculativa* is a conventional feature of practical works, which generally open with a historical or theoretical overview of their subject. In other cases, the logic of *musica speculativa* informs and structures the exposition of music itself. For example, Charles Butler's *The Principles of Musik in Singing and Setting* (1636) begins, unexceptionally, with a theoretical explanation of the modes.[48] Yet for a primer directed at actual singers and composers, Butler marshals a formidable arsenal for a seemingly perfunctory point: the first sentence is buttressed by three separate endnotes; a page and a half of text is followed by seven pages of annotations (in small type); and a conventional definition of the modes is backed up by references to Boethius, Aristotle, Augustine, Tullius, Plato, Macrobius, Isidore, Cassiodorus, Glareanus, Cicero, Plutarch, Timotheus, Quintilian, and Virgil. As we have seen with Butler's treatise on bees, his methods are exaggerated but not unusual. Although Boethius draws a fine line between *musica speculativa* and *musica practica,* the distinction in actual music primers in early modern England is much more muddied. Likewise, Thomas Morley's *Plaine and Easie Introduction to Practicall Musicke* (1597), a landmark of practical music instruction in England, though it asserts the Boethian model of music ("as for the division, music is either speculative or practical")[49], reveals a more hybrid approach in its actual exposition. As we will see, Morley's treatise, along with William Bathe's *A Briefe Introduction to the Skill of Song* (1596), demonstrates the pervasiveness of speculative rhetoric in *articulating* a pedagogical approach to music. Faced with the problem of sound that cannot be translated, Morley and Bathe fall back on *musica speculativa* and its tidy methods for dealing with the unwieldy properties of physical sound.

While Morley's place in the tradition of English composers is well-founded, modern scholarship on his *Introduction* has usually failed to notice the residual traces of *musica speculativa* in its representation of music performance and composition. Both Morley's and Bathe's treatises demonstrate the extent to which the disciplinization of practical music in early modern England required, at least on occasion, recourse to *musica speculativa* and its

---

47. Thomas Robinson, *The Schoole of Musicke: Wherein Is Taught the Perfect Method of True Fingering of the Lute* (1603), facsimile repr., ed. David Lumsden (Paris: Centre national de la recherche scientifique, 1971), pl. iv.

48. Charles Butler, *The Principles of Musik in Singing and Setting* (1636), facsimile repr. (New York: Da Capo, 1970), Ar-Br.

49. Thomas Morley, *A Plaine and Easie Introduction to Practicall Musicke* (1597), facsimile repr. (Amsterdam: Da Capo, 1969), "Annotations," J.

rhetorical strategies. Morley and Bathe are, after all, attempting to establish musical authority through printed *texts*. Because of the way academic disciplines have been organized since the twentieth century (Renaissance *musica practica* is closest to what is now called "music theory") and because the textuality of printed music is largely taken for granted (a standardized system of notation is quickly learned and ingrained), it has become conceptually easy for modern readers to dismiss the impact of *musica speculativa* on "real" musical thought and practice in Renaissance England.[50] Most histories of music frame speculative music as "largely a dead letter by the sixteenth century" that, like Hamlet's ghostly father, vanishes at the cock-crowing of the Enlightenment and Monteverdian ingenuity.[51] As Roger Bray notes, *musica speculativa,* and Boethius in particular, have "received a broadly unfavourable reception from modern musicologists," who generally argue or imply that "the ranging of music among the sciences hampered its development as an art."[52] However, the need to formalize practical music within a textual idiom leads writers like Morley and Bathe to emulate unapologetically the universalizing rhetoric of *musica speculativa,* even when these borrowings mean effacing musical sound.[53] More importantly, the treatises on practical music demonstrate how the mere act of putting music into text could activate the discursive strategies of *musica speculativa* and push music in the direction of metaphor. Morley's and Bathe's treatises document this textualization of music, whose effects had far-reaching consequences for the development of musical thought in the seventeenth century, and which effectively institutionalized the role of metaphor in musical language, whether speculative or performed.

Morley's *Introduction* is by far the most popular primer on practical music in early modern England, going through a second edition less than twenty

---

50. For a theoretical discussion of the problems attending the textual representation of music in early modern England, see Bruce R. Smith, *The Acoustic World of Early Modern England: Attending to the O-Factor* (Chicago: University of Chicago Press, 1999), especially 107–29.

51. John Caldwell, *The Oxford History of English Music,* (Oxford: Oxford University Press, 1991), 1:499.

52. Roger Bray, "Music and the Quadrivium in Early Tudor England," *Music and Letters* 76 (1995): 1. In the second quotation Bray is citing Paul Henry Lang, *Music in Western Civilization* (New York: Norton, 1941), 59.

53. Bray suggests that such an approach to music composition may have actually been institutionalized in English universities in the early sixteenth century, since candidates for music degrees at Cambridge and Oxford were required to submit a composition as part of their qualification ("Music and the Quadrivium"). See also Nan Cooke Carpenter, *Music in the Medieval and Renaissance Universities* (Norman: University of Oklahoma Press, 1958), 153–209.

years after its original publication.[54] Unlike the Renaissance works on *musica speculativa,* Morley's *Introduction* is firmly committed to the composition and performance of actual, heard music. The book's title page explicitly lists the work's three principal areas of instruction: (1) singing, (2) descant, and (3) composition.[55] In addition, the title page advertises "new songs of 2, 3, 4, and 5 parts" that appear throughout the treatise; Morley clearly intends his reader to imbibe the lessons of the treatise and apply them to the performance of extant songs, whether composed by him or others. Evidence of the early reception of the *Plaine and Easie Introduction* suggests that Morley's songs were in fact regularly performed and used as compositional models.[56] At the same time, Morley notes that his lessons are based on careful study of musical examples in current practice, rather than on speculative texts alone: "To my great griefe, then did I see the most part of mine owne precepts false and easie to be confuted by the workes of *Taverner, Fairfax, Cooper,* and infinite more ... & with what toyle & wearinesse I was enforced to compare the parts for trying out the value of some notes."[57] In this respect, Morley distinguishes his primer from other musical treatises that attempt to impose a monolithic set of rules, such as Thomas Ravenscroft's *A Briefe Discourse of the true (but neglected) use of Charact'ring the Degrees* (1617), which refers disparagingly to the "common *Practise*" as an impediment to instruction.[58] Indeed, much of the scholarship on Morley's *Introduction* in the last few decades has focused on its contribution to the development of compositional and notational methods in Renaissance England, firmly securing its place in the history of early modern musical practice, not musical thought.

However, Morley's text occasionally tells a different story. The work's title page reuses a woodcut originally designed for John Dee's *Mathematicall Preface*

---

54. On the proliferation of musical primers and practical treatises in early modern England, see Rebecca Herissone, *Music Theory in Seventeenth-Century England* (New York: Oxford University Press, 2000), 1–25; David C. Price, *Patrons and Musicians of the English Renaissance* (Cambridge: Cambridge University Press, 1981), 39–47.

55. As Morley is well aware, "descant" has multiple definitions in the sixteenth century. The most popular definition in late sixteenth-century England, which Morley adopts, defines descant as the singing of a "part extempore upon a plainsong," i.e., extemporizing a vocal part above a fixed melody. However, because descant involves a strict set of rules for voice leading and consonance, and because it can be realized as a distinct part in printed music, it was often considered a subject of composition. On the topic of descant and Renaissance performance practices, see Timothy J. McGee, *Medieval and Renaissance Music: A Performer's Guide* (Toronto: University of Toronto Press, 1985).

56. See, for example, John Irving, "Thomas Tomkins's Copy of Morley's *A Plain and Easy Introduction to Practical Music*," *Music and Letters* 71 (1990): 483–93.

57. Morley, *Plaine and Easie Introduction,* "To the curteous Reader," B.

58. Thomas Ravenscroft, *A Briefe Discourse of the true (but neglected) use of Charact'ring the Degrees* (London, 1617), 2A3.

(1570), a solidly speculative work. The illustration includes a conventional program for the four mathematical arts, placing music squarely alongside geometry, arithmetic, and astronomy (figure 3). At the top of this program the figures of Ptolemy and Marinus are prominently shown on either side of a large globe, with Ptolemy pointing one finger toward the stars and resting his other hand firmly on the globe, while Marinus measures a section of the globe with a compass. The image seems to suggest that the mathematical arts, including music, look "upward" toward philosophical and universal truth, a meaning that is corroborated by the emblematic banner underneath Ptolemy and Marinus: *virescit vulnere veritas,* itself an adaptation of Geffrey Whitney's *Choice of Emblemes* (1586), one of the earliest printed emblem books in English. Thus, as in conventional *musica speculativa,* the title page of Morley's *Introduction* represents music as an allegory for an underlying mathematical or philosophical *veritas.* Similarly, in the opening pages of the work, the narrative frame that Morley sets up is itself highly suggestive of an allegorical program: Philomathes tells his brother Polymathes that he has been publicly embarrassed for his ignorance of music, and he therefore wishes to learn music from Master Gnorimus. The etymological significance of the characters' names begs an allegorical reading: mathematics, through the Lover of Mathematics and Knowledge (*philo* + *mathes*), will be properly united with music by the entrance of Knowledge (*gnarus,* "knowing"), and this enterprise is warmly approved by One That Knows Much (*poly* + *mathes*).

The resonance of *musica speculativa* in Morley's treatise is not limited to its title page and opening frame. A brief glance at Morley's list of authorities at the beginning of his work parades most of the principal authorities on *musica speculativa* (Boethius, Zarlino, Gaffurio), and references to the same figures are scattered evenly throughout the work. More surprisingly, the rhetoric of *musica speculativa* occasionally inflects the method of music instruction itself, particularly in passages where the textuality of Morley's instructional system comes into conflict with the acoustic possibilities of music in the physical world. In these cases, as in the following exchange between Master Gnorimus and Philomathes over an exercise in sight-singing, the logic of mathematics functions as a convenient rhetorical device for bridging the gap between sound and text:

Ma. Now for the last tryall of your singing in continuall deduction sing this perfectly, and I will saie you understand plainsong well enough.
Phi. I know not how to beginne.
Ma. Why?

FIGURE 3. Title page from Thomas Morley, *A Plaine and Easie Introduction to Practicall Musicke* (1597). By permission of the Folger Shakespeare Library.

Phi. Because, beneath *Gam ut* there is nothing: and the first note standeth beneath *Gam ut*.

Ma. Whereas you saie, there is nothing beneath *Gam ut,* you deceive your selfe: For Musicke is included in no certaine bounds, (though the Musicions do include their songs within a certaine compasse.) And as you *Philosophers* say, that no number can be given so great, but that you may give a greater. And no poynt so small but that you may give a smaller. So there can be no note given so high, but you may give a higher, and none so lowe, but that you may give a lower... for if Mathematically you consider it, it is true as well without the compasse of the Scale, as within: and so may be continued infinitely.[59]

Here, Gnorimus presents Philomathes with a written note that lies outside the musical scale that he had earlier established, below "Gam ut," the lowest note on the scale. This apparent discrepancy between his textual system of musical notation and what can actually be sung in practice causes Gnorimus to admit that "music is included in no certain bounds," suggesting that practical music always exceeds its textual representation. Gnorimus averts this potential conflict between music and text by invoking the speculative discourse of philosophy and mathematics, whose rhetoric of infinity allows Morley to explain the acoustic range of actual music: "no point so small but that you may give a smaller." Nonetheless, Morley suggests in the next paragraph that even mathematics has its limitations against the experience of actual sound. Asked why the musical scale comprises only twenty notes, Gnorimus responds that "because that compasse was the reach of most voyces: so that under *Gam ut* the voice seemed as a kinde of *humming,* and above *E la* a kinde of constrained skricking."[60] Although mathematical rhetoric can comprehend an endless diatonic scale, it cannot account for what sounds are experienced *as music*. This is because the difference between singing and shrieking is fundamentally a cultural, subjective distinction, not a mathematical one, and because different human voices produce different timbres. Morley's explanation that the musical scale is based on the range of the human voice reminds his reader that practical music is ultimately an embodied phenomenon, fully realized in the physical, heterogeneous bodies of its performers and listeners.

Morley's difficulty in balancing the mathematical basis of the diatonic scale with its realization in vocal performance is representative of a larger

---

59. Morley, *Plaine and Easie Introduction,* 6.
60. Ibid., 7.

theoretical problem over the relationship between mathematics and music in the early modern period. Put simply, no single mathematical model could easily account for all the musical pitches that were included in standard practice.[61] Thus, on the one hand, professional musicians like Francis Pilkington represented the musical scale as a universal principle, "in its owne nature INFINITE; reaching from the base Earth (being as it were the GAM-UT or ground) to the highest E.LA of the incomprehensible heavens."[62] On the other hand, even the most speculative of theorists had trouble with mathematically sound harmonies that were indistinguishable from noise. More generally, the materiality of sound is a persistent problem for a standardized notational system for practical music, and Morley clearly does not want to dwell on the issue any more than is necessary: immediately after explaining the scale's origin in the human voice, Gnorimus impatiently tells Philomathes that "wee go from the purpose, and therefore proceede to the singing of your ensample."[63] In the instances where the semantics of music notation are allowed to follow their own logic, the discussion of music almost invariably slides into the mythological or allegorical mode:

> Ma. In this *Cantus*...there is also in the *Base* a Longe [i.e., a very long note] which must be sung nine Semibreefes, which is xxvii. Minymes.
> Phi. A time for an *Atlas* or *Typhoeus* to holde his breath, and not for mee or any other man now adayes.
> Ma. True, but I did set it downe of purpose, to make you understand the nature of the Moode.[64]

The fact that a human singer cannot hold a note for twenty-seven minims (beats of time) does not greatly trouble Morley's method of instruction, especially since a mythological figure ("an Atlas or Typhoeus") can neatly fill the gap between printed notation and performed music at times. (The fact that a string instrument can hold a note for twenty-seven minims is beside the point, since any instrument has material limitations that may not be reflected in a musical score.) Morley is clearly aware of the potential for his notational

---

61. See Clark and Rehding, *Music Theory and Natural Order*, 1–9. For a cogent, detailed exposition of the problem of harmonizing the scale in early modern Europe (though not for the mathematically disinclined), see Leeman L. Perkins, *Music in the Age of the Renaissance* (New York: W. W. Norton, 1999), 971–79.

62. Francis Pilkington, *The First Set of Madrigals and Pastorals of 3. 4. and 5. Parts* (1613), ed. Edmund H. Fellowes (London: Stainer & Bell, 1959), xv.

63. Morley, *Plaine and Easie Introduction*, 7.

64. Ibid., 20.

system to veer away from performed music, but he nonetheless argues for the efficacy of this system for musical practice: "Indeede wee doe not in Musicke consider the numbers by themselves, but set them for a signe to signifie the altering of our notes in the time."[65] The tendency to treat musical notation as a language—to transform it into a series of signs—marks both the meeting ground and the gap between Morley's text and the performative experience of music he is trying to teach.

The incongruity between musical notation and musical sound explains in part the appeal of *musica speculativa* for someone wishing to make definitive claims about music, even at the expense of actual sound. This is especially evident in Morley's representation of the proportions in music, which concerns the categorization and notation of what we now generally refer to as time signatures in music (e.g., 4/4 time). After explaining the five common proportions (dupla, tripla, quadrupla, sesquialtera, sesquitertia), Morley reproduces a table from Gaffurio's *De proportionibus musicis,* in which every possible numerical combination is geometrically represented and appropriately named (figure 4). The illustration, with its emphasis on visual and mathematical organization, typifies the sort of visual aids often found in Renaissance works on *musica speculativa.* The table's opacity—there are forty-five proportions identified on it—is quickly noted by Philomathes, who intuitively recognizes it as a thing different from musical sound: "Heere is a Table in deede contayning more than ever I meane to beate my brayns about. As for musick, the principal thing we seek in it, *is to delight the eare,* which cannot so perfectly be done in these hard proportions, as otherwise" (my emphasis). Gnorimus also notes the impracticality of this table for singing, but he nonetheless regards it as a worthy pedagogical tool: "If a man would ingulfe himselfe to learne to sing, and set downe all them which *Franchinis Gaufurius* hath set downe in his booke *De proportionibus musicis,* he should finde it a matter not onely hard, but almost impossible. But if you thinke you would be curious in proportions, and exercyse yourselfe in them at your leasure, heere is a Table where you may learne them at full."[66] The brief reference to Gaffurio acts as a signpost for more speculative study, but it also acknowledges the meeting ground between *musica speculativa* and *musica practica.* Morley turns the discussion back to examples of actual music, demonstrating the conventional use of musical proportions in two compositions by Renaldi and Striggio, but only after the idea of proportions has been contextualized within a speculative framework.

---

65. Ibid., 27.
66. Ibid., 33–34.

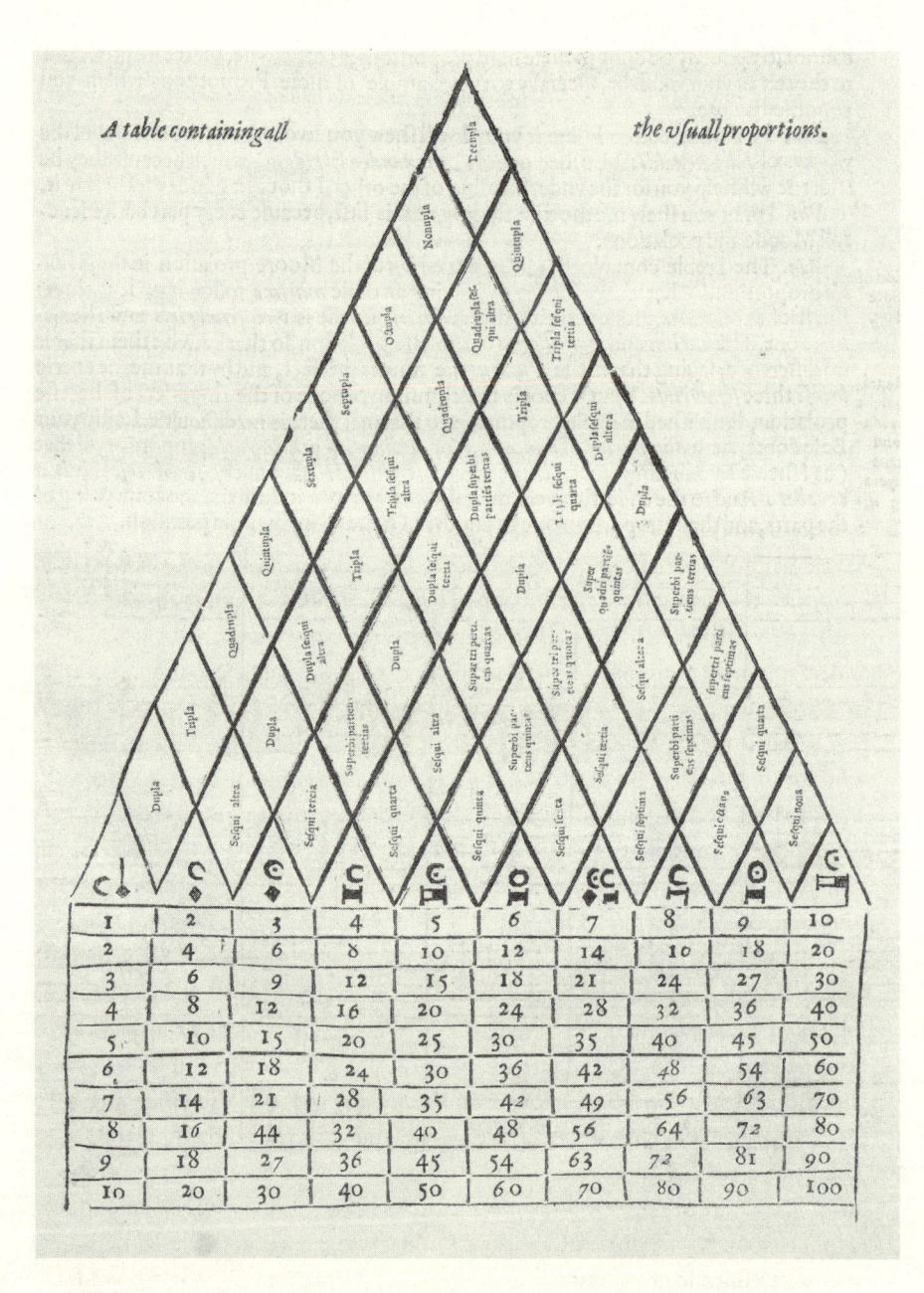

Figure 4. "A table containing all the usuall proportions," from Thomas Morley, *A Plaine and Easie Introduction to Practicall Musicke* (1597). By permission of the Folger Shakespeare Library.

Morley's representation of the relationship between *musica speculativa* and musical sound is not always coherent in the *Plaine and Easie Introduction*. On the one hand, Morley identifies a very real, causal relationship between speculative music's object of study and what one actually hears in the world: "*Speculative is that kinde of musicke* which by Mathematical helpes, seeketh out the causes, properties, and natures of soundes."[67] At other times, however, Morley seems to come close to admitting that he is merely trading in analogies when he reverts to speculative rhetoric, acknowledging that some musical precepts are "better conceived by deede than word."[68] Still, even in cases where the rhetoric of *musica speculativa* comes into open conflict with actual sound (usually by way of Philomathes' befuddled responses), Morley does not abandon speculative discourse. Rather, his representation of music suggests that the successful instruction of practical music is partially dependent on visual and allegorical modes of understanding. This idea is brought home by the musical "alphabets" that end the first section of the work. Here, a sequence of musical notes is matched with the letters of the English alphabet, usually with the prefatory phrase "Christes crosse be my speede, in all vertue to proceede," so that a musical precept is learned through a combination of aural memory and verbal logic.[69] In this way, Morley acknowledges the utility of visual and verbal systems for committing musical knowledge to memory—and, more importantly, for systematizing musical instruction.

William Bathe's *A Briefe Introduction to the Skill of Song* (1596) appears only a year before Morley's *Introduction,* yet it already presumes a significant body of practical music instruction:

Olde Musitions laid downe for Song, manifold and crabbed, confuse, tedious rules, as for example: though there be in all but sixe names, Ut, Re, Mi, Fa, Sol, La, hauing amongst them an easie order, yet could not they by rule declare, whether of these should bee attributed to euery Note, unlesse they had first framed the long ladder or skale of Gam-ut.[70]

---

67. Ibid., "Annotations," J.
68. Ibid., 25.
69. R. Alec Harman notes that this habit of joining musical examples to familiar texts was already a common pedagogical method. See Thomas Morley, *A Plain and Easy Introduction to Practical Music,* ed. R. Alec Harman (New York: Norton, 1953), 63n.
70. William Bathe, *A Briefe Introduction to the Skill of Song,* facsimile repr. (Kilkenny, Ireland: Boethius Press, 1982),A2v. All subsequent quotations of Bathe are from this edition. The exact date for the treatise has been the subject of debate. Kevin C. Karnes makes a persuasive argument that much of the treatise was composed between 1584 and 1586, even though the work was not published until 1596. See Bathe, *A Briefe Introduction to the Skill of Song,* ed. Kevin C. Karnes (Aldershot,

Bathe is speaking here of the habit of assigning syllable names (ut, re, mi) to the musical notes of a scale, a practice that he argues has been made almost incomprehensible by the fact that a single tone can have several names, depending on which key it appears in. His aim is to simplify the confusing assembly of rules in order to teach amateurs how to perform and sing music: "There was [one], that had... never practised to sing (for hee could not name one Note) who hearing of these rules, obtayned in short time, such profit by them, that he could sing a difficult song of himselfe, without any Instructor" (A3v). Thus, like Morley's treatise, Bathe's *Skill of Song* represents its origin in a lack of musical knowledge, while representing as its goal the performance of music by a general, "singing public." Yet for all its emphasis on music performance, Bathe's treatise represents music as something to apprehended through textual means as well as aural ones. In other words, music is read before being sung. Addressing the extant literature on *musica practica,* Bathe admits there is a great deal that escapes written instruction and that—until the appearance of Bathe—can only be learned by an imperfect process of hearing and vocalizing: "Many things are used in Song, for which [the practical music texts] give no rules at all, but committed them to dodge at it, harke to it, and harpe upon it" (A2v). In one sense, Bathe's treatise is remarkably prescient in articulating the "gappe" between acoustic, performed music and the written or spoken word. However, he responds to this "gappe" by asserting his own ability to close it: "For had they not opened the gappe, touching mee, it might very well hap that I should in no sort enter my selfe.... Nothing can at the beginning be perfected" (A3r). Further, Bathe suggests that a practice based on the faculties of ear and voice, which he calls "hearkening" and "harping," is inferior to learning from the printed text that he himself has set down: "There was another, who by dodging at it, hearkning to it, & harping upon it, could neuer be brought to tune sharps aright, who so soone as hee heard these rules set downe for the same, could tune them sufficiently well" (A3v).

Bathe charts a similar elision of musical sound and musical text on the first page of his treatise proper, which identifies four basic principles that will guide the correct performance of song:

> *To prepare for naming the Notes.* Practise to sunder the Vowels and Consonants, distinctly pronouncing them according to the manner of the place.

UK: Ashgate, 2005), 3–15. See also Jeremy L. Smith, *Thomas East and Music Publishing in Renaissance England* (Oxford: Oxford University Press, 2003), 80, 191.

To prepare for Quantitie. Practise to have the breath long to continue, and the tongue at libertie to runne.
To prepare for Time. Practise in striking to keepe a iust proportion of one stroke to another.
To prepare for Tune. Practise to haue your voice cleere, which when thou hast done, learne the rules following. (2A3r)

Within this scheme, the sounding, breathing body of the musician is circumscribed and ordered by an abstract mathematical and scientific system of performance: "pronouncing" becomes subject to "naming," "tongue" becomes "quantitie," "striking" becomes "time," and "voice" becomes "tune." Even where acoustic principles of performance can be discerned, Bathe's instructions show more concern for a clear understanding of a song's verbal text than for the quality of the voice itself: sung notes must be heard "distinctly," must always be appropriate to "the manner of the place" and in "just proportion," and must be enunciated by a "cleere" voice. Bathe further abstracts these rules for singing in the last sentence on the page, in terms that evoke *music speculativa:* "The skill of song doth consist in foure things: Naming. Quantitie. Time. Tune."

The experience of musical sound is always a factor in Bathe's text, however, and there are moments in the *Skill of Song* when music's sound complicates Bathe's systematic plan of instruction. For example, when explaining why the syllable "sol" is often used instead of "ut" in practice, Bathe grudgingly acknowledges that this is due to the fact that "sol" is a more euphonious sound: "And that euery *ut,* should bee named *sol,* which two things are used *euphoniae gratia,* and yet this name of *ut,* is most proper to the base or lowest part in the first place" (2A5v). Likewise, after diagramming the diatonic scale, Bathe implicitly acknowledges that the eight musical tones themselves need to be learned in "practise," by listening to another's voice or an instrument, before they can be accepted as "principle" (Bv). Bathe's treatise does, after all, offer some useful pedagogy in learning how to sight-read, including some tricks of tonal enunciation that are still used today.[71] Yet, as in Morley's *Introduction,* the need to formalize the study of music inevitably leads Bathe to adopt a brand of rhetoric that occasionally treats music as if it were something to be seen rather than heard. In these cases, Bathe's treatise resembles Renaissance writing on *musica speculativa,* especially in its tendency

---

71. One such method I recognize is Bathe's instruction to change temporarily the names of two notes in succession (e.g., fa fa to sol fa) in order to ingrain the actual sounds in memory, even though the changed names are not technically correct.

116   **CHAPTER 3**

to emblematize music and situate it within an elaborate, visual scheme, like Morley's diagram of the proportions. This aspect of Bathe's method is most strikingly evident in his "generall Table comprehending two parts in one," which attempts to set down the rules for consonance when composing a two-part composition (figure 5). This table—whose obscurity cannot be overstated—appears near the end of Bathe's treatise and consists of rows and columns of numbers that represent different musical intervals: "1" denotes a unison, "5" denotes a fifth, and so on. Bathe presents his table, which resembles the harmonic diagrams in speculative works, as comprehending nearly all two- and three-part compositions:

> This present table, may serve also, who so marketh it well, for 2 parts in one, without a plaine song, of all kinds, & in all waies for 3 parts in one, without a plainsong, or ground, the third part being under: of all kindes & of all wayes for 2 parts in one, upon 2 plain songs, or grounds at once, for maintaining reports, & other such things as these be. (C)

Moreover, as if this numeric table were not sufficient in itself, Bathe introduces another schematic for the composition of two- and three-part songs, a "Sword of Music" (*Gladius musicus*) that corresponds to the numeric table and on which is inscribed the verses: *Aggredior quo aderis cado cernis adesto mi Ihesu* and *Unum addas tollasque loco stet qua tuor addas* (figure 6). The verses on Bathe's *gladius* are less important for what they say than for what they encode. Through an elaborate system of correspondences, the number of words in each verse, the number of letters and vowels in each word, and the specific placement of each verse on the sword all signify the array of numbers of the preceding table:

> As the Sword now standeth, compting [counting] about upon the seven words, when you have found what woord serveth for the course, looke what vowels bee in it, and thereby you shall know the concords, that serveth for that course, as if the vowell bee A, it signifieth the unizon. If it be E, it signifieth the third. (C3v)

In this way, Bathe encapsulates all of the rules for musical consonance in two- and three-part compositions within a single figure, a feat of contrivance that he ensures is not lost on his reader: "Lo, thus are all the things expressed at large in the table, briefely contrived in the compasse of two verses" (C3v).

The modern editor of Bathe's *Skill of Song* describes the *gladius* as more remarkable than useful, and he notes its "forward-looking" relationship to

Rules of Song.

	6	8	11	10	9	8	7	6
The obser	5	5	7	6	5	4	3	2
uations of	4	1	6	5	4	3	2	1
the places		7	1	7	6	5	4	3
vp are sixe	3	2	6	7	1	2	3	4
	2	5	2	3	4	5	6	7
	1	1						

Places vp.	1	7	6	5	4	3	2
Courses vp. 1 / Courses downe.	1356	6	135	16	35	136	5
2	7	6	135	16	35	136	5	1356
3	6	135	16	35	136	5	1356	6
4	5	16	35	136	5	1356	6	135
5	4	35	136	5	1356	6	135	36
6	3	136	5	1356	6	135	16	35
7	2	5	1356	6	135	16	35	136
8 vt su: 1	1356	6	135	16	35	136	5

Places dovvn	1	2	3	4	5	6	7
The obser	1	1	2	3	4	5	6	7
uations of	2	5	6	7	1	2	3	4
the places	3	2	3	4	5	6	7	1
down are	4	7	1	2	3	4	5	6
sixe.	5	1	2	3	4	5	6	7
	6	5	6	7	8	9	10	11

FIGURE 5. "A generall Table comprehending two parts in one, of all kindes upon all plaine Songs," from William Bathe, *A Briefe Introduction to the Skill of Song* (1596). By permission of the William Andrews Clark Memorial Library, University of California, Los Angeles.

Two verses comprehending the foresaid Table, which for necessities sake of the matter, must be written crossing one another

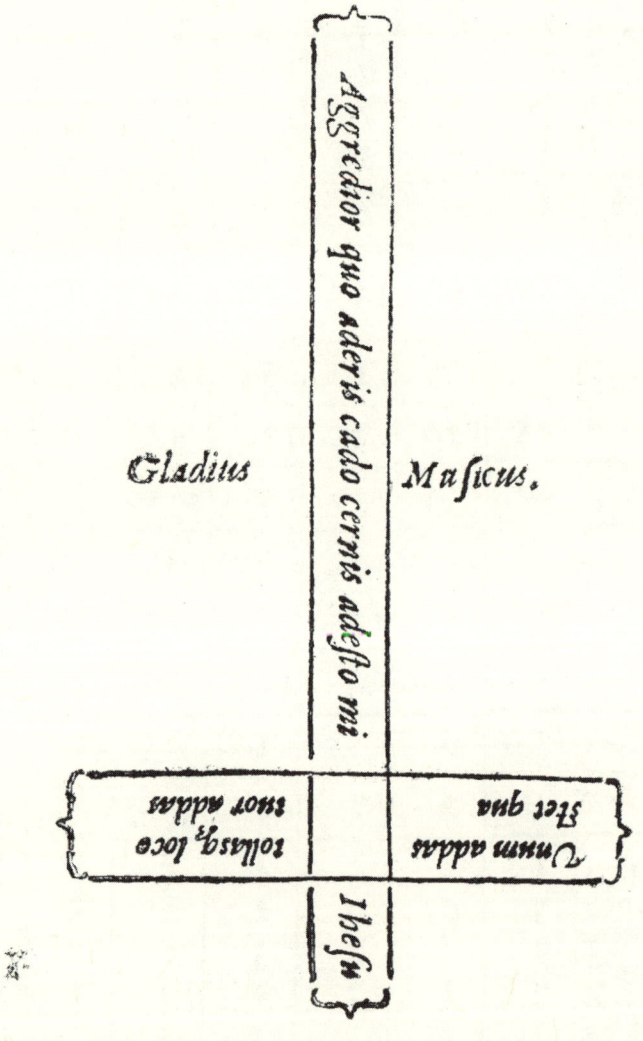

Aggredior quo aderis cado cernis adesto mi

Gladius   Musicus.

Vnum addas
Stet qua

tollasq; loce
tuor addas

Ihesu

In

FIGURE 6. "Gladius musicus," from William Bathe, *A Briefe Introduction to the Skill of Song* (1596). By permission of the William Andrews Clark Memorial Library, University of California, Los Angeles.

the compositional machines of Athanasius Kircher.[72] As a method of composition that is based on a combinatorial algorithm, however, Bathe's table and *gladius* also represent an attempt to link practical music back to a mathematical, speculative mode of discourse—an idea made palpably clear by the emblematic nature of Bathe's compositional diagrams. Bathe's *A Brief Introduction to the True Art of Music* (1584), written a few years before *Skill of Song* and generally considered the first music primer in English, is more deferential to the experience of sound. In this text, Bathe includes a separate section on "musick speculative" in which he comes dangerously close to revealing *musica speculativa* as an elaborate metaphor, in part simply because his writing on the subject is so clumsy. Bathe breaks convention in this early treatise by placing practical music before speculative music, remarking "that this tractation of musicke practice should go befoir the other of speculatione," in the same way that "reading must goe befoir gramer."[73] The absence of a section on speculative music in the 1596 treatise should not be taken to reflect, as has been suggested in one review of Bathe's *True Art of Music,* the conventional assumption that the development of music theory in the sixteenth and seventeenth centuries charts a simple decline of *musica speculativa* and a rise of *musica instrumentalis*.[74] Bathe's later treatise *incorporates* the rhetorical and textual strategies of *musica speculativa,* in a way that significantly affects the meaning and representation of practical music. *Musica speculativa* aids and abets the later treatise, helping it contain and control music's infinite variety.

Unruly Subjects: Teaching Music in Shakespearean Comedy

Shakespeare frequently returns to the Renaissance classroom in order to show its dependence on textual forms of authority, and music is a favorite subject through which Shakespeare's characters rehearse orthodox methods of education. In these instances, the tendency to teach "by the book" is often made to seem remarkably limiting, particularly in its willful ignorance of the extratextual effects of pedagogical practices. For example, in *Love's Labour's Lost,* arguably the most scholarly minded of Shakespeare's plays, the *logos* of academic discourse is repeatedly put into competition with its material,

---

72. Bathe, *Skill of Song,* ed. Karnes, 32–33.
73. William Bathe, *A Brief Introduction to the True Art of Music* (1584), ed. Cecil Hill (Colorado Springs: Colorado College Music Press, 1979), 1.
74. See Anne E. Waters's review in *Journal of Music Theory* 26 (1982): 351–52.

acoustic effects. The rhetoric of scholarly learning here literally *sounds* ridiculous. Such is the case in passages where the familiar language of sententiae spills over into rhyme, often at a dizzying pace:

> LONGUEVILLE. He weeds the corn and still lets grow the weeding.
> BIRON. The spring is near when green geese are a-breeding.
> DUMAINE. How follows that?
> BIRON.   Fit in his place and time.
> DUMAINE. In reason nothing.
> BIRON.   Something then in rhyme.
>
> (1.1.96–99)

Here, the aural quality of the maxim (its "rhyme") eclipses its verbal meaning, or "reason." In a similar way, Shakespeare draws attention to music's acoustic effects, as in the following musical "pun":

> ARMADO. How hast thou purchased this experience?
> MOTH. By my penny of observation.
> ARMADO. But O, but O—
> MOTH. "The hobby-horse is forgot."
>
> (3.1.21–24)

Moth's completion of Armado's exclamation ("but O") with a line from a popular song follows a logic of sound rather than sense. Armado's words *sound* like the phrase in a Robin Hood ballad, but in context they have nothing to do with it. Shakespeare reminds us that, in the acoustic world of the theater, spoken words may have an effect on listeners that has little or nothing to do with their verbal meaning. The same point is driven home a few lines earlier, when Moth's singing slips into nonsense language altogether:

> ARMADO. Warble, child; make passionate my sense of hearing.
> MOTH. [*sings*] Concolinel.
> ARMADO. Sweet air!
>
> (3.1.1–3)

Much editorial hand-wringing has been done to make sense of Moth's utterance, and interpretations of "concolinel" have ranged from the first two words of an Italian song to a corruption of an Irish phrase.[75] Yet for all their

---

75. Richard David summarizes the most popular readings of this line in his edition of the play. See *Love's Labour's Lost,* ed. Richard David (London: Methuen, 1985), 43n.

ingenuity, such explanations may be beside the point. Moth's strange word—typical of his language in the play—may simply be an utterance that revels in its own sonority, regardless of its possible linguistic meaning, and in this way it satisfies Armado's desire for sweet music.

In fact, the illegibility of "concolinel" may be precisely the point. The passage between Armado and Moth, like so many other moments in the play, ridicules the compulsion to make language and music classifiable. In his edition of the play, Richard David notes that Armado's request to "make passionate" his hearing may itself be a borrowing from Puttenham's *Arte of English Poesie,* in which the proportions of poetry are described in terms of a mathematical, visual conception of music:

> This proportion consisteth in placing of every verse in a staff or ditty by such reasonable distances as may best serve the ear for delight, and also to show the poet's art and variety of music... which manner of situation, even without respect of the rhyme, doth alter the nature of the poesy and make it either lighter or graver, or more merry or mournfull, and many ways passionate to the ear and heart of the hearer, seeming for this point that our maker by his measures and concords of sundry proportions doth counterfeit the harmonical tunes of the vocal and instrumental musics.[76]

Here, Puttenham represents the effects of music and poetry in such a concrete way as to render them mechanical: certain proportions produce "merry" feelings in the listener, others produce "mournfull" ones, and so on. In this context, the phrase "make passionate" is closest in meaning to "communicate," a point that makes the nonsensical exchange between Armado and Moth appear almost self-parodying. Musical rhetoric becomes the stuff of farce with Holofernes, whose declamation in the play's fourth act is spectacular in its mangling of Latin pastoral, Italian poetry, and musical language:

> HOLOFERNES. '*Facile precor gelida quando pecas omnia sub umbra ruminat*', and so forth. Ah, good old Mantuan! I may speak of thee as the traveller doth of Venice:
> *Venezia, Venezia,*

---

76. George Puttenham, *The Art of English Poesy* (1589), ed. Frank Whigham and Wayne A. Rebhorn (Ithaca, NY: Cornell University Press, 2007), 174. The passage occurs in book 2 ("Of Proportion"). Puttenham goes on to suggest that poetry and music are "sympathetic" arts, in the same way that audible sounds can be translated into visual signs. For a discussion of Puttenham's synthesis of poetry and music, see Henry Tompkins Kirby-Smith, *The Celestial Twins: Poetry and Music through the Ages* (Amherst: University of Massachusetts Press, 2000), 118–28.

Chi non ti vede, chi non ti prezia.
Old Mantuan, old Mantuan—who understandeth thee not, loves thee not. Ut, re, sol, la, mi, fa. Under pardon, sir, what are the contents? Or rather, as Horace says in his—what, my soul—verses? (4.2.86–94)

For Holofernes, reciting the notes of the gamut is simply one more exercise in textual citation that ranges from Mantuanus to Florio to Horace. However, Holofernes gets the gamut wrong: the names of the notes are correct, but their sequence is not, making them useless for singing. Holofernes seems to have read the gamut somewhere and memorized its names, but he does not have it in his ear. At the same time, the sound of academic discourse is for Holofernes a pleasure in itself, regardless of its incoherence or irrationality. Indeed, it may be one of the play's delicious ironies that the sonnet that Nathaniel reads in response ends with ambiguous praise for a lovesick musician: "'Celestial as thou art, O pardon, love, this wrong, / That singeth heaven's praise with such an earthly tongue'" (110–11).

In *Love's Labour's Lost,* Shakespeare dramatizes the point that the Renaissance music treatises try to conceal: namely, that academic discourse about music is often divorced from musical sound. This is nowhere more evident than in Holofernes' mangling of the gamut, which he treats as material for the demonstration of rhetorical *copia,* not for the actual singing of musical tones. It is hardly surprising at this point that Shakespeare associates Holofernes' "quantitative" approach to music with a similarly rigid attitude toward Ovid. In almost the same breath with which he recites the gamut, Holofernes critiques Berowne's letter with a mini-lecture on the classroom Ovid: "Here are only numbers ratified, but for the elegancy, facility, and golden cadence of poesy—*caret*. Ovidius Naso was the man. And why indeed 'Naso' but for smelling out the odoriferous flowers of fancy, the jerks of invention? *Imitari* is nothing" (4.2.113–17). Aside from the fact that he condemns an activity (*imitatio*) in which he zealously participates, Holofernes misses the point of Berowne's letter by dissecting its stylistic and etymological components. Shakespeare seems to be making a subtle point with this plodding scholar of music and Ovid. On the one hand, the rhetoric of academic discourse yields a pleasure of its own, if only for the person generating it. On the other hand, the systemization of music and Ovidian poetry invariably tends to obscure what it actually feels like to experience them. What else can we make of a self-professed authority on Ovid who cannot recognize a love letter?

In *Twelfth Night,* Shakespeare again shows how rhetorical uses of music and Ovid can reveal more about the speaker's own interests than about the works themselves. Just as allegorical rhetoric in philosophical and pedagogical texts works to transform music and Ovidian poetry into a version of divine, cosmological truth, a similar rhetoric can make music appear to reflect an individual's deepest feelings and desires. Shakespeare dramatizes the impulse to use music and Ovid as signs of a sublime interiority in the play's opening speech, arguably the most frequently quoted description of music in Shakespeare's works:

> If music be the food of love, play on,
> Give me excess of it that, surfeiting,
> The appetite may sicken and so die.
> That strain again, it had a dying fall.
> O, it came o'er my ear like the sweet sound
> That breathes upon a bank of violets,
> Stealing and giving odour.
> (1.1.1–7)

This speech is actually the *second* thing that happens in the play, and its immediate effect is to interpret the sound that the audience is already hearing. Here, Orsino rehearses the well-established association between music and love, and he invokes familiar descriptors of musical sound ("die," "dying," "strain," "sweet," "breathes," "validity," "pitch," "fall") to suggest his own internal passions.[77] His characterization of music as a sound that "breathes upon a bank of violets" (a phrase that has troubled modern editors) deftly pictorializes the music, so that music's excessiveness elides metaphorically into the excess of his own passion. In this way, Orsino "moralizes" the music as a reflection of his character. Similarly, Orsino translates Ovid's Actaeon into a figure for himself:

> O, when mine eyes did see Olivia first
> Methought she purged the air of pestilence;
> That instant was I turned into a hart,
> And my desires, like fell and cruel hounds,
> E'er since pursue me.
> (18–22)

To be sure, Orsino is not the first person to make use of Ovid's Actaeon to thematize his own frustrated desire; Petrarch makes the episode central to his *Rime Sparse*. More than Petrarch, however, Orsino demonstrates the capriciousness

---

77. On the Renaissance association of music and love, see Linda Phyllis Austern, "Love, Death and Ideas of Music in the English Renaissance," in *Love and Death in the Renaissance,* ed. Kenneth R. Bartlett, 17–36 (Ottawa: Dovehouse, 1991).

of using music and Ovid as allegories for something else, whether for cosmology, Christian theology, or erotic desire.[78]

Throughout the rest of the play, Shakespeare plays off the idea that music communicates an underlying meaning. Often, he again demystifies these acts of meaning making by joining them with instances of actual musical performance. When Orsino stops the music he had called for because it is "not so sweet now as it was before" (1.1.8), he may mean that he is tired of its plaintive narrative of a "dying fall." Or he may mean that the music no longer accords with his melancholy state of mind. In either case, Shakespeare presents two different reactions to music that literally sounds the same to his audience. A similar effect is achieved in act 2, when Orsino asks Feste for a particular song, which he describes as "old and plaine":

> The spinsters, and the knitters in the sun,
> And the free maids that weave their thread with bones,
> Do use to chant it. It is silly sooth,
> And dallies with the innocence of love,
> Like the old age.
>
> (2.4.43–47)

However, what follows is not a song about romantic innocence, but one which begins "Come away, come away death," and which Hollander has perceptively described as an "almost parodic version of the theme of death from unrequited love."[79] As we will see in chapter 5, Shakespeare achieves a similar effect in *The Winter's Tale,* when Autolycus performs a funeral dirge that he advertises as "a merry ballad." Context, in this case, is meaning—or what purports to be meaning. The play prompts its audience to hear this music differently than it is described in words, an experience that may be more or less pronounced depending on the musical performance itself. The experience of music is more complicated with Viola, who self-consciously uses music as a means of persuasion: early on she announces that she will gain favor with Orsino by "speak[ing] to him in many sorts of music" (1.2.54). At first glance, this would appear to rehearse the familiar association of rhetoric and music, à la Sidney and Puttenham. However, Viola's music reveals itself in practice to be much more dependent on its effect as an acoustic, *noisy*

---

78. On the role of Ovid in the play, see also Mary Ellen Lamb, "Ovid's *Metamorphoses* and Shakespeare's *Twelfth Night,*" in *Shakespearean Comedy,* ed. Maurice Charney, 63–77 (New York: New York Literary Forum, 1980).

79. Hollander, *Untuning of the Sky,* 157.

event. Asked by Olivia how she would court a woman, Viola responds that she would

> make me a willow cabin at your gate
> And call upon my soul within the house,
> Write loyal cantons of contemnèd love,
> And sing them loud even in the dead of night;
> Halloo your name to the reverberate hills,
> And make the babbling gossip of the air
> Cry out 'Olivia!'
>
> (1.5.237–43)

Viola's description of the soul that is "called upon" by a lover at first seems to invoke a Platonic model of love, while her reference to "cantons" evokes a kind of music that is intensely meaningful. In the course of the passage, however, this model of legible music gives way to a purely sonorous experience. The physical properties of the "reverberate hills" cause Viola's music to increase and multiply almost to the point of incoherence, so that the only perceived word is Olivia's name. Music at this point is meaningful only as a narcissistic mirror—as an acoustic phenomenon that can be allegorized endlessly as a flattering reflection of one's self.[80] Is it any wonder that Olivia responds so favorably?

The arbitrariness of musical allegories, already suggested by Orsino and Olivia, may also be at issue in the cryptic exchange between Feste and Malvolio in act 4. Here, in a passage that has often troubled the play's critics, Feste, disguised as Sir Topas, interrogates Malvolio, who is imprisoned in a dark room, about his opinion of Pythagorean metempsychosis:

> FESTE. What is the opinion of Pythagoras concerning wildfowl?
> MALVOLIO. That the soul of our grandam might haply inhabit a bird.
> FESTE. What thinkest thou of his opinion?
> MALVOLIO. I think nobly of the soul, and no way approve his opinion.
> FESTE. Fare thee well. Remain thou still in darkness. Thou shalt hold th'opinion of Pythagoras ere I will allow of thy wits, and fear to kill a woodcock lest thou dispossess the soul of thy grandam.
> (4.2.44–53)

---

80. Jonathan Bate suggests that the passage may in fact be an allusion to Ovid's Narcissus. *Shakespeare and Ovid* (Oxford: Oxford University Press, 1993), 148.

The dialogue between Feste and Malvolio plays out much like the dialogues between master and student in Renaissance books on musical instruction (Malvolio's oft-remarked name also resembles the typical neophyte in these works). Feste's "teaching" of Pythagoras in this scene derives from the last book of Ovid's *Metamorphoses,* in which the doctrine of metempsychosis is described at length and which Golding uses as the basis for his allegorical reading of Ovid's poem. But it is also worth remembering in this scene that Pythagoras is the Renaissance's most important authority for the doctrine of *musica speculativa,* particularly since Feste continues to torment Malvolio by singing a song. The fact that Feste's lecture on Pythagoras occurs as an act of force against Malvolio, the play's professed hater of music, implies the violence of these allegorizing traditions. After all, the "darkness" that Feste attributes to Malvolio in this passage is physical as well as intellectual. Thus Shakespeare subtly suggests that the learning of these systems of allegorical meaning may be less an effect of enlightenment than it is a product of forced discipline.

Through the humiliation of Malvolio, Shakespeare suggests that the "violence of allegory" (to adapt Gordon Teskey's phrase) operates on individual subjects as well as texts. In *The Taming of the Shrew,* Shakespeare again dramatizes the ideological ends of education, though in a way that maps the politics of the classroom onto a politics of gender relations. As many readers have noted, *The Shrew* is unusually reflective about practices of education, and while discussions of the play have understandably focused on the education of Katherine and the implications of her acquiescence to Petruchio in the final scene, the play is full of scenes of instruction, references to teaching and academic language, and allusions to schoolroom Latin texts. The play is set in Padua, well-known to Shakespeare's audience as a center of higher learning, and it begins, after a lengthy induction, with Lucentio's announcement of an academic program: "Here let us breathe, and haply institute / A course of learning and ingenious studies" (1.1.8–9). Lucentio's noble plan is soon derailed by the appearance of Bianca, but not before Shakespeare allows some discussion about the proposed course of study. Tranio, Lucentio's servant, is particularly quick to offer suggestions about the syllabus:

> Only, good master, while we do admire
> This virtue and this moral discipline,
> Let's be no stoics nor no stocks, I pray,
> Or so devote to Aristotle's checks
> As Ovid be an outcast quite abjured.
> Balk logic with acquaintance that you have,

And practise rhetoric in your common talk.
Music and poesy use to quicken you;
The mathematics and the metaphysics,
Fall to them as you find your stomach serves you.
No profit grows where is no pleasure ta'en.
(1.1.29–39)

In other words, Tranio advises, don't bury yourself in your books. Here he follows the advice given by Roger Ascham in *The Scholemaster* (1570), who writes that "learning should be always mingled with honest mirth and comely exercises."[81] Moreover, Tranio conspicuously singles out Ovid and music as examples of the kind of "mirthful" exercises that should temper serious philosophical study. In *The Scholemaster,* by contrast, Ascham initially groups music—following the long tradition of musical teaching established by Boethius—with the "bookish" mathematical sciences, noting that "some wits, moderate enough by nature, be many times marred by over-much study and use of some sciences, namely, music, arithmetic, and geometry."[82] Thus, the fact that Shakespeare's Tranio sees Ovid and music as producing more "pleasure" than "moral discipline" would seem to corroborate the point made by Jonathan Bate that "by the 1590s then, Ovid had become for many writers, readers, and playgoers a source of poetic and even licentious delight rather than moral edification."[83]

However, despite frequent pronouncements about the waning of earlier teaching methods at the end of the sixteenth century, the allegorizing tradition of music and Ovid is never entirely absent from *The Shrew.* When Petruchio presents Hortensio to Baptista as a possible music tutor for his daughter, he advertises him as "cunning in music and the mathematics / To instruct her fully in those sciences" (2.1.56–57). Our knowledge of Hortensio's true motives aside, his pretense at least promises a rigorous lesson in *musica speculativa*. In a similar way, characters in the play often speak as though they had learned their allegorical Ovid *too* well, as when Lucentio draws on a moralized reading of Ovid's Jupiter and Europa to articulate his own feelings for Bianca:

---

81. Roger Ascham, *The Scholemaster* (London, 1570), in *The Whole Works of Roger Ascham,* ed. J. A. Giles (New York: AMS Press, 1965), 3:139.

82. Ibid., 3:100. Ascham clearly means speculative music here rather than performed music, although his treatise is not always careful about distinguishing between the two. For example, in the same paragraph, Ascham cites Galen's warning that "much music marreth men's manners," even though Galen is likely referring to performed music. Later in the treatise, Ascham cites (performed) music as a healthy diversion, like dancing and sports, from classroom instruction.

83. Bate, *Shakespeare and Ovid,* 32.

> O yes, I saw sweet beauty in her face,
> Such as the daughter of Agenor had,
> That made great Jove to humble him to her hand
> When with his knees he kissed the Cretan strand.
> (1.1.161–64)

In a finely nuanced essay on the play's Ovidianism, Vanda Zajko argues that the allusion to Europa here refers most immediately to Ovid's amatory poetry, particularly the *Amores,* in which the story of Europa is used as a tool for seduction.[84] On this point Zajko explicitly departs from Bate's reading of the passage, which identifies the *Metamorphoses* as the principal intertext and which interprets the image of Jupiter as a symbol of "male humility."[85] I don't think the point here is simply to determine whether the *Amores* or the *Metamorphoses* is the proper lens through which to interpret Lucentio's use of Ovid, but rather the striking conjunction of two very different approaches to reading poetry. What Lucentio's allusion to Jupiter and Europa seems to show is how a reading of Ovid's Jupiter as humility or abasement—a move practiced by and learned from the allegorizing commentaries on Ovid—could be used to manipulate the terms of an erotic relationship. In this respect, Lucentio's allusion to Ovid is a fitting example of the kind of self-serving allegory that Francis Bacon decries in *De sapienta veterum:* "I know very well what pliant stuff fable is made of, how freely it will follow any way you please to draw it... that many, wishing only to gain the sanction and reverence of antiquity for doctrines and inventions of their own, have tried to twist the fables of the poet into that sense."[86] The uses of allegory, as Bacon and Shakespeare understood, extend well beyond the strictures of a Christianizing educational program.

The Taming of the Shrew systematically blurs the distinction between allegorical and ludic uses of music and Ovid, in part to show how the teaching of music and poetry can function as an exertion of social forms of power. The self-interested motives of music teaching are suggested in the first few lines of the play, when the Lord, having decided to abduct the sleeping Sly, instructs his servants to "procure [him] music ready when he wakes/ To make a dulcet and a heavenly sound" (ind. i.46–47), and again when he showers Sly

---

84. Vanda Zajko, "Petruchio is 'Kated': *The Taming of the Shrew* and Ovid," in *Shakespeare and the Classics,* ed. Charles Martindale and A. B. Taylor (Cambridge: Cambridge University Press, 2004), 37–38.
85. Bate, *Shakespeare and Ovid,* 124.
86. *The Works of Francis Bacon,* ed. James Spedding, (London: Longman, 1890), 6:695.

with slavish attention: "Wilt though have music? Hark, Apollo plays,/And twenty cagèd nightingales do sing" (ind. ii.33–34). Although the descriptions of music here invoke the orthodox language of universal harmony, the intent is clearly to use music as an instrument to deceive Sly and intensify his disorientation. Likewise, the Lord's description of Ovidian "pictures" evacuates the *Metamorphoses* of any moral pretense whatsoever, presenting it instead as mere erotic distraction:

> SECOND SERVINGMAN. Dost thou love pictures? We will fetch thee straight
>   Adonis painted by a running brook,
>   And Cytherea all in sedges hid,
>   Which seem to move and wanton with her breath
>   Even as the waving sedges play wi'th' wind.
> LORD. We'll show thee Io as she was a maid,
>   And how she was beguilèd and surprised,
>   As lively painted as the deed was done.
> THIRD SERVINGMAN. Or Daphne roaming through a thorny wood,
>   Scratching her legs that one shall swear she bleeds,
>   And at that sight shall sad Apollo weep,
>   So workmanly the blood and tears are drawn.
>
>   (ind. ii.47–58)

On the one hand, the Lord's manipulation of Sly can be read as a conservative lesson on the dangers of music and poetry for uneducated persons. Sly's ignorance of the difference between heavenly music and performed music, and his inability to read the moral lesson of Ovid's Io, "beguiled and surprised," as applicable to his own situation, naturally lead him to respond to music and Ovid in purely sensuous terms, a fact of which the Lord takes full advantage. On the other hand, the example of Sly makes apparent the problems posed by sensuous experience for *any* educational program. For if Daphne is the "picture" or "myrror of virginitee," as the allegorical readings describe her, she is still a picture, and one can always decide to dwell—as Ovid's Apollo clearly does—on the image of her delicately scratched legs. And, as we see, it is not only the uneducated Sly who is misled by music's sonorous promiscuity: the Lord himself mistakes the trumpet sounds announcing the arrival of the players for the sign of "some noble gentleman" (ind. i.71). The power that sensuous experience has in shaping our habits of learning is deftly summed up by Sly's admission that he must be a lord after all: "I see, I hear, I speak./I smell sweet savours, and I feel soft things./Upon my life, I am a lord indeed" (ind. ii.68–70).

The Lord's trick on Sly is thus a failed scene of instruction, according to the allegorists, since Sly does not undergo any positive moral transformation and since he forgets rather than reaffirms his social position. (It is hard to imagine what a "good" scene of instruction for Sly on these terms would look like, though presumably it would begin by curbing his rampant alcoholism.) In its failure, however, the episode reminds us of the stakes involved in music theory's policing of acoustic sound. As a committed sensualist (and likely illiterate), Sly will never be an ideal candidate for the ennobling effects of musical understanding; in Boethius's words, he is a "slave" to performance. In the next chapter, we will see how Shakespeare's Caliban also reverses the civilizing effects of music by immersing himself in the pleasures of musical sound, though in a manner that is entirely self-willed. In *The Shrew*, the failure to learn music usually stems from sheer obstinacy or incompetence. At the same time, when Shakespeare represents the orthodox attempt to teach music seriously, as spiritually or morally profitable, it almost always appears as a veil for the selfish application of power. This cynical view of humanist education is registered by the Lord's description of his actions as "practise" (32), a word that for Shakespeare can mean both thoughtful, methodical study, as when Titus says that "by still practice" he will learn to read Lavinia's body language (*Titus* 3.2.45), and covert manipulation, as when Henry V accuses his traitorous friends of having "practised on me for thy use" (*Henry V* 2.2.96). The Lord's treatment of Sly encompasses both meanings, and Shakespeare's staging of this episode at the beginning of the play prepares his audience to view the subsequent scenes of instruction with a strong degree of skepticism.

Shakespeare creates his own version of the humanist classroom in act 3, in the exchange between Bianca and her would-be tutors. Here, both Ovid and music are subjected to a dizzying display of willful distortions, in a way that again portrays education as a thinly disguised cover for male desire. Lucentio, disguised as a Latin tutor, begins his lesson by parsing lines from Ovid's *Heroides*:

> '*Hic ibat*', as I told you before—'*Simois*', I am Lucentio—'*hic est*', son unto Vincentio of Pisa—'*Sigeia tellus*', disguised thus to get your love—'*hic steterat*', and that Lucentio that comes a-wooing—'*Priami*', is my man Tranio—'*regia*', bearing my port—'*celsa senis*', that we might beguile the old pantaloon. (3.1.31–36)

Lucentio's mock translation of the lines, a seemingly innocuous passage from Penelope's letter to Ulysses describing the landscape of Troy, shows that he has read and understood Ovid's other work, the *Ars Amatoria*, which extols the value of secret communication between lovers and which Lucentio is actually seen reading later in the play. In this way, Lucentio undermines the humanist program by contaminating the *Heroides,* a standard classroom text, with the *Ars Amatoria,* a text that Erasmus had explicitly warned against. At the same time, as Patricia Phillippy has carefully shown, Ovid's *Heroides* was already an overly wrought text in sixteenth-century Europe, having been frequently moralized by Renaissance commentators as a compendium of positive and negative examples of feminine behavior.[87] Thus, Lucentio's twisting of Penelope's lines is simply another attempt, however clumsy, to accommodate Ovid's text to the desire to control women's actions.

A similar liberalness characterizes Hortensio's teaching of the musical scale, which follows soon after Lucentio's lesson:

> *Gam-ut* I am, the ground of all accord,
>   A—re—to plead Hortensio's passion.
> B—mi—Bianca, take him for thy lord,
>   C—fa, ut—that loves with all affection.
> D—sol, re—one clef, two notes have I,
> E—la, mi—show pity, or I die.
>
>   (3.1.71–76)

Hortensio reveals his amorous intentions by way of musical solmization, a method of teaching the musical scale using a combination of letter names and syllables that became gradually standardized in early modern printed texts on musical instruction. For instance, as we saw earlier in this chapter, Morley's *Plaine and Easie Introduction* begins its course on music with this same scale, which Philomathes asserts must be learned "forwards and backwards" before anything else can be studied. Neither point is lost on Bianca, who simultaneously rebuffs Hortensio's advances and points out the rudimentary nature of his lesson: "Why, I am past my gamut long ago" (69). Still, for all its disingenuousness, Hortensio's lesson is remarkable for its adherence to conventional pedagogical practices. His naming of the notes is technically correct, and his description of the first and fifth notes of the scale follows Morley almost verbatim. Likewise, the sexual competition between Lucentio and Hortensio is articulated in language that mimics actual contemporary debates about music:

> HORTENSIO. But, wrangling pedant, this Bianca is,
>   The patroness of heavenly harmony.

---

87. Patricia B. Phillippy, "'Loytering in love': Ovid's *Heroides,* Hospitality, and Humanist Education in *The Taming of the Shrew,*" *Criticism* 40 (1998): 30–38.

> Then give me leave to have prerogative,
> And when in music we have spent an hour
> Your lecture shall have leisure for as much.
> LUCENTIO. Preposterous ass, that never read so far
> To know the cause why music was ordained!
> Was it not to refresh the mind of man
> After his studies or his usual pain?
>
> (3.1.4–12)

The debate over academic prerogative quickly devolves into a series of insults, some of which recall Gosson's subtle sexual punning on "instrument" in *The Schoole of Abuse*: "Take you your instrument, play you the whiles" (22), and again, "tune your instrument" (25).[88] And, if the point were not clear enough: "Spit in the hole, man, and tune again" (39). The sexual implications of these lines are perhaps too decorously noted by the Norton editor of the play, who politely remarks that "Lucentio speaks contemptuously and may not be giving serious advice."

For all its bawdy humor, Bianca's lesson in *The Shrew* is a parody, not a travesty. As we have seen throughout this chapter, music and Ovid were regularly subjected to allegorical interpretations hardly less ingenious by early modern commentators wishing to stabilize and control their meaning. By using music theory and Ovidian poetry as thinly disguised veils for seduction, Shakespeare merely reverses the prevailing trend: he gives us a *de*moralized music and a *de*moralized Ovid, effectively exposing these two classroom subjects as instruments of masculine authority. Unlike the moralizing texts, however, *The Shrew* includes a figure whose awareness frustrates the aims of her instructors. Bianca's response to Horatio both deflates his romantic prospects and points out the strained ingeniousness of his presentation of musical theory: "Call you this gamut? Tut, I like it not. / Old fashions please me best. I am not so nice / To change true rules for odd inventions" (77–79). And although she gives Lucentio more encouragement, her response to him makes clear her unwillingness to play along with his game as a passive participant: "Now let me see if I can construe it. '*Hic ibat Simois*', I know you not—'*hic est Sigeia tellus*', I trust you not—'*hic steterat Priami*', take heed he hear us not—'*regia*', presume not—'*celsa senis*', despair not" (40–43). Bianca shows that she understands both the meaning and method of Lucentio's instruction, and this knowledge allows her to reconstrue Ovid's lines to express her own

---

88. I am indebted to Amanda Winkler for pointing out this aspect of Gosson's text.

intentions.[89] In this way, she successfully adopts the moralizing methods of her instructors in order to assert the importance of her own thoughts and feelings in the competition for her hand in marriage.

In drawing attention to her own experience, Bianca stands in sharp distinction to the tamed Katherine we see later in the play. Despite the fact that her father negotiates her marriage in her absence (though not in the way that he intends), Bianca establishes the satisfaction of her personal desires as the hurdle Lucentio must clear before marrying her. For example, her response to Lucentio's remark that he has been reading Ovid's *Ars Amatoria*—"may you prove, sir, master of your art" (4.2.9)—has often been read as a subtle challenge to Lucentio's ability to achieve simultaneous orgasm, which Ovid's text treats at length.[90] In this way, Bianca repeatedly refers to the physical experience of her own body, a habit that Katherine, by contrast, learns to shed by the end of the play. Katherine's admission in her final speech that women's bodies are "soft, and weak, and smooth" (5.2.169) does not refer to her own body, which at the very least is capable of smashing a lute atop a man's head. Rather, like the rest of her speech, it parrots the conventional, conservative rhetoric typically found in early modern texts on marriage. In other words, Katherine learns to substitute a practice of verbal repetition for the authority of her physical, subjective perceptions. Alexander Leggatt's comments on the difference between Bianca's and Katherine's education in the play are particularly instructive here:

> The taming plot presents in a deeper, more psychological way ideas that are handled superficially and externally in the romantic plot. Education is one such idea: Bianca is surrounded by instructors, none of whose credentials would bear examination; they have really come to win her, not to teach her.... But Petruchio, in his "taming-school"... really does teach Kate, and teaches her that inner order of which the music and the mathematics offered to Bianca are only a reflection.[91]

---

89. Heather James notes that, by showing a better understanding of Latin syntax and by carefully warning Lucentio about the dangers posed by Hortensio, Bianca actually surpasses her instructor's translation abilities. See "Shakespeare's Learned Heroines in Ovid's Schoolroom," in Martindale and Taylor, *Shakespeare and the Classics,* 70.

90. Ibid.

91. Alexander Leggatt, *Shakespeare's Comedy of Love* (London: Methuen, 1974), 49. In a similar reading of the play, Dennis S. Brooks argues that the difference between Bianca and Katherine at the end of the play shows the inferiority of conventional scholastic models of education (particularly the quadrivium and trivium) to "eikastic," or dramatic, forms of teaching. See his "'To show scorn her own image': The Varieties of Education in *The Taming of the Shrew,*" *Rocky Mountain Review of Language and Literature* 48 (1994): 7–32. While Brooks's observations about the different forms of

I wholly agree with Leggatt's claim that Petruchio teaches Katherine a kind of musical order, but I believe that this is only half the story. The music that Katherine learns is a kind of *speculative* music, apprehended through mathematical and cosmological precepts and not through reference to one's own experience of musical sound. It may be no coincidence that the first test of Katherine's obedience hinges on a cosmological fact—the difference between the sun and the moon—and that Katherine passes the test by subverting her physical perceptions to a masculine act of naming: "What you will have it named, even that it is,/And so it shall be still for Katherine" (4.6.22–23). Petruchio's "taming-school" models itself on the most reductive form of the humanist classroom, in which the relationship between instructor and student is shaped by a numbing process of repetition and enforced by the threat of physical punishment. Shakespeare allows his audience to witness the social and conjugal order that this type of learning makes possible, though not without giving us a sense of what is lost in the process.

Shakespeare revisits the humanist classroom in *As You Like It,* albeit in a more indirect fashion. The play begins with Orlando lamenting the fact that he has not been given a formal education:

> My brother Jaques he keeps at school, and report speaks goldenly of his profit. For my part, he keeps me rustically at home—or, to speak more properly, stays me here at home unkept; for call you that keeping for a gentleman of my birth, that differs not from the stalling of an ox? His horses are bred better, for besides that they are fair with their feeding, they are taught their manège. (1.1.4–10)

Orlando's conflation of feeding and teaching echoes Virgil's complaint about empty learning in the *Eclogues:* "Here is fat feeding and lean beasts." In this way he anticipates the play's exploration of pastoral and its concern with the effectiveness of different kinds of education. Like Orlando, Shakespeare's audience in this play never sees the inside of a traditional classroom. Instead, we are treated to a vision of the forest of Arden as nature's schoolroom: Duke Senior, echoing a theological commonplace, professes that he "finds tongues in trees, books in the running brooks,/Sermons in stones, and good in everything" (2.1.16–17).[92]

---

education represented in the play are carefully laid out, his conclusions depend on the assumption that Katherine's transformation into an obedient wife is desirable.

92. On the theological background of the idea of nature as teacher and its relation to the play, see Paul J. Willis, "'Tongues in trees': The Book of Nature in *As You Like It,*" *Modern Language Studies* 18 (Summer 1988): 65–74.

At the same moment that Shakespeare introduces Arden as a stand-in for the Renaissance classroom, the character Jaques is presented as its chief moralizer. Describing Jaques' reaction to a dying deer, the duke's men make apparent his propensity to turn every event in the forest into a worldly lesson:

> First, for his weeping into the needless stream;
> 'Poor dear,' quoth he, 'thou mak'st a testament
> As worldlings do, giving thy sum of more
> To that which had too much.' Then being there alone,
> Left and abandoned of his velvet friend,
> [']'Tis right,' quoth he, 'thus misery doth part
> The flux of company.' Anon a careless herd
> Full of the pasture jumps along by him
> And never stays to greet him. 'Ay,' quoth Jaques,
> 'Sweep on, you fat and greasy citizens,
> 'Tis just the fashion. Wherefore should you look
> Upon that poor and broken bankrupt there?'
> Thus most invectively he pierceth through
> The body of the country, city, court,
> Yea, and of this our life, swearing that we
> Are mere usurpers, tyrants, and what's worse,
> To fright the animals and to kill them up
> In their assigned and native dwelling place.
> (2.1.46–63)

This passage, one of the most frequently discussed in the play, has alternately been used as evidence of Jaques' pessimism, solipsism, sentimentality, compassion, wisdom, comicality, idealism, madness, or Pythagoreanism.[93] However, almost no critic I have read suggests a possible allusion to Ovid's Actaeon, despite the acknowledgment that Ovid pervades much of the rest of the play and despite Shakespeare's frequent use elsewhere of the dying deer as a reference to Actaeon.[94] Although the image of the deer is common in

---

93. See ibid., 68–69; Judy Z. Kronenfeld, "Shakespeare's Jaques and the Pastoral Cult of Solitude," *Texas Studies in Literature and Language* 18 (1976): 451–73; Winfried Schleiner, "Jaques and the Melancholy Stag," *English Language Notes* 17 (1980): 175–79.

94. The exception is Robert N. Watson, who also finds the passage suggestive of Actaeon, though he reads Actaeon—by way of Leonard Barkan's reading of Ovid and Giordano Bruno—as a figure for Jaques himself, not the deer. "As You Liken It: Simile in the Wilderness," *Shakespeare Survey* 56 (2003): 81–84. On the Ovidian elements in *As You Like It* and Shakespeare's frequent use of the deer metaphor, see Bate, *Shakespeare and Ovid*, 157–62, and James, *Shakespeare's Troy: Drama, Politics, and the Translation of Empire* (Cambridge: Cambridge University Press, 1997), respectively.

CHAPTER 3

Renaissance iconography, the lord's description shares with Ovid's account of Actaeon an emphasis on the deer's *tears,* particularly as they broach the limits of human communication:

> The wretched animal heaved forth such groans
> That their discharge did stretch his leathern coat
> Almost to bursting, and the big round tears
> Coursed one another down his innocent nose
> In piteous chase.
>
> (36–40)[95]

In addition, Shakespeare casts Jaques' reaction to the deer in terms that repeatedly call to mind the moralized reading of a classical text: the oak under which Jaques lies has as an "antic root" (31); the duke asks his men whether Jaques did "moralize this spectacle" (44); and the lords poke fun at Jaques' habit of contriving "a thousand similes" (45) while "commenting/Upon the sobbing deer" (65–66). Thus, if the sobbing deer points discreetly to Ovid's Actaeon (as I think it does), then Jaques' habit of "commenting" prolifically on it places him in a long line of Renaissance allegorizers of Ovid.

Jaques' moralizing response to the sobbing deer also hints at a particular attitude toward music. As I argued in chapter 1, Shakespeare's fascination with the transformed Actaeon stems in part from his interest in the problem of musical meaning. In *Titus Andronicus,* the speechless Lavinia—compared to Actaeon more than once in that play—demonstrates the ways in which words are forcefully imposed on nonverbal phenomena, like music. In a similar way, Jaques' eagerness to speak for the sobbing deer suggests that he is likely to interpret music as profoundly meaningful. And sure enough, when we first see him a few scenes later, he is listening to a musical performance with fervid intensity:

> JAQUES. More, more, I prithee, more.
> AMIENS. It will make you melancholy, Monsieur Jaques.
> JAQUES. I thank it. More, I prithee, more. I can suck melancholy out of
>   a song as a weasel sucks eggs. More, I prithee more. (2.5.9–12)

---

95. Cf. Golding, *Ovid's Metamorphoses,* 3.236–40: "When he saw his face/And horned temples in the brooke, he would have cryde alas,/But as for then no kinde of speach out of his lippes could passe./He sight and brayde: for that was then the speach that did remaine,/And downe the eyes that were not his, his bitter teares did raine."

Jaques' ability to "suck melancholy" from a pastoral, idyllic song shows his propensity to bend music's meaning to his will, in spite of the likelihood (suggested repeatedly in the scene) that he has little musical experience of his own.[96] A few lines later, the duke comments on the strangeness of Jaques' newfound interest in music: "If he, compact of jars, grow musical/We shall have shortly discord in the spheres" (2.7.5–6). Here, the duke's brief reference to Pythagorean *musica speculativa* suggests, in addition to Jaques' musical inexperience, the fact that the lessons of the humanist classroom have not been completely forgotten in Arden. Though he is constantly ridiculed by his companions, Jaques, Arden's resident allegorist, is only the most extreme case of an intemperate scholasticism that seeks to interpret all worldly phenomena according to a preconceived notion of human behavior and theological truths.

Through Jaques, Shakespeare demonstrates once again the shared interests of Ovidian allegory and speculative approaches to music. Though he seems to have had little musical experience, and even less previous regard for music, Jaques' handiness with maxims and his deftness with poetic verse allow him to presume to write music of his own. His contribution to Amiens's "Who Doth Ambition Shun" both heightens the song's moral sense and frames it as a commentary on the residents of Arden, while his verses come prepackaged with their own philological gloss: "'Tis a Greek invocation to call fools into a circle. I'll go sleep if I can. If I cannot, I'll rail against all the firstborn of Egypt" (2.5.53–55). Like Gresham's John Taverner, Jaques relies on his knowledge of classroom texts to compensate for his lack of musicianship. Likewise, his use of Ovidian material shows a familiarity with Renaissance mythographies and quotation books rather than a deep understanding of Ovid's poem: his pithy description of Touchstone as "knowledge ill-inhabited; worse than Jove in a thatched house" (3.3.7–8) alludes to Baucis and Philemon—likely inspired by Touchstone's description of himself as another "honest Ovid...among the Goths" (6)—but it ignores or forgets the original context of the episode in the *Metamorphoses,* in which the "thatched house" proves to be the most hospitable and reverent to Jove. In these cases, Jaques' approach to music and Ovid is to transform them into emblems. Like the Renaissance allegorists, Jaques rhetorically frames his subjects as *visual* phenomena that can easily be read as illustrations of a

---

96. A source for the particular song that Amiens sings in this scene ("Under the Greenwood Tree") has not been found, though "greenwood songs" were extremely common in sixteenth-century England. See Peter J. Seng, *The Vocal Songs in the Plays of Shakespeare* (Cambridge, MA: Harvard University Press, 1967), 70–76.

138　　CHAPTER 3

stable, articulate point.⁹⁷ This allegorical impulse helps explain the otherwise puzzling musical episode in 4.2, in which Jaques directs a procession of hunters:

> JAQUES. Which is he that killed the deer?
> FIRST LORD. Sir, it was I.
> JAQUES. [*to the others*] Let's present him to the Duke like a Roman conqueror. And it would do well to set the deer's horns upon his head for a branch of victory. Have you no song, forester, for this purpose?
> SECOND LORD. Yes, sir.
> JAQUES. Sing it. 'Tis no matter how it be in tune, so it make noise enough.
> LORDS. [*sing*] What shall he have that killed the deer?
> 　　　　His leather skin and horns to wear.
> 　　　　Then sing him home; the rest shall bear
> 　　　　This burden.
> 　　　　Take thou no scorn to wear the horn;
> 　　　　It was a crest ere thou wast born.
> 　　　　Thy father's father wore it,
> 　　　　And thy father bore it.
> 　　　　The horn, the horn, the lusty horn
> 　　　　Is not a thing to laugh to scorn.　　*Exeunt* (4.2.1–19)

Ross Duffin has persuasively suggested that the third line of the song is actually an interjection by Jaques.⁹⁸ In this way it matches his other efforts to create the procession's emblematic quality ("like a Roman conqueror," "a branch of victory"). Moreover, it underscores the fact that Jaques is not concerned with the particular acoustic effects of this music: for him, all music in a project like this is simply "noise enough." Whatever point he is trying to make with the procession, Jaques shows that he has learned well the strategies

---

　　97. The emblematic nature of the play as a whole has often been noted by critics. For example, Raymond B. Waddington argues that Jaques is only the most practiced of the play's many emblem makers and that Shakespeare designs the play itself as a series of meaningful emblems. "Moralizing the Spectacle: Dramatic Emblems in *As You Like It*," *Shakespeare Quarterly* 33 (1982): 155–63. See also E. Michael Thron, "Jaques: Emblems and Morals," *Shakespeare Quarterly* 30 (1979): 84–89. On the tradition of reading the play as an allegory, see also Maurice A. Hunt, *Shakespeare's "As You Like It": Late Elizabethan Culture and Literary Representation* (New York: Palgrave Macmillan, 2008), 11. For an insightful discussion of the idea that the play questions visuality (and, by extension, emblems and allegories themselves) as a reliable medium for truth, see Martha Ronk, "Locating the Visual in *As You Like It*," *Shakespeare Quarterly* 52 (2001): 255–76.
　　98. Ross W. Duffin, *Shakespeare's Songbook* (New York: W. W. Norton, 2004), 434.

of Renaissance allegory. If music is to teach something, it must work like a picture rather than sound.

Jaques' moralizing tendencies are especially provoked by Rosalind, in a way that clarifies the difference in their attitudes toward experience and learning. In their only exchange in the play, Jaques and Rosalind debate the value of experience—insofar as it is characterized by Jaques:

> JAQUES. I have neither the scholar's melancholy, which is emulation, nor the musician's, which is fantastical, nor the courtier's, which is proud, nor the soldier's, which is ambitious, nor the lawyer's, which is politic, nor the lady's, which is nice, nor the lover's, which is all these; but it is a melancholy of mine own, compounded of many simples, extracted from many objects, and indeed the sundry contemplation of my travels, in which my often rumination wraps me in a most humorous sadness.
>
> ROSALIND. A traveller! By my faith, you have great reason to be sad. I fear you have sold your own lands to see other men's. Then to have seen much and to have nothing is to have rich eyes and poor hands.
>
> JAQUES. Yes, I have gained my experience....
>
> ROSALIND. And your experience makes you sad. I had rather have a fool to make me merry than experience to make me sad—and to travel for it too! (4.1.10–26)

For all his claims to cosmopolitanism, Jaques' experience is remarkably bookish. His method of constructing his melancholy—"compounded of many simples, extracted from many objects"—follows closely the practice of writers like Robert Burton and Thomas Wright, whose massive treatises on melancholy are virtual compendiums of all previous writings on the subject. His melancholy is *not* quite his own, as he asserts. In a surprising book on Renaissance romance, Jeff Dolven shows how humanist writers endlessly wrestled with the question of travel (experience) as an alternative to classroom learning, since travel, though it was fraught with risks, offered an opportunity to go beyond the dry abstractions of textbook education.[99] Rosalind's sardonic comment—"and to travel for it too!"—implies that Jaques has incurred the expense of travel without going beyond the confines of bookish study, effectively reaping the disadvantages of both. In this respect, she echoes her earlier criticism of Orlando, whom she accuses of merely rehearsing poetic

---

99. Jeff Dolven, *Scenes of Instruction in Renaissance Romance* (Chicago: University of Chicago Press, 2007), 65–97.

conventions of love. More importantly, by contrasting Jaques' reaction to experience with her own—"I had rather have a fool to make me merry than experience to make me sad"—Rosalind separates Jaques from those members of Shakespeare's audience likely to respond to the play and its "fools" with delight rather than excessive moralization. In a single swipe, she divides the world into Casaubonian pedants and lusty theatergoers, squarely placing Jaques among the former.

The divide between Jaques and Shakespeare's audience, incisively summed up by Rosalind, is nowhere more apparent than in the play's dazzling use of songs, many of which are performed at the behest of Jaques himself. As David Lindley has shrewdly noted, the play "calls for more music than Shakespeare had ever previously demanded, yet, compared with almost all the songs [in other Shakespeare plays], those in this play have a curiously inessential quality."[100] In other words, the songs in *As You Like It* seem the least ripe for moralization, making Jaques' attempts to appropriate them for his own philosophizing seem especially strained. This resistance to interpretation is felt most strongly during songs like "It Was a Lover and His Lass," which appear in the play for little apparent reason other than to provide entertainment. Whether or not the songs in *As You Like It* were originally included to showcase the singing talents of Robert Armin, as has been suggested, Shakespeare takes the opportunity of the play's music to intensify the disjunction between a philosophical approach to music and the immediate experience of song. If, as Mark Booth suggests, the theatrical effect of performed songs is to create "some degree of identification between singer and audience"—in effect, to create a community of performers and listeners—then Jaques' response to them places him outside that community, even more so than his decision at the end of the play to leave the court altogether.[101]

Yet the play never closes the book on Jaques' moralizing practices. For one thing, Jaques' final judgments of his companions, though pithy, are remarkably accurate and insightful. More strikingly, the unexpected appearance of Hymen at the end of the play seems to move toward a highly symbolic view of music, not away from it. Many of the play's readers have commented on the strangeness of the final scene, which differs in tone and style from everything that has come before, particularly in its representation of music. In

---

100. David Lindley, *Shakespeare and Music* (London: Thomson, 2006), 190. Even John H. Long, who generally argues for the dramatic appropriateness of music in Shakespeare's plays, notes that "there is little apparent connection between the theme of the songs and the theme or moral of the novel.... The plot would suffer little damage if the songs were removed." *Shakespeare's Use of Music* (Gainesville: University of Florida Press, 1961), 1:139–40.

101. Mark Booth, *The Experience of Songs* (New Haven, CT: Yale University Press, 1981), 15.

contrast to the playful musical performances of the rest of the play, Hymen's songs are unusually didactic, and their lyrics introduce a speculative, Neoplatonic language not voiced by any other character, including Jaques: "Then is there mirth in heaven/When earthly things made even/Atone together" (5.4.97–99). The fact that Rosalind, who had earlier chastised Orlando for aping literary conventions, orchestrates this wedding masque (for that's essentially what it is) only makes the event more peculiar. It may be, as Jean Howard has suggested, that the appearance of Hymen at the end of *As You Like It* serves to emphasize the artificiality of marriage as a comic resolution.[102] Or, as Paul Willis has proposed, the emblematic quality of the scene is meant to remind us that, as fallen creatures, we can apprehend divine knowledge only indirectly—that all knowledge is heavily mediated.[103] (Indeed, as I will argue in chapter 6, Milton uses the occasion of a masque to make a similar point.) Whatever the reason, Shakespeare seems to have found the allegorical resources of the masque useful in this case, despite his awareness of allegory's tendency to close off the more unruly aspects of human experience. Lessons learned in the classroom, it appears, are not so easily forgotten.

---

102. The *Norton Shakespeare,* ed. Stephen Greenblatt (New York: W. W. Norton, 1997), 1593.
103. Willis, "'Tongues in trees,'" 71–72.

Chapter 4

Impolitic Noise
Resisting Orpheus from Julius Caesar *to* The Tempest

> Make people believe. The entire history of tonal music, like that of classical political economy, amounts to an attempt to make people believe in a consensual representation of the world. In order to replace the lost ritualization of the channelization of violence with the spectacle of the absence of violence. In order to stamp upon the spectators the faith that there is a harmony in order.
>
> —Jacques Attali, *Noise: The Political Economy of Music*

The political version of the theory of musical harmony is so ubiquitous in Renaissance England that it may be taken as a commonplace. In his archly conservative *The Boke named The Governour* (1531), for example, Sir Thomas Elyot firmly ties his program of political philosophy to the study of *musica speculativa*. Addressing the education of young boys destined to rule, Elyot instructs tutors to

> commende the perfecte understandinge of musike, declaringe howe necessary it is for the better attaynynge the knowlege of a publike weale: whiche, as I before haue saide, is made of an ordre of astates and degrees, and, by reason therof, conteineth in it a perfect harmony: whiche he shall afterwarde more perfectly onderstande, when he shall happen to rede the bokes of Plato, and Aristotle, of publike weales: wherin be written diuers examples of musike and geometrye. In this fourme may a wise and circumspecte tutor adapte the pleasant science of musike to a necessary and laudable purpose.[1]

---

1. Sir Thomas Elyot, *The Boke named The Governour* (1531), ed. Ernest Rhys (London: J. M. Dent, 1937), 28.

IMPOLITIC NOISE

About the mode of instruction, Elyot is absolutely clear: music is principally to be read, not heard. In this respect, his pedagogical approach to music is utterly orthodox. After warning his reader at length of the dangers of practical musical learning, Elyot directs his idealized tutor to the most abstract of philosophical texts. It is only *"in this fourme,"* Elyot concludes, that the true precepts of harmony will be understood. Moreover, once understood as abstract symbol, music reveals the natural order of government.

In this chapter I consider Shakespeare's exploration of musical harmony as a means of political representation. Elyot's treatise illustrates how smoothly the allegorizing rhetoric of *musica speculativa* moves from the classroom to the public sphere, where it presumes to explain the "ordre of astates and degrees."[2] As we saw in the last chapter, this rhetoric functions by obscuring the distinction between words about music and musical sound, so that music is made to seem naturally representative of an authorized narrative—of mathematics, cosmology, government, or anything else. In Neoplatonic writings, in particular, the postulation of secret or hidden meanings in music works to mystify—and therefore facilitate—the connection between the physical ("natural") world and universalizing ideologies of order. It is perhaps for this reason that, in Renaissance England, Neoplatonic formulations of music sometimes seem to be more prevalent in political contexts than in academic ones. Likewise, in Shakespeare's plays, Neoplatonic ideas of harmony are frequently invoked during moments when political actors attempt to legitimize or mythologize their power, even more so than in the scenes of instruction discussed in the last chapter. In this way, Shakespeare suggests that the ideological work performed by the rhetoric of *musica speculativa*, while useful in the classroom, is indispensable in the political arena.

In characteristic fashion, however, Shakespeare demonstrates the power of heard music to disrupt Neoplatonic models of harmony. Musical sound in the plays frequently grates against its rhetorical representation, exposing the political representation of harmony as a highly intricate shell game. Jacques Attali, the prolific French economist and former adviser to President Mitterand, famously claimed that "listening to music is listening to all noise, realizing that its appropriation and control is a reflection of power, that it

---

2. The idea of musical harmony as political order in the Renaissance is richly traced in Robin Headlam Wells, *Elizabethan Mythologies: Studies in Poetry, Drama, and Music* (Cambridge: Cambridge University Press, 1994), esp. 1–8. In addition to the chapter by Elyot discussed above, Headlam Wells adduces similar passages from La Primaudaye, Sir Thomas Browne, Richard Hooker, and Stephen Gosson.

is essentially political."[3] In plays from *Julius Caesar* to *The Tempest,* Shakespeare restores to music the "noisiness" that Attali sees as instrumental to its demystification. In this way, Shakespeare allows his audience to witness the political appropriation of music and compare it to their own listening experience, even, as we will see, at the risk of exposing his own plays as artificial constructions. Rather than make use of music's interpretive promiscuity to create a sense of dramatic unity, Shakespeare's plays often highlight the incongruence between language and musical sound—an incongruence that is always a possibility when someone attempts to describe an actual musical performance. As the teaching of music in early modern England makes clear, universalizing ideas about music are most persuasive when they are seen and read. They are constantly in danger of being unraveled by acoustic experience, and Shakespeare's political plays frequently exploit this vulnerability. In each case, the point is clear: we may all agree on the meaning of music, *until we are forced to hear it.*

Politicizing Harmony

Perhaps the most explicit example in Shakespeare's plays of *musica speculativa* being put into the service of political ideology occurs in *Troilus and Cressida,* when Ulysses famously scolds Agammemnon and the other Greek soldiers for their failure to observe political authority:

> The heavens themselves, the planets, and this centre
> Observe degree, priority, and place,
> Infixture, course, proportion, season, form,
> Office and custom, in all line of order.
> And therefore is the glorious planet Sol
> In noble eminence enthroned and sphered
> Amidst the other, whose med'cinable eye
> Corrects the ill aspects of planets evil
> And posts like the commandment of a king,
> Sans check, to good and bad. But when the planets
> In evil mixture to disorder wander,
> What plagues and what portents, what mutiny?
> ....

---

3. Jacques Attali, *Noise: The Political Economy of Music,* trans. Brian Massumi (1985; repr., Minneapolis: University of Minnesota Press, 1999), 6.

> Take but degree away, untune that string,
> And hark what discord follows.
> (1.3.85–110)

In this rhetorical tour de force, Ulysses sets up perfectly the traditional argument for musical harmony by articulating a model of cosmology founded on universal principles of proportion and form. The idea of the "untuned string" is a fitting analogy for dysfunctional government, but it is also presented as a real, physical manifestation of the universal principles of order that Ulysses cites as his ultimate authority. This double sense of the musical example replays the slippage between metaphor and sound that we find so often in writings about speculative music. Ulysses' appropriation of this rhetoric is also fitting insofar as his speech reflects a larger cultural project, in which Rome—and by extension, its imagined origins in Troy—is constantly mythologized as the antecedent of a nascent British empire. As Heather James has noted, literary representations of Troy in this period, such as Chapman's translation of the *Iliad,* "revitalized and politicized the epic ethos, however neoplatonized, in the Elizabethan consciousness of Troy."[4] While Shakespeare's *Troilus and Cressida* repeatedly discredits this project, as James persuasively argues, it does not do so in the scene with Ulysses. For one thing, Ovid is conspicuously absent here; in a play suffused with literary contamination, the ambivalent version of Ulysses in book 13 of the *Metamorphoses* notably does not encroach. (There is a reason why the passage is so easily excerpted.) Rather, the scene adheres faithfully, more or less, to a Neoplatonic ethos, and the traditional image of musical harmony, much like the image of the harp in Peacham's *Minerva Brittana,* functions neatly as a sign and guarantor of the naturalness of political authority.

Like the early modern pedagogical works on music, Ulysses' speech in *Troilus and Cressida* demonstrates how a "politics of interpretation" precedes and enables the politicization of music. If the "untuned string" that Ulysses invokes is a convenient emblem for his political ideology, part of the reason is that the experience of musical sound has become subordinate to its inscription in rhetoric. There is, after all, no music heard in this scene. Ulysses' injunction to his audience to "hark" does not actually implore them to listen with their ears. Rather, it forms part of a familiar rhetorical formula in which the imagined sound is already interpreted and understood before it is played, if at all: "And hark what discord follows." At the same time, the political appropriation

---

4. Heather James, *Shakespeare's Troy: Drama, Politics, and the Translation of Empire* (Cambridge: Cambridge University Press, 1997), 89.

146 CHAPTER 4

of music is extremely simplifying, even more so than the allegorical representations of music in works on *musica speculativa*. In its political guise, "music" is reduced to "harmony" or "proportion," the mathematical ratios that describe only the most consonant intervals on the musical scale. All other aspects of music—melody, chromaticism, dissonance—are relegated to the "evil mixture [that] to disorder wander[s]." Defined in this way, music is a powerfully conservative force, and in this context an encomium of music can sound much like its opposite. Ulysses' speech on harmony, for example, follows nearly point for point Gosson's critique of theatricality in *Playes Confuted:* "In a commonweale, if privat men be suffered to forsake theire calling because they desire to walke gentleman like in sattine & velvet, with a buckler at theire heeles, proportion is so broken, beutie dissolved, harmony confounded, & the whole body must be dismembred and the prince or the heade can not chuse but sicken."[5] Gosson's image of a "dismembred" commonwealth recalls his image of Musicke's "dismembered" body in his earlier tract, *The Schoole of Abuse*. In *Playes Confuted,* however, the abuses performed on music are now made to represent, not merely be a symptom of, the widespread decay of social order. Bad musicians are not just unruly subjects; they are bad *leaders*.

A similar lesson on political order initially appears to be enacted in Shakespeare's *Julius Caesar,* when the ghost of Caesar appears to Brutus. At the precise moment that the ghost vanishes, the musician Lucius, who had put himself to sleep with his own music, suddenly mutters, "The strings, my lord, are false" (4.2.341). John Hollander notes that this image of the "false" (untuned) strings acts as an appropriate commentary on the political disintegration of Brutus's faction. His reading of the line, which has been influential for a generation of critics, is instructive:

> The "disordered string" is ... an emblem of the unruled, unruly state.... Brutus, missing the import of this, comments, "He thinks he still is at his instrument," and shakes Lucius fully awake, inquiring after the phantom. But the meaning, I think, is clear, and the false strings suggest the discordant conspirators, now jangling and out of tune even among themselves. Brutus, who "in general honest thought/And common good to all, made one" of the varying faction he led, meets with the prophetic truth of the boy's half-dreamed image with a benevolently naturalistic interpretation of it.[6]

---

5. Stephen Gosson, *Playes Confuted in Five Actions* (1582), ed. Arthur Freeman (New York: Garland, 1972), 4G4r–4G4v.

6. John Hollander, *The Untuning of the Sky: Ideas of Music in English Poetry 1500–1700* (1961; repr., Princeton, NJ: Princeton University Press, 1993), 148–50.

The yoking together of musical and political dissonance here is consistent with *musica speculativa*. Hollander's description of the untuned strings as an "emblem" points directly to the visual, allegorical mode of the speculative treatises, and it is this framework that Hollander privileges in interpreting Shakespeare's play. At the same time, Brutus himself is criticized for failing to recognize the moral significance of the musical sentence. This framing of musical perception as an ethical problem—the idea that there are "good" and "bad" listeners of music, and that these differences reflect moral stature—is a phenomenon that the plays will address repeatedly. For now, it will be useful to note Hollander's suggestion (with the speculative treatises fully backing him) that Brutus's immediate, "naturalistic" response to music, and his concomitant failure to hear music *theoretically*, are indicative of his propensity for political error.

Yet for all its legibility, the allegorical reading of music in *Julius Caesar* may be more precarious than Hollander suggests. For one thing, Lucius gives a musical performance a few lines *before* the appearance of Caesar's ghost and before his pronouncement of "false strings." Hence, Shakespeare makes the interpretation of musical dissonance as political disharmony into a deliberately retrospective event; the actual performance of musical sound first occurs independently of a speculative or political context. Shakespeare further emphasizes the distance between the actual performance of music and the political reading of "false strings" by making Lucius unconscious of his own utterance:

> LUCIUS. The strings, my lord, are false.
> BRUTUS. He thinks he still is at his instrument.—
>   Lucius, awake!
> LUCIUS. My lord.
> BRUTUS. Didst thou dream, Lucius, that thou so cried'st out?
> LUCIUS. My lord, I do not know that I did cry.
> BRUTUS. Yes, that thou didst. Didst thou see anything?
> LUCIUS. Nothing, my lord.
> BRUTUS. Sleep again, Lucius. (4.2.341–49)

The fact that Lucius is oblivious to his music's significance may encourage us, as audience, to view him as an allegorical emblem, but only at the expense of removing ourselves at a readerly distance from the physical action of the play. In this case, the false strings are the *dramatist's* gesture to his audience about the meaning of the play. Brutus, who inhabits the drama, cannot be expected to share this perspective. Characters in an allegory, after all, do not usually see themselves as allegorical. Brutus's attempt to turn Lucius's utterance into a meaningful vision or prophecy fails ("Didst thou *see* anything?"), and only then is he forced to acknowledge the event as a mere coincidence. In this way, Brutus's experience of the music in this scene, markedly different from our own, obliquely points to the arbitrariness of political meanings that get attached to music by virtue of their temporal coincidence or symbolic resemblance. Drawing a political meaning from performed music, Shakespeare suggests, may be like wresting a prophetic vision from an overtired boy.

The rhetoric of speculative music, subtly deconstructed in *Julius Caesar*, also informs the attempt to order and make sense of worldly events in *Othello*. Ever since Lawrence Ross showed that the Clown's brief appearance in act 3 is not a "trivial scene" but an ironic nod to *musica mundana* ("music that may not be heard"), critics have noted the play's many references to speculative music.[7] Less apparent, however, has been the fact that Othello himself, more than any other character in the play, is deeply invested in the philosophical interpretation of music as universal order. For example, when Othello nostalgically recalls his military feats, he describes the actual music of battle as a reflection of heavenly events:

> Farewell the neighing steed and the shrill trump,
> The spirit-stirring drum, th'ear-piercing fife,
> The royal banner, and all quality,
> Pride, pomp, and circumstance of glorious war!
> And O, you mortal engines whose rude throats
> Th'immortal Jove's dread clamours counterfeit,
> Farewell! Othello's occupation's gone.
> (3.3.356–62)

More typically, Othello draws on speculative rhetoric to describe his changing relationship with Desdemona over the course of the play. When Othello meets Desdemona in Cyprus, he calls their eager kisses "the greatest discords... that e'er our hearts shall make" (2.1.195–96). Likewise, when he later condemns her supposed infidelity, Othello casts Desdemona as a degraded Orpheus, an "admirable musician... [who] will sing the savageness out of a bear" (4.1.180–81) and himself as a dehumanized creature whose "heart is turned to stone" (175), impervious to the civilizing effects

---

7. Lawrence J. Ross, "Shakespeare's 'Dull Clown' and Symbolic Music," *Shakespeare Quarterly* 17 (1966): 107–28. See also Rosalind King, "'Then murder's out of tune': The Music and Structure of *Othello*," *Shakespeare Survey* 39 (1987): 149–58.

of harmony. And again, when he learns that Roderigo has been killed by Cassio, he asserts that "murder's out of tune,/And sweet revenge grows harsh" (5.2.124–25).

It is important to note that Othello's musical references are not merely rhetorical flourishes—though they do attest to his fluency with language. Rather, Othello relies on music as real evidence of a natural order that gives meaning to his actions. In this respect, music is central to Othello's method of political self-representation, which equates actions with their representation. When he asserts that his "services... shall out-tongue" Brabanzio's accusations and that his "demerits/May speak unbonneted" (1.2.18–23), he suggests a transparency in language, much in the same way that he sees music as a reliable index of political order. However, as the play makes clear, music's meaning is profoundly unstable, especially when it is heard. In an insightful essay on the play's different kinds of music, Erin Minear argues that *Othello* demonstrates "the potential identity of music and noise," thereby making the point that "all music is noise (or all audible music, at any rate)."[8] In other words, the play exposes the distinction between music and noise as culturally constructed, and therefore any attempt to ground a political system in music runs the risk of being undone by the fact of musical performance. No one better understands the "noisiness" of music than Iago himself, who characterizes his plan to destroy Othello as the manipulation of a musical instrument: "I'll set down the pegs that make this music" (2.1.197). Most critics have read this line metaphorically, in the sense that Iago will make Othello's marriage "out of tune," or full of strife. I think there is a more literal sense here as well: by proposing to tamper with the "pegs" of a musical instrument, Iago suggests that he will control the actual sounds of the play—the material, acoustic aspects of this marital "music"—rather than resort to "mere prattle without practice" (1.1.25).

As someone who understands the effects of musical sound, independent of its symbolic meaning, Iago is able to use music powerfully to his advantage. He succeeds in getting Cassio drunk, in part by singing a medley of English drinking songs. Such music is "noisy" in the full sense of the word: in addition to being literally loud, its nonsensical lyrics—"And let me the cannikin clink, clink/And let me the cannikin clink" (2.3.60–61)—follow a logic of sound more than sense. The acoustic aspects of its composition—its rhythm, tempo, melody—are designed to accompany and encourage the regular alternation of singing and drinking. It is, after all, drinking music. In a more

---

8. Erin Minear, "Music and the Crisis of Meaning in *Othello*," *Studies in English Literature* 49 (2009): 364.

subtle fashion, Iago successfully raises doubts in Othello's mind about Cassio's character by playing on the difference between language and sound:

> OTHELLO. Is he not honest?
> IAGO. Honest, my lord?
> OTHELLO. Honest? Ay, honest.
> IAGO. My lord, for aught I know.
> OTHELLO.   What dost thou think?
> IAGO. Think, my lord?
> OTHELLO. 'Think, my lord?' By heaven, thou echo'st me
>   As if there were some monster in thy thought
>   Too hideous to be shown! Thou dost mean something.
>   (3.3.105–12)

Othello's insistence that language must "mean something" causes him to react uncomfortably to Iago's seemingly hollow, "echoing" words. For him, sound with meaning can only be "monstrous." The fact that Iago carefully modulates the sound of his voice is registered by Othello himself: "These stops of thine fright me the more" (125). Othello's description of Iago's pauses as "stops" also suggests the "stops," or holes, in a musical wind instrument, as when Hamlet commends men who "are not a pipe for Fortune's finger / To sound what stop she please" (*Hamlet* 3.2.63–64), or when he sardonically instructs Guildenstern how to play the "stops" on a recorder (3.2.331). In this respect, Shakespeare suggests that Iago's singing performances and vocal tricks are all of a piece. Iago exploits the promiscuity of musical sound, knowing full well that Othello will scramble to find a meaning for it—whether it be the "close dilations" of the heart (*Othello* 3.3.128), or, soon enough, the "proof" (195) of Desdemona's infidelity.

Iago's musical game is a cruel one, but he is not the only one in the play who seems to mock Othello's belief in music's meaning. When the musicians gather outside Othello's house to serenade his wedding morning, the Clown turns them away with a series of puns that play on the confusion of music and noise:

> CLOWN. Are these, I pray you, wind instruments?
> MUSICIAN. Ay, marry are they, sir.
> CLOWN. O, thereby hangs a tail.
> MUSICIAN. Whereby hangs a tale, sir?
> CLOWN. Marry, sir, by many a wind instrument that I know. But masters, here's money for you, and the general so likes your music that he desires you, for love's sake, to make no more noise with it.

MUSICIAN. Well, sir, we will not.
CLOWN. If you have any music that may not be heard, to't again; but, as they say, to hear music, the general does not greatly care.
MUSICIAN. We ha' none such, sir.
CLOWN. Then put up your pipes in your bag, for I'll away. (3.1.6–18)

Rosalind King, noting that "Nonesuch" is also the name of a popular sixteenth-century ballad, reads the scene as evidence of Cassio's ineptness in choosing crude music to accompany the "harmony of true partnership." Minear, on the other hand, reads the Clown's request for "music that may not be heard" as a comment on the hollowness of ideas of celestial harmony.[9] I think that both readings are in play here, but I believe there is also another sense for the Clown's remarks—one that speaks directly to Othello's approach to music and marriage. In *The Art of English Poesy* (1589), George Puttenham devotes one of his longest chapters to epithalamiums, which he defines as "ballads at the bedding of the bride." At the risk of offending "chaste and honorable ears," Puttenham explains that the "tunes of the songs were very loud and shrill, to the intent there might no noise be heard out of the bedchamber by the screaking and outcry of the young damsel feeling the first forces of her stiff and rigorous young man, she being as all virgins tender and weak."[10] From this point of view, Cassio is guilty of bad timing rather than indecorum, since he provides nighttime music instead of an aubade. More importantly, epithalamiums, according to Puttenham, are literally "loud and shrill" because they mimic the messy, physical negotiations of the marriage bed. In this respect, Othello's rejection of epithalamium music suggests that he is uncomfortable with the unadorned representation of female sexuality. It is notable, for one thing, that Othello is one of the few characters in the play who never refers directly to his sexual relationship with Desdemona. When he does hint at it, he does so by denying "the palate of his appetite" (1.3.261). This rejection of bodily "appetite" is central to Othello's method of political self-representation, which works by sublimating both music and sexuality. For example, Othello's eloquent self-defense at the duke's court locates his appeal to Desdemona in his ability to "tell" his impressive military actions, and not in the physical features that seem to be the personal obsession of Iago and Brabanzio. Thus, the Clown's lewd transformation of "tale" into

---

9. King, "'Then murder's out of tune,'" 155; Minear, "Music and the Crisis of Meaning," 364.
10. George Puttenham, *The Art of English Poesy*, ed. Frank Whigham and Wayne A. Reborn (Ithaca, NY: Cornell University Press, 2007), 139. There may also be here the suggestion of public bedding rituals that typically included "ribald songs" and loud, obscene charivari, which, like epithalamiums, raucously drew attention to the bride's loss of virginity. See Lawrence Stone, *The Road to Divorce: England 1530–1987* (Oxford: Oxford University Press, 1990), 101.

"tail" participates in a larger movement in the play that subverts Othello's attempt to sublimate the physical aspects of his marriage and that foregrounds a noisy, bodily conception of music.

While Othello's efforts to control his public image ultimately fail, he is at least aided by Desdemona, who also subscribes to the idea that music is fundamentally meaningful.[11] By contrast, in *Richard II,* Richard's frequent turn to Neoplatonic rhetoric as a means of framing political events increasingly comes off as an inward, solipsistic activity.[12] When he first learns of Bolingbroke's rebellion, he is quick to cast it in cosmological terms, with himself as "the searching eye of heaven" (3.2.33). Likewise, when he is summoned by Bolingbroke in the next scene, he draws on moralized readings of Ovid and music to frame the event as an assault on the natural order:

Down, down I come like glist'ring Phaethon,
Wanting the manage of unruly jades.
In the base court: base court where kings grow base
To come at traitors' calls, and do them grace.
In the base court, come down: down court, down King,
For night-owls shriek where mounting larks should sing.
(3.3.177–82)

There may be a submerged musical pun here in the repetition of "down" and "base": by moving down the musical scale toward the "bass," Richard ultimately lands on the gam-ut, the lowest note of the scale, often figured in speculative diagrams as *terra,* or "earth"—the endpoint of Phaëthon's disastrous ride. As the play progresses, however, the gap between Richard's rhetorical abilities and political power grows larger, making his appeals to heavenly providence seem increasingly hollow. At his lowest point in the play, Richard himself comments on the meaninglessness of musical harmony in relation to

---

11. Desdemona's music has been well discussed in criticism of the play. While critics disagree on whether her performance of the "Willow" song distances her audience or allows them to identify with her, most acknowledge that her references to music and her singing raise the issue of music's expressiveness. See Minear, "Music and the Crisis of Meaning," 364–67; David Lindley, *Shakespeare and Music* (London: Thomson, 2006), 146–53; King, "'Then murder's out of tune,'" 156–58; Lisa Hopkins, "'What did thy song bode, lady?': *Othello* as Operatic Text," *Shakespeare Yearbook* 4 (1994): 61–70; Winifred Maynard, *Elizabethan Lyric Poetry and Its Music* (Oxford: Clarendon, 1986), 155–73; F. W. Sternfeld, *Music in Shakespearean Tragedy* (London: Routledge, 1963), 23–52.

12. See also A. D. Nuttall, "Ovid's Narcissus and Shakespeare's *Richard II:* The Reflected Self," in *Ovid Renewed: Ovidian Influences on Literature and Art from the Middle Ages to the Twentieth Century,* ed. Charles Martindale, 137–50 (Cambridge: Cambridge University Press, 1988); Pierre Iselin, "Myth, Memory, and Music in *Richard II, Hamlet,* and *Othello,*" in *Reclamations of Shakespeare,* ed. A. J. Hoenselaars, 173–86 (Amsterdam: Rodopi, 1994).

his own political fortunes: "Music do I hear./Ha, ha; keep time! How sour sweet music is/When time is broke and no proportion kept" (5.5.42–44). Like Othello's musical phrases, Richard's invocations of harmony are not simply rhetorical *sprezzatura,* but assertions that there *is,* in Attali's words, "a harmony in order." In this way, the pathos of Richard's final scene stems from the realization (more his than ours) that the association between the "sweet" music that he can still hear and the terms of his sovereignty has been nothing more than a willful construction, and that there is no music, earthly or heavenly, that can stop a more skillful politician from "wash[ing] the balm from an anointed king" (3.2.51).

Shakespeare's kings frequently invoke Neoplatonic ideas of harmony to assert their place in the natural order, though often without calling attention to the disjunction between musical and political realities. For example, when the dying Henry calls for "some dull and favourable hand [to] whisper music to [his] weary spirit" (*2 Henry IV* 4.3.134–35), he, like Richard before him, invokes the idea of music's spiritual nature to sanctify his reign. However, the play does not punish Henry for his rhetoric in the same way that Richard is punished—by being made a figure of pathetic disillusionment—in his play. Likewise, in *2 Henry VI,* the king's use of musical dissonance to describe his warring subjects does not make him seem politically naive: "How irksome is this music to my heart!/When such strings jar, what hope of harmony?" (2.1.59–60).[13] In one sense, these musical references function as straightforward metaphors, unproblematized because they come across as affectations of speech. At the same time, their metaphoricity derives partly from the fact that, in these plays, *any* claim to universal order is usually exposed as political posturing. This is especially the case in assertions of royal legitimacy, as when Prince Henry announces that he will succeed the dying King John:

I am the cygnet to this pale faint swan,
Who chants a doleful hymn to his own death,
And from the organ-pipe of frailty sings
His soul and body to their lasting rest.
         (*King John* 5.7.21–24)

Here, Henry's attempt to romanticize the transfer of power by invoking an idea of natural music rings hollow, not merely because swan song is a common conceit in Renaissance poetry, but because the play by this point has

---

13. There may, however, be a subtle joke on the meaning of music in the subsequent line: "What means this noise?" (62).

shredded any sense of the naturalness of royal authority. Even though Henry promises a more hopeful reign, the play makes clear that his ascension has been effected more by accident and political maneuvering than by heavenly design. In this context, the appeals to harmony come off as little more than disingenuous attempts to ceremonialize the messy, chaotic business of English politics.

In *The Merchant of Venice,* Shakespeare documents a more effective use of the political and ideological dimensions of musical orthodoxy, particularly in its capacity to marginalize and silence alternative modes of experience. Here, in the play's last act, Shakespeare offers his most eloquent précis of the doctrine of *musica speculativa:*

> There's not the smallest orb which thou behold'st
> But in his motion like an angel sings,
> Still choiring to the young-eyed cherubins.
> Such harmony is in immortal souls,
> But whilst this muddy vesture of decay
> Doth grossly close it in, we cannot hear it.
>   (5.1.59–64)

Lorenzo's speech faithfully adheres to conventions of *musica speculativa,* including the Boethian categories of music: *musica mundana* (the music of the spheres) and *musica humana* (the harmony of the soul). At the same time, the speech emphasizes the allegorical nature of speculative discourse: the "muddy vesture of decay" that Lorenzo describes is essentially the same "fictive veil" that the Renaissance moralizers ascribe to earthly matter and sensuous poetry. Indeed, the idea of the moralized Ovid is made explicit a few lines later, when Lorenzo adduces the "feigning," or allegorizing, poet:

> Therefore the poet
> Did feign that Orpheus drew trees, stones, and floods,
> Since naught so stockish, hard, and full of rage
> But music for the time doth change his nature.
>   (78–81)

By contextualizing Lorenzo's redaction of *musica speculativa* in terms of the allegorical Ovid ("the poet" of Orpheus), Shakespeare suggests—with hardly less subtlety than John Taverner in his Gresham College lectures—that the two discourses are imaginatively and ideologically linked.

As a definition of music, Lorenzo's speech is as orthodox an articulation of Renaissance *musica speculativa* as one will find in Shakespeare. W. H. Auden echoes many critics when he writes that "anyone at the time, if asked, 'What is music?' would have given the answer stated by Lorenzo to Jessica in the last scene of *The Merchant of Venice*."[14] While Auden may be going too far (there were many who had different answers to the question, as we have seen), he is right that Lorenzo's answer is what someone would have been *supposed* to say. Yet musical orthodoxy need not be taken as the play's—or Shakespeare's—final answer on the subject. By placing Lorenzo's speech in a dramatic context, Shakespeare activates the traditional rhetoric of *musica speculativa* in a way that demonstrates its contingency.[15] Lorenzo's encomium is not, after all, a self-contained set piece, though it is often excerpted as such. His speech is a direct response to Jessica's statement, "I am never merry when I hear sweet music" (5.1.69). These are striking words, in part because they are the last words Jessica says in the play, but also because they express, with surprising directness, a radically subjective view of musical experience. Perhaps at no other moment does Jessica more resemble her father, Shylock, who two scenes earlier gives an incisive account of musical subjectivity:

> Some men there are love not a gaping pig,
> Some that are mad if they behold a cat,
> And others when the bagpipe sings i'th' nose
> Cannot contain their urine; for affection,
> Mistress of passion, sways it to the mood
> Of what it likes or loathes.
>
> (4.1.46–51)

In many of the early modern attacks on music, the bagpipe (or hornpipe) is singled out as an example of loud, degraded music, in contrast to Neoplatonic models of musical harmony. In this respect, Shylock's description of music purposefully emphasizes its noisiness, while his references to bodily functions (nose, urine) make indelible the idea of music's physicality. Moreover, his pun on "mood/mode" (which I have not seen acknowledged in any edition of the play) evokes and challenges the theory of musical modes often put forth by poetic theorists like Puttenham. For Shylock, music's effect is

---

14. W. H. Auden, *The Dyer's Hand* (New York: Random House, 1948), 500–501.
15. Marc Berley also makes a clear distinction between Shakespeare's and Lorenzo's views of music; his reading of the play's music is instructive. *After the Heavenly Tune: English Poetry and the Aspiration to Song* (Pittsburgh: Duquesne University Press, 2000), 83–124.

not determined by its internal properties (its "mode"), as Puttenham would argue, but by the whims and fancies of its listeners (their "moods"). It is this radical subjectivity, which Shylock sees exemplified by music, that he posits—mistakenly, tragically—as untouchable by Venetian law.

Shylock's assertion of musical subjectivity in the trial scene comes close to Portia's point in 3.2 that music's meaning is determined by its context, though in Shylock's case musical subjectivity is more explicitly tied to the play's concerns about religious difference. It is no accident that Shylock asserts subjectivity in music in the same breath in which he asserts his preference not to eat pork: "Some men there are love not a gaping pig." Indeed, many perceptive readers of the play have sensed that Shylock's attitude toward music is inseparable from his status as the play's Jewish character. In his masterful reading of the play's theological framework, Lawrence Danson refers to Shylock's "spiritual tone-deafness"—a figurative phrase that the play literalizes—and concludes that Shylock "wilfully prefers his silent entombment in the flesh."[16] From the standpoint of conservative Christian theology, Danson's assessment is undoubtedly correct: Jewishness, fleshiness, and musical unorthodoxy form a veritable "axis of evil" that the play conspicuously expunges. The political implications of musical preference are made explicit in Lorenzo's final words about music, which seem directed to Shylock as much as Jessica:

> The man that hath no music in himself,
> Nor is not moved with concord of sweet sounds,
> Is fit for treasons, stratagems, and spoils.
> The motions of his spirit are dull as night,
> And his affections dark as Erebus.
> Let no such man be trusted. Mark the music.
> (5.1.82–87)

Here, in true speculative fashion, Lorenzo connects the idea of moral and social degeneracy, signified by the Boethian categories of *musica humana* and *musica practica,* to the fact of *musica mundana,* the "motions" of spiritual and planetary bodies. In effect, he universalizes religious difference. At the same time, his short command to Jessica to listen again ("Mark the music") suggests the willfulness involved in understanding this conception of musical harmony. To hear music as universal harmony is to make a politically

---

16. Lawrence Danson, *The Harmonies of "The Merchant of Venice"* (New Haven, CT: Yale University Press, 1978), 183, 188.

and ideologically inflected choice. Or, more accurately, to hear music as universal harmony is not to *hear* music at all. Since the promiscuousness of musical sound opens the door to subjectivity in feeling—and thus radical unorthodoxy—then, conversely, political harmony depends crucially on an act of translating musical sound into something other than itself—most likely, a visual or textual representation of music as divine or mathematical order. In other words, political harmony comes at the expense of silencing music. And, in *The Merchant of Venice,* it comes at the expense of silencing Jessica.

Music's Body and Shakespearean Romance

Does music have a body? The question may seem absurd, especially in the absence of our modern understanding of acoustics. Yet as it turns out, the rejection of the idea that music has a substance—the rejection of its materiality—is a crucial step in the early modern attempt to pin down music's meaning. For example, Robert Burton, in *The Anatomy of Melancholy* (1621), can describe music's effect on its listeners only after he has framed it as a voice that "speaks without a mouth" (*sine ore loquens*).[17] For all its emphasis on physiological processes, Burton's treatise finds music intelligible only when it has been sublimated as insubstantial air. In much the same way, Shakespeare's final romances (*Cymbeline, Pericles,* and *The Tempest*) stage the construction of a legible, coherent meaning in music and the concomitant denial of music's substantiality. Much attention has been given to the presence of Neoplatonic ideas about music in these late plays; less noticed is the amount of *work* done, often conspicuously, to keep music's material nature at bay.[18] In these instances, music's body is continually in danger of intruding, and its presence is a constant threat to the coherent theory of political harmony—the fundamental distinction between "good" and "bad" listeners of music—that underpins the plays' symbolic economies.

The idea of music's body is simultaneously evoked and evaded in *Cymbeline,* a play that always seems to be gazing on, recording, clothing, dismembering, or dumping its *actual* physical, human bodies. The traditional

---

17. Robert Burton, *The Anatomy of Melancholy* (1621), ed. Holbrook Jackson (London: J. M. Dent, 1975), 116.

18. The relationship between music and Neoplatonism in the romances has been well discussed. See John P. Cutts, "Music and the Supernatural in *The Tempest:* A Study in Interpretation," *Music and Letters* 39 (1958): 347–58; Catherine M. Dunn, "The Function of Music in Shakespeare's Romances," *Shakespeare Quarterly* 20 (1969): 391–405; Headlam Wells, *Elizabethan Mythologies,* 63–80.

view that music inwardly moves the passions is raised early in the play, but through a distinctively negative example. Cloten, attempting to soften Innogen's feelings toward him, clumsily calls for music in terms that suggest its instrumentality: "I would this music would come. I am advised to give her music o' mornings; they say it will penetrate.... Come on, tune. If you can penetrate her with your fingering, so; we'll try with tongue too" (2.3.10–13). While Shakespeare's pun on musical penetration here may cause us to snicker at Cloten's unabashed lewdness, it underscores the fact that Cloten really expects music to have a physical presence. His idea of musical penetration is not figurative. Little surprise, then, when Cloten describes music as a physical phenomenon brought about by vibrating, resounding bodies (or body parts): "If this penetrate I will consider your music the better; if it do not, it is a vice in her ears which horse hairs and calves' guts nor the voice of unpaved eunuch to boot can never amend" (24–27). Here, Cloten identifies music with the material components of its production—"horse hairs and calves' guts." As such, his attempt to sway Innogen with music is an utter failure: "I have assailed her with musics, but she vouchsafes no notice" (35–36). The play affirms its musical orthodoxy here by holding up for ridicule its most bodily listener, whose misunderstanding of music is so complete that he grammatically declines it as a plural noun.

Shakespeare offers a more traditional vision of music later in the play, and it hides the bodily traces of music as conspicuously as Cloten dwells on them. Immediately after Cloten is reduced to a body without a head, Shakespeare stages a striking scene of invisible, disembodied music:

> GUIDERIUS. I have sent Cloten's clotpoll down the stream
> In embassy to his mother. His body's hostage
> For his return.
>   *Solemn music*
> BELARIUS. My ingenious instrument!—
> Hark, Polydore, it sounds. But what occasion
> Hath Cadwal now to give it motion? Hark!
> (4.2.185–89)

Although Belarius addresses the "instrument" of music, no instrument is ever seen. Instead, historical narrative replaces the image of musical performance: "Since death of my dear'st mother / It did not speak before" (191–92). For Guiderius, the memory of his mother's death acts as a strong interpretive context, making the musical instrument appear to be expressive: first it "sounds," then it "speaks." At this moment, Belarius goes further and gives a short lecture on musical decorum:

> All solemn things
> Should answer solemn accidents. The matter?
> Triumphs for nothing and lamenting toys
> Is jollity for apes and grief for boys.
> Is Cadwal mad?
>
> (192–96)

The lesson here is short but clear: music independent of meaning is a form of madness. (There is an echo of Horatio's remark in *Hamlet* that Ophelia's "speech is nothing.") The purpose of Belarius's lecture seems to be to purge music of its corporeal effects and to reinscribe meaning, or "matter," as the core of music's essence. Once the importance of musical representation is reestablished, then—and only then—does Shakespeare permit physical bodies to be brought onto the stage: "*Enter Arviragus, with Innogen dead, bearing her in his arms*" (196 s.d.). The play's dense trafficking of human bodies and corpses, now situated in the context of symbolic music, invites an emblematic reading, and the image of Arviragus carrying Innogen, like the other corporeal images that follow, has received its share of allegorical interpretations, ranging from a reading of the scene as a political commentary on tyranny to a Neoplatonic analysis of the scene as a figuration of the myth of Eros and Psyche.[19]

The play's most conventional example of a musical emblem comes in the final act, in which Posthumus is given a prophetic vision of his—and Britain's—future through the ghosts of his dead ancestors. While the echoes of Virgil's *Aeneid* in the scene have been noted, the staging is also remarkable for its use of music in giving the vision a narrative shape:

> *Solemn music. Enter, as in an apparition,* SICILIUS *Leonatus (father to Posthumus, an old man) attired like a warrior, leading in his hand an ancient matron, his wife, and* MOTHER *to Posthumus, with music before them. Then, after other music, follows the two young Leonati,* BROTHERS *to Posthumus, with wounds as they died in the wars.* (5.5.123 s.d.)

---

19. The Neoplatonic reading of the play is developed at length in Peggy Muñoz Simonds, *Myth, Emblem, and Music in Shakespeare's "Cymbeline": An Iconographic Reconstruction* (Newark: University of Delaware Press, 1992).

As David Quint has written, empire loves a parade. Speculative music, it seems to me, loves a dream vision. Shakespeare manages to include both here, and the effectiveness of the scene suggests the extent to which Neoplatonic representations of music depend on a static system of visual signs for their persuasiveness. Or, conversely, if the play's dismembering and confusion of physical bodies threaten to undo its endorsement of Jacobean, nationalist propaganda, as Heather James has proposed, then a similarly uncontrolled obsession with corporeality and instrumentality threatens to undermine a Neoplatonic reading of the play's musical episodes. The play handles this threat and maintains the integrity of its musical symbolism (if just barely) by carefully managing its theatrical bodies: by ultimately distinguishing between the bodies of Posthumus and Cloten, by affirming the physical hardiness and "princely blood" of Guiderius and Arviragus, and, in its most Neoplatonic moment, by eschewing physical bodies altogether in favor of a parade of insubstantial ghosts.

In its staging of ghosts, *Cymbeline* shares with *Pericles,* which also makes a musical dream vision the centerpiece of its final act. In *Pericles,* however, the tension between performed music and *musica speculativa* works to a different effect. In this play, Shakespeare again suggests the strained relationship between Renaissance *musica speculativa* and musical sound, but in a way that undermines conventional claims about music's effect on the emotions. As in *Cymbeline,* the idea of music's harmonizing ability is suggested in *Pericles* in the context of melancholia, through the character of Pericles, who is described by Helicanus as "a man who for this three months hath not spoken/To anyone, nor taken sustenance/But to prorogue his grief" (scene 21, lines 18–20). The idea of melancholia is made explicit by Helicanus a few lines later when he refers to Pericles' "melancholy state" (206). And, in line with seventeenth-century textbook representations of melancholy, Lysimachus proposes a musical cure for the king's illness.[20] Marina, Pericles'

---

20. The idea of music as a cure for melancholy is a commonplace in early modern writing on the passions. See Penelope Gouk, "Music, Melancholy, and Medical Spirits in Early Modern Thought," in *Music as Medicine: The History of Music Therapy since Antiquity,* ed. Peregrine Horden, 173–94 (Aldershot, UK: Ashgate, 2000); Linda Phyllis Austern, "'The conceit of the minde': Music, Medicine and Mental Process in Early Modern England," *Irish Musical Studies* 4 (1996): 133–51; Wilfrid Mellers, "The Double Man: John Dowland, Hamlet, and Seventeenth-Century Melancholy," *Margin* 7 (1988): 53–64; F. David Hoeniger, "Musical Cures of Melancholy and Mania in Shakespeare," in *Mirror up to Shakespeare: Essays in Honor of G. R. Hibbard,* ed. J. C. Gray, 55–67 (Toronto: University of Toronto Press, 1984); Bridget Gellert Lyons, *Voices of Melancholy: Studies in Literary Treatments of Melancholy in Renaissance England* (New York: Barnes & Noble, 1971).

unrecognized daughter, is presented to him in language lifted from early modern medical accounts of music's effect on the passions:

> She questionless, with her sweet harmony
> And other chosen attractions, would allure,
> And make a batt'ry through his deafened ports,
> Which now are midway stopped.
>
> (34–37)[21]

The rhetoric of *musica speculativa* here, together with Gower's remark in the act's prologue that Marina "sings like one immortal," sets the stage for a spectacular demonstration of music's restorative abilities. It is all the more striking, then, when this music spectacularly fails. Marina's musical performance, which goes on at length, fails to evoke even the smallest response from Pericles, causing Lysimachus to ask, "Marked he your music?" (68) In this way, the play evokes the idea of speculative music only to demonstrate its distance from performed sound.

The failure of Marina's music in *Pericles* holds up for review speculative claims about music's effect on the body, and about music's body itself. Early modern writing on melancholy frequently uses different notions of music's corporeality in order to make generalizations about human processes that cannot be seen. For example, like Burton, Thomas Wright raises the question of music's body in his discussion of melancholy. Unlike Burton, however, Wright does not avoid the problem of music's material nature:

> How musicke stirreth up these passions, and moveth so mightily these affections? What hath the shaking or ratificiall crispling of the ayre (which is in effect the substance of musicke) to doe with rousing up choller, afflicting with melancholy, jubilating the heart with pleasure, elevating the soul to devotion...what qualitie carie simple single sounds and voices, to enable them to worke such wonders?[22]

---

21. The Norton edition of the play replaces Q1's "allure" with "alarum," on the reasoning that "allure" carries a sexual sense, inappropriate to the scene. While "allure" may have this meaning in some contexts, it appears in early modern descriptions of music's power that are not necessarily sexually suggestive.

22. Thomas Wright, *The Passions of the Minde in Generall* (1604), ed. Thomas O. Sloan (Urbana: University of Illinois Press, 1971), 168.

Echoing Benedick's question in *Much Ado About Nothing*—"Is it not strange that sheep's guts should hale souls out of men's bodies?" (2.3.53–55)—Wright locates music's "substance" precisely in the physical aspects of its production. Moreover, instead of making it easier to generalize music's effect on its listeners, the focus on music's body leads Wright to make one of his most radical pronouncements about the subjectivity of musical experience: "I cannot imagine, that if a man never had heard a Trumpet or a Drum in his life, that he would at the first hearing bee moved to warres."[23]

Pericles repeatedly highlights the idea of music's incorporeality, particularly in scenes where music has a different effect from what is expected. Shortly before the final act, the audience learns that Marina's voice has the immediate effect of driving men to religion—a problem, since she works in a brothel:

> FIRST GENTLEMAN. Did you ever hear the like?
> SECOND GENTLEMAN. No, nor never shall do in such a place as this, she being once gone.
> FIRST GENTLEMAN. But to have divinity preached there—did you ever dream of such a thing?
> SECOND GENTLEMAN. No, no. Come, I am for no more bawdy houses. Shall 's go hear the vestals sing?
> FIRST GENTLEMAN. I'll do anything now that is virtuous, but I am out of the road of rutting for ever. (scene 19, lines 1–9)

The scene, while playable as farce, describes the spiritually harmonizing effects of Marina's voice in Orphic terms, and there is a subtle echo of Macrobius's *Dream of Scipio* that suggests again a reading of Marina's voice as *musica mundana*. Yet the scene of Marina's heavenly singing is never staged. Her divine music is not given corporeal presence, much like the vestal music whose bodily source cannot be seen (since vestal virgins were not allowed to be seen by men). Their music is, quite literally, disembodied. As in *Cymbeline,* an orderly, Neoplatonic vision of music requires leaving behind the earthly—and usually female—sources of its production. Even when music is performed, as when the doctor Cerimon uses music to resuscitate Thaisa, its source is rhetorically obscured: "The still and woeful music that we have,/ Cause it to sound" (scene 12, lines 86–87). Here, the invisibility of musical performers (at least in the play's text) helps to mystify the medicinal and spiritual effects of music, which Cerimon predictably calls a "secret art" (29).[24]

---

23. Ibid., 171.
24. F. Elizabeth Hart argues against the emendation of "rough" to "still" in this passage, provocatively suggesting that the idea of "rough magic" fits into a pattern of allusions to the rites of

In its close adherence to Neoplatonic representations of music, *Pericles* is Shakespeare's most straightforward attempt to theatricalize *musica speculativa*. Hence the distinctly Pythagorean moment at the end of the play, when Pericles hears the music of the spheres:

> PERICLES. Give me my robes. I am wild in my beholding.
>   O heavens, bless my girl! But hark, what music?
>   . . . .
>   How sure you are my daughter. But what music?
> HELICANUS. My lord, I hear none.
> PERICLES. None? The music of the spheres! List, my Marina.
> LYSIMACHUS. It is not good to cross him. Give him way.
> PERICLES. Rar'st sounds. Do ye not year?
> LYSIMACHUS. Music, my Lord?
> PERICLES. I hear most heav'nly music.
>   It raps me unto list'ning, and thick slumber
>   Hangs upon mine eyelids. Let me rest.
>
> (scene 21, lines 208–20)

The actual representation of *musica mundana*—or, in this case, a character's experience of *musica mundana*—is unusual for Shakespeare. Together with the spectacular failure of Marina's attempt to cure her father's melancholy with music, Pericles' epiphanic hearing of heavenly music obliquely points to a subtle but important link between Renaissance ideas of melancholy and conventional *musica speculativa*. Namely, *Pericles* shows how the mystification of melancholy both encourages and depends on a notion of incorporeal music that transcends its own physical production. Although some editors of the play insert a stage direction for performed music in this scene, I believe that the absence of heard music here may be purposeful. By making Pericles' outburst the only sign of celestial music in this scene, the play sustains the belief that music's redemptive, curative power is not to be located in its material, acoustic aspects (as someone like Cloten would have it) but in an intangible, incorporeal space that can be apprehended only by the mind. This is allegory's version of music. Thus it is not surprising that the end of the play is presided over by Apollo and Diana, in full allegorical garb. While Shakespeare does not problematize *musica speculativa* in *Pericles* as overtly as he does elsewhere, he lays bare the ideological dependencies between music

---

an easternized Diana of Ephesus. This would seem to enhance the mystifying rhetoric in the scene. "Cerimon's 'Rough' Music in *Pericles*, 3.2," *Shakespeare Quarterly* 51 (2000): 313–31.

and allegory that I traced in the previous chapter. Indeed, the play urges repeatedly an allegorical interpretation of itself, nowhere more so than in the closing speech by the historical Gower:

> In Pericles, his queen, and daughter seen,
> Although assailed with fortune fierce and keen,
> Virtue preserved from fell destruction's blast,
> Led on by heav'n, and crowned with joy at last.
> (scene 22, lines 110–13)

Gower's explicit moralization suggests that early modern allegory, with its doctrinal rejection of sensuous experience, is the ideal—if not the only—context for the representation of speculative music. At the same time, if two centuries of critical and audience ambivalence toward the play is to be trusted, then the heavy machinery of this moralizing apparatus is not always persuasive or compelling from a theatrical perspective. That may be precisely the point.

Teaching Caliban

In its transferal of music from the familiar shores of Britain and Italy to an unknown island inhabited by airy spirits and fleeting visions, *The Tempest* confirms the synergy between Neoplatonic interpretations of music and a veiling of music's bodily production. At the same time, *The Tempest* is as dexterous in its handling of Neoplatonic ideas of harmony as *Pericles* is clumsy. Since at least the eighteenth century, the play has been perennially popular on the stage, in part because of its elaborate use of magic and music. A nineteenth-century advertisement for a production in Leeds, for example, disproportionately highlights the magical and musical episodes of the play, suggesting that audiences found them the most appealing.[25] However, while it uses music to good theatrical effect, the play also presents a scathing critique of artistic power. The deep ambivalence over Prospero's magic that has dogged the play's critical history has also made it a popular choice for postcolonial productions of Shakespeare.[26] This ambivalence partly explains

---

25. David Lindley, "Music for *The Tempest* in Leeds in 1865" (conference paper presented at the Music in Shakespeare conference, University of Leeds, September 2002).
26. For a detailed account of these productions, see the discussion of the play's twentieth-century stage history in *The Tempest,* ed. Virginia Mason Vaughan and Alden T. Vaughan (London: Thomson, 1999), 112–24.

the play's choice of Ovidian models. Shakespeare does not draw on Orpheus or Pythagoras, who—along with Hermes, Moses, and others—constituted for many Renaissance writers the principal magi in a line of initiates that stretched back to Adam.[27] Instead, the Ovidian figures who loom over the play are Circe and Medea, both of whom are associated in the Renaissance with a mystical, morally suspect power.[28] By raising serious concerns about the moral uses to which magic is put, *The Tempest* interrogates the ideological and political ends of Neoplatonic systems of thought—and of art forms, such as the masque, that rely heavily on Neoplatonic ideas. Moreover, in identifying music and Ovidian allegory as instruments of power, Shakespeare renders deeply problematic the claims to authority made on their behalf. In these cases, teaching music is hardly different from commanding it.

Almost as soon as it begins, *The Tempest* suggests the collusion between pedagogical methods and political power. The history of the relationship between Caliban, Miranda, and Prospero is revealed to be full of scenes of instruction, which Miranda describes in language that echoes much Renaissance writing on music:

> Abhorrèd slave,
> Which any print of goodness wilt not take,
> Being capable of all ill! I pitied thee,
> Took pains to make thee speak, taught thee each hour
> One thing or other. When thou didst not, savage,
> Know thine own meaning, but wouldst gabble like
> A thing most brutish, I endowed thy purposes
> With words that made them known.
>
> (1.2.354–61)

Miranda's description of Caliban's first sounds as a "brutish gabble," which she attempts to transform into articulate language, recalls the early modern attacks on music as a "bleating of brute beastes." Although music is not

---

27. Penelope Gouk, *Music, Science and Natural Magic in Seventeenth-Century England* (New Haven, CT: Yale University Press, 1999), 12. See also D. P. Walker, *The Ancient Theology: Studies in Christian Platonism from the Fifteenth to the Eighteenth Century* (London: Duckworth, 1972), 1–25. For an argument that Shakespeare does in fact model Prospero on Orpheus, see Peggy Muñoz Simonds, "'Sweet power of music': The Political Magic of 'The Miraculous Harp' in Shakespeare's *The Tempest*," *Comparative Drama* 29 (1995): 61–90.

28. On the Renaissance reception of Circe, see Merritt Y. Hughes, "Spenser's Acrasia and the Circe of the Renaissance," *Journal of the History of Ideas* 4 (1943): 381–99; Leonora Leet Brodwin, "Milton and the Renaissance Circe," *Milton Studies* 6 (1974): 46–54; Judith E. Browning, "Sin, Eve, and Circe: *Paradise Lost* and the Ovidian Circe Tradition," *Milton Studies* 26 (1991): 135–58.

explicitly named here, the violent encounter between Miranda's "words" and Caliban's "gabble" recalls the scenes of musical meaning making in *Titus Andronicus* and *Hamlet*. In *The Tempest,* moreover, the clash between sound and words is represented as a colonial encounter: "The red plague rid you/For learning me your language!" (367–68). While Caliban's response to Miranda frames language as a colonization of sound, the play does not uniformly represent music as the triumph of civilized society over unruly noise, despite the fact that most early modern histories of music link the discovery of music with advances in civilization. Rather, the play develops a complex relationship between language, sound, and music, avoiding a hierarchical ordering of language and sound in favor of a more unsettled relationship.[29]

The tension between sound and meaning is established the first time we hear music in the play, when Ariel and the other spirits sing "dispersedly" around Ferdinand:

ARIEL.	Come unto these yellow sands,
	And then take hands;
	Curtsied when you have and kissed—
	The wild waves whist—
	Foot it featly here and there,
	And, sweet sprites, bear
	The burden. Hark, hark!
SPIRITS. (*dispersedly*)	Bow-wow!
ARIEL.	The watch-dogs bark.
SPIRITS.	Bow-wow!

---

29. For this reason I feel that colonial models are inadequate for interpreting the play's representation of magic. It is notable, for one thing, that many readings of the play's colonialist politics focus on Prospero's power over vision, not sound or music. See, for example, Meredith Skura, "Discourse and the Individual: The Case of Colonialism in *The Tempest*," *Shakespeare Quarterly* 40 (1989): 42–69; Stephen Greenblatt, *Shakespearean Negotiations* (Berkeley: University of California Press, 1988), 142–63; *The Tempest,* ed. Stephen Orgel, (Oxford: Oxford University Press, 1987); Paul Brown, "'This thing of darkness I acknowledge mine': *The Tempest* and the Discourse of Colonialism," in *Political Shakespeare: New Essays in Cultural Materialism,* ed. Jonathan Dollimore and Alan Sinfield, 48–71 (Manchester: Manchester University Press, 1985). Since the 1990s, criticism has richly expanded the field of the play's politics, both geographically and historically, though these readings also typically map the relationship between Prospero and Caliban onto other hierarchical relationships (e.g., England and Ireland, England and the Ottoman Empire, social classes within England, men and women of color). See Irene Lara, "Beyond Caliban's Curses: The Decolonial Feminist Literacy of Sycorax," *Journal of International Women's Studies* 9 (2007): 80–98; Jerry Brotton, "'This Tunis, sir, was Carthage': Contesting Colonialism in *The Tempest*," in *Post-Colonial Shakespeares,* ed. Ania Loomba and Martin Orkin, 23–42 (London: Routledge, 1998); Andrew Hadfield, *Literature, Travel, and Colonial Writing in the English Renaissance 1545–1625* (Oxford: Clarendon, 1998), 242–54; Barbara Fuchs, "Conquering Islands: Contextualizing *The Tempest*," *Shakespeare Quarterly* 48 (1997): 45–62.

ARIEL. Hark, hark, I hear,
The strain of strutting Chanticleer
Cry 'cock-a-diddle-dow'.
  (1.2.378–90)

As a sonorous event, Ariel's performance oscillates between the formalism of a recognizable song and the ambient, natural sounds of barking dogs and crowing cocks. In this way, the scene muddies the distinction between music and unstructured, nonhuman sound. Shakespeare intensifies the illegibility of this music by "dispersing" the burden of Ariel's song (that is, assigning it to different voices around the stage). A musical burden, or refrain, typically organizes a song both structurally and thematically: it gives formal shape to the musical composition and expresses the meaning of its verse, as when Lucrece says that she will "burden-wise...hum on Tarquin still." By multiplying the song's burden and spreading it among different voices singing at different times, Shakespeare deprives it of its formal purpose.[30] Thus Ariel's song strains against meaning both in the nonsensicality of its verbal text ("Hark, hark," "Bow-wow") and in its confusion of what would otherwise be a recognizable acoustic, musical pattern.[31]

Shakespeare's dispersal of musical form in the play's second scene is instrumental in his representation of music as a magical art. In other words, while the audience sees the blending of musical and natural sound as an exercise of Prospero's magical power, the indeterminacy of this music is experienced by Ferdinand as mystical phenomenon: "Where should this music be? I'th' air or th'earth?/It sounds no more; and sure it waits upon/Some god o'th' island" (1.2.391–93). Ferdinand's response here is instructive: in the absence of a clear sight line to its source, music is more easily perceived as divine. Shakespeare is not the only stage director to have understood this theatrical effect: it was Richard Wagner, who, when staging his *Ring* cycle in 1869, first decided to place the orchestra underneath the stage, completely invisible to the audience. In addition to giving music an "otherwordly" effect, especially desirable for the opera's depiction of cosmic events, this staging also made

---

30. This lack of musical clarity is reflected by the different views on how to stage this scene. In the 1999 Arden edition of the play, the editors note the disagreement among critics over whether to render "Hark, hark" as a musical refrain or to make "Bow-wow" the only repeated sound from the other spirits. Vaughan and Vaughan, *Tempest*, 177.

31. Michael Neill deftly traces the play's punning on the musical and physical senses of "burden," noting how the play complicates a simple Neoplatonic reading. See "'Noises,/Sounds, and sweet airs': The Burden of Shakespeare's *Tempest*," *Shakespeare Quarterly* 59 (2008): 36–59. His essay, which appeared after I had written this chapter, also notes the play's frequent blurring of the boundary between music and noise.

it easier for audiences to hear music as *narrative*. Something similar happens when Ferdinand hears Ariel's second song, which increases his sense of disorientation but which also gives him snippets of possible meaning:

> ARIEL. Full fathom five thy father lies.
>   Of his bones are coral made;
> Those are pearls that were his eyes;
>   Nothing of him that doth fade
> But doth suffer a sea-change
> Into something rich and strange.
>   Sea-nymphs hourly ring his knell:
> SPIRITS. Ding dong.
> ARIEL. Hark, now I hear them.
> SPIRITS.   Ding dong bell.
> (1.2.400–408)

Again, Ferdinand identifies the murkiness of music's source as a sign of its divinity: "This is no mortal business, nor no sound/That the earth owes. I hear it now above me" (410–11). This sense of music's intentionality allows Ferdinand to make connections, however tenuous, between the music he hears and his own situation: "The ditty does remember my drowned father" (409). Reasonable enough, except that Ferdinand's father is very much alive. Here, the semblance of meaning, encouraged by the song's resemblance to funeral bells, is enough to inspire a false belief. Later in the play, a similar conflation of music and meaning confirms Alonso's belief that *his* son is dead:

> The winds did sing it to me, and the thunder,
> That deep and dreadful organ-pipe, pronounced
> The name of Prosper. It did bass my trespass.
> Therefor my son i'th' ooze is bedded...
> (3.3.97–100)

Again, the confusion of natural sound, music, and words ("Prosper") creates the sense of prophecy. In both scenes Shakespeare makes an important point about music's suasiveness: it is the *expectation* that music is narrative that allows for moments of magical hearing.

Through the play's staging of strange music, Shakespeare gives his audience a double view of music's place in the world. On the one hand, the magical episodes allow the audience to see firsthand the harmonizing, civilizing effects of music that are usually described in speculative texts. This way of seeing and hearing the play's music informs David Lindley's observation that "for many critics over the years it has been *The Tempest*'s exemplification of the neoplatonic view of music's power which has been central to their readings of the play."[32] On the other hand, by calling attention to Prospero's agency in engineering these scenes, Shakespeare suggests that music, because it can work unseen, is a useful tool for making magical phenomena seem credible. This is not to say that the connections between Renaissance musical and magical thought rest on theatrical shows alone. In her impressive study of early modern science, for example, Penelope Gouk has shown the real overlaps between speculative music, harmonic theory, mathematics, acoustic theory, and natural science that undergird much serious writing on magic in the period.[33] Nonetheless, for Shakespeare's Ferdinand, it is the indefiniteness of Ariel's music, rather than its formal or harmonic structure, that gives evidence of its magical quality. In this way the play shows that the Neoplatonic collapsing of the distinction between human and natural agency can be realized as a perceptible event—in the careful blending of human and natural sound. On this effect of sound on Renaissance magical thought, Gouk notes that "the magical universe is one which arises from a predominantly oral-aural perception of the world, where knowledge is chiefly communicated through voice and speech. Words in this context are indistinguishable from actions, and have a power far beyond their literal meaning. Sound places man in the middle of the universe, which is conceived of animistically because *all sounds suggest voices.*"[34] In other words, in a magical universe all sounds are

---

32. Lindley, *Shakespeare and Music*, 218.

33. Gouk, *Music, Science and Natural Magic*. See also Gary Tomlinson, *Music in Renaissance Magic: Toward a Historiography of Others* (Chicago: University of Chicago Press, 1993). Gouk's and Tomlinson's emphasis on the connections between magic, Neoplatonism, and natural philosophy stems in part from their attempt to qualify earlier studies that pit magic against the emergence of "rational" thought in the seventeenth century. In this respect, their work offers a valuable corrective to the study of magic in Michel Foucault, *The Order of Things: An Archaeology of the Human Sciences* (New York: Pantheon, 1970) and Brian Vickers, "Analogy versus Identity: The Rejection of Occult Symbolism, 1580–1680," in *Occult and Scientific Mentalities in the Renaissance*, ed. Brian Vickers, 95–163 (Cambridge: Cambridge University Press, 1984). Other valuable studies on Renaissance magic and music include Ioan P. Couliano, *Eros and Magic in the Renaissance* (Chicago: University of Chicago Press, 1987) and D. P. Walker, *Spiritual and Demonic Magic from Ficino to Campanella* (London: Warburg Institute, 1958).

34. Gouk, *Music, Science and Natural Magic*, 17, my emphasis. It should be noted that Gouk is describing here Walter Ong's conception of magical thought, which she ultimately finds too limiting: "However, no simple correlation between magic and non-literacy on the one hand and between science and literary on the other can in fact be made. Vision plays a profoundly important role in non-literate cultures, while hearing and the other senses continue to shape the perception of all literate societies in powerful if little-understood ways" (18). See Walter J. Ong, *Ramus, Method and the Decay of Dialogue* (Cambridge, MA: Harvard University Press, 1958) and *The Presence of the Word* (New Haven, CT: Yale University Press, 1970).

intended. Like Butler's musical bees, the effectiveness of Prospero's music is such that it seems to grow organically from its natural environment, and it is this characteristic that gives it its prophetic quality.

The Tempest proliferates a magical model of music in its frequent blurring of noise and meaning. Music in the play sounds from different locations on and around the stage, visibly and invisibly, from mortal and immortal beings, in verbal and nonverbal settings, in sleeping and waking states. In a world where "all sounds suggest voices" and where sounds permeate every acoustic space, the boundaries between music, sound, and language quickly break down. At this point, Prospero's island begins to feel like the theater itself, and the question most often asked by the play's characters—What is this music?—becomes the audience's question as well. This conjunction of onstage and audience confusion is nowhere better demonstrated than in the murder-plot scene in act 2, in which a single musical performance is heard differently by each character and by the audience:

> Enter ARIEL, *with music and song*
> ARIEL. My master through his art foresees the danger
> That you his friend are in—and sends me forth,
> For else his project dies, to keep them living.
> *[He] sings in Gonzalo's ear*
> While you here do snoring lie,
> Open-eyed conspiracy
> His time doth take.
> If of life you keep a care,
> Shake off slumber, and beware.
> Awake, awake!
> ANTONIO. Then let us both be sudden.
> GONZALO. Now, good angels
> Preserve the King!
>
> (2.1.293–303)

What is this music heard by Shakespeare's audience, but not heard *as* music by the play's characters? Once awakened, Alonso admits to hearing "nothing" (309), while Gonzalo recalls only "a humming,/And that a strange one too" (313–14). What do they hear? Does Gonzalo hear the sense of Ariel's song, a warning against "open-eyed conspiracy"? Does he hear the nonverbal sound of the music, as a senseless "humming"? Sebastian is quick to identify the sound, though we are never told what he really hears: "Even now we heard a hollow burst of bellowing,/Like bulls, or rather lions. Did't not wake you?/It struck mine ear most terribly" (307–9). Shakespeare's audience will recognize these statements as false: there are no bellowing bulls or lions. Yet Sebastian's instinct to contextualize the strange noise demonstrates the fact that power in *The Tempest* is often tantamount to the ability to turn music's promiscuity to one's advantage. Prospero, after all, has a vested interest in maintaining the gap between the meaning of Ariel's song and its actual aural reception. If Antonio or Gonzalo had fully understood Ariel's song, Prospero's plan would have failed. In this sense, the play frames the ambiguity and illegibility *that is the condition of music* as constitutive of Prospero's—and the dramatist's—power.

It is tempting to apply an Orphic reading to the *The Tempest* whenever characters hear music differently. Lorenzo's argument in *The Merchant of Venice* that "naught so stockish, hard, and full of rage/But music for the time doth change his nature" (5.1.80–81) is a very Orphic sentiment, articulating the Neoplatonic idea that the inability to be moved by harmonious music is a sign of moral degeneracy. This explanation seems to account for the different responses to Ariel's music in *The Tempest*. Sebastian and Antonio, intending murder, presumably hear no music while they are awake. Alonso, not quite a murderer, hears no music while he is asleep. Gonzalo, "honest" but compromised by his passivity, hears music only as an indistinct "humming." In this way, differences in moral stature correspond with differences in hearing. When Caliban first meets Stephano and Trinculo, he rejects as noisome their "scurvy" music (2.2.53). However, after getting drunk on Stephano's "celestial liquor" (2.2.109), he becomes a devoted listener of their crude, noisy drinking songs. Thus united, this trio of drunk, murderous musicians plays the role of Ovid's Bacchantes, who murder Orpheus in a drunken rage, while their earthy, raucous music becomes a perversion of the heavenly music of Prospero, the play's Orpheus figure and "musician-king."[35]

Despite the attractiveness of Orpheus as a model, however, the play's Ovidianism is much more complex in its relation to Neoplatonic ideas of music. Specifically, Shakespeare draws on Ovidian figures who have an ambiguous moral status in the Renaissance in order to complicate a conventional symbolic reading of Prospero's music. Two episodes merit special attention in this regard: Ariel's performance of music for Ferdinand in act 1, discussed above, and Prospero's recantation in act 5. First, Ferdinand's first words to Miranda have long been recognized as an echo of Virgil's Aeneas in book 1 of the *Aeneid*: "Most sure the goddess/On whom these airs attend" (1.2.425–26). Accordingly, Ferdinand's meeting with Miranda has been read as the first step

---

35. The phrase is from Wells, *Elizabethan Mythologies*, 63.

in the reestablishment of a legitimate political authority, modeled on Aeneas's reestablishment of Trojan rule in Italy.[36] However, Ferdinand's reaction to Ariel's music a few lines earlier suggests Circean music:

> This music crept by me upon the waters,
> Allaying both their fury and my passion
> With its sweet air. Thence I have followed it—
> Or it hath drawn me rather.
>
> (1.2.395–98)

Like his problematic literary ancestor, Ferdinand is remarkably susceptible to feminine charms. His sensual description of music's "sweetness" and the passivity suggested in his parenthetical remark are closer to representations of Circean music in Ovid, Ariosto, and Spenser than to accounts of Orpheus. (This Circean undertone is confirmed by Milton's imitation of this scene in *Comus*, which I discuss at length in chapter 6.) Thus Shakespeare's habitual contamination of Virgil with Ovid occurs here in tandem with a Circean contamination of the Neoplatonic Orpheus—and of Virgil's Neptune, who calms the seas in the opening of the *Aeneid*.

The disorienting effects of Prospero's music also suggest another Ovidian, Circean model, which has seldom been recognized as a source for the play. In book 14 of the *Metamorphoses*, Ovid introduces the figure of Canens (literally, "one who sings") in terms that recall Orpheus: "She used to move woods and rocks, soften wild beasts, stop the long rivers with her singing, and stay the wandering birds" (*silvas et saxa movere/ et mulcere feras et flumina longa morari/ ore suo volucresque vagas retinere solebat,* 14.338–40). Circe conceives a passion for Picus, betrothed to Canens, and with her "magic song" (*carmine cantato,* 369) disorients and scatters Picus's attendants. Through her music, the heavens are darkened, thick fogs spring from the ground, and the wandering Picus is left alone to face Circe. Picus rebuffs her, so Circe transforms him into a picus bird. Her music becomes a loud, harrowing noise that continues to terrify Picus's men:

> The stones also seemed to voice hoarse bellowings; the baying of dogs was heard, the ground was foul with dark, crawling things, and the thin shades of the silent dead seemed to be flitting about. The astounded crowd quaked at the monstrous sights and sounds.

---

36. See James, *Shakespeare's Troy,* 189–221.

et lapides visi mugitus edere raucos
et latrare canes et humus serpentibus atris
squalere et tenues animae volitare silentum:
attonitum monstris vulgus pavet.
(14.409–12)

Stormy skies, misty fogs, baying dogs, airy spirits, wandering statesmen, disorienting sound: Ovid's episode catalogs the effects of Prospero's music. Ovid points up the anti-Orphic bent of Circe's music by making the entire scene take place while Canens is singing. Like the Bacchantes' noisy shrieking, the sheer sound of Circe's music overwhelms the Orphic voice, and, like Orpheus's dismembered head, Canens exits the poem singing a dying lament. By modeling Prospero's magic on Circe's music and evoking a Virgilian context—Picus is retrospectively another epic wanderer, one who cannot resist feminine power—Shakespeare creates a network of associations that severely problematize an Orphic reading of Prospero, rendering the meaning of his "heavenly music" profoundly ambiguous.[37]

Shakespeare also draws on Ovid's Medea to represent Prospero's magic. Prospero's incantation in the play's last act has long been recognized as an imitation of Golding's translation of the *Metamorphoses:* "Ye Charmes and Witchcrafts, and thou Earth which both with herbe and weed...ye Elves of Hilles, of Brookes, of Woods alone,/Of standing Lakes" (*Ovid's Metamorphoses,* 7.263–65). Although Shakespeare omits the references to witchcraft, Prospero's language is clearly inspired by Medea's: "Ye elves of hills, brooks, standing lakes and groves,/And ye that on the sands with printless foot/Do chase the ebbing Neptune" (5.1.33–35). Jonathan Bate argues that this imitation prompts Shakespeare's audience to recognize that Prospero's magic "is, for all its apparent whiteness, the selfsame black magic as that of Medea," thus morally tainting the play's representation of magic and problematizing the reading of Prospero's art as redemptive.[38] While Prospero's kinship with

---

37. Although Jonathan Bate notes the relevance of Ovid's Circe to other parts of the play, he does not mention the Picus episode. The allusion would seem to bolster Bate's point that allusions to Aeneas in *The Tempest* pertain more to the "metamorphic" episodes in the *Aeneid,* which Ovid dwells on and which include the digression on Picus in the *Metamorphoses.* See Jonathan Bate, *Shakespeare and Ovid* (Oxford: Oxford University Press, 1993), 243–46. The idea that Circe is more Homeric than Ovidian may partly account for her absence in studies of the play's Ovidianism. Leonard Barkan, for example, refers to Circe as an "un-Ovidian myth of transformation." *The Gods Made Flesh: Metamorphosis and the Pursuit of Paganism* (London: Yale University Press, 1986), 273.

38. Bate, *Shakespeare and Ovid,* 252. Other readers, however, argue that the allusion to Medea doesn't morally inflect Prospero's "white magic." See *The Tempest,* ed. Frank Kermode (London: Arden, 1954), 149; Barbara Howard Traister, *Heavenly Necromancers: The Magician in English Renaissance*

CHAPTER 4

Medea has been much debated, less notice has been given to his invocation of music at the end of this speech, an element not found in Medea's incantation:

> But this rough magic
> I here abjure. And when I have required
> Some heavenly music—which even now I do—
> To work mine end upon their senses that
> This airy charm is for, I'll break my staff,
> Bury it certain fathoms in the earth,
> And deeper than did ever plummet sound
> I'll drown my book. *Solemn music.*
> (5.1.50–57)

Prospero's reference to "heavenly music" directly suggests *musica mundana,* and it evokes the Neoplatonic idea of cosmological harmony. Yet we might be wary of ascribing an Orphic meaning too easily in a scene that is so heavily contextualized through Ovid's Medea. In the same passage, Prospero describes his music as an "airy charm," using a word whose Latin cognate (*carmen*) Ovid repeatedly uses for Medea and Circe, and almost never for Orpheus.

The rest of Prospero's recantation is full of musical "puns": plucked, grave, rough, air, staff, deep, sound. In this way the speech plays on the indefiniteness between music and language that characterizes Prospero's magic. The precariousness of the ties between music and words, and the instability of musical meaning, approach a breaking point in the wedding masque that Prospero stages in act 4. In chapter 6, I show how Milton locates the hermeneutic instability of the court masque in its dependence on musical symbolism and Ovidian typology. In *The Tempest,* Shakespeare also uses the masque to demonstrate the slipperiness of music and Ovidian allegory, but he levels a more sweeping blow at Neoplatonic symbolism itself, which he portrays as theatrically constructed. For example, Shakespeare suggests the Neoplatonic program of Prospero's masque at the same time that he shows its dependence on performance in the stage direction that ends the masque: "*Enter certain reapers, properly habited. They join with the nymphs in a graceful dance; towards the end whereof* PROSPERO *starts suddenly and speaks; after which, to a strange hollow and confused noise, they heavily vanish*" (4.1.138 s.d.). Conventionally, the

---

Drama (Columbia: University of Missouri Press, 1984); John S. Mebane, *Renaissance Magic and the Return of the Golden Age: The Occult Tradition and Marlowe, Jonson, and Shakespeare* (Lincoln: University of Nebraska Press, 1989).

"graceful dance" of the nymphs should symbolize the restoration of social and political harmony that Prospero wants to associate with the marriage of Miranda and Ferdinand, but the performance of this message is disrupted by the real fact of political rebellion: "I had forgot that foul conspiracy/Of the beast Caliban and his confederates" (139–40). The flimsiness of the masque may render it futile or trifling, as some readers have suggested.[39] Yet Prospero is quick even to moralize its sudden disruption, which he uses to articulate a Neoplatonic vision of change:

> Our revels now are ended. These our actors,
> As I foretold you, were all spirits, and
> Are melted into air, into thin air;
> And like the baseless fabric of this vision,
> The cloud-capped towers, the gorgeous palaces,
> The solemn temples, the great globe itself,
> Yea, all which it inherit, shall dissolve;
> And, like this insubstantial pageant faded,
> Leave not a rack behind.
>
> (148–56)

Rather than subvert the performative aspect of the masque to its poetic text (as someone like Ben Jonson would be inclined to do), he allegorizes the "confused noise" of his masque's disintegration, thus preserving a symbolic pattern of harmony and noise that many of the play's readers have identified with *The Tempest* itself.[40] In this respect, Prospero reveals the extent to which Neoplatonism crucially depends on its ability to fashion to its advantage the gap between performance and text, between musical sound and musical meaning—in effect, to make this gap into a sign of its explanatory power rather than its weakness.

Prospero's moralization also reminds his audience of one of the central aims of the court masque, and of speculative music: to instruct.[41] Just as

---

39. For example, see Robert Egan, *Drama within Drama: Shakespeare's Sense of His Art* (New York: Columbia University Press, 1975), 108–10; David Lindley, "Music, Masque and Meaning in *The Tempest*," in *The Court Masque*, ed. David Lindley, 47–59 (Manchester: Manchester University Press, 1984).

40. For Jonson's approach to music in the masque, see Mary Chan, *Music in the Theatre of Ben Jonson* (Oxford: Oxford University Press, 1980). Jonson's ambivalence toward dramatic performance is well-known. See Jonas Barish, *The Antitheatrical Prejudice* (Berkeley: University of California Press, 1981), 132–54.

41. The masque's reliance on Neoplatonic ideas and speculative music, as well as its reputation as a form of instruction, is nicely outlined in Peter Walls, *Music in the English Courtly Masque, 1604–1640* (Oxford: Clarendon, 1996), 7–14.

he designs his masque as a lesson on sexual and social self-regulation for Miranda and Ferdinand, consonant with his political ideology, early modern *musica speculativa* represents its subject as a lesson in political and religious universalism. In Sir Thomas Browne's words, music is "an Hieroglyphical and shadowed lesson of the whole World, and creatures of God."[42] Given the centrality of instruction in *musica speculativa,* it is not surprising that Prospero's masque is disrupted by his most recalcitrant student. Initially, Caliban seems to be an ideal candidate for the civilizing power of music: in Lorenzo's words, a "savage" ready to be tamed and made "modest" by music's "sweet power." However, through Caliban, Shakespeare turns the Orphic model inside out. Although music clearly "moves" Caliban, it does not make him a better political subject:

> Be not afeard. The isle is full of noises,
> Sounds, and sweet airs, that give delight and hurt not.
> Sometimes a thousand twangling instruments
> Will hum about mine ears, and sometimes voices
> That if I then had waked after long sleep
> Will make me sleep again; and then in dreaming
> The clouds methought would open and show riches
> Ready to drop upon me, that when I waked
> I cried to dream again.
>
> (3.2.130–38)

The passage is striking. Instead of bringing Caliban into harmony with Prospero's government, music inspires in him fantasies of power. Caliban's response may be a perversion of the Orphic model, but its rhetorical power is as compelling as any other description of music in the play.[43] More importantly, Caliban's description of the island's acoustic world does not draw a distinction between music, language, and natural sound. His speech is partly modeled on Ovid's Ariadne, who in the *Heroides* also half sleeps on an island permeated with natural and human sounds, some of them perceived as musical.[44] Unlike

---

42. Sir Thomas Browne, *Religio Medici* (1642), vol. 1 of *The Works of Sir Thomas Brown,* ed. Geoffrey Keynes (Chicago: University of Chicago Press, 1964), 88.

43. Bate suggests that Caliban may be modeled in part on Ovid's Polyphemus in book 13 of the *Metamorphoses,* another savage creature who has the ability to describe nature through beautiful poetry (*Shakespeare and Ovid,* 247–48). In a quite different manner, Annabel Patterson suggests that the eloquence of Caliban's response is evidence of Shakespeare's preference for "popular" egalitarian politics over monarchial rule. See *Shakespeare and the Popular Voice* (Oxford: Blackwell, 1989), 155.

44. Cf. Ovid, *The Heroides,* trans. Grant Showerman (Cambridge, MA: Harvard University Press, 1977): " 'Twas the time when the earth is first besprinkled with crystal rime, and songsters hid in the

Ariadne, however, and unlike his Italian companions, Caliban recognizes the confusion of natural and musical sound as a source of pleasure rather than fear, and his expression of this pleasure marks him with a radical subjectivity unmatched by any other character in the play. In this way Caliban joins a small group of musical "dissidents" in Shakespeare—Hippolyta, Jessica, Ophelia—whose experience of music falls outside of the prescribed effects normally described in orthodox music theory and outside of the larger symbolic patterns of the plays in which they appear. Put simply, their habits of musical listening do nothing to bolster the music of the spheres.

Caliban's appropriation of music for his own pleasure demonstrates the mutual dependence of musical and colonial readings of the play, which have traditionally been represented as mutually exclusive.[45] Prospero may not have supreme control over music's production, but he is an expert colonizer of its meaning. At the same time, the precariousness of Prospero's empire of the ear reminds us of the vexed relationship between Neoplatonic theories of harmony and musical sound in early modern England. This conflict puts a different slant on scholarly attempts to pin down the actual musical settings for the play's many songs. For example, in their discussions of "Full Fathom Five," Howell Chickering and Jacquelyn Fox-Good each scrutinize the available contemporary setting by Robert Johnson, coming to different conclusions about whether the song melodically or harmonically expresses the idea of continual transformation.[46] While their readings shed light on Johnson's compositional practice and its subtle effects on a modern audience, arguments about melodic and harmonic signification are something of a bun fight when compared with the play's larger struggles over musical meaning. Prospero's musical power does not stem from his manipulation of harmonic or numerical figures—even though he may claim to do so. His power derives more substantially on his ability to control the context through which music is interpreted in the first place. In this way, Prospero's "project" (epilogue, 12)

---

branch begin their plaint. Half waking only and languid from sleep, I turned upon my side and put forth hands to clasp my Theseus" (10.7–10). Ovid's word for the sound of the birds, *queror,* can mean both a complaint and a musical warble; Showerman wisely splits this into "songsters" and "plaint." As so often in Ovid's poetry, the meaning of a word is transformed before our eyes: as Ariadne gradually wakes up, the meaning of *queror* shifts from the innocent music of the birds to the complaint she will deliver against Theseus.

45. Lindley also sees the critical debate over the play as mirroring a musical conflict in the play, although he identifies the conflict as a "transition" between symbolic and rhetorical interpretations of music in seventeenth-century England (*Shakespeare and Music,* 228).

46. Howell Chickering, "Hearing Ariel's Songs," *Journal of Medieval and Renaissance Studies* 24 (1994): 131–72, and Jacquelyn Fox-Good, "Other Voices: The Sweet, Dangerous Air(s) of Shakespeare's *Tempest,*" *Shakespeare Studies* 24 (1996): 241–74.

mirrors the project of *musica speculativa,* which not only addresses the quantitative and philosophical bases of music but also institutionalizes a site of instruction—usually, but not always, the printed book—in which music, if it is to be understood correctly, must be read.

The example of Prospero shows that the figure of Orpheus is important not only for what it says about music but for *how* it allows to music to say. The value of Neoplatonizing, universal representations of music is that they purport to delve into the most fundamental questions of acoustic experience, when in fact they transpose the discussion of music to a noiseless sphere of discourse where problems can be worked out in visual and linguistic terms. Indeed, the appeal of allegorical rhetoric can be gauged by its presence in the writing of someone openly contemptuous of *musica speculativa.* In his *Sylva sylvarum,* Francis Bacon asserts that the "cause" of musical sympathy "is dark, and hath not been rendered by any; and therefore would be better contemplated." Referring to numerical relationships between musical notes, Bacon writes that "the just and measured proportion of the air percussed, towards the baseness or trebleness of tones, is one of the greatest secrets in the contemplation of sounds."[47] Although we would be hard-pressed to find someone less congenial to Neoplatonic views of music than Bacon, his use of the Neoplatonic rhetoric of secrecy at key moments demonstrates its usefulness in bridging sensuous experience with the exactness of scientific explanation. Bacon's description of music's mysteriousness appears, not surprisingly, in the section of *Sylva sylvarum* in which he categorizes the different kinds of music and their effects in different nations. Thus, although Bacon grounds his claims about music in observable scientific experiments, his desire to demonstrate the universality of music's effects on its listeners makes the speculative rhetoric of the allegorists—especially their postulation of a "veiled" world—irresistible.[48]

---

47. Francis Bacon, *Sylva sylvarum; or, A Natural History in Ten Centuries* (1626), ed. J. Spedding et al. (London, 1857), vol. 2, experiments 103, 183.

48. Bacon's description of music in this part of the *Sylva* echoes his characterization of mythology in *De sapientia veterum,* which he also describes as "veiled" and "dark." The allegorical and speculative rhetoric in Bacon's writing should qualify Penelope Gouk's assertion that Bacon rejected the relationship between musical sounds and mathematical proportions. See "Music in Francis Bacon's Natural Philosophy," in *Francis Bacon: Terminologia e fortuna nel XVII secolo,* ed. Martha Fattori, 139–54 (Rome: Edizioni dell'Ateneo, 1985). See also Gouk, "Some English Theories of Hearing in the Seventeenth Century," in *The Second Sense: Studies in Hearing and Musical Judgment from Antiquity to the Seventeenth Century,* ed. Michael Fend, Charles Burnett, and Penelope Gouk (London: Warburg Institute, 1991), 98–99. On the role of rhetoric and mysticism in Bacon's writing, see also Lisa Jardine, *Francis Bacon: Discovery and the Art of Discourse* (Cambridge: Cambridge University Press, 1972); Paolo Rossi, *Francis Bacon: From Magic to Science,* trans. S. Rabinovitch (Chicago: University of Chicago Press,

IMPOLITIC NOISE 179

Bacon again broaches a mystifying, Neoplatonic rhetoric when he describes music in *The New Atlantis*. Here, he is more explicit about the ideological aspirations of his scientific research: "We represent and imitate all articulate sounds and letters, and the voices and notes of beasts and birds." This idea of a fully capable acoustic notational system vivifies the universalizing bent of *musica speculativa,* and it unleashes a fantasy of awesome power that sets as its goal "the knowledge of Causes, and secret motions of things; and the enlarging of the bounds of Human Empire, to the effecting of all things possible."[49] As his choice of words suggests, Bacon's project has political overtones, and his speculative rhetoric helps create the illusion—if not the fact—of the expansive reach of his natural philosophy. Speculative music's rhetoric of universality enables Bacon to carve a conceptual space in which sensuous experience, scientific experiment, individual subjectivity, and national interests all converge, thus making his paradoxical joining of Aristotelian acoustic theory with Platonic philosophy seem natural. In this chapter I have shown how Shakespeare repeatedly returns to the language of Neoplatonic music, both to demonstrate its political and ideological appropriation and to expose its limitations. The allegorization of music is not only a useful prop for Christian theology, conservative academic institutions, or entrepreneurial book publishers; it offers a powerful rhetorical tool with which to control music's promiscuity and make music emblematic of the political state itself. Moreover, in order to be politically effective, the relationship between sense experience and knowledge depends on a certain degree of mystification—a sense of mystery, as Susan Bruce has noted, "which Bensalem and the *New Atlantis* so studiously preserve."[50] In this context, the political capital of *musica speculativa* is clear. As a set of rhetorical strategies, it enables its proponents to situate the experience of musical sound *within a structure of power,* in which scientific experiment or any other textual model is understood as authoritative. The singular achievement of *musica speculativa* is its ability to take the illegibility—the "noise"—of musical sound and code it as a veil for its own meanings. If there is a "politics of music" in Renaissance England, whether theological, cultural, or textual, then it would seem to dictate, as Prospero and Bacon evidently realized, that music's noise must not only be controlled. It must also be made secret.

1968); D. P. Walker, "Francis Bacon and Spiritus," in *Science, Medicine and Society in the Renaissance,* ed. A. G. Debus, 2:121–30 (New York: Science History Publications, 1972).

49. Francis Bacon, *New Atlantis* (1627) in *Three Early Modern Utopias,* ed. Susan Bruce (Oxford: Oxford University Press, 1999), 177.

50. Ibid., xxxiv.

CHAPTER 5

Shakespeare's Idolatry
Psalms and Hornpipes in The Winter's Tale

> Recognizing idols for what they are does not break their enchantment.
>
> —W. H. Auden

Shakespeare's exposure of the interests propping up *musica speculativa* suggests the hollowness of universalizing notions of music. By repeatedly demonstrating that the Renaissance allegories of music and Ovid *are* allegories, in the service of specific political and cultural viewpoints, the plays and poems cultivate a profound skepticism about texts that profess to explain the true nature of music. At the same time, by emphasizing the fundamental disparity between musical sound and narratives of harmony, Shakespeare fuels the notion that listening to music is an essentially sensuous experience, ultimately dependent for its meaning on the whims and fancies of its human listeners. Insofar as Shakespeare prompts his audience to hear music apart from its sublimating contexts, he defines a model of acoustic experience that is independent of any moral or civic program. Musical sound, thus evacuated of Platonic moralizing, is hardly less than an idolatrous ravishment.

In this chapter I show how *The Winter's Tale* rehearses the early modern theology of iconoclasm, effectively stoking anxieties in Jacobean England that music had become an inappropriate object of mystical devotion. Even more than *The Tempest,* which is generally considered the most musical of Shakespeare's romances, *The Winter's Tale* intervenes in contemporary debates over the moral and theological status of music, images, and the theater. Criticism of the play since the late twentieth century has noted its engagement with Protestant ideology, particularly in the play's famous transformation scene, in which a painted statue is made the object of quasi-religious devotion. Huston Diehl, in a number of pieces on *The Winter's Tale* and the Reformation theater, argues that the play self-consciously "raises the specter of idolatry... in order to liberate theater from the charge it is idolatrous."[1] Diehl's suggestion of a "liberated" theater is a strong response to critics who suggest that the play, especially in its mysterious conclusion, stages and endorses the sacramental practices of the medieval church. However, in arguing for or against the idolatrous nature of Shakespeare's theater, readers of *The Winter's Tale,* including Diehl, construe the play's theological engagements almost exclusively in terms of the *image.* Consequently, the place of music in the debate over iconoclasm has been left out of the discussion. This is not a negligible omission, since, as I hope to show, the ambiguous representation of music in the play does not merely reflect or reproduce the problem of the idolatrous image. Rather, Shakespeare's use of music in *The Winter's Tale* renders indeterminate the boundary between idolatry and *all* sensory experience, regardless of its moral content.

Shakespeare's suggestion of an idolatrous theater in *The Winter's Tale* hinges on his use of "superstition," a word that appears only twice in the play and that punctuates two crucial moments of recognition: Antigonus's visionary dream of Hermione's ghost at the play's midpoint and Perdita's encounter with the statue in the final scene. In both cases, Shakespeare invites his audience to reflect on the credibility of the theatrical image by stressing its artificiality. In the first instance, the appearance of Hermione's ghost is rendered through a conspicuous narrative "set piece," while in the second instance the statue is presented as a freshly painted thing, "but newly fixed" (5.1.47). However, only in the statue scene does Shakespeare use a musical

---

1. Huston Diehl, "'Strike all that look upon with marvel': Theatrical and Theological Wonder in *The Winter's Tale,*" in *Rematerializing Shakespeare: Authority and Representation on the Early Modern English Stage,* ed. Bryan Reynolds and William N. West (New York: Palgrave, 2005), 21. See also Diehl's excellent work on the English Reformation theater in *Staging Reform, Reforming the Stage: Protestantism and Popular Theater in Early Modern England* (Ithaca, NY: Cornell University Press, 1997), especially 125–55. In an essay from 2008, Diehl argues that Paulina fulfills the role of a Pauline preacher, who uses both theatricality and incisive rhetoric to encourage conversion. See "'Does not the stone rebuke me?': The Pauline Rebuke and Paulina's Lawful Magic in *The Winter's Tale,*" in *Shakespeare and the Cultures of Performance,* ed. Paul Yachnin and Patricia Badir, 69–82 (Aldershot, UK: Ashgate, 2008). For other work on the play's response to Reformist ideology, see Michael O'Connell, *The Idolatrous Eye: Iconoclasm and Theater in Early Modern England* (Oxford: Oxford University Press, 2000), 138–42; T. G. Bishop, *Shakespeare and the Theatre of Wonder* (Cambridge: Cambridge University Press, 1996); Julia Reinhard Lupton, *Afterlives of the Saints: Hagiography, Typology, and Renaissance Literature* (Stanford: Stanford University Press, 1996).

performance to create the effect of a mystical metamorphosis—the play's theatrical coup de grâce:

> Music; awake her; Strike!
> 'Tis time. Descend. Be stone no more. Approach.
> Strike all that look upon with marvel.
> (5.3.98–100)

Here, Paulina's double use of "strike," first as musical command and second as a description of the statue's arresting presence, rhetorically conflates the musical and visual effects of the metamorphic moment. Ironically, the centrality of music in this scene has gone largely unremarked by critics of the play's iconoclasm, despite the fact that this music is the crowning gesture in Paulina's theatrical production—and despite the fact that it evokes a model of natural magic that would have hardly been uncontroversial. Conversely, readers of the play who take notice of the music in the final scene generally ascribe to it a symbolic meaning. Northrop Frye, in a well-known essay on the play's symbolic structure, reads the music of the final scene as a symbol for human nature before the Fall. For Frye, the scene's music serves to identify the statue's metamorphosis as an allegory for divine will, identified in the play with the god Apollo.[2] In similar fashion, most studies of the play, even those that examine its political and theological resonances, generally retain Frye's symbolic reading of the play's music. Stephen Orgel, for example, suggests that the play's musical resurrection "sound[s] much more like Renaissance apologias for theatre than like any version of religious experience."[3] In these cases, the idea of a sublimating music helps insulate the play's conclusion—and its overt theatricality—from any serious entanglement with theological controversy.

Yet as we have seen in the preceding chapters, music in Shakespeare rarely functions as straightforward symbol. The Neoplatonic notion of music as divine harmony is countered, if not actually overpowered, by the

---

2. Northrop Frye, "Recognition in *The Winter's Tale*," in *Fables of Identity* (New York: Harcourt, 1963), 110, 117. The tendency to read music in these plays in terms of a Neoplatonic symbolism has been particularly enduring. See J. M. Nosworthy, "Music and Its Function in the Romances of Shakespeare," *Shakespeare Survey* 11 (1958): 60–69; Mary Chan, *Music in the Theatre of Ben Jonson* (Oxford: Clarendon, 1980), 317–18; David Armitage, "The Dismemberment of Orpheus: Mythic Elements in Shakespeare's Romances," *Shakespeare Survey* 39 (1986): 123–33.

3. *The Winter's Tale,* ed. Stephen Orgel (Oxford: Oxford University Press, 1996), 260. By suggesting that Paulina's claim focuses on the "therapeutic quality" of music, Orgel identifies orthodox *musica humana*—particularly as represented by writers like Thomas Wright and Burton—as the most natural context for interpreting the play's music.

play's frequent representation of music as sensuous artifice. In this way, the questionable status of music in the play resembles the moral ambiguity of Ovid's Pygmalion as a figure for the play's regenerative conclusion. As Mary Ellen Lamb has shown, the contrary perceptions of Ovid in the Renaissance as moral allegory or immoral eroticism are intensified in the case of Pygmalion, who "represented both transcendent myth and smutty joke" for many early modern readers.[4] For Lamb, the idea of a degenerate Ovidianism in *The Winter's Tale* is exemplified by Autolycus, the ballad-peddling rogue whom Shakespeare derives from book 11 of the *Metamorphoses*. At the same time, Autolycus's immediate effect in the play is to encourage an exceptionally idolatrous attitude toward music: his ballads are bawdy, morally barren, and received with near-hysterical devotion. Thus, *as* musician, Autolycus is an ideal lightning rod for Puritan critiques of art. To the extent that Autolycus's musical performances in the play's pastoral scene contaminate Paulina's musical spell in the finale—and I will suggest that they do—Shakespeare fractures his play's aesthetic economy and plants the seeds for a morally ambivalent reception of the play by his own audience. As in *The Tempest,* Shakespeare constructs the play's fissures precisely around the audience's relationship to musical sound, so that an interrogation of music's meaning makes problematic any authoritative reading of the play's iconoclasm. However, in contrast to the earlier works, *The Winter's Tale* reenvisions the noncongruity between music and language as a source of power rather than crisis. Shakespeare sustains the conflict between music and language, along with the conflict between different Renaissance Ovids, in order to derive a new kind of theatrical pleasure that is not reducible to Neoplatonic precepts. Music's inscrutability, Shakespeare seems to suggest, is not a cipher for something mysterious, but something to be enjoyed on its own terms. In this way, Shakespeare's dual use of iconoclastic and Ovidian rhetoric in *The Winter's Tale* works to reimagine *as productive* the gap between music and language, but it does not dispel, interpret, or sublimate that gap.

---

4. Mary Ellen Lamb, "Ovid and *The Winter's Tale:* Conflicting Views toward Art," in *Shakespeare and Dramatic Tradition: Essays in Honor of S. F. Johnson,* ed. W. R. Elton and W. B. Long (Newark: University of Delaware Press, 1989), 73. Lamb offers a persuasive account of the contrasting readings of Ovid's Pygmalion in the Renaissance, especially the moralizing interpretations of Renaissance mythographers and the eroticizing interpretations of antitheatrical polemicists. Her argument, which aligns the two Renaissance readings of Ovid with the two kinds of art practiced by Paulina and Autolycus, has richly informed my own reading of the play. My difference with her essay, on the extent to which Paulina's and Autolycus's art can be distinguished from each other, is discussed at length below.

Musical Idolatry, 1601–11

There is perhaps no better demonstration of music as idolatrous ravishment in Jacobean England than the case of John Bull. While taking an extended leave of absence from his duties as music professor at Gresham College in 1602, the virtuosic composer and organist took the opportunity to travel abroad:

> Dr. Bull took occasion to go incognito into France and Germany. At length hearing of a famous musician belonging to a certain cathedral... he applied himself as a novice to him, to learn something of his faculty, and to see and admire his works. This musician, after some discourse had passed between them, conducted Bull to a vestry, or music school, joyning to the cathedral, and shew'd to him a lesson or song of forty parts, and then made a vaunting challenge to any person in the world to add one more part to them; supposing it to be so compleat and full, that it was impossible for any mortal man to correct, or add to it. Bull thereupon desiring the use of ink and rul'd paper (such as we call musical paper) prayed the musician to lock him up in the said school for two or three hours; which being done, not without great disdain by the musician, Bull in that time, or less, added forty more parts to the said lesson or song. The musician thereupon being called in, he viewed it, tried it, and retry'd it. At length he burst out into a great ecstasy, and swore by the great God, that *he, that added those forty parts, must either be the devil, or Dr. Bull, etc.* Whereupon Bull making himself known, the musician fell down and ador'd him.[5]

This apocryphal anecdote first appears in print in Anthony Wood's *Fasti Oxonienses* (1690) and, despite its dubious origins, was canonized fifty years later in John Ward's massive book on the Gresham faculty. Although no record of the story appears until several years after Bull's death, it illustrates the iconic status that Bull enjoyed during his lifetime. Bull's reputation as an organist of remarkable ability began to take shape in 1586, when he became a gentleman of the Chapel Royal and made a favorable impression on the archbishop of Canterbury. By 1596 he was making regular use of the title "Dr. John Bull, Organist of Her Majesty's Chapel." As noted earlier, it was a mark of Bull's favored status under Queen Elizabeth that, when he was appointed to the

---

5. John Ward, *Lives of the Professors of Gresham College* (London, 1740), 200.

Gresham professorship, he received special permission from the queen to give his lectures in English only; the other professors were required by statute to lecture in English and Latin. Bull's reputation reached its high point in 1613 with the publication of *Parthenia,* which Janet Pollack has called "the most important of all early publications of English keyboard music." In this volume, the commendatory poem by George Chapman identifies Bull, along with William Byrd and Orlando Gibbons, as the most important—and the most English—of the nation's composers.[6]

Despite his enormous popularity in England and abroad, Bull did not lack detractors. We have already seen John Taverner's systematic attempt to discredit Bull's qualifications as an instructor of speculative music, after Taverner himself assumed the post of Gresham music professor in 1609. At the same time, Bull's reputation as a composer did not go unchallenged. John Ward notes that the story of Bull's messianic appearance at St. Omer's Cathedral (a location that itself might have suggested Catholic sympathies) was discredited almost as soon as it was heard: "That part of the story relating to the *forty parts,* said to have been added by Dr. Bull in *two or three hours,* has been rejected by our best artists in music, as a thing wholly improbable. And the account they give of it, as handed down to them by tradition, is this; that the lesson or song, when delivered to the doctor, consisted of *sixteen parts,* to which he added *four others.*"[7] This "correction" is as telling as the story itself, since a twenty-part song would hardly have been remarkable when compared to other polyphonic works of the period; the revised story appears to be an attempt to diminish the reputation of Bull's virtuosity altogether. Bull's successor at Gresham College, John Taverner, lobbed a more incisive attack on Bull's talent by disparaging musicians whose fame rested on "industry," a phrase that would have likely evoked the memory of Bull's compositional skills. In this vein, Taverner openly criticized the state of contemporary English music:

[We content] our selves for the most part with any ordinary stuff, which when it is the best is but some light ayre, commonly without either conceit or life or almost shadow of any true and natural passion; only laboring a kind of fruitless curiosity in making diverse parts

---

6. See Janet Pollack, "A Reevaluation of *Parthenia* and Its Context" (PhD diss., Duke University, 2001). Bull was also included in John Case's *Apologia* (1588) in a short list of England's greatest musicians.
7. Ward, *Lives of the Professors,* 200.

answerable one to the other, whenas indeed none of them answer the Argument which should be their chief ground. And so they only fill the ear without ever delighting the mind.[8]

Taverner's jab at "light ayres" may be a response to the growing popularity of English songbooks in Jacobean England, such as Dowland's, yet his references to "fruitless curiosity" and "diverse parts" suggest more directly Bull himself, who would have been well-known to Taverner's audience for his skill in polyphonic composition ("making diverse parts answerable one to the other").

It should not be surprising that Bull's musicianship was occasionally challenged, given the long-standing suspicion of polyphonic music among Reformist writers. In fact, antipathy toward Bull in the seventeenth century often appears—when it does appear—as an expression of Protestant iconoclasm. At the end of one of his lectures, after describing the effects of "heavenly musicke," Taverner inserts an uncharacteristic digression on the Reformist debate over church music:

> Some might object, that this use of musicke in divine service was a thing onely used among Heathen nations and therefore... still heathenish, Whereas indeed though the Pagans did generally use itt in their ceremonies, yet heere in allsoe the Divell, whoe as one saith, is Gods ape, in his impious & presumptuous imitating of divers thinges which belong properly to the true God, did craftily abuse them, prophanely mixing musicke & other divine rites in his diabolicall ~~superstition~~ idolatry.[9]

Taverner's criticism of contemporary English music as idolatrous is typical of Reformist attacks on music. Although he goes on to reject the idea that all music should be removed from the church, his implication is clear: there are some who, like the devil or "God's ape," compose music that is not an earthly reflection of divine harmony but a demonic perversion of it. By contrast, a more generous allusion to Bull in Jacobean England may be found in Samuel Rowley's *When You See Me, You Know Me,* first performed in 1604. Here,

---

8. John Taverner, lectures 2 and 8a, Gresham College Music Lectures, 1610, Sloane Manuscript 2329, British Library, London.

9. Taverner, Gresham College Music Lectures, lecture 7. I have reproduced the manuscript correction made in the text, as evidence of the fact that the two terms were interchangeable for Taverner. The emendation is one of several in the manuscript, which may have been in the process of being prepared for publication.

Rowley gives considerable attention to the historical figure of Christopher Tye, the sixteenth-century composer whom the play represents as an unusually skillful musician:

> Doctor, I thanke you and commend your cunning,
> I oft haue heard my Father merrily speake,
> In your hye praise, and thus his Highnesse sayth,
> England, one God, one truth, one Doctor hath
> For Musicks Art, and that is Doctor *Tye,*
> Admir'd for skill in Musickes harmonie.[10]

Rowley's description of Tye's "cunning" and "skill" echoes contemporary references to Bull, though without Taverner's negative remarks. Moreover, Rowley makes a point of contextualizing his praise of Tye, who was thought to have been Prince Edward's music tutor, within contemporary debates over music. In the play, Edward tells Tye: "Truely I love it [music] yet there are a sort/Seeming more pure than wise, that will upbrayd at it,/ Calling it idle, vaine, and frivolous" (2036–38). This reference to "a sort...that will upbrayd" music is more appropriate to Bull than to Tye, since Reformist polemic on music had not yet taken this shape in the 1540s. (Also, Bull had been identified as a music tutor to Princess Elizabeth, and possibly the late Prince Henry, in the dedication to *Parthenia*.) In this way, the passage in *When You See Me*—unique in the play for its seeming irrelevance to the plot—betrays a topical allusiveness that seems to speak concernedly to theological issues that would understandably have attended James's accession to the throne.

What begins to emerge from these early Jacobean references to music are two very different conceptions of Bull that correspond to a broader contemporary debate over music: on the one hand, a national musical icon, worthy of being grouped with William Byrd and Orlando Gibbons by the compiler of *Parthenia,* and on the other, a musical charlatan, whose compositions are without substance and who performs his greatest feats behind locked doors. Clearly Bull was a convenient lightning rod for debates about music's idolatrous nature, especially when these debates intensified. Less expected is the degree to which Bull himself, whether intentionally or not, *encouraged* the perception of his work as idolatrous. For example, Christopher Field, in an excellent essay on Renaissance compositional practices, notes that Bull was distinctive among English composers for his habit of exploring harmonic

---

10. Samuel Rowley, *When You See Me, You Know Me* (1605), ed. F. P. Wilson (London: Malone Society, 1952), 2081–86.

progressions that had been thought to be theoretical possibilities, not practical ones.[11] One of Bull's keyboard works, which Field suggests may have been presented at one of Bull's lectures at Gresham College, is composed so that it progresses through the entire circle of fifths, including all twelve hexachord classes; Renaissance musical practice only considered three of the hexachords to be practically feasible, with the other nine being placed in the realm of *musica ficta,* or "feigned music." Thus, one of the effects of this harmonic experiment is a glaring affront to the conventional distinction between speculative music and practical music, especially as it is visually represented on the page. In fact, the transgressive nature of the piece has led some scholars to question whether it was intended for performance at all (although Field argues persuasively that it was). For a contemporary of Bull's, the problem may have been understood somewhat differently: by blurring the distinction between speculative and actual music, Bull was arguably attempting to disrupt the boundary between the abstract music that was the provenance of the heavens (and the exposition of which was the provenance of someone like Taverner) and his own, humanly composed *and performed* music.

The experimental, mystical nature of Bull's hexachord composition is a quality which one finds often in his work. In her authoritative study of *Parthenia,* Janet Pollack points out the conspicuous references to emblems and "hieroglyphicks" in the dedication, which, along with the work's many allusions to historical and literary events, imbue the collection with a teasingly mysterious significance.[12] Another sign of Bull's ambiguous reputation as national icon and mystical figure may be found in the portrait which hangs in the Faculty of Music at Oxford, produced in 1589 and generally considered to be the only extant authentic portrait of Bull. The portrait contains a number of curiosities, the most striking of which is a depiction of a skull, crossbones, and hourglass in the portrait's top right corner; the image has generally been interpreted as a reference to Bull's involvement in the hermetic sciences.[13] The most compelling example of Bull's tendency toward mystical self-representation is a set of compositions found in a thin manuscript volume in the British Library. In one of these compositions, "Sphera mundi," which appears to have been intended for *some* kind of performance, a speculative and celestial meaning is openly suggested. For example, the unexplained

---

11. Christopher D. S. Field, "Jenkins and the Cosmography of Harmony," in *John Jenkins and His Time: Studies in English Consort Music,* ed. Andrew Ashbee and Peter Holman, 1–74 (Oxford: Clarendon Press, 1996).

12. Pollack, "Reevaluation of *Parthenia.*"

13. *New Grove Dictionary of Music and Musicians,* ed. Stanley Sadie (London: Macmillan, 1980), s.v. "John Bull."

inscription on the left side of the score, "Firmamentem Cæli," evokes the typical, allegorizing representations of music as celestial harmony.[14] Moreover, the score itself is composed as a visual emblem, self-consciously staging its importance as a mystical, inscrutable work. Many of the other compositions in the manuscript are also presented through visually intricate scores, some of them even more elaborate than "Sphera mundi." In this respect, Bull's musical innovativeness, as it is showcased in the manuscript, appears to be as much a function of emblematic mysticism as it is a demonstration of compositional originality. While Bull's unique virtuosity as a performer and composer established his reputation as an English musical icon, his particular method of musical composition invites his audience to apprehend his music *as* icon—as visual image, with all of the attendant mystical and sensuous qualities that would encourage its interpretation as an object of idolatrous devotion.

Bull's musicianship, as it was constructed both by himself and his audiences in the seventeenth century, bears much in common with Paulina's theatrical artistry in the final scene of *The Winter's Tale,* not only in its eerie deployment of synesthesia, but also in the way its heavy-handed mysticism provokes an iconoclastic response among Reformist ideologues. Thus, by attending to the most controversial aspects of Bull's self-presentation around this time, we are in a better position to see how far Shakespeare brings his final scene into dangerous territory. After all, Paulina does not merely tempt her audience to regard a statue as an object of devotion. Like the apocryphal Bull at St. Omer's, she stages in a "chapel" a mysterious, musical performance that ends with a rapturous scene of recognition. At the same time, as I will show in the following pages, Paulina's musical spell is only the climax of a series of moments in *The Winter's Tale* that encourages the audience to view the play in iconoclastic terms. The play's deployment of ghosts, moving statues, and "winter's tales" makes a strong appeal to the audience's imagination, but it does so in a way that exposes the audience's credibility in the theater as essentially superstitious and fallible. In the chapter's final section, I go on to discuss the many associative links between Autolycus's and Paulina's music—some of which will be more apparent after the preceding discussion—to show how Shakespeare collapses the distinction between virtuosity and profanity. Just as the fabled musician at St. Omer's delivers both a rapturous account of Bull's virtuosity and a possible indictment of his transgressiveness, so does *The Winter's Tale* muddy the distinction between its two principal theatricalists. Although Huston Diehl suggests that Shakespeare would presumably have

---

14. British Library Royal Manuscript 24.f.25, 6r.

wanted to distance himself from the painter Giulio Romano, "a sixteenth-century Italian artist whose name links him to Rome and whose reputation was based on his daring ambition to rival God's own artistry,"[15] it is the specter of a musical magician that haunts both the play's pastoral episode and the final transformation scene, ultimately deferring a conclusive distinction between idolatry and faith.

Pauline Iconoclasm and Ovidian Heresy

At the beginning of act 5, shortly before unveiling the statue of Hermione, Paulina extracts a promise from Leontes to defer to herself the choice of a second wife, if any:

> She shall not be so young
> As was your former, but she shall be such
> As, walked your first queen's ghost, it should take joy
> To see her in your arms.
> (5.1.78–81)

Paulina's instructions are strongly opposed by Leontes' advisors, who are anxious about a crisis of succession. Paulina manages to persuade, in part by stoking Leontes' guilt, but also by conjuring a ghostly image of Hermione that appeals to both eyes and ears:

> Were I the ghost that walked I'd bid you mark
> Her eye, and tell me for what dull part in't
> You chose her. Then I'd shriek that even your ears
> Should rift to hear me.
> (63–66)

Prefiguring the scene of the statue's transformation, Paulina animates her own imagined ghost by a crafty act of ventriloquism ("Were *I* the ghost... *I'd* bid you"). The affective power of this speaking image profoundly influences Leontes, who had already begun to conceive of Hermione in remarkably theatrical terms:

> No more such wives, therefore no wife. One worse,
> And better used, would make her sainted spirit

---

15. Diehl, "'Strike all that look upon with marvel,'" 26–27.

Again possess her corpse, and on this stage,
Where we offenders mourn, appear soul-vexed,
And begin, 'Why to me?'

(56–60)

Here, the evocation of "the stage" coincides with a highly suspect image of sainthood, effectively suggesting a collaboration between the theater and idolatrous practices. In this way, the play suggests that Paulina's persuasive power over Leontes hinges on her ability to spur his superstitious imagination. At the same time, the play makes clear to its own audience the fatuousness of Paulina's rhetoric of ghostly possession by associating it with a belief the audience knows to be false, at least in part: Paulina swears that Antigonus did "perish with the infant" (44), and so the discovery of an heir would be as "monstrous" (41) as a ghost. In this way, the scene dramatizes the suasive power of ghostly images while prodding the audience to recognize, with an iconoclastic sensibility, the spuriousness of these imagined scenarios.

Paulina's conspicuous use of ghostly images in her injunction to Leontes problematizes the suggestion that she is the play's "Pauline" lecturer, since a truly Pauline figure would be expected to remove the veil from superstitious practices. On the one hand, as Diehl has argued, Paulina's careful manipulation of Leontes' reaction to the imagined ghost of Hermione—and, later, to the statue itself—might be interpreted as an intricate lesson to Shakespeare's audience on how to discriminate between legitimate and idolatrous habits of belief.[16] On the other, the play strains against its own revelations of "true" and "false" images. Rather than assuming a simple didactic role, the play puts its audiences in a compromised position by encouraging them to act superstitiously. For example, although Paulina's representation of Hermione's ghost may anticipate the play's final scene, it also evokes a comparison with her husband's ghostly encounter in act 3. The first appearance of Hermione's ghost in the play is described by Antigonus in terms that suggest the collusion of theatrical and idolatrous practices:

Come, poor babe.
I have heard, but not believed, the spirits o'th' dead
May walk again. If such thing be, thy mother
Appeared to me last night, for ne'er was dream
So like a waking. To me comes a creature,
Sometimes her head on one side, some another.

---

16. Diehl, "'Strike all that look upon with marvel.'"

> I never saw a vessel of like sorrow,
> So filled and so becoming. In pure white robes
> Like very sanctity she did approach
> My cabin where I lay, thrice bowed before me,
> And, gasping to begin some speech, her eyes
> Became two spouts. The fury spent, anon
> Did this break from her: 'Good Antigonus,
> Since fate, against thy better disposition,
> Hath made thy person for the thrower-out
> Of my poor babe according to thine oath,
> Places remote enough are in Bohemia.
> There weep, and leave it crying; and for the babe
> Is counted lost for ever, Perdita
> I prithee call't. For this ungentle business,
> Put on thee by my lord, thou ne'er shalt see
> Thy wife Paulina more.' And so with shrieks
> She melted into air. Affrighted much,
> I did in time collect myself, and thought
> This was so, and no slumber. Dreams are toys,
> Yet for this once, yea superstitiously,
> I will be squared by this.
>
> (3.3.14–40)

Like Paulina's injunction to Leontes, Antigonus's vision evokes the image of a sainted spirit, "in pure white robes" and lapsing into ghostly "shrieks." Also like Paulina, Antigonus refers to Apollonian prophecy as a guarantor of the dream's credibility: "I do believe / Hermione hath suffered death, and that / Apollo would . . . it should here be laid" (40–43). In both cases, Shakespeare emphasizes the effect of theatrical narrative on belief. The strangeness of the vision ("sometimes her head on one side, some another"), together with the eerie nature of its sound ("gasping," "shrieks"), compels Antigonus to regard the image of Hermione as authentic. At the same time, Shakespeare's audience is led to believe, at least for the time being, that the vision is real and purposeful: *we* see the ghost of Hermione through Antigonus's language, and we are encouraged to regard its appearance at this point in the play as a natural and necessary part of the play's outcome.

Still, despite the dramatic appeal of Antigonus's vision, its credibility is at odds with other aspects of the play's formal structure. At first, Shakespeare constructs a series of echoes between the Delphic oracle, Antigonus's dream, and Hermione's statue that suggest a prophetic relationship between the three events: Hermione's first words to Perdita ask the precise question her ghost had answered for Antigonus: "Where hast thou been preserved? Where lived?" (5.3.125). Likewise, Paulina's oracular statement—"Our Perdita is found" (121)—repeats and reverses the ghost's words to Antigonus: "For the babe/Is counted lost for ever, Perdita/I prithee call 't" (3.3.31–33). This echoing effect in Paulina's language is either profoundly uncanny or a Shakespearean slip, since the naming of Perdita took place in Bohemia, not Sicily.[17] On the one hand, Paulina's knowledge of Perdita's name is less mysterious when we recognize (as Hermione seems to) her words as a translation of the oracle itself: "That which is lost be not found" (3.2.133–34). On the other hand, rationalizing Paulina's words only makes those of Antigonus more mysterious, since he leaves Sicily *before* the oracle is read. Of course, the question of whether Antigonus's ghost is real may seem a red herring, an ingenious attempt to fracture the play's dramatic economy. Yet the play prompts such a question by making two pointed references to "superstition": first when Antigonus declares the legitimacy of the ghost, and again when Perdita defends her worshipful stance toward the statue. Antigonus acknowledges that he is superstitious, while Perdita denies it. The play, remarkably, validates both of these claims, insofar as the animation of Hermione's statue (who is then presumed to have been alive for sixteen years) collapses the authenticity of the ghost seen by Antigonus. In this way, the effect of the play's final scene is to deflect the charge of idolatry from Perdita to Antigonus.

Tempting as it may be to dismiss the imputation of idolatry to Antigonus as one of the play's many casualties, the play works hard to convince its audience that the "false" ghost, who compels Antigonus to take Perdita to Bohemia, is a crucial part of the oracle's fulfillment. On both dramatic and rhetorical grounds, the narrative of Antigonus's dream is as persuasive as anything else in the play (man-eating bears excepted), while Paulina's repeated references to "profane" magic in the final scene bring to mind the possibility that idolatry is to be found elsewhere. As in Antigonus's final speech and in her own injunction to Leontes, Paulina's presentation of the statue suggests a theatrical experience that borders on the profane:

> Either forbear,
> Quit presently the chapel, or resolve you
> For more amazement. If you can behold it,

---

17. Certainly the idea that Hermione should not know Perdita's name may be too literal minded, and the possible inconsistencies in the plot can be explained with only moderate difficulty. However, the fact that a rationalizing explanation is required at all to account for the play's verbal echoes seems to me itself significant.

> I'll make the statue move indeed, descend,
> And take you by the hand. But then you'll think—
> Which I protest against—I am assisted
> By wicked powers.
>
> (5.3.85–91)

Julia Reinhard Lupton argues that, once we realize Hermione has been alive all along, any sense of magic in the final scene subsides into a purely symbolic register: "The play's rationalizing deflation of its carefully staged mystery definitively undercuts the Catholic iconography the scene so powerfully evokes, enacting the movement from the Church to its Reform."[18] However, a symbolic reading will not do for Antigonus's vision of Hermione's ghost, nor for the audience's reception of it. Prompted by Paulina herself to make judgments about the play's many mysterious images in terms of an increasingly iconoclastic stance, Shakespeare's audience is pressured to reflect on the ghostly image that it earlier found so persuasive. The problem of distinguishing between sacred and profane images in the play becomes maddeningly vexed, muddying the already ambiguous boundary between idolatry and symbolic reception.

The theological ambiguity of Paulina's magic is refracted and compounded by the play's imitation of Ovid's Pygmalion, whose story of an animated statue is the model for Shakespeare's most radical departure from his source. The Ovidian myth, whose meaning for *The Winter's Tale* has been often debated, was itself interpreted in Renaissance England alternately as a moral fable on the virtue of faith (Pygmalion's statue comes to life because of Venus's gracious approval of his prayers) and as one of the most obscene episodes in the *Metamorphoses*. Part of the grounds for a lascivious reading of the episode stems from the fact that the metamorphosis of Pygmalion's statue occurs during an act of lovemaking:

> Ut rediit, simulacra suae petit ille puellae
> incumbensque toro dedit oscula: visa tepere est;
> admovet os iterum, manibus quoque pectora temptat:
> temptatum mollescit ebur positoque rigore
> subsidit digitis ceditque, ut Hymettia sole
> cera remollescit tractataque pollice multas
> flectitur in facies ipsoque fit utilis usu.

---

18. Lupton, *Afterlives of the Saints*, 216.

dum stupet et dubie gaudet fallique veretur,
rursus amans rursusque manu sua vota retractat.
corpus erat! saliunt temptatae pollice venae.
(10.280–89)

When he returned he sought the image of his maid, and bending over the couch he kissed her. She seemed warm to his touch. Again he kissed her, and with his hands also he touched her breast. The ivory grew soft to his touch and, its hardness vanishing, gave and yielded beneath his fingers, as Hymettian wax grows soft under the sun and, moulded by the thumb, is easily shaped to many forms and becomes usable through use itself. The lover stands amazed, rejoices still in doubt, fears he is mistaken, and tries his hopes again and yet again with his hand. Yes, it was real flesh! The veins were pulsing beneath his testing finger.

Here, Ovid conflates the softening of the statue with the sexual "hardening" of Pygmalion. Shakespeare replays this double act of petrification (albeit in chastened form) by emphasizing the hardening effect that Hermione's statue has on her audience, especially Leontes: "Does not the stone rebuke me/ For being more stone than it?" (5.3.37–38). In both cases, the act of metamorphosis is rendered morally ambiguous insofar as it transfers attention to the imagination of the viewer. In Ovid's poem, the statue's transformation, which also happens to be the most "pornographic" moment of the story, elides into—and is nearly indistinguishable from—Pygmalion's fantasies of agalmatophilia.[19] Although Shakespeare mostly avoids any sexual undertones in his version,[20] the ambiguous physical movement of Hermione (up until the point where she steps down from the pedestal) suggests

---

19. The suggestive bawdiness of this line is more apparent in the Latin, since *pollex* has a sexual sense in addition to "thumb." William S. Anderson notes that Ovid's sources for the story were overtly obscene. See his *Ovid's Metamorphoses, Books 6–10* (Norman: University of Oklahoma Press, 1972), 496. See also Brooks Otis, *Ovid as an Epic Poet* (Cambridge: Cambridge University Press, 1966), 389.

20. However, a connection between Ovidian tumescence and Shakespearean petrification may be strengthened by the intervention of John Marston's *Metamorphosis of Pigmalions Image* (1598), in which a pornographic conception of stoniness is the poem's major conceit. See Lynn Enterline, *The Rhetoric of the Body from Ovid to Shakespeare* (Cambridge: Cambridge University Press, 2000), 125–51. See also Lori Humphrey Newcomb, "'If that which is lost be not found': Monumental Bodies, Spectacular Bodies in *The Winter's Tale*," in *Ovid and the Renaissance Body*, ed. Goran V. Stanivukovic (Toronto: University of Toronto Press, 2001), 244, who sees evidence of an association between stoniness and male penetrative ability in Ovid's story, at least for an early readership.

that the perception of the statue's humanity is merely an effect of self-deluding "fancy":

> PAULINA. No longer shall you gaze on't, lest your fancy
>   May think anon it moves.
> LEONTES.   Let be, let be!
>   Would I were dead but that methinks already.
>   What was he that did make it? See, my lord,
>   Would you not deem it breathed, and that those veins
>   Did verily bear blood?
>
> (5.3.60–65)

The indeterminacy of Hermione's physical presence at this moment—is her breathing really perceptible?—strangely recalls Leontes' inability earlier in the play to locate physical proof of Hermione's fidelity.[21] In the absence of conclusive evidence, Leontes' ravings about the statue's apparent liveliness appear—like his earlier ravings about Hermione's promiscuity—as mad as Pygmalion.

Renaissance detractors of Ovid often pointed to the salaciousness of the Pygmalion episode as evidence of the poet's moral bankruptcy. While Shakespeare often draws attention to this aspect of Ovid in many of the plays (the Ovidian music lesson in *Taming of the Shrew* is one example), there is another, less-discussed aspect of the Pygmalion story that bears directly on the theological politics of *The Winter's Tale*. In Ovid's version, the metamorphosis of statue into woman depends crucially on the manner of *prayer:*

> Festa dies Veneris tota celeberrima Cypro
> venerat, et pandis inductae cornibus aurum
> conciderant ictae nivea cervice iuvencae,
> turaque fumabant, cum munere functus ad aras
> constitit et timide 'si, di, dare cuncta potestis,
> sit coniunx, opto,' non ausus 'eburnea virgo'
> dicere, Pygmalion 'similis mea' dixit 'eburnae.'
>
> (10.270–76)

---

21. The emphasis on breath here also recalls Ovid's myth of Deucalion and Pyrrha, which has also been cited as a possible source for Hermione's transformation scene. See Jonathan Bate, *Shakespeare and Ovid* (Oxford: Oxford University Press, 1993), 233–34, and Francois Laroque, "A New Ovidian Source for the Statue Scene in *The Winter's Tale*," *Notes and Queries New Series* 31 (1984): 215–17.

And now the festal day of Venus had come, which all Cyprus thronged to celebrate; heifers with spreading horns covered with gold had fallen 'neath the death-stroke on their snowy necks, and the altars smoked with incense. Pygmalion, having brought his gift to the altar, stood and falteringly prayed: 'If ye, O gods, can give all things, I pray to have as wife—' he did not dare add 'my ivory maid,' but said, 'one like my ivory maid.'

To an early modern reader, the ostentatious paganism of the scene, with its gold-covered calves and incense, might appear as a perfect example of idolatrous worship, recalling as it does the biblical scene in Exodus that inspired the Decalogue and, hence, the original proscription against idolatry. However, as if in response to the possible charge of idolatry, Pygmalion makes a crucial (if insincere) distinction between the breathing woman that he hopes for and the stony lady he has perversely courted—"one *like* my ivory maid." Despite his fetishizing impulses, Pygmalion does not fully collapse the distinction between divine and human creations. In this respect he is distinguished from Phaëthon, Ovid's supreme idolater, who attempts to erase the difference between heavenly and earthly action in one fell swoop. In Ovid's words, Phaëthon is "one who greatly dared" (*excidit magnis ausis*, 2.328), while Pygmalion is "not daring" (*non ausus*).

Shakespeare alludes to the choice made by Pygmalion in his description of Hermione's ghost and statue. Just as Pygmalion makes the crucial decision to ask for someone "like" his ivory woman, Antigonus prefaces the narrative of his prophetic vision by announcing that "ne'er was dream/So *like* a waking" (3.3.17–18, my emphasis).[22] The word "like" is repeated twice in the next four lines, both times as a description of Hermione's ghost. The same word appears several times in the final scene, in each instance as a reference to the statue's uncanny effect on its audience: "So her dead likeness I do well believe/Excels what ever yet you looked upon,/Or hand of man hath done" (5.3.15–17). Hence, the same word that makes Pygmalion's prayer acceptable to Venus also links ghost, statue, and woman in *The Winter's Tale*. As much as the play prompts its own audience to choose sides with Antigonus or Paulina on the grounds of a wakened iconoclasm, it rhetorically conflates the two mysterious visions of Hermione in the play, almost to the point of collapsing the safe distance of "likeness" (the idea that something seems *like* Hermione) into a sense of identification (the perception that something

---

22. Arthur Golding, for example, also emphasizes the word "like" in his translation of the passage.

is Hermione). Shakespeare avoids giving his audience a stable vantage point for distinguishing between likeness and identity, instead engaging their complicity in a particular form of theatrical idolatry. In this way, the play comes close to Ovid's Pygmalion, who avoids heresy by saying "like," without meaning it. What is remarkable and unexpected about Shakespeare's play, as we shall see, is the way in which it brings the audience's experience of music into its meditation on the meaning of idolatry. The idea that music contains meaning may simply be a delusion that stems from the sense that it "sounds like" something else, either through a kind of acoustic imitation or through an ingrained habit of convention. Imagined like this, the habit of listening to music for a deeper meaning is no different from worshipping at the foot of a painted statue. *He, that added those forty parts, must either be the devil, or Dr. Bull.*

Autolycus and the End of Pastoral

At first glance, music in *The Winter's Tale* promises to recover the distinction between sacred and profane art. The first three acts, which chart the familial and civic disintegration in Sicily, are marked by a consistent pattern of *noise*: the brash interruption of Mamillius's "softly" recited winter's tale (2.1.32), the "ear-deaf'ning voice o'th' oracle,/Kin to Jove's thunder" (3.1.9–10), and the "savage clamour" of the storm that greets the Sicilians in Bohemia (3.3.55). The destruction of the Sicilians in Bohemia is itself described by the shepherd's son in terms that suggest a perverse parody of a musical performance, with the sounds of nature and man rhythmically answering each other with increased intensity: "But to make an end of the ship—to see how the sea flap-dragoned it! But first, how the poor souls roared, and the sea mocked them, and how the poor gentleman roared, and the bear mocked him, both roaring louder than the sea or weather" (3.3.90–94). The extent to which Shakespeare constructs the acoustic world of the play's first half as exclusive of harmonious music can be gauged by the change he makes to his literary source, Robert Greene's *Pandosto*. In Greene's text, the transferal of the infant daughter from her native kingdom is marked by sweet-sounding music and lullabies: "After that they had set all things in order, the shepherd went to his sheep with a merry note, and the good wife learned to sing lullaby at home with her young babe."[23] Shakespeare replaces the wife's lullaby

---

23. Robert Greene, *Pandosto, The Triumph of Time* (1588), in *Narrative and Dramatic Sources of Shakespeare*, ed. Geoffrey Bullough (London: Routledge, 1957), 175.

in *Pandosto* with a cacophony of shrieks and tempests, at the same time calling attention to the acoustic difference between the source text and the play: "The day frowns more and more. Thou'rt like to have/A lullaby too rough" (3.3.53–54). By contrast, Paulina's music in the last scene, although it is not described, is almost universally understood as harmonious. Taken this way, the alternation between noise and music encourages a Neoplatonic reading of the play, in which the noisiness of the first three acts signifies moral and civic disorder, and the instrumental harmony of the final scene symbolizes the sanctity of Paulina's magic—and, more generally, the redemptive nature of the play's ending.[24]

Taken symbolically, music in *The Winter's Tale* offers a moral and aesthetic clarity denied by the play's visual and rhetorical structure. Such a reading would be tempting—and traditionally has been—were it not for the radical deconstruction of music that Shakespeare exercises in act 4. Here, in the play's famous pastoral scene, Shakespeare frenetically rehearses the conflicting ways in which music relates to its verbal contexts, effectively undermining any stable definition of musical meaning. The fact that this deconstruction occurs in the context of pastoral is not incidental: pastoral, more than other genres, generates and relies on a highly symbolic, sublimating notion of music. Paul Alpers, for example, calls attention to the "harmony between human and natural music" in Theocritus's first idyll, which he sees as representative of the pastoral ideal.[25] Pastoral's conflation of actual (human) music with ideal (natural) music maps neatly onto the categories of *musica practica* and *musica humana,* thus bolstering a speculative conception of music. For this reason it is not surprising that Alpers, who largely adopts Frye's reading of *The Winter's Tale,* considers act 4 to be exemplary of pastoral, rather than subversive of it.[26] However, the play's pastoralism is not immune from the iconoclastic skepticism that surrounds it. As Lupton has provocatively suggested, the anxiety over idolatry that dominates the play's theological meditations conjoins with an antipathy toward pagan models, especially when the use of pagan sources tends toward mystification.[27] Pastoral music thus becomes another object of iconoclastic doubt rather than an escape from it. Instead of securing a redemptive reading of the play à la Frye, music—both alluded to and performed in act 4—pushes the idea of a sublimated art to its breaking point.

---

24. See Armitage, "Dismemberment of Orpheus."
25. Paul Alpers, *What Is Pastoral?* (Chicago: University of Chicago Press, 1996), 24.
26. Ibid., 204–22.
27. See Lupton, *Afterlives of the Saints.*

Shakespeare's careful references to Apollo in *The Winter's Tale* are a subtle index to the play's demystification of both music and pastoral. For example, the sound of Apollo's oracle in act 3 is associated not with Apollonian harmony but with a violent assault on the ears of its audience: "The burst/And the ear-deaf'ning voice o'th' oracle,/Kin to Jove's thunder, so surprised my sense/That I was nothing" (3.1.8–11). In a more subtle fashion, Shakespeare raises again the expectation of divine music in the Ovidian catalog that Florizel recites to Perdita in act 4, only to end on a markedly "human" note:

> Apprehend
> Nothing but jollity. The gods themselves,
> Humbling their deities to love, have taken
> The shapes of beasts upon them. Jupiter
> Became a bull, and bellowed; the green Neptune
> A ram, and bleated; and the fire-robed god,
> Golden Apollo, a poor humble swain,
> As I seem now.
>
> (4.4.24–31)

The catalog of godly transformations, which Shakespeare adapts freely from the tale of Arachne in book 6 of the *Metamorphoses,* is intended by Florizel to justify Perdita's dressing up as a pastoral goddess.[28] Yet the poetic form of the catalog sets up a pattern of rhythmic and analogical correspondences that calls attention to what precisely is missing: Jupiter becomes a bull and "bellows," Neptune becomes a ram and "bleats." The pattern should logically continue as "the fire-robed god,/Golden Apollo, a poor humble swain,/*And sang*," as the classical Apollo typically does in his pastoral manifestations. Instead of completing the pattern with an image of Apollonian music, however, Shakespeare moves the focus back to Florizel himself ("As I seem now"), a very human singer courting a very human (and somewhat skeptical) listener. The Apollo evoked by Florizel is not the authoritative figure of prophecy and harmony, but simply a philandering god among others who bellow and bleat rather than sing. In this way, Shakespeare uses Apollo, who functions metonymically as a representative of both music and pastoral, to raise the expectation of a

---

28. Phebe Jensen also remarks on the significance of Arachne as a figure for iconoclasm. "Singing Psalms to Horn-Pipes: Festivity, Iconoclasm, and Catholicism in *The Winter's Tale,*" *Shakespeare Quarterly* 55, no. 3 (Fall 2004): 279–306. Many readers have commented on the dark undertones of the interchange between Florizel and Perdita, not least because of its preoccupation with Ovidian rape scenes.

sublimated art and then foreclose on it. The scene abandons the possibility of musical sublimity, exposing pastoral metamorphosis (as Ovid's Arachne does) as a convenient pretense for an illicit courtship.

Shakespeare's demystification of pastoral, performed through a degradation of Apollo, anticipates Milton's "On the Morning of Christ's Nativity," in which the impotence of Apollonian prophecy is made to represent the obsolescence of classical pastoral:

> The oracles are dumb,
> No voice, or hideous hum
> Runs through the archèd roof in words deceiving.
> Apollo from his shrine
> Can no more divine,
> With hollow shriek the steep of Delphos leaving.
> No nightly trance, or breathèd spell,
> Inspires the pale-eyed priest from the prophetic cell.
>   (173–80)[29]

Here, Milton presents the hollowness of pagan pastoral as a musical problem through the image of Apollo fleeing Delphos "with hollow shriek[ing]," but also through an especially garish rhyme: "Apollo from his shrine/ Can no more divine." In the next chapter, I suggest that Milton's *Maske* represents *all* earthly, acoustic music as inherently fallen; in the Nativity Ode, the representation of hollow music serves primarily as a foil for the "true" music of the angelic choirs that herald the coming of the Son. In this way, the *synchronous* condition of hearing false prophecy (that is, of listening superstitiously) is conflated with the *diachronic* condition of living in a postlapsarian world. Thus Polixenes' comment in act 1 that "we were as twinned lambs that did frisk i'th' sun" (1.2.69) captures pastoral's nostalgic impulse, but the play immediately links this sentiment with an acute sense of loss. Likewise, the absence of Apollonian music in the play reminds us that, despite the change of seasons, the play still operates in a fallen world: divine oracles fall on deaf ears, innocent servants are eaten by bears, and a pastoral goddess is revealed to be a "pranked up" shepherd's daughter. In other words, music in the play functions less as a symbol of regeneration than a reminder of loss. This systematic deferment of heavenly music cultivates in Shakespeare's audience an active

---

29. *John Milton,* ed. Stephen Orgel and Jonathan Goldberg (Oxford: Oxford University Press, 1991).

iconoclasm—one that is doctrinally linked to the strand of Pauline theology that insists on reminding us, "We were not as we are now."

While references to Apollo and classical mythology go far in undercutting the play's pastoral, Shakespeare's most sustained attack on a symbolic reading of music unquestionably centers on Autolycus. Insofar as Autolycus's ballads and impromptu musical performances provide a cover for his thievery, his art is truly profane.[30] The bawdiness of his songs, never fully covert, makes a mockery of the idea of redemptive harmony. At the same time, Autolycus is the play's most overtly Ovidian character, and Shakespeare makes a point of asserting Autolycus's literary roots: "My father named me Autolycus; who, being as I am, littered under Mercury, was likewise a snapper-up of unconsidered trifles. With die and drab purchased this caparison, and my revenue is the silly cheat" (4.3.24–28). In this respect, Shakespeare follows Ovid's account in book 11 of the *Metamorphoses* of the figure Autolycus, who is "littered" by Mercury and who inherits his father's characteristic deviousness:[31]

alipedis de stirpe dei versuta propago
nascitur Autolycus furtum ingeniosus ad omne,
candida de nigris et de candentibus atra
qui facere adsuerat, patriae non degener artis.
                          (11.312–15)

A son was born to the wing-footed god, Autolycus, of crafty nature, well versed in cunning wiles. For he could make white of black and black of white, a worthy heir of his father's art.

Here again, Shakespeare takes the opportunity to raise and frustrate the expectations of a sublime, Apollonian musician. Ovid's Autolycus, who is the product of a double rape, is one half of a set of twins fathered by Mercury and Apollo: Autolycus is fathered by Mercury and Philammon is fathered by Apollo. Although many readers note that Shakespeare's Autolycus combines aspects of both Autolycus and Philammon, the play carefully avoids making any direct connection between Autolycus and Apollo. Instead, the only

---

30. Like Falstaff, Autolycus has historically enjoyed his share of disparaging critics. See especially Frank Kermode, *William Shakespeare: The Final Plays* (London: Longmans Green, 1963), and David Kaula, "Autolycus's Trumpery," *Studies in English Literature* 16 (1976): 287–303.

31. Homer's *Odyssey* has also been cited as a source for Shakespeare's Autolycus. See Merritt Y. Hughes, "A Classical vs. a Social Approach to Shakespeare's Autolycus," *Shakespeare Association Bulletin* 15 (1940): 222. Ovid's references to a divine rape and to the musician Philammon, however, come much closer to Shakespeare's musical rogue than Homer's Autolycus does.

qualities linking the two figures cast Apollo in a decidedly negative light: a seemingly profane art and an ability to deceive people for ignoble purposes. Ovid's Mercury impregnates Chione after magically inducing her to sleep, while Apollo accomplishes the same thing a few hours later by disguising himself as an old woman. Like Apollo, Shakespeare's Autolycus is a master of disguise who can pass as a ragged beggar or a noble courtier at will and who uses the occasion of a sheepshearing festival to rob its participants. In this way, Shakespeare confirms temporarily the most disapproving Reformist attitudes toward festivity, and, through the figure of Autolycus, he conflates and localizes a complex of iconoclasm, antipastoralism, and skepticism about music's putative power of redemption.

The case against music is bolstered by Autolycus's music itself. Historically, critics of *The Winter's Tale* have often dismissed Autolycus's songs as a simple backdrop that effects a change of tone in the play. Frye, for example, rhapsodizes the effect of Autolycus's first song as a comic inversion of the first half of the play: "We find ourselves in Bohemia with spring imagery bursting out of Autolycus's first song.... If Leontes is an imaginary cuckold, Autolycus, the thieving harbinger of spring, is something of an imaginary cuckoo."[32] For others, however, Autolycus's songs are simply extraneous. In an early essay entitled "Extraneous Song in Elizabethan Drama after the Advent of Shakespeare," which set the tone for at least two generations of the play's critics, Louis B. Wright makes Autolycus the standard-bearer of all vain, trifling songs that are of no value to the study of Shakespearean drama: "Autolycus is a clown and only a clown. His performances are pure clownery; his songs are merely extraneous clown songs with no dramatic value outside the clown scenes which are themselves extraneous."[33] Although the sheer repetitiveness of this claim makes it seem to protest too much, the rejection of Autolycus's songs is not surprising given their bawdiness. Autolycus's music evokes images of pastoral innocence and rebirth, helping to effect the play's dramatic change of tone, but this music is almost always tainted with "smutty" eroticism. His first song, which opens the play's pastoral episode, is replete with images of spring and rebirth: "daffodils begin to peer," "the sweet o'the year," "the sweet birds," "the lark, that tirra-lirra chants" (4.3.1–9). However, the last line of the song presents this pastoral warmth as

---

32. Frye, "Recognition in *The Winter's Tale*," 108.
33. Louis B. Wright, "Extraneous Song in Elizabethan Drama after the Advent of Shakespeare," *Studies in Philology* 24 (1927): 264. See also Peter J. Seng, *The Vocal Songs in the Plays of Shakespeare* (Cambridge, MA: Harvard University Press, 1967), 242, and John H. Long, *Shakespeare's Use of Music: The Final Comedies* (Gainesville: University of Florida Press, 1961), 71, who, although they find Autolycus significantly more agreeable, nonetheless see much of his music as mere pictorial backdrop.

a backdrop for sexual frolicking: "While we lie tumbling in the hay" (12). Likewise, the sensuality of Autolycus's songs is not limited to their texts alone; their acoustic, physical aspects often point to a latent eroticism beneath the seemingly innocent pastoral verse. For example, although his fourth song, "Lawn as White as Driven Snow," is generally dismissed as a typical peddler's song, a seventeenth-century setting for the song indicates the potential for a musical eroticism that, with the appropriate embellishment, borders on the obscene. Here, the peddler's "pins" and "poaking-stickes" are set to a quick, "pecking" staccato phrase that interrupts the predominantly lilting movement of the song.[34] In this respect, Wilson's setting is an excellent example of musical text painting, and an exuberant performance of the song's staccato section would certainly drive home the point of its latent bawdry. The song's refrain on "what maids lack" is particularly suggestive: the phrase, repeated four times, follows an ascending melodic line that climaxes each time on "lack," producing an agitated sound at the thought of what maidens "lack from head to heel."

The kind of performative prurience made possible through Autolycus's songs does little to deflect an iconoclastic attitude toward music. Moreover, the fact that Autolycus's music finds an eager audience in the play seems only to confirm the susceptibility of the average listener, as in the servant's rapturous praise of Autolycus's art:

> He hath songs for man or woman, of all sizes. No milliner can so fit his customers with gloves. He has the prettiest love songs for maids, so without bawdry, which is strange, with such delicate burdens of dildos and fadings, 'Jump her, and thump her'; and where some stretch-mouthed rascal would, as it were, mean mischief and break a foul gap into the matter, he makes the maid to answer, 'Whoop, do me no harm, good man'; puts him off, slights him, with 'Whoop, do me no harm, good man!' (4.4.190–98)

---

34. John Wilson, *Cheerful Ayers or Ballads* (1660), reprinted in Long, *Shakespeare's Use of Music*, 80. Because of the date of Wilson's setting, Seng argues that it is hardly probable that it was the original music for the ballad (*Vocal Songs*, 240). Nosworthy and Pafford, on the other hand, contend that Wilson's setting (if it is not the original one) is unlikely to have differed significantly from the setting that Shakespeare would have known. See Nosworthy, "Music and Its Function," 65; J. H. P. Pafford, "Music, and the Songs in *The Winter's Tale*," *Shakespeare Quarterly* 10 (1959): 168. Whether or not Wilson's setting is truly original, it suggests a possible way in which a seventeenth-century musician may have interpreted the song. Moreover, the sexual suggestiveness of the song's "pins" and "poaking-stickes" is reinforced by contemporary analogues, one of which advises maids who are "troubled with an itching" to come to the speaker/peddler for a "cure" (cited in Seng, *Vocal Songs*, 241).

The specifically idolatrous nature of this zeal for bawdy music is made explicit a few lines later, when the same servant describes the effect of Autolycus's songs: "He hath ribbons of all the colours i'th' rainbow; points more than all the lawyers in Bohemia can learnedly handle, though they come to him by th' gross... why, he sings 'em over as they were gods or goddesses" (202–6). The servant's passing reference to Bohemian lawyers in his praise of music may not be accidental. Alfred Thomas has suggested that, far from being a remote, almost imaginary location, Bohemia was for many people in Renaissance England, including Shakespeare, an important site for the mingling of Catholic and Protestant followers and their beliefs.[35] Thus, if Shakespeare's decision to trade Sicily for Bohemia reflects, at least in part, a recognition of Bohemia's significance in the controversy between Catholic and Protestant theologies, then it should certainly intensify the question of Autolycus's musical idolatry. Indeed, the specter of idolatry hovers over the ballads themselves, which Autolycus advertises as fantastical accounts of supernatural transformations:

> Here's another ballad, of a fish that appeared upon the coast on Wednesday the fourscore of April, forty thousand fathom above water, and sung this ballad against the hard hearts of maids. It was thought she was a woman, and was turned into a cold fish for she would not exchange flesh with one that loved her. The ballad is very pitiful, and as true. (4.4.265–70)

In his edition of the play, J. H. P. Pafford notes that early modern ballads typically include fantastical subjects, but he argues that Autolycus's description of a magical metamorphosis here is so ridiculous that Shakespeare's audience is likely to be "moved to laughter both by the ridiculous extravagances themselves and by the ridiculous credulity of the peasants."[36] While Autolycus's ballad is certainly outrageous, its account of a woman "pitifully" transformed by a lover's jealousy also looks ahead to the play's final scene, in which Paulina asks her onstage audience (and, to an extent, Shakespeare's audience) to take "as true" the metamorphosis of a painted statue into a breathing woman. William Carroll has suggested, for instance, that while Autolycus's ballad "mocks" the idea of transformation, it also "anticipates our

---

35. Alfred Thomas, *A Blessed Shore: England and Bohemia from Chaucer to Shakespeare* (Ithaca, NY: Cornell University Press, 2007).
36. *The Winter's Tale,* ed. J. H. P. Pafford (London: Methuen, 1963), 106n.

own wishes during the final act of the play."[37] Sure enough, many of the subjects that permeate the final act of the play—metamorphosis, death, sexuality, regeneration—emerge in Autolycus's songs in act 4. Thus the seemingly vulgar music of the play's pastoral episode, even if it does not contaminate the final transformation scene, forms another connection between the idolatrous art of Autolycus's thievery and the illusion-making power of Paulina's sacramental theater.

The most striking suggestion of an affinity between Autolycus's and Paulina's art occurs in the fifth, and longest, song in act 4. Here, as he does so often in the plays, Shakespeare sets up a conflict between musical performance and verbal context, in this case by framing the performance of a traditionally mournful song as "merry" entertainment:

AUTOLYCUS. Why, this is a passing merry one, and goes to the tune of 'Two Maids Wooing a Man'. There's scarce a maid westward but she sings it. 'Tis in request, I can tell you.
MOPSA. We can both sing it. If thou'lt bear a part thou shalt hear; 'tis in three parts.
DORCAS. We had the tune on't a month ago.
AUTOLYCUS. I can bear my part, you must know, 'tis my occupation. Have at it with you:
   [*They sing.*]
AUTOLYCUS.   Get you hence, for I must go
              Where it fits not you to know.
DORCAS.   Whither?
MOPSA.   O whither?
DORCAS.   Whither?
MOPSA.   It becomes thy oath full well
              Thou to me thy secrets tell.
DORCAS.   Me too. Let me go thither.
MOPSA.   Or thou go'st to th' grange or mill,
DORCAS.   If to either, thou dost ill.
AUTOLYCUS.   Neither.
DORCAS.   What neither?
AUTOLYCUS.   Neither.

---

37. William C. Carroll, *The Metamorphoses of Shakespearean Comedy* (Princeton, NJ: Princeton University Press, 1985), 212.

Dorcas.	Thou hast sworn my love to be.
Mopsa.	Thou hast sworn it more to me.
	Then whither goest? Say, whither?

(4.4.277–96)

Dorcas's admission that she knows the "tune," but not the words, for this song is not remarkable. Musical settings were regularly joined to multiple song texts, and printings of early modern ballad texts often refer to older songs whose tunes can be used with "newer" lyrics.[38] In this way, Shakespeare subtly reminds his audience of the promiscuity of song settings, suggesting yet again that musical scores may illuminate very little about any particular text. Even so, Autolycus's description of the song as a "merry ballad," as well as his choice of accompanying tune, is peculiar in light of the historical record. The only extant musical setting for the ballad, which appears in a seventeenth-century songbook for lute and viol, is decidedly plaintive. Stylistically, it resembles contemporary settings for songs like Ophelia's "How Should I Your True Love Know" and Desdemona's "Willow" song; to Peter Seng's ears, the setting "sounds more like a funeral march than a merry tune."[39] Edward Cappell, one of the most musically inclined early readers of Shakespeare, praises the song for its joviality, but he does so by severing it from its musical context: "[The song] is of wonderful sweetness, and *musical without music,* as are all the songs of this Poet in general."[40] In this respect, Cappell is merely following Autolycus, who glosses over the elegiac qualities of the song and asks his audience to sing it to "Two Maids Wooing a Man"—a tune that has never been discovered and may simply be one of the play's fictive creations. Autolycus, after all, is describing a song he wishes to sell. Like Paulina in the succeeding act, he carefully manipulates the conditions of a musical performance in order to encourage a particular reaction from his listeners, but he also relies on his audience's ability to adapt the experience of musical sound to their own preconceived notions about its meaning. Put another way, if the

---

38. Ross W. Duffin, *Shakespeare's Songbook* (New York: Norton, 2004), 13. See also Claude Simpson, *The British Broadside Ballad and Its Music* (New Brunswick, NJ: Rutgers University Press, 1996).

39. Seng, *Vocal Songs,* 245. The setting I am referring to is the one which appears (along with a second verse) in a New York Public Library manuscript, "Songs unto the Violl and Lute," Drexel 4175 (no. 59), reproduced in John P. Cutts, "An Unpublished Contemporary Setting of a Shakespeare Song," *Shakespeare Survey* 9 (1956): 86–89. Cutts argues that the setting, which appears with other settings by Robert Johnson, was also probably composed by Johnson, who composed several original settings for songs in Shakespeare's plays.

40. Edward Cappell, *Notes and Various Readings to Shakespeare* (n.d., 1779–83?), cited in Seng, *Vocal Songs,* 243, my emphasis.

meaning of Hermione's transformation at the end of the play hinges on an interpretation of Ovid's Pygmalion as either transcendent fable or "smutty joke," then it also depends, as does the judgment of Autolycus' ballads, on the way one listens to music.

The suggestiveness of Autolycus's song is more pronounced in the second verse, which Shakespeare does not include. As soon as Autolycus, Mopsa, and Dorcas are done singing the first verse, the Clown interrupts with a reference to additional verses: "We'll have this song out anon by ourselves" (4.4.297). The second verse appears in a seventeenth-century manuscript collection of ballads, housed in the New York Public Library:

neuer more for lasses sake
will I dance at fare or wake
Ah mee oh Ah mee Ah mee
who shall then ware a rated shooe
or what shall the bagpipe doe
recant or elce you slay mee
recant or elce you slay me
if thou leaue our Andorne greene
where shall fill or frize be seene
sleeping what sleeping sleeping
no Ile warrant the sitting sadly
or Idely walking madly
in some darke in some darke
in some darke Corner weeping
in some darke darke Corner weeping.[41]

This is a far cry from the "merry" ballad that Autolycus advertises. What is especially striking about this second verse is the way in which it adumbrates, in narrative fashion, the effects of Hermione's absence in the play. The singer's avowal that he will shun ritual festivity and romantic courtship echoes Leontes' promise to Paulina in act 5 that he will never remarry. Likewise,

---

41. "Songs unto the Violl and Lute," reproduced in Cutts, "Unpublished Contemporary Setting." Cutts remarks that "though one is naturally apprehensive about claiming that this second verse originally belonged to *The Winter's Tale*, there are certain indications tending to the belief that this may have been so.... Obviously, from the Clown's last words, there was more to the song than is presented here" (86–88). Pafford, on the other hand, notes that "lyrics and stage songs were often expanded in broadsheets in the 17th century...and these verses may be post-1611 expansions" (*Winter's Tale*, 108). It seems to me that the resonances in the second verse produced by Cutts with the rest of *The Winter's Tale* (which I discuss below) are too coincidental not to have been known to Shakespeare when he chose to insert this song into the play.

the ballad's image of a mourning woman who walks madly recalls Antigonus's vision of Hermione shortly before his death. The singer's ambiguous statement that he is only "sleeping," and his prediction that he will end up "sitting sadly... in some darke Corner," also connotes Hermione, who at the end of the play is discovered to have been "sitting" quietly for sixteen years. The suggestiveness of the ballad in its entirety, more than can be comfortably attributed to coincidence, brings Autolycus's music remarkably close to Paulina's mysterious performance in the final scene. At the same time, the ballad itself reminds us of the difference between these two kinds of music: "what shall the bagpipe doe." Where, in other words, will we be able to hear bagpipe music, when only psalms are to be played (because you are dead)? For a moment, the question is moot, as funereal lament appears in the middle of raucous festivity and the distinction between sacred and profane music—and between Autolycus's and Paulina's art—imaginatively collapses.

To be sure, my reading of Autolycus's music makes much use of an absent text. Yet it is precisely the fact that Shakespeare deliberately excludes the second verse of "Get You Hence" that makes the performance of the song open to the widest possible range of interpretations and responses. Instead of eliciting a uniform reaction to Autolycus's musical performance, the unperformed verses hover just outside the confines of the play as a teasing, disruptive context that lingers in the ear of an audience member who may remember having heard the song before. This is, after all, a song that many in the audience *know*. In his discussion of music in *The Winter's Tale,* David Lindley points out how the popularity of the song makes it difficult to gauge its effect on Shakespeare's original audience. I cite his comments at length, since they raise other problems in the song's performance history:

> The song survives in two manuscripts, and contains ornamentation of the vocal line which, one might think, would make it more appropriate to courtly professional singers than to Autolycus and two shepherdesses. Even in the version Duffin advances, stripped of this elaboration, the song seems to me not to have the character of a popular song that might readily have been got by heart and sung to other lyrics, as the text implies this is.... It is, of course, possible that this setting was not intended for theatrical use, or that it was composed for a later production of the play, but if it is indeed the song heard by the original audience, then its character is somewhat surprising.... Its relative musical sophistication requires that we suspend for the duration of the song the impression we have already formed of the naive characters of the two shepherdesses. Instead the song becomes a self-contained set piece, to

be indulged in for its own sake, rather than being a direct expression of the dramatic situation or of the character of its singers. For these reasons I am inclined to believe that this is unlikely to have been the setting rendered at the original performances—but it must remain a possibility that Shakespeare was happy to insert what, in modern terms, one might call a "production number," and that it offers a further ingredient in this scene's exploration of the relationships between courtly sophistication and rural simplicity.[42]

With his typical sensitivity and ear for musical nuance, Lindley here lays out the many incongruities of the song's performance. However, I am less inclined to believe that these incongruities demand an aesthetically satisfying "answer," in the form of either an authentic, more "popular" setting for the song that remains to be found, or a habit of listening that momentarily forgets the dramatic context and hears the song as a "self-contained set piece." Such answers are only necessary for audiences who believe that the relationship between music and the dramatic text must always be harmonious. Shakespeare seems to be interested in a different effect here, and he constructs the pastoral scene so that there is virtually no way to stage its music without provoking either a sharp sense of ambivalence or a willful inattention to the play's inconsistencies. Put another way, the scene both represents and triggers the audience's idolatrous habits of listening to music. Moreover, by prompting his audience to hear music apart from its dramatic context, Shakespeare outlines a mode of listening to music that is independent of any redemptive or moral structure. The meaning of this music, if there is any, is finally created in the individual ears of those who hear it.

Taken this way, the radical subjectivity of musical experience in *The Winter's Tale* would seem to validate Protestant claims about music's worthlessness. The indeterminacy of musical sound, its sensuousness, and its independence from language all make it a precarious vehicle for securing dramatic or aesthetic unity, much less for imparting theological orthodoxy. As he has done so many times before, Shakespeare contaminates the aesthetic economy of the play's final scene by stoking the most troubling suspicions about music's meaning. On the one hand, it becomes impossible to hear the music in the transformation scene simply as Neoplatonic symbol. There is something troubling about a character named Paulina who conspicuously uses music to stage a version of Ovid's Pygmalion. On the other hand, the play asserts its

---

42. David Lindley, *Shakespeare and Music* (London: Thomson, 2006), 167–68.

own moral authority by privileging Leontes' reaction to art in the final scene over his earlier, destructive iconoclastic tendencies. How then, we might ask, *do* we hear music, if not as sublimated allegory or fleshly sound?

I believe that the play does suggest a different way of hearing music, although the suggestion is so brief that it has often been overlooked. While poring over the ingredients for the sheepshearing festival, Shakespeare's Clown gives a fleeting—but striking—portrait of one of the singers:

> Three pound of sugar, five pound of currants, rice—what will this sister of mine do with rice? But my father hath made her mistress of the feast, and she lays it on. She hath made me four-and-twenty nosegays for the shearers—three-man-song-men, all, and very good ones—but they are most of them means and basses, but one Puritan amongst them, and he sings psalms to hornpipes. I must have saffron to colour the warden pies; mace; dates, none—that's out of my note; nutmegs, seven; a race or two of ginger. (4.3.35–43)

In the space of two lines—indeed, in the margins of a grocery list—Shakespeare evokes with full force the Reformist controversy over music. The psalms had been the primary battleground over which religious debates about music were waged, and the tradition of metrical psalm settings that took hold in the sixteenth century, in which the clarity of the text takes precedence over the musical line, represented for many Reformists the limits of what was tolerable in church music. Moreover, insofar as it was considered a didactic form of entertainment, psalm singing, both domestic and public, was often presented as a moral alternative to "scurrilous" music, such as popular ballads.[43] In this respect, Shakespeare's psalm-singing Puritan is utterly confounding. Instead of choosing a metrical setting, he picks for his music the hornpipe, which had the reputation in England as the noisiest, most sensuous of instruments, and which was especially singled out for censure in the Reformist attacks on music.[44] The conflation of psalms and hornpipes here

---

43. For an account of the cultural significance of psalm singing in early modern England, see Nicholas Temperley, "'If any of you be mery let hym synge psalmes': The Culture of Psalms in Church and Home," in *"Noyses, sounds, and sweet aires": Music in Early Modern England,* ed. Jessie Ann Owens, 90–100 (Washington, DC: Folger Shakespeare Library, 2006).

44. See, for example, Phillip Stubbes's description of morris dancing: "Then have they their Hobby-horses, dragons & other Antiques, togither with their baudie Pipers and thundering Drummers to strike up the devils daunce withall, them marche these heathen company towards the Church and Churchyard, their pipers pipeing, their drummers thundring, their bels jyngling, their handkerchefs swinging about their heds like madmen... like devils incarnate with such a confuse noise, that no man can hear his own voice," *Anatomie of Abuses* (1583), ed. Arthur Freeman (New York: Garland,

negatively echoes the second verse of "Get You Hence," in which the genre of musical lament is defined against the music of bagpipes ("what shall the bagpipe doe"). Even without the noise of hornpipes, the Puritan's voice is an oddity in itself: he is neither a "mean" (tenor) nor a "bass," and in this way he confounds the four-voice structure of practical music systems such as Morley's. (The other reading of this line implies that he sings in a higher register, thereby ascribing to him a more "feminine" voice.) He is a walking—or, rather, a singing—contradiction, collapsing the boundaries between sacred and profane art, between masculine and feminine voices, between ordered systems of music and shrill noise.

As someone who throws into confusion nearly every category of music, Shakespeare's Puritan stands as an embodiment of the impossibility of pinning down music's meaning. Milton, as I show in the next chapter, would later theologize this aspect of music as a consequence of the Fall. Shakespeare does not explain away the instability of musical meaning in this way, even though the idea of the Fall is evoked at several moments in *The Winter's Tale*. Rather, he is content to leave it as an experience in its own right. Even more, he suggests that the ambiguity of musical meaning, rather than precluding its enjoyment, may actually be a source of its pleasure. Far from the horrifying spectacle of music's meaningless in *Titus Andronicus,* the image of this overly happy Puritan in Shakespeare's last pastoral stands as a strangely comforting acknowledgment of the fact that music is nothing like a language. As someone who would have no scruples against singing "the hundred psalms to the tune of 'Greensleeves,'" providing a literal realization of Mistress Ford's criticism in *The Merry Wives of Windsor,* he may also be a distant relative of Falstaff's. This peculiar fellow hovers just outside the boundaries of the play, somewhere with Hippolyta's Spartan hounds and Jessica's deviant ear, as a reminder of the radical subjectivity of musical experience. A disenchanted idolater, he may also be a figure for a way of seeing and hearing Shakespearean drama itself—not as something to be solved, but as something to be seen and heard, superstitiously.

1973), M2r–v. Christopher R. Wilson and Michela Calore suggest a meaning of "hornpipe" as a type of dance. *Music in Shakespeare: A Dictionary* (London: Athlone, 2005), 218. However, the instrument of the same name was in common use.

Chapter 6

The Reforming of Reformation
Milton's A Maske

> Surely, if [Pythagoras] held any doctrine of the harmony of the spheres, or taught that the heavens revolve in unison with some sweet melody, it was only as a means of suggesting allegorically the close interrelation of the orbs and their uniform revolution in accordance with the laws of destiny for ever. In this he followed the example of the poets, or (what is almost the same thing) of the divine oracles, who never display before the eyes of the vulgar any holy or secret mystery unless it be in some way cloaked or veiled.
>
> —"On the Harmony of the Spheres"
>
> The Bible... answers dubiously and darkly to the common reader.
>
> —*Areopagitica*

Unlike Shakespeare's dismantling of moralized music, Milton's comments on music and Scripture in the *Prolusions* and *Areopagitica* constitute a defense of allegory, based on a careful understanding of figuration. Just as the Bible represents divine truth elliptically or "darkly," music—as it is understood and experienced by a human audience—has a figural relation to cosmological and divine knowledge, not a literal one. And while Milton couches his defense with references to the "vulgar" or "common reader," his other remarks in the same lecture on harmony suggest that this figural way of understanding truth is essential for almost *any* human reader or auditor: only Pythagoras, who was "worthy to hold converse with the gods themselves," could hear the true music of the spheres directly.[1] Thus, for Milton, figuration, defined as an indirect and imperfect way of presenting immutable concepts through poetic or musical forms, is necessary for the human attainment of

---

1. *The Complete Prose Works of John Milton*, ed. Don M. Wolfe (New Haven, CT: Yale University Press, 1953), 1:238. All quotations of "On the Harmony" are from this edition.

knowledge, which on earth must always be considered incomplete. In this way, Milton acknowledges the instability of musical meaning that Shakespeare had repeatedly demonstrated in plays from *Titus Andronicus* to *The Winter's Tale,* but he finally deems this instability as the condition of knowledge itself.

In this chapter I suggest that Milton's conception of music and knowledge in his early writings elucidates a subtle, but ardent, defense of figuration in *A Maske*—one that powerfully answers the radically deconstructive approach to music taken by Shakespeare. Like "On the Harmony" and *Areopagitica, A Maske* represents earthly music both as a heavily mediated form and as an indispensable component of human understanding. Moreover, in some ways strikingly similar to Shakespeare, Milton expresses this complex attitude toward music and figuration through a concurrent exploration of theatricality and Ovidian typology. Like music, Ovidian poetry and theatricality are frequently characterized in Renaissance England (in both laudatory and proscriptive contexts) as opaque, indirect forms of representation; as we have seen in chapter 3, the representation of both music and the *Metamorphoses* as truth hidden under a fictive veil is a common rhetorical move in Renaissance England. As I will show in the following pages, Milton also emphasizes—though with considerably different goals than the allegorists'—the performative and dynamic aspects of theater, Ovid, and music in *A Maske,* thereby demonstrating their shared status as intensely sensuous and imperfect modes of apprehending truth.

Much Milton criticism in the last twenty years has focused on the complex evolution of typology and iconology in his prose and poetry.[2] Attention to Milton's representation of music contributes to these studies by holding up for examination Milton's own self-conscious evaluation of the usefulness of figural and iconological forms of representation. Equally important, as I will show, *A Maske* identifies figuration as a central concern of Reformist ideology. Ovid and music were themselves often politicized and moralized in early modern antitheatrical literature, a fact of which Milton was well aware. Stephen Gosson had included Ovid in his attack on plays and music, and Prynne had also cited Ovid as an example of an immoral poet in *Histriomastix,* published the year before *A Maske.* Critical work on early modern antitheatricalism has seldom explored in depth the inclusion of music and Ovid in the Puritan attacks on the theater, even though these sections of the tracts often sparked the most violent responses at the time of publication.[3]

---

2. See, for example, essays by Stella P. Revard, Kent R. Lehnhof, Raymond B. Waddington, and Lauren Shohet in *Milton Studies* 41 (2002).

3. See, for example, Stephen Buhler's account of William Prynne's trial in "Counterpoint and Controversy: Milton and the Critiques of Polyphonic Music," *Milton Studies* 36 (1998): 22–25. The

This is an unfortunate omission, since the debates over music and Ovid bring into sharp focus a sustained hostility toward figuration and performance that is crucially relevant to Milton's engagement with Protestant ideology. Early modern antitheatricalism systematically articulates a strong suspicion about pedagogical modes that rely on fictive, sensuous veils to impart divine precepts. For this reason, heavily mediated discourses such as music and Ovidian allegory routinely fall under Reformist censure. In *A Maske,* Milton's attitude toward knowledge and figuration leads to a sympathetic (at least in part) representation of music, Ovid, and theatricality, and his sustained attention to these three subjects prompts us to consider the basis of their frequent proscription in Reformist polemic. In this respect, by unleashing Puritan, Prynnian rhetoric in the vicinity of Ovid and music, *A Maske* illuminates some of the ideological currents that inform early modern antitheatricalism.

By showing how *A Maske* interrogates Puritan antitheatrical polemic, this chapter revises the prevalent critical notion that Milton "reforms" the Stuart court masque. David Norbrook suggests that, by radically departing from standard masque practices, Milton "rethink[s] masque conventions in the light of an apocalyptic Protestant ideology" and attempts to reinstate "a new moral purity and integrity in art." Likewise, Leah Marcus argues that *A Maske* is "designed... to win arts and pastimes back from the domination of the court and the Laudian wing of the church" and make them more compatible with Puritan political and moral ideology. It is certainly the case that the court masque, as a genre, embodied precisely those elements most disturbing to Puritan sentiment: theater, mixed dancing, women actors, emphasis on visual spectacle, lavish monetary expenditure, and the replenishment of royalist iconography. It is also evident that Milton assigns the most conventional masque idioms not to the masque proper but to the central figure of the antimasque. As Norbrook remarks, "Milton puts the defence of 'high solemnities' in the mouth of the antimasque villain while his heroine calls for the redistribution of wealth." Thus, whether taking Comus as an emblem for financial excess, sexual immorality, or Laudian politics, these interpretations generally presume that Comus the "antimasque villain" represents those elements which Reformist ideology—and Milton—ultimately reject.[4]

---

preeminent study of early modern antitheatricalism remains Jonas Barish's *The Antitheatrical Prejudice* (Berkeley: University of California Press, 1981), but see also Jean E. Howard, *The Stage and Social Struggle in Early Modern England* (London: Routledge, 1994) and Laura Levine, *Men in Women's Clothing: Anti-Theatricality and Effeminization, 1579–1642* (Cambridge: Cambridge University Press, 1994).

4. David Norbrook, "The Reformation of the Masque," in *The Court Masque,* ed. David Lindley (Manchester: Manchester University Press, 1984), 106–7; Leah S. Marcus, *The Politics of Mirth: Jonson, Herrick, Milton, Marvell, and the Defense of Old Holiday Pastimes* (Chicago: University of Chicago

However, Milton does not purge the masque of its intense reliance on figuration and iconology, even as he acknowledges that these "magic structures" may be championed and co-opted by someone like Comus.[5] Rather, Milton identifies the imperfect nature of these modes as a direct consequence of the Fall. In the first two parts of the chapter, I show how *A Maske* uses theatricality and Ovidian allusion to demonstrate the radical instability of figurative knowledge, in a way that makes complete "moral purity in art" impossible. In the chapter's last section, I suggest that Milton uses music—in many ways the most figurative art form—to confirm this instability, but in a way that establishes figuration as essential to *any* postlapsarian aesthetic. This acceptance of figurative "dubiousness" emphasizes the precariousness of Milton's project (because it denies authoritative claims to universal meaning), but it also enables Milton to stage a *critique* of the antitheatrical tracts for their refusal to acknowledge the impact of original sin on the transmission of knowledge. In the case of music, much Milton criticism has generally aligned Milton's sympathies with Protestant ideology as put forth in the antitheatrical tracts. Stephen Buhler, discussing the repression of polyphony in *Paradise Lost,* argues that "the controversies over counterpoint—and Milton's participation in them—help to illustrate Milton's developing and sustained allegiances to Puritan principles."[6] Yet, the aesthetic-theological politics of Milton's masque may be ideologically closer to a work like *Areopagitica,* in which the narrow proscription of classical authors and music is cited as reason for "reforming the reformation itself." Despite Milton's obvious Puritan sympathies and his need to "reform" the court masque, *A Maske* responds to Protestant ideology more fully—and more critically—than has previously been recognized.

"Subtle Incongruities": *A Maske* and Antitheatricality

When Milton's Lady ironically tells Comus to "enjoy [his] dear wit, and gay rhetoric" (790), she effectively sums up his crime as a devotion to figurative,

---

Press, 1986), 20. Marcus recognizes Milton's desire to reconcile aspects of Comus's art with his own theological outlook, although she generally upholds the oppositional Puritan-Laudian schematic by aligning Milton with contemporary Protestant ideology. See also Martin Butler, *The Stuart Court Masque and Political Culture* (Cambridge: Cambridge University Press, 2008), 352–57.

5. On the phenomenological aspect of mediation in the Stuart masque, particularly Milton's *Comus,* see Lauren Shohet, "Figuring Chastity: Milton's Ludlow Masque," in *Menacing Virgins: Representing Virginity in the Middle Ages and Renaissance,* ed. Kathleen Coyne Kelly and Marina Leslie, 146–64 (Newark: University of Delaware Press, 1999).

6. Buhler, "Counterpoint and Controversy," 18.

theatrical language.[7] In this way, Milton arms his heroine with contemporary antitheatrical polemic in order to establish a recognizable opposition between theatrical representation and plain, Puritan "honesty." Throughout *A Maske*, the Lady draws on Puritan political and moral ideology to vilify Comus on the basis of his mutability, manipulation of vision, and ability to transform others—all qualities that traditionally distinguish the Stuart masque. For example, when the Lady rebukes Comus for pretending to be a shepherd, she calls him "false traitor" and "imposter" (690, 762). William Prynne says as much about actors in *Histriomastix:* "What else is an *hypocrite, in his true etimologie, but a Stage-player, or one who acts anothers part*."[8] The Lady goes on to say:

> Hence with thy brewed enchantments, foul deceiver,
> Hast thou betrayed my credulous innocence
> With vizored falsehood, and base forgery,
> And wouldst thou seek again to trap me here
> With lickerish baits fit to ensnare a brute?
>
> (696–700)

Here, "vizor" suggests "mask," and "base forgery" recalls the Platonic bias against the theater, often cited in the tracts, in which theater's mimetic nature makes it an inferior, "base" copy of an original. This Platonic distrust of appearances underscores the Lady's statement that Comus "canst not touch the freedom of my mind/With all thy charms, although this corporal rind/Thou hast immanacled" (663–65). The Lady's reference to "corporal rind" sustains Comus's allusion to Ovid's Daphne in the preceding lines (by recuperating a latent pun on rind/skin in the *Metamorphoses*), but in a way that deflates the Ovidian comparison: Comus may transform the Lady into a second Daphne, but only on the insignificant level of corporal surfaces. Thus, by filtering Comus's rhetoric through Protestant ideology, the Lady not only counters Comus's use of allusion; she also undermines the mode of figuration that enables him to traffic in fictive iconographies in the first place.

At the same time, the attempt to vilify Comus via a Puritan critique of theatricality is risky business. By aligning the Lady with contemporary Reformist attitudes, Milton makes her vulnerable to a more damaging textual

---

7. All quotations of Milton's works (excepting "On the Harmony") are from *John Milton,* ed. Stephen Orgel and Jonathan Goldberg (Oxford: Oxford University Press, 1991), unless otherwise noted. Translations of Milton's Latin poetry are my own.

8. William Prynne, *Histriomastix: The Players Scourge or Actors Tragedie* (1633), ed. Arthur Freeman (New York: Garland, 1974), 158.

contamination: the most radical Puritan antitheatrical rhetoric, which seeks to dissolve the theater entirely. Indeed, early twentieth-century Milton criticism suggests the extent to which *A Maske* is susceptible to contamination by Reformist polemic. Enid Welsford writes that "there is in *Comus* a subtle incongruity between the symbolism and the idea that it is meant to symbolise, and of this incongruity Milton seems to be entirely unaware. He could not see that the masque, whose presiding deity was Hymen, was a most unsuitable vehicle for the unfolding of the 'sage and serious doctrine of virginity.'"[9] This reading of the Lady's harsh rhetoric, although it problematically denies the possibility of Milton's awareness of his masque's incongruities, foregrounds the fact that the masque is fully realized only in performance. Milton's Lady, for all her rebukes, *is* acting in a masque after all, and within this performative context mimesis is unavoidable. Welsford's sense of a "subtle incongruity" hits at a conflict between content and context in *A Maske* that must be considered—namely, what the Lady argues as being beyond theatrical representation *is* being represented. In contrast to Welsford's reading, arguments about *A Maske* as "Puritan" or "anti-Laudian" often avoid the problem of how one can articulate a rejection of figuration and appearance, particularly in a dramatic medium. Such arguments tacitly assume that Milton's masque is somehow exempt from contemporary Puritan antitheatricality. For example, Maryann McGuire acknowledges the relevance of William Prynne's notoriously antitheatrical *Histriomastix* to Milton's masque, but she then confidently asserts that "Milton was no Prynne" in order to avoid the possibility of literary or ideological contamination.[10] Accordingly, when Milton's Lady rejects the argument that beauty "must be shown/In courts, at feasts, and high solemnities" (745–46), we are expected not to dwell on the fact that she herself is conspicuously on display to the Bridgewater court. McGuire admits Prynne's applicability to *masques,* only to foreclose on his applicability to *A Maske.*

Milton does not, however, evade the potential conflict between the Lady's argument and the physical occasion of its utterance. Rather, he intensifies this conflict by making theatrical self-consciousness (at least for the

---

9. Enid Welsford, *The Court Masque* (Cambridge: Cambridge University Press, 1927), 320. Many early critics also find Milton's Lady too prudish. See Sir Walter Raleigh, *Milton* (New York: Putnam, 1900), 28, and Douglas Bush, *The Renaissance and English Humanism* (1933; repr., Toronto: University of Toronto Press, 1968), who remarks that "one would rather live with Comus than the Lady" (108).

10. Maryann C. McGuire, *Milton's Puritan Masque* (Athens: University of Georgia Press, 1983), 22. See also William S. Miller Jr., *The Mythography of Milton's "Comus"* (New York: Garland, 1988), 169–212.

audience) nearly unavoidable, as in the Lady's final repudiation of Comus's theatricality:

> Enjoy your dear wit, and gay rhetoric
> That hath so well been taught her dazzling fence,
> Thou art not fit to hear thyself convinced;
> Yet should I try, the uncontrollèd worth
> Of this pure cause would kindle my rapt spirits
> To such a flame of sacred vehemence,
> That dumb things would be moved to sympathize,
> And the brute Earth would lend her nerves, and shake,
> Till all thy magic structures reared so high,
> Were shattered into heaps o'er thy false head.
> (790–99)

As the Lady calls attention to Comus's "dazzling fence," which she brands as lacking substance, she also implies the performativity of her own response. For one thing, the effects of the "sacred vehemence" she describes are remarkably Orphic. While such language gestures toward prophecy, the Orphic parallel firmly places the Lady in the context of a listening *audience:* like Orpheus, Milton's Lady stands before an enraptured audience that will be "moved to sympathize" if she is successful. By emphasizing the dramatic nature of the Lady's utterance, Milton comes close to suggesting the self-contradictory theatricality of much radical antitheatricalism itself, which, as Jonas Barish has noted, often constitutes the very thing it aims to suppress.[11] In a sense, the sincerity of the Lady's argument depends on a deliberate unawareness of its occasional context—an unawareness that is far less appropriate to a masque performance than to a book like *Histriomastix.* As Stephen Orgel points out, theatrical self-consciousness is systemically more pronounced in the court masque than in any other dramatic genre; the hero of a Stuart masque conventionally triumphs by virtue of "*know[ing]* that he is an actor in a masque and is conscious of the presence and significance of the audience."[12] The masque, which for Orgel is radically self-conscious, is for Milton's Lady a remarkably unreflexive event.

In threatening to bring down Comus's "magic structures," the Lady reiterates a brand of antitheatricality typical of Ben Jonson in his attacks on

---

11. See Barish, *Antitheatrical Prejudice,* 83–89.
12. Stephen Orgel, *The Jonsonian Masque* (Cambridge, MA: Harvard University Press, 1967), 13, my emphasis.

Inigo Jones, whose magic structures Jonson begrudged as the most popular element of the Stuart masque.[13] Similar to Jonson's expressions of "unresolved ambivalence" toward the stage,[14] the Lady's implicit criticism of the masque paradoxically belies the fact that she is one of the principal entertainers of the evening: the magic structures falling on Comus's head would presumably fall on hers too. This self-referential backfiring, which nearly amounts to a dramatic contradiction, may very well suggest the stage's inherent limitation: the masque cannot represent an attack on figuration without undermining its own message. In this way Milton demonstrates the masque's profound inability to advance a strict, Puritan aesthetic. Even further, Milton's dramaturgy during the temptation scene shows how the rejection of figuration might be indistinguishable from its authorization. In performance, the Lady's immobility and silence can register iconologically as a reminder of monarchical form. As the silent center and object of many of the spoken and sung words in the second half of the masque, the Lady takes on the visual qualities of the Stuart masque's sustaining icon: the "non-dramatic" monarch or other royal figure who conventionally "stays in the center of the masque universe" and silently authorizes the entertainment that is taking place.[15] Thus, even if the Lady's silence is intended as an assertion of the superiority of contemplation over linguistic display, *A Maske* exposes the impotence of silence when placed in a theatrical context. Taken all together, the Lady's silence and immobility effectively suggest the only logical outcome of her vehement antitheatricalism. The Lady's antitheatrical rhetoric, taken to its extreme conclusion, is ultimately self-negating, and the fact that she is literally stuck to her chair even after Comus is expelled suggests that a public condemnation of theatricality fatally ignores the condition of its utterance. It is worth noting that the Lady has no more lines for the rest of the masque. As she sits stuck to her chair in a gum of self-contradiction, forced to repudiate theatricality and demonstrate its effectiveness simultaneously, she visually emblematizes what a Puritan poetics, in the most radical Prynnian sense, must be.

---

13. For an excellent discussion of Jonson's antitheatricalism, see Barish, *Antitheatrical Prejudice*, 132–54. See also D. J. Gordon, "Poet and Architect: The Intellectual Setting of the Quarrel between Ben Jonson and Inigo Jones," in *The Renaissance Imagination*, ed. Stephen Orgel, 77–101 (Berkeley: University of California Press, 1975).

14. Barish, *Antitheatrical Prejudice*, 133.

15. Orgel, *Jonsonian Masque*, 18. Joseph Loewenstein also notes that the Lady's immobility recalls "the ironic image of the monarch enthroned in the royal seat" (*Responsive Readings: Versions of Echo in Pastoral, Epic, and the Jonsonian Masque* [New Haven, CT: Yale University Press, 1984], 139). Although it runs somewhat counter to my claims, his argument that this identification actually suggests a deficiency in royalist masque convention (by forestalling the more dynamic aspect of the quest) is persuasive.

Figuring Ovid

Milton compounds the problematizing effects of the masque's theatricality with a sustained use of Ovid that emphasizes the pitfalls of figural representation. In this respect, Milton astutely identifies the proscription of Ovid in the antitheatrical tracts as an attack on figuration. At the same time, Milton makes figural representation in his masque unavoidable. In the previous section I suggest how the masque's iconographic and theatrical modes (the *appearance* of the Lady as an Orphic or monarchical figure) can undercut its poetic or argumentative ones (the Lady's antitheatrical polemic).[16] The masque's Ovidianism operates in much the same way, since, as Milton shows, poetic allusions to Ovid can spawn a series of figural or iconological associations that exceed any single ideological or political message.

Early in the masque, Milton's Lady alludes to two Ovidian myths that, despite their tragic associations, function largely as innocent poetic metaphors:

> Sweet Echo, sweetest nymph that liv'st unseen
> Within thy airy shell
> By slow Meander's margent green,
> And in the violet-embroidered vale
> Where the love-lorn nightingale
> Nightly to thee her sad song mourneth well.
> (230–35)

As Richard DuRocher has noted, the Lady's allusion to Philomela ("the love-lorn nightingale") is potentially gloomy: in the *Metamorphoses*, Philomela becomes a nightingale only after Tereus has brutally raped her and removed her tongue.[17] The apparent figural similarity between the nightingale and Milton's Lady, who both sing a sad song to Echo, does not suggest a happy outcome. In context, however, the Lady's allusions do not evoke any real sense

---

16. Cedric Brown suggests that the text of *A Maske* is primarily intended for reception in a *poetic* (literary) mode rather than a theatrical or iconological one, citing the fact that Milton made several strategic changes and elaborations for the 1637 publication. See *John Milton's Aristocratic Entertainments* (Cambridge: Cambridge University Press, 1985), 132–52. The distinction is not trivial, since reading the *Maske* poetically leads Brown and many other critics to assert the work's "ardently, idealistically reformist spirit" (2), thus foregoing the possibility of a critique of Reformist ideology. Still, Brown sensitively points out a number of dramatically "awkward" moments that Milton's emendations create—an effect that Milton may very well have intended.

17. Richard DuRocher, *Milton and Ovid* (Ithaca, NY: Cornell University Press, 1985), 50–51. DuRocher also notes the dark implications of the Lady's invocation to Echo, comparing it to Ovidian soliloquies "in which an isolated female character reveals her wavering personality."

CHAPTER 6

of danger or compromise her intended meaning. Rather, they are contained by a pastoral, lyrical tradition that keeps tragedy at bay.[18] A darker Ovidianism comes to the foreground with the entrance of Comus. Comus's association with Circe, his intemperate sensuality, and his transformative powers all encourage Milton's audience to see him as an Ovidian prototype. Likewise, when Comus first hears the Lady singing, he imaginatively evokes an Ovidian world that is far more morally suspect than Philomela or Echo:

> I have oft heard
> My mother Circe with the Sirens three,
> Amidst the flowery-kirtled Naiades
> Culling their potent herbs, and baleful drugs,
> Who as they sung, would take the prisoned soul,
> And lap it in Elysium; Scylla wept,
> And chid her barking waves into attention,
> And fell Charybdis murmured soft applause.
> (252–59)

Comus's references to Circe and the Sirens, and his own self-identification with Scylla, register Milton's construction of the antimasque through Ovidian models. Citing Scylla's transformation into a self-consuming monster in the *Metamorphoses,* DuRocher recognizes the moral appropriateness of Ovid's Scylla as a figure for Comus, since "for Milton the 'restless' circularity of the process—to flee, but drag along what one flees; to be self-fed and self-consumed—is both the condition and the horror of evil."[19] Thus, while Milton makes associations between the Lady and Ovid's Philomela and Echo, his use of Ovidian typology in his representation of Comus initially distinguishes pastoral humility from sensuous, "restless" mutability.

The tendency to view Comus as an Ovidian prototype—and his seduction as an Ovidian plot—is partly an effect of the masque's iconographic mode.

---

18. However, Loewenstein notes that often "Milton's associations with echo have an odd morbidity, as if he recognized only the lamenting strain in the traditions of echo," suggesting that this darker strain of the pastoral-echo tradition profoundly inflects the Lady's performance of her song (*Responsive Readings,* 142). On the role of Ovid in *A Maske,* see Davis P. Harding, *Milton and the Renaissance Ovid* (Urbana, IL: University of Illinois Press 1946), 58–66; DuRocher, *Milton and Ovid,* 47–58; Leonora Leet Brodwin, "Milton and the Renaissance Circe," *Milton Studies* 6 (1974): 21–83. See also Judith E. Browning's article "Sin, Eve, and Circe: *Paradise Lost* and the Ovidian Circe Tradition," *Milton Studies* 26 (1991): 135–58. Although Browning's article focuses on the Ovidian elements in *Paradise Lost,* her discussion of Ovid's Scylla and Circe has been particularly helpful for the present chapter.

19. DuRocher, *Milton and Ovid,* 49.

In other words, Comus's legibility as a Circe or Scylla figure is enhanced by a mode of aesthetic reception, endemic to the Stuart court masque, in which the characters on stage are "read" as mythical or allegorical personifications.[20] However, in contrast to masque convention, Milton's recourse to Ovid does not ultimately stabilize the allegorical meanings in *A Maske*. As Comus elaborates his attempt to seduce the Lady, he incorporates the Ovidian associations so far established into a larger pattern that serves *his* immoral designs. For example, even though Comus recognizes a "sacred delight" in the Lady's pastoral singing, such delight does not reform him. Instead, Comus's memory of Circe and the Sirens contaminates that delight and refigures it as sensual. He imagines the Lady as someone who improves on, but does not redeem, the sensuous qualities of Circe, Sirens, and Scylla ("and she shall be my queen," 265). In this respect, Comus's attempt to seduce the Lady is tantamount to his representation of her as an Ovidian *figura*. The example of Ovid's Scylla is especially illustrative of Comus's subversive use of allusion. In book 14 of the *Metamorphoses*, Glaucus attempts to seduce the virgin Scylla and appeals to Circe for help. When Circe offers herself instead and is rejected, she poisons Scylla's favorite wading pool and transforms her into the half-woman, half-Cerberean monster that terrorizes Odysseus. Like Ovid's Glaucus, Comus is enchanted by the Lady and appeals to Circean magic to trap her. Additionally, Circe's "liquors brewed," mentioned in Ovid (*latices pressi, Met.* 14.56), become Comus's "brewed enchantments" (*A Maske*, 696), and her "charm, dark with its maze of uncanny words" (*obscurum verborum ambage novorum...carmen, Met.* 14.57–58) suggests his "dear wit, and gay rhetoric" (*A Maske*, 790). Like his mother, Circe, Comus draws on occult magic to pollute a virgin and transform her into the object of her own horror. In the process, Comus promiscuously invests the figure of Ovid's Scylla—already identified with himself—with the Lady's own plight.

The special violence of Comus's allusiveness is that he repeatedly uses Renaissance moralizations of Ovid for immoral purposes. Whereas Renaissance moralizations often attempt to control the meaning of classical poetry and assimilate it to a Christian ideology, Comus takes advantage of the inherent figurativeness (and hence, the potential instability) of this mode of allegory. Although Ovid's Scylla is a helpless victim, the moralized Scylla of the Renaissance mythographies is appetitive; the slipperiness of this allegorical association opens up an imaginative space for Comus through which he

---

20. See Barbara K. Lewalski, "Milton's *Comus* and the Politics of Masquing," in *The Politics of the Stuart Court Masque,* ed. David Bevington and Peter Holbrook, 296–300 (Cambridge: Cambridge University Press, 1998).

can suggest the Lady's susceptibility to temptation. Judith Browning notes that the Renaissance moralizations of Scylla "associate her Circean 'pollution' with her inability to withstand 'bewitching pleasure,'"[21] and Comus evokes a similar association when, having "immanacled" the Lady in his hall with "charms," he tempts her with "all the pleasures/That fancy can beget on youthful thoughts" (664–69). In this way, the Renaissance Scylla not only provides Comus with a model for his own seduction plot; it also enables him to imagine the Lady—who parallels Ovid's Scylla—as someone who both succumbs to *and is a figure for* appetite. After all, Comus does not intend to rape the Lady. He attempts to seduce her and make her a willing accomplice in her own pollution. To this end, Comus encourages his audience to see the Lady not as chastity (as she is conventionally known) but as appetite. Comus's allegorical Ovidianism (in contrast to a lyrical use of Ovid), aided by the Renaissance moralizations, particularly enables him to shift the masque's figural politics in a way that aligns the Lady (and not merely himself) with Ovid's Scylla. The Lady's nondramatic immobility in performance corroborates this mode of Ovidian association: "fixed, and motionless" in Comus's chair just as Ovid's Scylla is fixed in the water with her barking dogs, the Lady replicates Scylla's fate (819). Likewise, the "glutinous heat" that binds the Lady to her chair (917) recalls the gluttonous heat that Renaissance mythographers associate with Circe and Scylla.[22] This is Ovidianism with a vengeance: in a medium as intensely iconographic as the Stuart masque, where visual association is nearly equivalent to meaning, Comus's "posing" of the Lady as Scylla amounts to an imaginative rape. His Ovidian "moralization" of the Lady engenders an iconological pollution of her before the actual event, effectively evacuating the Renaissance allegories of their moral efficacy by using their colorful rhetoric to stage an immoral scene.

Through Comus's manipulation of Ovidian *figurae,* Milton appears to confirm temporarily the depiction of Ovidian poetry in the antitheatrical tracts as morally unsalvageable. On the one hand, Comus's allusiveness does much to justify Puritan suspicion of Ovid, since for him Ovidian mythology provides a literary model for sexual corruption. On the other hand, Protestant critiques of Ovid (and, to a lesser extent, of Virgil) also reject the allegorization of classical poets by expressing a deep-seated suspicion of veiled, "figured" truth, regardless of how morally conservative that truth may be. Milton's masque initially bolsters this suspicion by suggesting that the Renaissance moralizations, rather than having strict control over poetry's meaning,

---

21. Browning, "Sin, Eve, and Circe," 139.
22. Harding, *Milton and the Renaissance Ovid,* 59.

actually depend on a mode of figuration which is profoundly unstable and susceptible to abuse. Comus's eagerness to use this instability to his advantage, demonstrated in the allusions to Scylla, is even more pronounced in his reference to Ovid's Daphne:

> Nay lady sit; if I but wave this wand,
> Your nerves are all chained up in alabaster,
> And you a statue, or as Daphne was
> Root-bound, that fled Apollo.
> (659–62)

This allusion serves Comus in two ways. First, it allows him (and the audience) to imagine at least a half-successful outcome to his pursuit of the Lady, since Daphne ultimately became the symbol of Apollo's poetic power. Second, and more importantly, by aligning the Lady with Ovid's most famous poetic *figura*, Comus emphasizes the Lady's role—entirely appropriate to the masque genre—*as figure*. It is precisely amid the shifting meanings of *figura/forma* that Ovid's Apollo is able to possess Daphne. Once transformed into poetic and corporal figure, Daphne "consents" to Apollonian ownership: "The laurel waved her new-made branches, and seemed to move her head-like top in full consent" (*factis modo laurea ramis/adnuit utque caput visa est agitasse cacumen*, 1.566–67). Similarly, Comus's figurations of the Lady allow him to "read" her as a second Daphne or, even worse, a second Gallathea, "all chained up in alabaster" (*A Maske* 660).[23]

Milton's reference to Daphne hints at the reason for Ovid's particular aptness for subversive allusion and for his prominence in the antitheatrical tracts. Ovid's Daphne episode plays on the potential conflict between form and content (Apollo's selfish interpretation of the tree's nodding is one of the masterstrokes in the *Metamorphoses*), a conflict that Ovid develops throughout the rest of his poem. This instability of figural meaning, which Puritan polemicists rightly suspect as being encouraged by Ovidian poetry,

---

23. DuRocher, on the other hand, while acknowledging Comus's "depth of imaginative power and ethical perversion," argues that the Lady is never contaminated by Comus's Ovidianism: "To anyone familiar with Ovid's myth, however, Comus's attempt to heighten his putative mastery over the Lady by the comparison [to Daphne] must seem vain, if not ludicrous. Daphne actually avoided Apollo's seduction precisely by becoming 'root-bound,' and her transformation into the laurel, though unwelcome, was not a result of Apollo's power" (*Milton and Ovid*, 51–52). Yet it is precisely the "ludicrousness" of Comus's Ovidian perversions, I argue, that reveals the potentially radical instability of Ovidian figuration in the poem, which Comus seeks to exploit. By contaminating the myth of Daphne and Apollo with that of Pygmalion (which DuRocher does not note), Comus takes the elements in the Daphne and Apollo story that do not support his sinister agenda and reworks them to his advantage.

makes deception in poetry possible. Milton glosses this possibility of deception in the exchange between the two brothers by showing how even the most straightforward articulation of ideology may be contaminated by the masque's Ovidian figurations. Realizing they have lost their sister, the Second Brother fears that she is "within the direful grasp/Of savage hunger, or of savage heat" (357–58). After learning of his sister's predicament from the Attendant Spirit, the Elder Brother correctly identifies his sister's capturer as a metamorphic power:

> But evil on itself shall back recoil,
> And mix no more with goodness, when at last
> Gathered like scum, and settled to itself
> It shall be in eternal restless change
> Self-fed, and self-consumed....
>
> (593–97)

Like someone versed in the antitheatrical tracts, the Elder Brother indicates his distaste for metamorphosis by equating moral evil with "eternal restless change." As DuRocher correctly notes, the Elder Brother's depiction of evil ("self-fed, and self-consumed") points to Comus's earlier self-identification with Ovid's Scylla.[24] However, the Elder Brother cannot control his own metaphors, since his words also suggest the image of the Lady herself, who at this moment is visually surrounded (as Ovid's Scylla is) by a rout of barking monsters. The Lady, "within the direful grasp" of a Scylla figure, is also in danger of being read *iconologically* as the Scylla of the Renaissance mythographers.[25] This iconological identification, whose persuasiveness must be recognized as an effect of the masque's visual, performative nature, frustrates the easy *poetic* association of Comus with Scylla that the Elder Brother attempts to convey.[26] Thus, poetic terms in the masque that would enable an easy

---

24. Ibid., 48.

25. Cf. George Sandys, *Ovid's Metamorphosis Englished, Mythologized, and Represented in Figures* (1632), ed. Karl K. Hulley and Stanley T. Vandersall (Lincoln: University of Nebraska Press, 1970): "*Circe* was said to bee the daughter of *Sol* and *Persis*, in that lust proceeds from heat and moisture, which naturally incites to luxury; and getting the dominion, deformes our soules with all bestial vices; alluring some to inordinate Venus; others to anger, cruelty, and every excesse of passion." Brodwin argues that Milton's treatment of Circe differs from the Renaissance moralizations of Circe, asserting that the Homeric source is the version closest to Milton's ("Milton and the Renaissance Circe," 23). Browning, however, in her study of *Paradise Lost*, notes Milton's habit of specifically evoking Ovidian versions of Scylla with Circe in the poem ("Sin, Eve, and Circe").

26. For an analogous example of how visual, iconographic meanings may override textual ones in the masque, see Orgel's discussion of Hunnis's *The Ladie of the Lake* (*Jonsonian Masque*, 39–42).

distinction between chastity and contagion threaten to collapse into each other by way of their figural semblance when the masque is performed.

Milton raises the crisis of figuration to its highest pitch at the end of the temptation scene by making a striking parallel between the Lady and Ovid's Philomela. The Lady's final assertion that she will raise "such a flame of sacred vehemence,/That dumb things would be moved to sympathize" (795–96) echoes Protestant formulations of inspiration, but it also imitates Ovid's Philomela immediately after her rape by Tereus:

> ipsa pudore
> proiecto tua facta loquar: si copia detur,
> in populos veniam; si silvis clausa tenebor,
> inplebo silvas et conscia saxa movebo;
> audiet haec aether et si deus ullus in illo est!
> (6.544–48)

I will myself cast shame aside and proclaim what you have done. If I should have the chance, I would go where people throng and tell it; if I am kept shut up in these woods, I will fill the woods with my story and move the very rocks to pity. The air of heaven shall hear it, and, if there is any god in heaven, he shall hear it too.

The Ovidian quotation here recalls the Attendant Spirit's earlier reference to the Lady as a "poor hapless nightingale" and the reference to "love-lorn nightingale" in the Lady's song—except that the metaphor now carries all its tragic associations. Whereas earlier the Lady could unproblematically allude to Philomela within the context of pastoral, at this point in the masque it is much more difficult to ignore the Lady's role as a second Philomela. In a sense, Milton's Lady is tricked into "speaking" Ovid. The fact that Ovidian quotation and antitheatrical rhetoric converge in the Lady's final speech suggests that her repudiation of Comus has somehow backfired. Paradoxically, Ovidian quotation and Puritan polemic *are* saying the same thing here, in that they both pressure a reading of the Lady as already contaminated. For one thing, Philomela's statement in the *Metamorphoses* that she will move rocks to pity is directed at a condition (rape) that Ovid represents as "unspeakable" (*nefas*).[27] Thus, although Milton's Lady refers to a subject (chastity) that she believes to be beyond the representational limits of the stage, the

---

27. Lynn Enterline, *The Rhetoric of the Body from Ovid to Shakespeare* (Cambridge: Cambridge University Press, 2000), 3.

Ovidian context makes her ensuing silence indistinguishable from the shame (*pudor*) that Philomela casts aside. For Ovid's Philomela, it is the violation of chastity, not its essence, that is truly unspeakable. At the same time, Puritan polemic as put forth by Prynne categorizes the Lady as a "notorious whore" by virtue of her performance in a masque. Under this harsh view of theatricality, the Lady's "sacred vehemence" represented on stage would look very much like Comus's "dazzling fence" and would undoubtedly evoke more Ovidian resonances. Given this impasse, Milton seems to suggest a profound weakness of Protestant ideology—or at least of its articulation—in the face of figural representation. Stuck between Comus's profligate Ovidianism and the radical Puritanism of her own arguments, between a figural context that reads silence as *pudor* and an ideology that suspects female declamation as "whorish," Milton's Lady finds herself with no critical space in which to move.[28] To put it glibly, she finds herself between Scylla and Charybdis.

The Different Musics of *A Maske*

The failure to appreciate the urgency of the Lady's ideological dilemma, represented by her immobility, inevitably leads to a failure to appreciate her very real need for deliverance. Such a failure causes Stanley Fish to remark, after a lengthy discussion on the meaning of haemony, that the Lady is "fixed but free."[29] However, just as haemony as a magical device is insufficient in *A Maske*, the "fixed but free" argument would hardly satisfy the Earl of Bridgewater as to why his daughter cannot return home. The point is that Milton has created an ideological and aesthetic crux in which allegorical Ovidianism, royalist iconography, and zealous antitheatricalism all compete for the meaning of the Lady's theatrical presence. Milton's awareness that neither an inward reversion to the "freedom of [the Lady's] mind" nor a prophecy-inspired shattering of magic structures is an acceptable *occasional* solution (that is, they will not get us to the evening's festive dances) suggests that they

---

28. In the same vein, Marcus reads the Lady's immobility as a visual representation of the "Puritan dilemma in the face of Laudian power—the plight of those who were locked into rigid rejection of all arts and pastimes because those which were most culturally conspicuous seemed tainted with political and sexual corruption" (*Politics of Mirth,* 198). Whereas Marcus's interpretation is primarily informed by political context, my argument is more directed at the Lady's poetic and rhetorical effects. In this respect, I argue that the Lady's harsh absolutism and antitheatricalism are as much (if not more) responsible as Laud for her immobility.

29. Stanley Fish, "Problem Solving in *Comus*," in *Illustrious Evidence: Approaches to English Literature of the Early Seventeenth Century,* ed. Earl Miner (Berkeley: University of California Press, 1975), 127.

are insufficient moral responses as well, if we believe that *A Maske* sustains its moral-ideological trial through the end. Indeed, the masque continues to work out the difficulties of figuration raised in the scenes with Comus, and it finally resolves these issues in the context of a third, related contemporary debate: the controversy over music. Milton's masque, it should be noted, ends with a dense sequence of musical interludes: the musical invocation to Sabrina, the spell that frees the Lady from her chair, the restoration of the children to their parents, and the song that the Attendant Spirit sings as he returns to the heavens. As Louis Martz suggests, music in *Comus* "gives one the power to penetrate disguises, guard from evil, and rescue from enchantment.... Music serve[s] to create a harmony in which the oppositions of life are reconciled."[30] We should not take Martz's reference to "harmony" to conclude that music for Milton is merely a metaphysical conceit or a metaphor for rejuvenation—in the masque, the *performance* of music exemplifies the need for figural modes of knowledge in a postlapsarian world.

There are many reasons why music is, for Milton, an appropriate context for the close examination of Protestant ideology. Through its constitutive performativity—the fact that it cannot be reduced to verbal rhetoric or visual icon—music achieves an illustrative force that effectively clarifies the theological and political debates over Ovid and theater as arguments over the transmission of knowledge. As we have seen in chapter 1, the Reformist debate over music that is exemplified by Stephen Gosson's *Schoole of Abuse* focuses on music's perceived illegibility in the face of elaborate polyphony and hieroglyphic notation. What is being attacked in these tracts is not just complex harmonization or church polyphony but any type of music that has the effect of undermining the text's authority. Music independent of language is no different from bestial noise, and Thomas Becon's argument that polyphony in church services forces singers to "barke a counterpoynt as it were a number of dogges" comes close to Milton's characterization of Comus and Circe, who change people "into some brutish form of wolf, or bear,/Or ounce, or tiger, hog, or bearded goat" (70–71).[31]

Milton had often considered the relationship between music and language in his early poems, in which he frequently praises music's ability to complement and give emotional force to things expressed in poetry. In his much-maligned "The Passion," for example, in which Milton professes to "set my harp to notes of saddest woe" (9), he portrays the relationship between music and language as wholly sympathetic: "Me softer airs befit, and softer strings/Of

---

30. Louis Martz, "The Music of *Comus*," in Miner, *Illustrious Evidence*, 108.
31. Thomas Becon, *The Reliques of Rome* (London, 1563), 121v.

lute, or viol still, more apt for mournful things" (27–28). The fact that Milton had actually played the viol suggests that he is not merely waxing metaphorical; rather, the lines attest to the belief in music's expressiveness, as well as the idea that music and poetry could be complementary activities *within* a single person—somewhat like (as Milton would later characterize his prose writing) performing related activities with the left and right hands. Likewise, in his sixth *Elegy* ("To Charles Diodati"), Milton again alludes to music's ability to speak a kind of poetic truth through the sounds produced by an instrument: "Phoebus silently creeps into your heart... through eyes of girls and through sounding fingers" (*tacitum per pectora serpere Phoebum...perque puellares oculos digitumque sonantem,* 45–47). Unlike "The Passion," however, the sixth *Elegy* associates performed music specifically with lyric poetry: epic poetry requires the avoidance of wine, Ovidian poetry, and the strains of the lyre, just as Ulysses avoids the "womanish sounds" (*foeminei soni,* 74) of the Sirens.

In "Ad patrem," Milton again represents music and language as complementary activities, although here the relationship between the two arts is more strained and marked by an underlying sense of competition. Here, addressing himself to his father, a composer, Milton defends his decision to be a poet by representing music and poetry as nearly indistinguishable activities. The poem begins by pitting the "thin sounds" (*tenues soni*) and "empty words" (*vacua verba*) of ineffective poetry against the ennobled *carmen* that Milton hopes to present to his father as a sign of gratitude. The word *carmen*, which can be translated as either "poem" or "song," appears eleven times in the first half of the poem; its precedence in the poem over other forms of music, such as *cantus,* suggests that Milton sees music and poetry as inextricably joined. In this respect, the poem takes part in the nostalgic attempt—well rehearsed in early modern England—to restore the union of music and poetry that was believed to have existed in the ancient past.[32] Accordingly, Milton's lofty aspiration that his poetry will achieve sublimity coincides with his vision of poetry that is fully wedded to music: "My sweet poems, joined with the smooth-speaking lute, will sound through the stars and the vaulted reach of the twin poles" (*Dulcia suaviloquo sociantes carmina plectro, / Astra quibus, geminique poli convexa sonabunt,* 33–34).

---

32. Of course, the idea that Milton's poetry actually incorporates musical idioms and styles—often with reference to the influence of Italian musical styles on Milton—has been fruitfully discussed. See Diane McColley, *Poetry and Music in Seventeenth-Century England* (Cambridge: Cambridge University Press, 1997), 175–217; Louise Schleiner, *The Living Lyre in English Verse from Elizabeth through the Restoration* (Columbia: University of Missouri Press, 1984), 102–57; Gretchen Ludke Finney, *Musical Backgrounds for English Literature: 1580–1650* (New Brunswick: Rutgers University Press, 1962), 175–219.

Despite the poem's vision of a harmonious union of music and poetry, however, Milton suggests that music *without* poetry is morally deficient. For example, Milton's choice of words implies that music is noble when it resembles poetry: "sweet-speaking" (*suaviloquens*), "measured" (*modulamen*), "meter" (*numerus*). This idea is made explicit at the end of the poem's section on music, in which Milton firmly distinguishes between song and purely instrumental music:

> Denique quid vocis modulamen inane juvabit,
> Verborum sensusque vacans, numerique loquacis?
> Silvestres decet iste choros, non Orphea cantus,
> Qui tenuit fluvious & quercubus addidit aures
> Carmine, non cithara...
>
> (50–54)

Therefore who will enjoy melody deprived of voice, feelings without words or the rhythms of speech? Such music is fit for woodland revelers, not the singer Orpheus, who held rivers and gave ears to oak trees through songs, not through the cithara.

Here, Milton's derisive reference to "woodland singers" may be a subtle echo of Spenser's "woody Nymphes," who idolatrously worship Una in book 1 of *The Faerie Queene*. More suggestively, Milton's pointed reference to the cithara recalls Boethius's disparaging characterization of instrumental musicians in *De institutione musica*: "Those of the class which is dependent upon instruments...such as kitharists...are excluded from comprehension of musical knowledge, since, as was said, they act as slaves."[33] It also alludes, I believe, to Vincenzo Galilei's damning portrait of citharists in his *Dialogo della musica antica e della moderna* (1581), which Milton is likely to have known. In this work, Galilei blames citharists for being among the first to separate music from poetry: "The cithara players of those times began— either for the purpose of somehow surpassing those who sang to the cithara or of escaping the need of always having a singer with them...to seek a way of somehow delighting the ear with the mere sound of the instrument, without the aid of the voice."[34] This is the same criticism made by Gosson

---

33. Boethius, *Fundamentals of Music*, trans. Calvin M. Bower, ed. Claude V. Palisca (New Haven, CT: Yale University Press, 1989), 51. The passage is discussed at greater length in chapter 3.

34. Cited in Oliver Strunk, *Source Readings in Musical History* (New York: W. W. Norton, 1950), 308–9.

in *The Schoole of Abuse:* at a crucial point in time, willful musicians, drunk on instrumental sound and on their desire for innovation, stripped music of its linguistic meaning and corrupted it. In this light, the subtext of Milton's poem, carefully suggested by his choice of musical terms, seems to suggest his sympathies with Reformist ideals.[35]

Most readers of Milton view *A Maske* as also upholding the Reformist attitude toward music, noting that the characters' descriptions of Comus echo the conventional attacks on music.[36] For example, when the Elder Brother says that his sister has "no gross ear" (458), he suggests that the Lady's chastity depends on her ability to discriminate among different kinds of sound, an observation that is consistent with the masque's repeated references to ears and hearing. This sensitivity to various kinds of music arguably explains Milton's removal of the word "counterpoint" from the Lady's song to Echo at the beginning of the masque. In the Bridgewater manuscript, the Lady's song has "Sweet queen of parley, daughter of the sphere. / So mayst thou be translated to the skies / And hould a Counterpointe to all heav'ns harmonies" (241–43), whereas in the 1637 publication of the masque, Milton replaces "hould a Counterpointe" with "give resounding grace."[37] As Stephen Buhler suggests, "Milton apparently decided, counterpoint should not be approvingly mentioned in a song that" is clearly monodic. The settings that Henry Lawes wrote for the masque's songs, Buhler notes, conform well to the "pattern advanced by the Reformist critique of polyphony."[38] Nonetheless, readings of *A Maske* as simply extolling a "monodic," Reformist style tend to downplay the many other kinds of music that are sanctioned by the masque, including the loud "jigs" and "rural dance" which are foregrounded by the Lady's return to the court (952).[39] Moreover, while Milton clearly

---

35. On the relationship between "Ad patrem" and Reformist ideology, see also Peter C. Herman, "Milton and the Muse-Haters: *Ad patrem, L'Allegro/Il Penseroso,* and the Ambivalences of Poetry," *Criticism* 37 (1995): 37–56; M. N. K. Mander, "The *Epistola ad patrem:* Milton's Apology for Poetry," *Milton Quarterly* 23 (1989): 158–65.

36. See Buhler, "Counterpoint and Controversy"; Norbrook, "Reformation of the Masque"; and Mary Elizabeth Basile, "The Music of *A Maske,*" *Milton Quarterly* 27 (1993): 86–98.

37. For the Bridgewater text of the Lady's song to Echo, see *Milton's Dramatic Poems,* ed. Geoffrey Bullough and Margaret Bullough (London: Athlone, 1978).

38. Buhler, "Counterpoint and Controversy," 26–27. See also Peter Walls, "'Comus': The Court Masque Questioned," in *The Well Enchanting Skill: Music, Poetry, and Drama in the Culture of the Renaissance,* ed. John Caldwell, Edward Olleson, and Susan Wollenberg, 107–13 (Oxford: Clarendon, 1990).

39. Likewise, in his essay on *Comus,* John Creaser argues that positive, royalist imagery runs throughout the masque, going so far as to say that "the final scene is not a charmingly parochial touch, but a symbol of vice-regal authority." "'The present aid of this occasion': The Setting of *Comus,*" in Lindley, *Court Masque,* 113.

evokes Lawes through the figure of the Attendant Spirit ("a swain,/That to the service of this house belongs," 84–85), he is careful to distinguish this figure from the other, equally necessary "artists" that preside over the Lady's resuscitation. Before examining the role of music in the masque's final scene, however, it will be useful to consider briefly Milton's treatment of music in a few other representative works.

In "At a Solemn Music," Milton distinguishes between heavenly and earthly music:

> That we on earth with undiscording voice
> May rightly answer that melodious noise;
> As once we did, till disproportioned sin
> Jarred against nature's chime, and with harsh din
> Broke the fair music that all creatures made
> To their great Lord, whose love their motion swayed
> In perfect diapason, whilst they stood
> In first obedience, and their state of good.
>
> (17–24)

The pun on "broken" at line 21 is particularly revealing: in technical terms, "broken" music consists of several parts played by different instruments (hence the term "broken consort").[40] Even if such music is written monodically, each part is still heard distinctly, thus approaching the effects of conventional polyphony. Milton is aiming at more than a mere poetic conceit: by "breaking" its "first obedience" to God, humanity necessarily distanced itself from the "undisturbèd song of pure concent" (6) in which multiple voices are indistinguishable from perfect unity. Broken or polyphonic music should not accordingly be rejected, but recognized as an imperfect imitation (figuration) of divine harmony. This imitative music will not be made perfect "till God ere long/To his celestial consort us unite,/To live with him, and sing in endless morn of light" (26–28). Milton's poem thus defines the inherent difference between heavenly and earthly music as ontological, and it authorizes the figure-making activity of the imagination ("high-raised fantasy," 5) as a noble striving toward the divine ideal.

---

40. The validity of this musical meaning of "broken" in the seventeenth century has been questioned, but see *Troilus and Cressida* 3.1.50–55, where "broken music" clearly seems to have been understood in relation to "part-music." Polyphony, of course, should not be confused with polyvocality (music with several voices); see Buhler, "Counterpoint and Controversy," 18–19, for the association of "partial" music with "counterpoint" in Renaissance England.

A similar distinction is made in *Arcades,* only this time the focus is on hearing rather than performing music. Here, music has the power to draw "the low world in measured motion .../After the heavenly tune, which none can hear/Of human mould with gross unpurgèd ear" (71–73). As a "lesser god" (79), the poem's Genius of the Wood can hear the celestial harmony, but only "in deep of night when drowsiness/Hath locked up mortal sense" (61–62), presumably when imagination or fantasy is given reign over the faculties of sun-clad reason ("mortal sense"). At the same time that the poem commends earthly music's aspiration toward perfection, it *also* emphasizes a dissociation between the "inimitable sounds" (78) of divine music and human (or semi-divine) music made by "inferior hand or voice" (77). A much harsher view of earthbound music appears in *Lycidas,* where Milton denounces the empty ceremony of the Laudian church:

What recks it them? What need they? They are sped;
And when they list, their lean and flashy songs
Grate on their scrannel pipes of wretched straw,
The hungry sheep look up, and are not fed,
But swoll'n with wind, and the rank mist they draw,
Rot inwardly, and foul contagion spread.
(122–27)

These lines closely follow Gosson's critique of polyphony in *The Schoole of Abuse* (both allude to Virgil's *Eclogues*), and the references to "scrannel pipes" and "swoll'n wind" echo the Protestant bias against wind instruments. But Milton seems more critical of the *use* such music is put to than of any inherent moral deficiency in it; the "oaten flute" and "rough" satyrs' dances are positively mentioned in the description of Lycidas's youth (33–34). Moreover, as in "At a Solemn Music" and *Arcades,* Milton carefully distinguishes between heavenly and earthly music: the Apollonian music that interrupts the poem is "of a higher mood" than the shepherd's piping (87), and heaven's "unexpressive nuptial song" is apprehensible to Lycidas only after death (176).

Milton's persistent classification of music in the early poems adumbrates the idea that earthly music is ontologically inferior since it can gesture toward celestial harmony but never articulate it.[41] In this respect, polyphonic music is

---

41. Marc Berley also argues that early poems such as "L'Allegro" and *Arcades* are concerned with making distinctions between divine and earthly music, although he tends to emphasize less than I do the value Milton attaches to performed, audible music. See his excellent chapter on the influence of

different from monody in degree, not kind—both are expressive figurations of heaven's "*un*expressive nuptial song" (my emphasis). However, to respond to music's inarticulateness by overregulating it (as if attempting to pin down its meaning) or by shunning it altogether (as a vain or idolatrous figuration) is for Milton clearly inappropriate, as he indicates in *Areopagitica* (1644):

> If we think to regulate printing, thereby to rectify manners, we must regulate all recreations and pastimes, all that is delightful to man. No music must be heard, no song be set or sung, but what is grave and Doric.... It will ask more than the work of twenty licensers to examine all the lutes, the violins and the guitars in every house.... And who shall silence all the airs and madrigals that whisper softness in chambers?... The villages also must have their visitors to inquire what lectures the bagpipe and the rebec reads, even to the balladry and the gamut of every municipal fiddler. (251)

Milton's mock proposal to inspect every fiddler's "gamut" (range of notes) is a sardonic answer to Gosson's contempt for the historical creation of new musical strings.[42] Milton revises Gosson's near-hysterical list of musical innovations so that it is the attempted *control* of music that threatens to spin into confusion. Music's (especially polyphonic music's) indeterminacy with respect to language, which underscores the Protestant proscription on polyphony, is in fact extremely consonant (no pun intended) with Milton's representation of Truth in *Areopagitica:*

> Truth indeed came once into the world with her divine master, and was a perfect shape most glorious to look on; but when he ascended, and his apostles after him were laid asleep, then straight arose a wicked race of deceivers, who, as that story goes of the Egyptian Typhon with his conspirators, how they dealt with the good Osiris, took the virgin Truth, hewed her lovely form into a thousand pieces and scattered them to the four winds. (263)

In the musical sense of the word, Milton's Truth is distinctly "partial." Accordingly, Milton's ardent rejection of the Puritan attitude toward music

---

musica speculativa on Milton's poetry in *After the Heavenly Tune: English Poetry and the Aspiration to Song* (Pittsburgh: Duquesne University Press, 2000), 141–205.

42. "Gamut" is the lowest note, or the lowest string of a violin, so that to inspect the "gamut" of every fiddler, as Milton says, would require inspecting every string on every string instrument.

in *Areopagitica* reflects his more general theme that Reformist attitudes in England may have gone too far, threatening to make England "the latest and the backwardest scholars, of whom God offered to have made us the teachers" (265).

Areopagitica provides an instructive context for Milton's attitude toward music in *A Maske,* which is less deferential to Protestant ideology than has generally been recognized. For one thing, Milton's removal of "counterpoint" at line 243 may suggest a Reformist attitude toward polyphony, but it may also suggest—somewhat at odds with Reformist attitudes—a fundamental incongruity between heavenly music and Echo's earthly music. In musical practice, "counterpoint" implies two lines of equal stature, which does not accord with Milton's conception of earthly (or semidivine) music in the early poems. For its own part, *A Maske* maintains distinctions between heavenly and earthly experience, particularly in the case of the Attendant Spirit, whose language closely resembles Milton's representation of earth in *Areopagitica:* "But for such,/I would not soil these pure ambrosial weeds,/With the rank vapours of this sin-worn mould" (15–17). The Attendant Spirit's identification with Henry Lawes is an appropriate compliment, since, as Milton suggests in sonnet 13, Lawes's essentially homophonic style represents a noble striving for the heavenly ideal of unity between words and music. Yet by associating Lawes with specifically divine music, *A Maske* also enables the articulation of a *positive* relationship between heavenly music and its inferior, earthly figuration. In other words, Milton's praise of Lawes and monody is not restrictive. After all, while the Attendant Spirit shows a marked preference for the monodic style of the Lady's song (a preference which would have registered as a charming joke in performance, since he composed it), he is still content to listen to the "barbarous dissonance" of Comus's music for "a while" (550–51).

Even more than *Areopagitica,* Milton's "On the Harmony of the Spheres" explicitly addresses the distinction between divine and earthly music, in language which frequently resonates with the poetry of *A Maske.* In his early essay, Milton defends the well-known Pythagorean theory of *musica mundana* as a useful allegory: "Surely, if he held any doctrine of the harmony of the spheres... it was only as a means of suggesting allegorically the close interrelation of the orbs" (235). Under this interpretation, earthly music is desirable because it approximates or figures heavenly harmony, not because it can boast a literal identification with it. Building on this defense of figurative knowledge, Milton describes the rejection of Pythagorean theory in terms that are remarkably similar to Comus's defense of pleasure:

> If you rob the heavens of this music, you devote those wonderful minds and subordinate gods of yours to a life of drudgery, and condemn them

to the treadmill. And even Atlas himself would long since have cast down the burden of the skies from his shoulders to its ruin, had not that sweet harmony soothed him with an ecstasy of delight as he panted and sweated beneath his heavy load. Again, the Dolphin would long since have wearied of the stars and preferred his proper element of the sea to the skies, had he not well known that the singing spheres of heaven far surpassed Arion's lyre in sweetness. And we may well believe that it is in order to tune their own notes in accord with that harmony of heaven to which they listen so intently, that the lark takes her flight up into the clouds at daybreak and the nightingale passes the lonely hours of night in song. (237)

In this paragraph, the Aristotelian dismissal of *musica mundana* amounts to both a rejection of figurative knowledge and a harsh asceticism reminiscent of the Lady's attack on Comus. Taken together with *A Maske* (a comparison made more appealing by Milton's reference to the "lonely nightingale"), "On the Harmony" proffers a critique of the Protestant bias against theatricality and allegory, insofar as it suggests that Protestant ideology crucially misunderstands the relationship between divine truth and human understanding. Milton argues that only an indirect and imperfect apprehension of divine truth is possible on earth, which explains why heavenly music can never be experienced as actual sound: "The fault is in our own deaf ears, which are either unable or unworthy to hear these sweet strains" (238). As in *Areopagitica*, Milton here applies the idea of the Fall (registered by his specific use of the word *incusare*) to construct a defense of figuration. In other words, the Fall makes figured truth—and earthly music—necessary, rather than things to be rejected for their lack of plainness. In language that strongly recalls the description of the Attendant Spirit in *A Maske*, Milton again in "On the Harmony" evokes Pythagoras to suggest that figured knowledge is a gift from heaven itself: "Pythagoras alone among men is said to have heard this music—if indeed he was not rather some good spirit and denizen of heaven, sent down perchance by the gods' behest to instruct mankind in holiness and lead them back to righteousness" (238). Like the Attendant Spirit, Milton's Pythagoras represents cloaked, "disguised" knowledge. The singularity of Pythagoras's aural experience makes his gift of harmony valuable while confirming the ontological distance between heavenly and earthly music.

While consideration of Milton's early writings on music effectively reorients the Lady's antitheatrical polemic as a debate over figuration, we should note that *A Maske* advocates a defense of earthly music on its own terms as well. Along these lines, Milton's critique of Reformist polemic in *A Maske* might best be summarized in a line shortly before the invocation to Sabrina. Here, the Attendant Spirit reveals that the Lady can be freed only through an earthly water nymph who must be "right invoked in *warbled song*" (854, my emphasis). "Warbled" here is a loaded word: it appears consistently in Reformist polemic as an indicator of immoral, seductive sound. In *Histriomastix*, Prynne refers to chromatic harmony as "a dishonest art of warbling the voice."[43] In Henry Burton's sermon against conformity to the English cathedrals, he calls their musical service a "Long Babylonish Service, so bellowed and warbled out, as the hearers are but little the wiser."[44] Likewise, Christopher Dow's attack on Burton sarcastically calls attention to his "distaste" for music that is "bellowed and warbled out."[45] And in Owen Feltham's *Resolves* (1631), a text that is particularly uncongenial to music's sensuous qualities, a "warble" is nothing short of demonic: "Damned Sathan! that with Orphean ayres, and dextrous warbles, lead'st us to the Flames of Hell."[46] In these contexts, "warble" appears to denote a kind of utterance that undermines language (particularly scriptural language) in favor of purely physical sound.[47] This preference for sensuous experience partly explains warbling's "fallen" associations in certain Miltonian contexts. In book 2 of *Paradise Lost* (in a passage that echoes Feltham's *Resolves*), for example, Milton characterizes the insincere praise that the fallen angels render to God as "warbled hymns" (2.242). In a very different setting, Milton's first sonnet, "warbling" becomes the sign of amorous (not necessarily chaste) love: "O nightingale, that on yon bloomy spray/Warblest at eve, when all the woods are still" (1–2). As here, "warbling" occurs frequently in Ovidian contexts in Renaissance poetry, particularly those that allude to Philomela. Marlowe's translation of Ovid's *Amores* has in the invocation a call to the "elegian muse, that warblest amorous lays."[48] In *The Complainte of Phylomene* (1576), George Gascoigne uses alliteration to emphasize the pure sonority of Philomela's irregular, yet melodious, lament: "And many a note, she warbled wondrous

---

43. Prynne, *Histriomastix*, 275.
44. Henry Burton, *For God, and the King* ([Amsterdam], 1636), 160.
45. Christopher Dow, *Innovations Unjustly Charged upon the Present Church and State* (London, 1637), 9.
46. Owen Feltham, *Resolves* (London, 1631), 86.
47. This sense of "warble" is corroborated a few years after Milton's masque in a poem by Edmund Waller that is addressed, somewhat coincidentally, to Henry Lawes himself. Praising Lawes for his (presupposed) rejection of florid ornamentation in musical settings, Waller writes, "Let those which only warble long,/And gargle in their throats a song,/ Content themselves with *Ut, re, mi*:/Let words, and sense, be set by thee." Henry Lawes, *Ayres and Dialogues* (London, 1653), preface, lines 25–28.
48. Christopher Marlowe, *Ovid's Elegies*, in *The Complete Poems and Translations*, ed. Stephen Orgel (London: Penguin, 1971), 1.33.

wel."[49] Likewise, Shakespeare describes Lucrece after she has been raped as a "lamenting Philomel [who] had ended/The well-tuned warble of her nightly sorrow" (1079–80). As the special province of rebel angels, concupiscent lovers, and mutilated women, "warbled" song is, in these particular contexts, "fallen" song. Through its resonance in Marlowe, Gascoigne, and Shakespeare, "warbled song" returns Milton's audience to the scene of Ovid's Philomela and to the kind of sensuous Ovidianism that characterizes Comus himself.

This is not to say that "warble" does not carry positive connotations, particularly in Milton's early poems and elsewhere in *Paradise Lost*. Yet even in these cases, "warble" often appears in contexts that emphasize the distance between heaven and fallen humanity. In *Arcades,* for example, the "warbled string" represents the Genius of the Wood's attempt to imitate, but not replicate, "the heavenly tune, which none can hear" (87, 72). Likewise, in "On the Morning of Christ's Nativity," "divinely-warbled voice" signals an unprecedented, startling conjunction of heavenly song and earthly sensuous experience, by which the "crystal spheres" almost "have power to touch our senses" (96, 125, 127); only an event as momentous as Christ's nativity can effect such a conjunction. In "L'Allegro," "warbling" comes to stand for a kind of utterance that calls attention to its own sonority, irrespective of the words that only partially structure it. Here, Milton contrasts a "warbling" Shakespeare with "learnèd" Jonson, anticipating Samuel Johnson's famous portrayal of Shakespeare as a wandering Atalanta entranced by the sonorous indeterminacy of language (132–34). As John Guillory has noted, this section of "L'Allegro" bears more affinity with Comus's artistry than with the Attendant Spirit's or the Lady's.[50] Milton's deliberately ambivalent moralization of "warbling" can be gauged by its proximity to the word "lapse" in *Paradise Lost* (a similar association between "warble" and "lap" occurs in "L'Allegro"):

And liquid lapse of murmuring streams; by these,
Creatures that lived, and moved, and walked, or flew,
Birds on the branches warbling; all things smiled,
With fragrance and with joy my heart o'erflowed.
(8.263–66)

---

49. George Gascoigne, *The Complainte of Phylomene,* ed. William L. Wallace (Salzburg: Institut für Englische Sprache und Literatur, University of Salzburg, 1975), 90.

50. See John Guillory, *Poetic Authority: Spenser, Milton, and Literary History* (New York: Columbia University Press, 1983), 68–93. Guillory does not, however, note the resonance of "warbled song" in *Comus* with "warbling" Shakespeare in "L'Allegro"; rather, his reading of *Comus* proffers the whole Sabrina episode as a reversion to Spenserian (and occasionally Ovidian) influence.

For prelapsarian Adam, the "warbling" sounds of birds are unproblematic because they are intelligible, just as every speech or sound act in heaven is immediately articulate ("my tongue obeyed and readily could name," 272). In the same way, the soundful "lapse of murmuring streams" has an unqualified innocence. After the Fall, however, "warbling" sound becomes inarticulate and "lapse" assumes its negative meaning. Although evocative of heavenly experience, postlapsarian warbling (and earthly music in general) represents the loss of simultaneity between uttering and "naming" that Adam once enjoyed.[51]

In a poem that bears such a heavy intertextual relationship with contemporary attacks on music and theater, as well as with Milton's other early poems, the characterization of the Attendant Spirit's song as "warbled" has far-reaching implications. "Warbled song," as early modern antitheatricalism rightly suspects, does not presuppose the inviolability of language, but rather calls attention to the gap between sound and word through its own imperfect imitation. Thus, by making "warbled song" a prerequisite for the Lady's freedom, Milton recognizes the fallen condition of his human protagonists and ties the masque's divine resolution to a kind of music that Reformist polemic repeatedly condemns. Remarkably, Milton's careful rendering of "warbled" music evokes both the perception of divine presence that Martin Luther himself professed to hear in birdsong *and* the knowledge that warbled song is, as Luther also pointed out, *voiceless* song. As in the case of Philomela, who becomes a nightingale *after* she has been raped and rendered speechless by Tereus, "warbled song" in *A Maske* follows the double assault on the Lady's body and voice and the painful demonstration of her insufficiency. Warbled song, as Ovid's Philomela and Shakespeare's Lavinia (and soon Milton's Lady) will attest, is first and foremost a sign of loss.

Whether or not Henry Lawes's music for *A Maske* is strictly monodic in its composition (as has been argued), the work repeatedly tempts its audience to hear this music as earthly and sensuous; Milton's emphasis on shepherds' "play" (958) and "court guise" (962) in the closing songs is closer to the raucous wedding masque of Shakespeare's *Winter's Tale* than to the angelic (homophonic) choirs of the Nativity Ode. In fact, the musical associations at the end of the masque do not support a strict adherence to rigid, Puritan aesthetics. The invocation to Sabrina includes the appeal to "songs of sirens sweet" (878), recalling Comus's earlier praise of Siren (polyphonic) music, and the "mincing Dryades" (964) at the end of the masque recall Becon's characterization of polyphonic music as "mynsed." As David Lindley has

---

51. See, however, "Il Penseroso," where the speaker's reference to Orpheus's "warbled" notes forms part of a vision of divine reunion (106). Here, "warbling" is a distinctly sound-producing—not language-producing—activity, but one that points beyond the realm of sensuous experience.

shown in his study of the musical politics of the court masque, a performance of *A Maske* would have intensified the correspondences between Comus's music and the celebratory music at the end (in contrast to the music composed by Lawes): "The musical markers of social class and moral probity slip and slide in this masque. The problem is embodied in the person of Henry Lawes himself... [who] is disguised as a shepherd, but employs a musical language in the masque's surviving songs which is emphatically removed from the taint of the popular."[52] In effect, Milton "tricks" our ears, capitalizing on music's performance in the masque in order to loosen the traditional associations between monody and "divine," unfallen song. The point is not only that performed music introduces indeterminacy of signification (which it surely does) but also that Milton is aware of this indeterminacy and attributes it to music's ontological status after the Fall. For Milton, music's indeterminacy results from its status as an imitation of celestial sound that is inaudible on earth.

As imitation, "warbled song" is for Milton profoundly theatrical and figural. Likewise, Sabrina's appearance in the masque is intensely theatrical in a way that emphasizes earthly, sensuous experience:

Thrice upon thy finger's tip,
Thrice upon thy rubied lip,
Next this marble venomed seat
Smeared with gums of glutinous heat
I touch with chaste palms moist and cold,
Now the spell hath lost his hold.

(914–19)

Sabrina's focus on the Lady's fingertip and lip suggests rejuvenation of the senses of touch and taste which the Lady's ascetic Puritanism had stifled. Finger and lip also signify the two body parts that perform earthly music, either on a string instrument or by singing. This implicit sanctioning of sensuous experience (especially musical experience), which is fulfilled by the "jigs" and "rural dance" at the end of the masque, corresponds to the dense profusion of mythological, mostly Ovidian figures that characterize the invocation to Sabrina and the closing hymeneal scene. As Christopher Kendrick has noted,

---

52. David Lindley, "The Politics of Music in the Masque," in Bevington and Holbrook, *Politics of the Stuart Court Masque*, 282. Peter Walls also notes that the actual music given to the Attendant Spirit introduces an unusually ambiguous mode of musical signification in the masque, although he finally concludes that "by and large, however, the use of music and dance corresponds to normal masque usage." *Music in the English Courtly Masque, 1604–1640* (Oxford: Clarendon, 1996), 298.

"[Sabrina's] presence lifts at least part of the fairy world from Comus' copious ambit."[53] But Milton does more than "lift" Comus's stock figures: he rechannels the musical and Ovidian elements of the antimasque in order to free the Lady, thus authorizing the modes of figuration and performativity—which Comus had abused—as necessary and valuable aspects of human experience. It is this acceptance of figuration and theatricality, despite their moral ambivalence, that arguably stands behind the Attendant Spirit's warning to the Lady's brothers that "without [Comus's] rod reversed,/And backward mutters of dissevering power,/We cannot free the Lady" (816–18).

A Maske intuits an ideological connection between the Puritan critiques of classical poetry and polyphonic music, and it finds the basis of this connection to be a deep-seated anxiety over the fundamental indeterminacy of artistic expression. Again, the masque shares this outlook with *Areopagitica*, where the defense of "wanton" Ovid appears in close conjunction with the defense of musical innovation (241–42). In this work, as in *A Maske*, the mythological figure of Psyche stands as a reminder of the distance between heaven and humanity and of the inapprehensibility of divine knowledge; like Truth in a thousand pieces, knowledge is represented here as "those confused seeds which were imposed upon Psyche as an incessant labour to cull out and sort asunder" (247). Humanity's fallen nature partly explains why Milton unanxiously presents Cupid and Psyche, and Venus and Adonis, at the end of *A Maske* as analogous—but not identical—examples of love. In both cases, men and women imitate divinity in a way that creates an unending proliferation of voices and *figurae*. This mode of figuration is certainly precarious and creates an "incessant labour," as the example of Comus makes clear, but a "marble-like" retreat into nonperformative contemplation impedes the reintegration of Truth rather than furthers it. Milton's rejection of an aesthetics based on Puritan ideology in *A Maske* reminds us that we are after all in a fallen world, and it is a fact of our fallen condition that we speak and hear several voices. In doing so, Milton forecloses on the rigidly antitheatrical and antifigural rhetoric of the Lady's attacks on Comus. Despite his need to repudiate an intemperate sensuality, and despite his need to reform the masque in the face of Laudian politics, Milton recognizes that Reformist extremism—whether directed against theater, Ovid, or music—can lead to a debilitating stasis, as the Lady's immobility iconologically suggests.

---

53. Christopher Kendrick, "Milton and Sexuality: A Symptomatic Reading of *Comus*," in *Re-Membering Milton: Essays on the Texts and Traditions*, ed. Mary Nyquist and Margaret W. Ferguson (New York: Methuen, 1987), 51.

Selected Bibliography

Primary Sources

Agrippa, Henry Cornelius. *Of the Vanitie and Uncertaintie of Artes and Sciences.* 1569. Translated by James Sanford. Edited by Catherine M. Dunn. Northridge: California State University Press, 1974.

———. *Opera.* 2 vols. Hildesheim: Verlag, 1970.

Ascham, Roger. *The Whole Works of Roger Ascham.* Edited by J. A. Giles. Vol. 3, *The Scholemaster.* 1570. New York: AMS Press, 1965.

Bacon, Francis. *The Works of Francis Bacon.* Edited by James Spedding. 6 vols. London: Longman, 1890.

Bate, Jonathan, ed. *The Romantics on Shakespeare.* London: Penguin, 1992.

Bathe, William. *A Briefe Introduction to the Skill of Song.* 1596. Facsimile reprint. Kilkenny, Ireland: Boethius Press, 1982.

———. *A Briefe Introduction to the Skill of Song.* 1596. Edited by Kevin C. Karnes. Aldershot, UK: Ashgate, 2005.

———. *A Brief Introduction to the True Art of Music.* 1584. Edited by Cecil Hill. Colorado Springs: Colorado College Music Press, 1979.

Becon, Thomas. *The Jewel of Joy.* 1553. In *The Catechism of Thomas Becon,* edited by John Ayre. Cambridge: Cambridge University Press, 1844.

———. *The Reliques of Rome.* London, 1563.

Boethius. *Fundamentals of Music.* Translated by Calvin M. Bower. Edited by Claude V. Palisca. New Haven, CT: Yale University Press, 1989.

Browne, Sir Thomas. *The Works of Sir Thomas Browne.* Edited by Geoffrey Keynes. Vol. 1, *Religio medici.* 1642. Chicago: University of Chicago Press, 1964.

Bullinger, Heinrich. *Fiftie Godlie and Learned Sermons.* 1577. Translated by H. I. In *The Decades of Henry Bullinger,* edited by Thomas Harding. Cambridge: Cambridge University Press, 1849–52.

Burton, Robert. *The Anatomy of Melancholy.* 1621. Edited by Holbrook Jackson. London: J. M. Dent, 1975.

Butler, Charles. *The Feminine Monarchie; or, A Treatise concerning bees and the due ordering of them.* London, 1609.

———. *The Principles of Musik in Singing and Setting.* 1636. New York: Da Capo, 1970.

[Byron, Lord, and Percy Bysshe Shelley]. "Byron and Shelley on the Character of Hamlet." 1829. In *The Romantics on Shakespeare,* edited by Jonathan Bate. London: Penguin, 1992.

Caldwell, Edward, ed. *Documentary Annals of the Reformed Church of England.* 2 vols. Oxford: Oxford University Press, 1844.

Campion, Thomas. *A New Way of Making Fowre Parts in Counterpoint.* 1613. Edited by Christopher R. Wilson. Aldershot, UK: Ashgate, 2003.

SELECTED BIBLIOGRAPHY

Case, John. *The Praise of Musicke.* London, 1586.
Clarke, Mary Cowden. *The Girlhood of Shakespeare's Heroines.* New York, 1852.
Coleridge, Samuel. *Literary Remains.* 1836–39. In *The Romantics on Shakespeare,* edited by Jonathan Bate. London: Penguin, 1992.
Dow, Christopher. *Innovations Unjustly Charged upon the Present Church and State.* London, 1637.
Elyot, Sir Thomas. *The Boke named The Governour.* 1531. Edited by Ernest Rhys. London: J. M. Dent, 1937.
The Fable of Ovid Treting of Narcissus. London, 1560.
Faucit, Helena. *On Some of Shakespeare's Female Characters.* Edinburgh: Blackwood, 1885.
Feltham, Owen. *Resolves.* London, 1631.
Gaffurius, Franchinus. *De harmonia musicorum instrumentorum opus.* 1518. Translated by Clement A. Miller. Rome: American Institute of Musicology, 1977.
Gascoigne, George. *The Complainte of Phylomene.* 1576. Edited by William L. Wallace. Salzburg: Institut für Englische Sprache und Literatur, University of Salzburg, 1975.
Golding, Arthur. *Shakespeare's Ovid being Arthur Golding's Translation of the Metamorphoses.* Edited by W. H. D. Rouse. London: Centaur, 1961.
Gosson, Stephen. *Playes Confuted in Five Actions.* 1582. Edited by Arthur Freeman. New York: Garland, 1972.
———. *The Schoole of Abuse.* 1579. Edited by Arthur Freeman. New York: Garland, 1973.
Goethe, J. W. von. *Wilhelm Meister's Apprenticeship.* 1796. In *The Romantics on Shakespeare,* edited by Jonathan Bate. London: Penguin, 1992.
Greene, Robert. *Pandosto, The Triumph of Time.* 1588. In *Narrative and Dramatic Sources of Shakespeare,* edited by Geoffrey Bullough. London: Routledge, 1957.
Hazlitt, William. *Characters of Shakespeare's Plays.* 1817. London: Oxford University Press, 1966.
Hiatt, Charles. *Ellen Terry and Her Impersonations.* London: Bell, 1898.
Hoffmann, E. T. A. "Review of Beethoven's Fifth Symphony." In *E. T. A. Hoffmann's Musical Writings,* edited by David Charlton, translated by Martyn Clarke, 234–51. Cambridge: Cambridge University Press, 1989.
Hooker, Richard. *Of the Lawes of Ecclesiastical Polity.* Edited by Georges Edelen. In *The Folger Library Edition of the Works of Richard Hooker,* edited by W. Speed Hill, vols. 1–4. Cambridge, MA: Belknap, 1977.
Jameson, Anna. *Shakespeare's Heroines: Characteristics of Women Moral, Poetical and Historical.* 1833. London: G. Bell, 1978.
Lake, Arthur. *Sermons with Some Religious and Divine Meditations.* London, 1629.
Lavinius, Peter. *P. Ovidii Nasonis poete ingeniosissimi Metamorphoseos libri XV.* Lyon, 1527.
Lodge, Thomas. *A Reply to Gosson's "Schoole of Abuse."* ca. 1579. Edited by Arthur Freeman. New York: Garland, 1973.
Luther, Martin. *Symphoniae jucundae.* 1538. Translated by Ulrich S. Leupold. In *Music in the Western World: A History in Documents,* edited by Piero Weiss and Richard Taruskin, 100–103. New York: Schirmer, 1984.
Macrobius. *Commentary on the Dream of Scipio.* Translated by William Harris Stahl. New York: Columbia University Press, 1990.
Morley, Thomas. *A Plaine and Easie Introduction to Practicall Musicke.* 1597. Facsimile reprint. Amsterdam: Da Capo, 1969.

Ovid. *The Heroides.* Translated by Grant Showerman. Cambridge, MA: Harvard University Press, 1977.

———. *Metamorphoses.* Translated by Frank Justice Miller. Cambridge, MA: Harvard University Press, 1984.

Peend, Thomas. *The Pleasant Fable of Hermaphroditus and Salmacis.* London, 1565.

Pilkington, Francis. *The First Set of Madrigals and Pastorals of 3. 4. and 5. Parts.* 1613. Edited by Edmund H. Fellowes. London: Stainer and Bell, 1959.

Prynne, William. *Histriomastix: The Players Scourge or Actors Tragedie.* 1633. Edited by Arthur Freeman. New York: Garland, 1974.

Puttenham, George. *The Art of English Poesy.* 1589. Edited by Frank Whigham and Wayne A. Rebhorn. Ithaca, NY: Cornell University Press, 2007.

Ravenscroft, Thomas. *A Briefe Discourse of the true (but neglected) use of Charact'ring the Degrees.* London, 1617.

Robinson, Thomas. *The Schoole of Musicke: Wherein Is Taught the Perfect Method of True Fingering of the Lute.* 1603. Facsimile reprint. Edited by David Lumsden. Paris: Centre national de la recherche scientifique, 1971.

Rowley, Samuel. *When You See Me, You Know Me.* 1605. Edited by F. P. Wilson. London: Malone Society, 1952.

Sandys, George. *Ovid's Metamorphosis Englished, Mythologized, and Represented in Figures.* 1632. Edited by Karl K. Hulley and Stanley T. Vandersall. Lincoln: University of Nebraska Press, 1970.

Strachey, Edward. *Shakespeare's "Hamlet."* London, 1848.

Stubbes, Phillip. *The Anatomie of Abuses.* 1583. Edited by Arthur Freeman. New York: Garland, 1973.

Swetnam, Joseph. *The Araignment of Lewde, Idle, Froward and Unconstant Women.* London, 1615.

Taverner, John. Gresham College Music Lectures. 1610. Sloane Manuscript 2329. British Library, London.

Tinctoris, Johannes. *The Art of Counterpoint.* 1477. Translated by Albert Seay. Rome: American Institute of Musicology, 1961.

Ward, John. *Lives of the Professors of Gresham College.* London, 1740.

Wilson, Thomas. *The Arte of Rhetorique.* 1553. Edited by Thomas J. Derrick. New York: Garland, 1982.

Wingate, Charles E. L. *Shakespeare's Heroines on the Stage.* New York: Crowell, 1895.

Wood, Anthony. *Fasti Oxonienses.* Oxford, 1790.

Wright, Thomas. *The Passions of the Minde in Generall.* 1604. Edited by Thomas O. Sloan. Urbana: University of Illinois Press, 1971.

Secondary Sources

Abbate, Carolyn. *Unsung Voices: Opera and Musical Narrative in the Nineteenth Century.* Princeton, NJ: Princeton University Press, 1991.

Adelman, Janet. *Suffocating Mothers: Fantasies of Maternal Origin in Shakespeare's Plays.* New York: Routledge, 1992.

Allen, D. C. *Mysteriously Meant: The Rediscovery of Pagan Symbolism and Allegorical Interpretation in the Renaissance.* Baltimore: Johns Hopkins University Press, 1970.

SELECTED BIBLIOGRAPHY

Alpers, Paul. *What Is Pastoral?* Chicago: University of Chicago Press, 1996.

Ammann, Peter J. "The Musical Theory and Philosophy of Robert Fludd." *Journal of the Warburg and Courtauld Institutes* 30 (1967): 198–227.

Anderson, William S. *Ovid's Metamorphoses, Books 6–10*. Norman: University of Oklahoma Press, 1972.

Armitage, David. "The Dismemberment of Orpheus: Mythic Elements in Shakespeare's Romances." *Shakespeare Survey* 39 (1986): 123–33.

Attali, Jacques. *Noise: The Political Economy of Music*. Translated by Brian Massumi. 1985. Reprint, Minneapolis: University of Minnesota Press, 1999.

Auden, W. H. *The Dyer's Hand*. New York: Random House, 1948.

Austern, Linda Phyllis. "'Alluring the auditorie to effeminacie': Music and the Idea of the Feminine in Early Modern England." *Music and Letters* 74 (1993): 343–54.

———. "'The conceit of the minde': Music, Medicine and Mental Process in Early Modern England." *Irish Musical Studies* 4 (1996): 133–51.

———. "Love, Death and Ideas of Music in the English Renaissance." In *Love and Death in the Renaissance,* edited by Kenneth R. Bartlett, 17–36. Ottawa: Dovehouse, 1991.

———. "Music and the English Renaissance Controversy over Women." In *Cecilia Reclaimed: Feminist Perspectives on Gender and Music,* edited by Susan C. Cook and Judy S. Tsou, 52–69. Urbana: University of Illinois Press, 1994.

———. "'My mother musicke': Music and Early Modern Fantasies of Embodiment." In *Maternal Measures: Figuring Caregiving in the Early Modern Period,* edited by Naomi J. Miller and Naomi Yavneh, 239–81. Aldershot, UK: Ashgate, 2001.

———. "Nature, Culture, Myth, and the Musician in Early Modern England." *Journal of the American Musicological Society* 51 (1998): 1–47.

———. "'Sing againe Syren': The Female Musician and Sexual Enchantment in Elizabethan Life and Literature." *Renaissance Quarterly* 42 (1989): 420–48.

———. "The Siren, the Muse, and the God of Love: Music and Gender in Seventeenth-Century English Emblem Books." *Journal of Musicological Research* 18 (1999): 95–138.

———. "''Tis nature's voice': Music, Natural Philosophy and the Hidden World in Seventeenth-Century England." In *Music Theory and Natural Order from the Renaissance to the Early Twentieth Century,* edited by Suzannah Clark and Alexander Rehding, 30–67. Cambridge: Cambridge University Press, 2001.

Barish, Jonas. *The Antitheatrical Prejudice*. Berkeley: University of California Press, 1981.

Barkan, Leonard. *The Gods Made Flesh: Metamorphosis and the Pursuit of Paganism*. London: Yale University Press, 1986.

Barzun, Jacques. *The Use and Abuse of Art*. Princeton, NJ: Princeton University Press, 1974.

Basile, Mary Elizabeth. "The Music of *A Maske.*" *Milton Quarterly* 27 (1993): 86–98.

Bate, Jonathan. *Shakespeare and Ovid*. Oxford: Oxford University Press, 1993.

Berley, Marc. *After the Heavenly Tune: English Poetry and the Aspiration to Song*. Pittsburgh: Duquesne University Press, 2000.

Bishop, T. G. *Shakespeare and the Theatre of Wonder*. Cambridge: Cambridge University Press, 1996.

Bloom, Gina. *Voice in Motion: Staging Gender, Shaping Sound in Early Modern England*. Philadelphia: University of Pennsylvania Press, 2007.

Boyd, Morrison Comegys. *Elizabethan Music and Musical Criticism*. 2nd ed. Philadelphia: University of Pennsylvania Press, 1962.
Bradley, A. C. *Shakespearean Tragedy*. Edited by John Russell Brown. 1904. Reprint, New York: St. Martin's, 1992.
Bray, Roger. "Music and the Quadrivium in Early Tudor England." *Music and Letters* 76 (1995): 1–18.
Brodwin, Leonora Leet. "Milton and the Renaissance Circe." *Milton Studies* 6 (1974): 21–83.
Brooks, Dennis S. "'To show scorn her own image': The Varieties of Education in *The Taming of the Shrew*." *Rocky Mountain Review of Language and Literature* 48 (1994): 7–32.
Brown, Cedric. *John Milton's Aristocratic Entertainments*. Cambridge: Cambridge University Press, 1985.
Brown, Paul. "'This thing of darkness I acknowledge mine': *The Tempest* and the Discourse of Colonialism." In *Political Shakespeare: New Essays in Cultural Materialism*, edited by Jonathan Dollimore and Alan Sinfield, 48–71. Manchester: Manchester University Press, 1985.
Browning, Judith E. "Sin, Eve, and Circe: *Paradise Lost* and the Ovidian Circe Tradition." *Milton Studies* 26 (1991): 135–58.
Buhler, Stephen. "Counterpoint and Controversy: Milton and the Critiques of Polyphonic Music." *Milton Studies* 36 (1998): 18–40.
Bush, Douglas. *Mythology and the Renaissance Tradition in English Poetry*. New York: Norton, 1963.
Calogero, Elena Laura. "'Sweet aluring harmony': Heavenly and Earthly Sirens in Sixteenth- and Seventeenth-Century Literary and Visual Culture." In *The Music of the Sirens*, edited by Linda Phyllis Austern and Inna Naroditskaya, 140–75. Bloomington: Indiana University Press, 2006.
Camden, Carroll. "On Ophelia's Madness." *Shakespeare Quarterly* 15 (1964): 247–55.
Carpenter, Nan Cooke. *Music in the Medieval and Renaissance Universities*. Norman: University of Oklahoma Press, 1958.
Carroll, William C. *The Metamorphoses of Shakespearean Comedy*. Princeton, NJ: Princeton University Press, 1985.
Chan, Mary. *Music in the Theatre of Ben Jonson*. Oxford: Oxford University Press, 1980.
Chickering, Howell. "Hearing Ariel's Songs." *Journal of Medieval and Renaissance Studies* 24 (1994): 131–72.
Chua, Daniel K. L. *Absolute Music and the Construction of Meaning*. Cambridge: Cambridge University Press, 1999.
Cohen, H. F. *Quantifying Music: The Science of Music at the First Stage of the Scientific Revolution, 1580–1650*. Dordrecht: D. Reidel, 1984.
Couliano, Ioan P. *Eros and Magic in the Renaissance*. Chicago: University of Chicago Press, 1987.
Cutts, John P. "Music and the Supernatural in *The Tempest*: A Study in Interpretation." *Music and Letters* 39 (1958): 347–58.
———. "An Unpublished Contemporary Setting of a Shakespeare Song." *Shakespeare Survey* 9 (1956): 86–89.
Dahlhaus, Carl. *The Idea of Absolute Music*. Translated by Roger Lustig. Chicago: University of Chicago Press, 1989.

Danson, Lawrence. *The Harmonies of "The Merchant of Venice."* New Haven, CT: Yale University Press, 1978.

———. *Tragic Alphabet: Shakespeare's Drama of Language.* New Haven, CT: Yale University Press, 1974.

Davis, Richard Beale. *George Sandys: Poet Adventurer.* New York: Columbia University Press, 1955.

Dent, Edward J. "Shakespeare and Music." In *A Companion to Shakespeare Studies,* edited by Harley Granville-Barker and G. B. Harrison, 137–62. New York: Macmillan, 1934.

Diehl, Huston. "'Does not the stone rebuke me?': The Pauline Rebuke and Paulina's Lawful Magic in *The Winter's Tale.*" In *Shakespeare and the Cultures of Performance,* edited by Paul Yachnin and Patricia Badir, 69–82. Aldershot, UK: Ashgate, 2008.

———. *Staging Reform, Reforming the Stage: Protestantism and Popular Theater in Early Modern England.* Ithaca, NY: Cornell University Press, 1997.

———. "'Strike all that look upon with marvel': Theatrical and Theological Wonder in *The Winter's Tale.*" In *Rematerializing Shakespeare: Authority and Representation on the Early Modern English Stage,* edited by Bryan Reynolds and William N. West, 19–34. New York: Palgrave, 2005.

Dolven, Jeff. *Scenes of Instruction in Renaissance Romance.* Chicago: University of Chicago Press, 2007.

Doran, Madeleine. "Some Renaissance 'Ovids.'" In *Literature and Society,* edited by Bernice Slote, 44–62. Lincoln: University of Nebraska Press, 1964.

Dubrow, Heather. *The Challenges of Orpheus: Lyric Poetry and Early Modern England.* Baltimore: Johns Hopkins University Press, 2007.

Duffin, Ross W. *Shakespeare's Songbook.* New York: W. W. Norton, 2004.

Dunn, Catherine M. "The Function of Music in Shakespeare's Romances." *Shakespeare Quarterly* 20 (1969): 391–405.

Dunn, Leslie C. "The Lady Sings in Welsh: Women's Song as Marginal Discourse on the Shakespearean Stage." In *Place and Displacement in the Renaissance,* edited by Alvin Vos, 51–67. Binghamton, NY: SUNY Press, 1995.

———. "Ophelia's Songs in *Hamlet:* Music, Madness, and the Feminine." In *Embodied Voices: Representing Female Vocality in Western Culture,* edited by Leslie C. Dunn and Nancy A. Jones, 50–64. Cambridge: Cambridge University Press, 1994.

DuRocher, Richard. *Milton and Ovid.* Ithaca, NY: Cornell University Press, 1985.

Egan, Robert. *Drama within Drama: Shakespeare's Sense of His Art.* New York: Columbia University Press, 1975.

Enterline, Lynn. *The Rhetoric of the Body from Ovid to Shakespeare.* Cambridge: Cambridge University Press, 2000.

Field, Christopher D. S. "Jenkins and the Cosmography of Harmony." In *John Jenkins and His Time: Studies in English Consort Music,* edited by Andrew Ashbee and Peter Holman, 1–74. Oxford: Clarendon, 1996.

Fineman, Joel. *The Subjectivity Effect in Western Literary Tradition.* Cambridge, MA: MIT Press, 1991.

Finney, Gretchen Ludke. *Musical Backgrounds for English Literature: 1580–1650.* New Brunswick, NJ: Rutgers University Press, 1962.

Fischer, Sandra K. "Hearing Ophelia: Gender and Tragic Discourse in *Hamlet*." *Renaissance and Reformation/Renaissance et Réforme* 26 (1990): 1–11.
Fish, Stanley. "Problem Solving in *Comus*." In *Illustrious Evidence: Approaches to English Literature of the Early Seventeenth Century,* edited by Earl Miner, 115–31. Berkeley: University of California Press, 1975.
Folkerth, Wes. *The Sound of Shakespeare.* London: Routledge, 2002.
Foucault, Michel. *Madness and Civilization: A History of Insanity in the Age of Reason.* Translated by Richard Howard. New York: Vintage Books, 1988.
Fox-Good, Jacquelyn. "Ophelia's Mad Songs: Music, Gender, Power." In *Subjects on the World's Stage: Essays on British Literature of the Middle Ages and the Renaissance,* edited by David G. Allen and Robert A. White, 217–38. Newark: University of Delaware Press, 1995.
———. "Other Voices: The Sweet, Dangerous Air(s) of Shakespeare's *Tempest*." *Shakespeare Studies* 24 (1996): 241–74.
Frye, Northrop. *Fables of Identity.* New York: Harcourt, 1963.
Garside, Charles, Jr. *The Origins of Calvin's Theology of Music: 1536–1543.* Philadelphia: American Philosophical Society, 1979.
Godwin, Joscelyn. *Music, Mysticism and Magic: A Sourcebook.* London: Routledge, 1986.
———. *Robert Fludd: Hermetic Philosopher and Surveyor of Two Worlds.* Boulder, CO: Shambhala, 1979.
Goehr, Lydia. "'Music has no meaning to speak of': On the Politics of Musical Interpretation." In *The Interpretation of Music: Philosophical Essays,* edited by Michael Krausz, 177–90. Oxford: Clarendon, 1993.
Gordon, D. J. "Poet and Architect: The Intellectual Setting of the Quarrel between Ben Jonson and Inigo Jones." In *The Renaissance Imagination,* edited by Stephen Orgel, 77–101. Berkeley: University of California Press, 1975.
Gouk, Penelope. "Music in Francis Bacon's Natural Philosophy." In *Francis Bacon: Terminologia e fortuna nel XVII secolo,* edited by Martha Fattori, 139–54. Rome: Edizioni dell'Ateneo, 1985.
———. "Music, Melancholy, and Medical Spirits in Early Modern Thought." In *Music as Medicine: The History of Music Therapy since Antiquity,* edited by Peregrine Horden, 173–94. Aldershot, UK: Ashgate, 2000.
———. *Music, Science and Natural Magic in Seventeenth-Century England.* New Haven, CT: Yale University Press, 1999.
———. "Some English Theories of Hearing in the Seventeenth Century." In *The Second Sense: Studies in Hearing and Musical Judgment from Antiquity to the Seventeenth Century,* edited by Michael Fend, Charles Burnett, and Penelope Gouk, 95–113. London: Warburg Institute, 1991.
Graham, Jean E. "'Virgin ears': Silence, Deafness, and Chastity in Milton's *Maske*." *Milton Studies* 36 (1999): 1–17.
Green, Douglas E. "Interpreting 'Her Martyr'd Signs': Gender and Tragedy in *Titus Andronicus*." *Shakespeare Quarterly* 40 (1989): 317–26.
Greenblatt, Stephen. *Shakespearean Negotiations.* Berkeley: University of California Press, 1988.
Guillory, John. *Poetic Authority: Spenser, Milton, and Literary History.* New York: Columbia University Press, 1983.

SELECTED BIBLIOGRAPHY

Harding, Davis P. *Milton and the Renaissance Ovid*. Urbana: University of Illinois Press, 1946.

Hart, F. Elizabeth. "Cerimon's 'Rough' Music in *Pericles*, 3.2." *Shakespeare Quarterly* 51 (2000): 313–31.

Hartwig, Joan. "Cloten, Autolycus, and Caliban: Bearers of Parodic Burdens." In *Shakespeare's Romances Reconsidered,* edited by Carol McGinnis Kay and Henry E. Jacobs, 91–103. Lincoln: University of Nebraska Press, 1978.

Headlam Wells, Robin. *Elizabethan Mythologies: Studies in Poetry, Drama, and Music.* Cambridge: Cambridge University Press, 1994.

Heninger, S. K. *Touches of Sweet Harmony: Pythagorean Cosmology and Renaissance Poetics.* San Marino, CA: Huntington Library, 1974.

Herissone, Rebecca. *Music Theory in Seventeenth-Century England*. New York: Oxford University Press, 2000.

Herman, Peter C. "Milton and the Muse-Haters: *Ad patrem, L'Allegro/Il Penseroso,* and the Ambivalences of Poetry." *Criticism* 37 (1995): 37–56.

Hoeniger, F. David. "Musical Cures of Melancholy and Mania in Shakespeare." In *Mirror up to Shakespeare: Essays in Honor of G. R. Hibbard,* edited by J. C. Gray, 55–67. Toronto: University of Toronto Press, 1984.

Hollander, John. *The Untuning of the Sky: Ideas of Music in English Poetry 1500–1700.* Princeton, NJ: Princeton University Press, 1961.

Hopkins, Lisa. "'What did thy song bode, lady?': *Othello* as Operatic Text." *Shakespeare Yearbook* 4 (1994): 61–70.

Hoppe, H. R. "John Bull in the Archduke Albert's Service." *Music and Letters* 35 (1954): 114–15.

Howard, Jean E. *The Stage and Social Struggle in Early Modern England*. London: Routledge, 1994.

Huffman, William H. *Robert Fludd and the End of the Renaissance*. London: Routledge, 1988.

Hughes, Merritt Y. "Spenser's Acrasia and the Circe of the Renaissance." *Journal of the History of Ideas* 4 (1943): 381–99.

Hulse, Clark. *Metamorphic Verse: The Elizabethan Minor Epic*. Princeton, NJ: Princeton University Press, 1981.

Hunt, Maurice A. *Shakespeare's "As You Like It": Late Elizabethan Culture and Literary Representation*. New York: Palgrave Macmillan, 2008.

Irving, John. "Thomas Tomkins's Copy of Morley's *A Plain and Easy Introduction to Practical Music.*" *Music and Letters* 71 (1990): 483–93.

Iselin, Pierre. "Music and Difference: Elizabethan Stage Music and Its Reception." In *French Essays on Shakespeare and His Contemporaries,* edited by Jean-Marie Maguin and Michèle Willems, 96–113. Newark: University of Delaware Press, 1995.

———. "Myth, Memory, and Music in *Richard II, Hamlet,* and *Othello.*" In *Reclamations of Shakespeare,* edited by A. J. Hoenselaars, 173–86. Amsterdam: Rodopi, 1994.

James, Heather. "Ovid and the Question of Politics in Early Modern England." *ELH* 70 (2003): 343–73.

———. "Shakespeare's Learned Heroines in Ovid's Schoolroom." In *Shakespeare and the Classics,* edited by Charles Martindale and A. B. Taylor, 67–85. Cambridge: Cambridge University Press, 2004.

———. *Shakespeare's Troy: Drama, Politics, and the Translation of Empire*. Cambridge: Cambridge University Press, 1997.

Javitch, Daniel. "Rescuing Ovid from the Allegorizers." *Comparative Literature* 30 (1978): 97–107.
Jensen, Phebe. "Singing Psalms to Horn-Pipes: Festivity, Iconoclasm, and Catholicism in *The Winter's Tale.*" *Shakespeare Quarterly* 55 (2004): 279–306.
Jorgens, Elise Bickford. *The Well-Tun'd Word: Musical Interpretations of English Poetry, 1597–1651*. Minneapolis: University of Minnesota Press, 1982.
———. "The Singer's Voice in Elizabethan Drama." In *Renaissance Rereadings: Intertext and Context,* edited by Maryanne Cline Horowitz, Anne J. Cruz, and Wendy A. Furman, 33–47. Urbana: University of Illinois Press, 1988.
Judd, Cristle Collins. *Reading Renaissance Music Theory: Hearing with the Eyes.* Cambridge: Cambridge University Press, 2000.
Kahn, Coppélia. "The Rape in Shakespeare's *Lucrece.*" *Shakespeare Studies* 9 (1976): 45–72.
Keilen, Sean. *Vulgar Eloquence: On the Renaissance Invention of English Literature.* New Haven, CT: Yale University Press, 2006.
Kendrick, Christopher. "Milton and Sexuality: A Symptomatic Reading of *Comus.*" In *Re-Membering Milton: Essays on the Texts and Traditions,* edited by Mary Nyquist and Margaret W. Ferguson, 43–73. New York: Methuen, 1987.
Kim, Hyun-Ah. *Humanism and the Reform of Sacred Music in Early Modern England.* Aldershot, UK: Ashgate, 2008.
King, Rosalind. "'Then murder's out of tune': The Music and Structure of *Othello.*" *Shakespeare Survey* 39 (1987): 149–58.
Kirby-Smith, Henry Tompkins. *The Celestial Twins: Poetry and Music through the Ages.* Amherst: University of Massachusetts Press, 2000.
Kronenfeld, Judy Z. "Shakespeare's Jaques and the Pastoral Cult of Solitude." *Texas Studies in Literature and Language* 18 (1976): 451–73.
Lamb, Mary Ellen. "Ovid's *Metamorphoses* and Shakespeare's *Twelfth Night.*" In *Shakespearean Comedy,* edited by Maurice Charney, 63–77. New York: New York Literary Forum, 1980.
———. "Ovid and *The Winter's Tale:* Conflicting Views toward Art." In *Shakespeare and Dramatic Tradition: Essays in Honor of S. F. Johnson,* edited by W. R. Elton and W. B. Long, 69–87. Newark: University of Delaware Press, 1989.
Leggatt, Alexander. *Shakespeare's Comedy of Love.* London: Methuen, 1974.
LeHuray, Peter. *Music and the Reformation in England, 1549–1660.* Cambridge: Cambridge University Press, 1978.
LeHuray, Peter, and James Day, eds. *Music and Aesthetics in the Eighteenth and Early-Nineteenth Centuries.* Cambridge: Cambridge University Press, 1981.
Leppert, Richard. *The Sight of Sound: Music, Representation, and the History of the Body.* Berkeley: University of California Press, 1993.
Lerner, Laurence. "Ovid and the Elizabethans." In *Ovid Renewed: Ovidian Influences on Literature and Art from the Middle Ages to the Twentieth Century,* edited by Charles Martindale, 121–35. Cambridge: Cambridge University Press, 1988.
Leverenz, David. "The Woman in *Hamlet:* An Interpersonal View." In *Representing Shakespeare: New Psychoanalytic Essays,* edited by Murray M. Schwartz and Coppélia Kahn, 110–128. Baltimore: Johns Hopkins University Press, 1980.
Levine, Laura. *Men in Women's Clothing: Anti-Theatricality and Effeminization, 1579–1642.* Cambridge: Cambridge University Press, 1994.

Lewalski, Barbara K. "Milton's *Comus* and the Politics of Masquing." In *The Politics of the Stuart Court Masque,* edited by David Bevington and Peter Holbrook, 296–320. Cambridge: Cambridge University Press, 1998.

Lindley, David. "Music, Masque and Meaning in *The Tempest.*" In *The Court Masque,* edited by David Lindley, 47–59. Manchester: Manchester University Press, 1984.

———. "The Politics of Music in the Masque." In *The Politics of the Stuart Court Masque,* edited by David Bevington and Peter Holbrook, 273–95. Cambridge: Cambridge University Press, 1998.

———. *Shakespeare and Music.* London: Thomson, 2006.

Loewenstein, Joseph. *Responsive Readings: Versions of Echo in Pastoral, Epic, and the Jonsonian Masque.* New Haven, CT: Yale University Press, 1984.

Long, John H. *Shakespeare's Use of Music: The Final Comedies.* Gainesville: University of Florida Press, 1961.

Lupton, Julia Reinhard. *Afterlives of the Saints: Hagiography, Typology, and Renaissance Literature.* Stanford: Stanford University Press, 1996.

Lyne, Raphael. "Golding's Englished *Metamorphoses.*" *Translation and Literature* 5 (1996): 183–200.

Lyons, Bridget Gellert. "The Iconography of Ophelia." *ELH* 44 (1977): 60–74.

———. *Voices of Melancholy: Studies in Literary Treatments of Melancholy in Renaissance England.* New York: Barnes & Noble, 1971.

Mace, Dean T. "Marin Mersenne on Language and Music." *Journal of Music Theory* 14 (1970): 2–34.

Major, John M. "*Comus* and *The Tempest.*" *Shakespeare Quarterly* 10 (1959): 177–84.

Mander, M. N. K. "The *Epistola ad patrem:* Milton's Apology for Poetry." *Milton Quarterly* 23 (1989): 158–65.

Manifold, J. S. *The Music in English Drama from Shakespeare to Purcell.* London: Rockliff, 1956.

Marcus, Leah S. *The Politics of Mirth: Jonson, Herrick, Milton, Marvell, and the Defense of Old Holiday Pastimes.* Chicago: University of Chicago Press, 1986.

Marder, Elissa. "Disarticulated Voices: Feminism and Philomela." *Hypatia* 7 (1992): 148–66.

Martz, Louis. "The Music of *Comus.*" In *Illustrious Evidence: Approaches to English Literature of the Early Seventeenth Century,* edited by Earl Miner, 93–113. Berkeley: University of California Press, 1975.

Maus, Katharine Eisaman. "Taking Tropes Seriously: Language and Violence in Shakespeare's *Rape of Lucrece.*" *Shakespeare Quarterly* 37 (1986): 66–82.

Maynard, Winifred. *Elizabethan Lyric Poetry and Its Music.* Oxford: Clarendon, 1986.

Mazzio, Carla. *The Inarticulate Renaissance: Language Trouble in an Age of Eloquence.* Philadelphia: University of Pennsylvania Press, 2009.

McClary, Susan. *Feminine Endings: Music, Gender, and Sexuality.* Minneapolis: University of Minnesota Press, 1991.

McColley, Diane. *Poetry and Music in Seventeenth-Century England.* Cambridge: Cambridge University Press, 1997.

McCullen, Joseph T., Jr. "The Functions of Songs Aroused by Madness in Elizabethan Drama." In *A Tribute to George Coffin Taylor: Studies and Essays, Chiefly Elizabethan, by His Students and Friends,* edited by Arnold Williams, 185–96. Chapel Hill: University of North Carolina Press, 1952.

McGee, Timothy J. *Medieval and Renaissance Music: A Performer's Guide.* Toronto: University of Toronto Press, 1985.

McGuire, Maryann C. *Milton's Puritan Masque.* Athens: University of Georgia Press, 1983.

Mebane, John S. *Renaissance Magic and the Return of the Golden Age: The Occult Tradition and Marlowe, Jonson, and Shakespeare.* Lincoln: University of Nebraska Press, 1989.

Mellers, Wilfrid. "The Double Man: John Dowland, Hamlet, and Seventeenth-Century Melancholy." *Margin* 7 (1988): 53–64.

———. *Harmonious Meeting: A Study of the Relationship between English Music, Poetry and Theatre, c. 1600–1900.* London: Dobson Books, 1965.

———. "John Bull and English Keyboard Music." *Music Quarterly* 40 (1954): 548–71.

Metz, G. Harold. *Shakespeare's Earliest Tragedy: Studies in "Titus Andronicus."* Madison, NJ: Fairleigh Dickinson University Press, 1996.

Meyer-Baer, Kathi. *Music of the Spheres and the Dance of Death: Studies in Musical Iconology.* New York: Da Capo, 1984.

Minear, Erin. "Music and the Crisis of Meaning in *Othello.*" *Studies in English Literature* 49 (2009): 355–70.

Montrose, Louis. *The Purpose of Playing: Shakespeare and the Cultural Politics of the Elizabethan Theatre.* Chicago: University of Chicago Press, 1996.

Naylor, Edward W. *Shakespeare and Music.* London: J. M. Dent, 1896.

Neill, Michael. "'Noises,/Sounds, and sweet airs': The Burden of Shakespeare's *Tempest.*" *Shakespeare Quarterly* 59 (2008): 36–59.

Noble, Richmond. *Shakespeare's Use of Song.* Oxford: Oxford University Press, 1923.

Norbrook, David. "The Reformation of the Masque." In *The Court Masque*, edited by David Lindley, 94–110. Manchester: Manchester University Press, 1984.

Nosworthy, J. M. "Music and Its Function in the Romances of Shakespeare." *Shakespeare Survey* 11 (1958): 60–69.

Nuttall, A. D. "Ovid's Narcissus and Shakespeare's *Richard II:* The Reflected Self." In *Ovid Renewed: Ovidian Influences on Literature and Art from the Middle Ages to the Twentieth Century,* edited by Charles Martindale, 137–50. Cambridge: Cambridge University Press, 1988.

Oakley-Brown, Liz. *Ovid and the Cultural Politics of Translation in Early Modern England.* Aldershot, UK: Ashgate, 2006.

———. "Translating the Subject: Ovid's *Metamorphoses* in England 1560–67." In *Translation and Nation: Towards a Cultural Politics of Englishness,* edited by Roger Ellis and Liz Oakley-Brown, 48–84. Clevedon, UK: Multilingual Matters, 2001.

O'Connell, Michael. *The Idolatrous Eye: Iconoclasm and Theater in Early Modern England.* Oxford: Oxford University Press, 2000.

Ong, Walter J. *Orality and Literacy: The Technologizing of the Word.* London: Routledge, 1988.

Orgel, Stephen. *The Jonsonian Masque.* Cambridge, MA: Harvard University Press, 1967.

Pafford, J. H. P. "Music, and the Songs in *The Winter's Tale.*" *Shakespeare Quarterly* 10 (1959): 161–75.

Palisca, Claude. *Humanism in Italian Renaissance Musical Thought.* New Haven, CT: Yale University Press, 1985.

Patrick, J. Max. "The Problem of Ophelia." In *Studies in Shakespeare,* edited by Arthur D. Matthews and Clark M. Emery, 139–44. Coral Gables, FL: University of Miami Press, 1953.

Patterson, Annabel. *Shakespeare and the Popular Voice.* Oxford: Blackwell, 1989.

Pattison, Bruce. *Music and Poetry of the English Renaissance.* London: Methuen, 1948.

Pearcy, Lee T. *The Mediated Muse: English Translations of Ovid, 1560–1700.* Hamden, CT: Archon, 1984.

Perkins, Leeman L. *Music in the Age of the Renaissance.* New York: W. W. Norton, 1999.

Peyré, Yves. "Niobe and the Nemean Lion: Reading *Hamlet* in the Light of Ovid's *Metamorphoses.*" In *Shakespeare's Ovid,* edited by A. B. Taylor, 126–134. Cambridge: Cambridge University Press, 2000.

Phillippy, Patricia B. "'Loytering in love': Ovid's *Heroides,* Hospitality, and Humanist Education in *The Taming of the Shrew.*" *Criticism* 40 (1998): 30–38.

Pillow, Kirk. *Sublime Understanding: Aesthetic Reflection in Kant and Hegel.* Cambridge, MA: MIT Press, 2000.

Pollack, Janet. "A Reevaluation of *Parthenia* and Its Context." PhD diss., Duke University, 2001.

Price, David C. *Patrons and Musicians of the English Renaissance.* Cambridge: Cambridge University Press, 1981.

Pruett, James. "Charles Butler—Musician, Grammarian, Apiarist." *Musical Quarterly* 49 (1963): 498–509.

Rainbow, Bernarr. "Bathe and His Introduction to Musicke." *Musical Times* 123 (1982): 243–47.

Ronk, Martha. "Locating the Visual in *As You Like It.*" *Shakespeare Quarterly* 52 (2001): 255–76.

Ross, Lawrence J. "Shakespeare's 'Dull Clown' and Symbolic Music." *Shakespeare Quarterly* 17 (1966): 107–28.

Rowe, Katherine A. "Dismembering and Forgetting in *Titus Andronicus.*" *Shakespeare Quarterly* 45 (1994): 279–303.

Rubin, Deborah. *Ovid's "Metamorphoses" Englished: George Sandys as Translator and Mythographer.* New York: Garland, 1985.

Sachs, Klaus-Jürgen. "Boethius and the Judgement of the Ears: A Hidden Challenge in Medieval and Renaissance Music Theory." In *The Second Sense: Studies in Hearing and Musical Judgement from Antiquity to the Seventeenth Century,* edited by Charles Burnett, Michael Fend, and Penelope Gouk, 169–98. London: Warburg Institute, 1991.

Schleiner, Louise. *The Living Lyre in English Verse from Elizabeth through the Restoration.* Columbia: University of Missouri Press, 1984.

Schleiner, Winfried. "Jaques and the Melancholy Stag." *English Language Notes* 17 (1980): 175–79.

Scholes, P. S. *The Puritans and Music.* New York: Russell and Russell, 1962.

Seng, Peter J. *The Vocal Songs in the Plays of Shakespeare.* Cambridge, MA: Harvard University Press, 1967.

Shohet, Lauren. "Figuring Chastity: Milton's Ludlow Masque." In *Menacing Virgins: Representing Virginity in the Middle Ages and Renaissance,* edited by Kathleen Coyne Kelly and Marina Leslie, 146–64. Newark: University of Delaware Press, 1999.

Showalter, Elaine. "Representing Ophelia: Women, Madness, and the Responsibilities of Feminist Criticism." In *Shakespeare and the Question of Theory,* edited by Patricia Parker and Geoffrey Hartman, 77–94. New York: Methuen, 1985.

Simonds, Peggy Muñoz. *Myth, Emblem, and Music in Shakespeare's Cymbeline: An Iconographic Reconstruction.* Newark: University of Delaware Press, 1992.

——. "'Sweet power of music': The Political Magic of 'The Miraculous Harp' in Shakespeare's *The Tempest.*" *Comparative Drama* 29 (1995): 61–90.

Simpson, Claude. *The British Broadside Ballad and Its Music.* New Brunswick, NJ: Rutgers University Press, 1996.

Skura, Meredith. "Discourse and the Individual: The Case of Colonialism in *The Tempest.*" *Shakespeare Quarterly* 40 (1989): 42–69.

Smith, Bruce R. *The Acoustic World of Early Modern England: Attending to the O-Factor.* Chicago: University of Chicago Press, 1999.

——. "The Contest of Apollo and Marsyas: Ideas about Music in the Middle Ages." In *By Things Seen: Reference and Recognition in Medieval Thought,* edited by David L. Jeffrey, 81–107. Ottawa: University of Ottawa Press, 1979.

——. "Hearing Green." In *Reading the Early Modern Passions,* edited by Gail Kern Paster, Katherine Rowe, and Mary Floyd-Wilson, 147–68. Philadelphia: University of Pennsylvania Press, 2004.

Smith, Jeremy L. *Thomas East and Music Publishing in Renaissance England.* Oxford: Oxford University Press, 2003.

Steinberg, Michael P. *Listening to Reason: Culture, Subjectivity, and Nineteenth-Century Music.* Princeton, NJ: Princeton University Press, 2004.

Sternfeld, F. W. *Music in Shakespearean Tragedy.* London: Routledge, 1963.

Stevens, John. *Music and Poetry in the Early Tudor Court.* Cambridge: Cambridge University Press, 1979.

Temperley, Nicholas. "'If any of you be mery let hym synge psalmes': The Culture of Psalms in Church and Home." In *"Noyses, sounds, and sweet aires": Music in Early Modern England,* edited by Jessie Ann Owens, 90–100. Washington, DC: Folger Shakespeare Library, 2006.

Teskey, Gordon. *Allegory and Violence.* Ithaca, NY: Cornell University Press, 1996.

Thomas, Alfred. *A Blessed Shore: England and Bohemia from Chaucer to Shakespeare.* Ithaca, NY: Cornell University Press, 2007.

Thron, E. Michael. "Jaques: Emblems and Morals." *Shakespeare Quarterly* 30 (1979): 84–89.

Tomlinson, Gary. *Music in Renaissance Magic: Toward a Historiography of Others.* Chicago: University of Chicago Press, 1993.

Traister, Barbara Howard. *Heavenly Necromancers: The Magician in English Renaissance Drama.* Columbia: University of Missouri Press, 1984.

Tribble, Evelyn. "Glozing the Gap: Glossing Traditions and *The Shepheardes Calendar.*" *Criticism* 34 (1992): 155–72.

Trubowitz, Rachel. "Sublime/Pauline: Denying Death in *Paradise Lost.*" In *Imagining Death in Spenser and Milton,* edited by Patrick Cheney, Elizabeth Jane Bellamy, and Michael Schoenfeldt, 131–50. New York: Palgrave Macmillan, 2003.

Vickers, Nancy. "'The blazon of sweet beauty's best': Shakespeare's *Lucrece.*" In *Shakespeare and the Question of Theory,* edited by Patricia Parker and Geoffrey Hartman, 95–115. New York: Methuen, 1985.

Waddington, Raymond B. "Moralizing the Spectacle: Dramatic Emblems in *As You Like It.*" *Shakespeare Quarterly* 33 (1982): 155–63.

Walker, D. P. *The Ancient Theology: Studies in Christian Platonism from the Fifteenth to the Eighteenth Century.* London: Duckworth, 1972.

———. "Francis Bacon and *Spiritus.*" In *Science, Medicine and Society in the Renaissance,* edited by A. G. Debus, 2:121–30. New York: Science History Publications, 1972.

———. *Spiritual and Demonic Magic from Ficino to Campanella.* London: Warburg Institute, 1958.

Walls, Peter. "'Comus': The Court Masque Questioned." In *The Well Enchanting Skill: Music, Poetry, and Drama in the Culture of the Renaissance,* edited by John Caldwell, Edward Olleson, and Susan Wollenberg, 107–13. Oxford: Clarendon, 1990.

———. *Music in the English Courtly Masque, 1604–1640.* Oxford: Clarendon, 1996.

Watson, Robert N. "As You Liken It: Simile in the Wilderness." *Shakespeare Survey* 56 (2003): 79–92.

Welsford, Enid. *The Court Masque.* Cambridge: Cambridge University Press, 1927.

Willis, Paul J. "'Tongues in trees': The Book of Nature in *As You Like It.*" *Modern Language Studies* 18 (Summer 1988): 65–74.

Wilson, Christopher R., and Michela Calore. *Music in Shakespeare: A Dictionary.* London: Athlone, 2005.

Winkler, Amanda Eubanks. *O Let Us Howle Some Heavy Note: Music for Witches, the Melancholic, and the Mad on the Seventeenth-Century English Stage.* Bloomington: Indiana University Press, 2006.

Winn, James Anderson. *Unsuspected Eloquence: A History of the Relations between Poetry and Music.* New Haven, CT: Yale University Press, 1981.

Zajko, Vanda. "Petruchio is 'Kated': *The Taming of the Shrew* and Ovid." In *Shakespeare and the Classics,* edited by Charles Martindale and A. B. Taylor, 33–48. Cambridge: Cambridge University Press, 2004.

INDEX

Adelman, Janet, 62
Agrippa, Cornelius, 23, 25, 27
allegory. *See* music: allegory and; Ovid: allegory in
Alpers, Paul, 199
animal sounds, 10, 25, 41, 67–68, 167, 172–73, 200, 229. *See also individual animals*
antitheatricalism, 21, 214–20. *See also* Reformism
Apollo, 182, 200–203. *See also under* Ovid: *Metamorphoses*
Ariosto, 172
Armin, Robert, 140
Ascham, Roger, 127
Attali, Jacques, 142–44, 153
Auden, W. H., 155, 180
Austern, Linda Phyllis, 63, 78

Bach, C. P. E., 57
Bacon, Francis, 128, 178–79
bagpipes, 155, 209, 212
ballads, 50, 57, 151, 202–9, 211. *See also* songs
Barish, Jonas, 219
Bate, Jonathan, 127–28, 173
Bathe, William, 82, 104–5, 113–19
Becon, Thomas, 24–25, 27, 229
bees, 8–10
Bersuire, Pierre, 81, 84
biblical text, 81
birds, 18–19, 29–30, 43, 68, 71–73, 238–41
body
    female, 19, 31–36, 42–43, 69, 76
    music's, 157–64
    physical human, 157–64
Boethius, 89, 96, 104, 107, 127, 130, 231
Bohemia, 198, 205
Bonham Carter, Helena, 60
Booth, Mark, 140
Bradley, A. C., 64–65
Bray, Roger, 105
broken consort, 233

Browne, Sir Thomas, 26, 176
Browning, Judith, 224
Bruce, Susan, 179
Buhler, Stephen, 216, 232
Bull, John, 96–97, 102, 184–90
Bullinger, Heinrich, 25
Burton, Henry, 238
Burton, Robert, 139, 157, 161
Butler, Charles, 8–10, 15, 104, 170
Byrd, William, 185, 187

Calvin, Jean, 23–24
Campion, Thomas, 4
Cappell, Edward, 207
Carroll, William, 205
Case, John, 20, 26, 27, 98–99
Catholicism, 194, 205. *See also* iconography
Chapel Royal, 184
Chapman, George, 145, 185
chastity, 66, 227–28
Chaucer, 82
Chickering, Howell, 177
Christianity. *See also* Reformism
    Ovid and, 81, 84
    Pythagoras and, 99–101
Chua, Daniel, 53
cithara, 231
Coleridge, Samuel, 50, 59
colonialism, 166
counterpoint, 236

Dahlhaus, Carl, 55–56
Danson, Lawrence, 43, 156
David, Richard, 121
Dee, John, 106
deer, 135–36, 138
Diehl, Huston, 181, 189, 191
dogs, 14–15, 29–31, 45, 75, 166–67
Dolven, Jeff, 82, 139
Dow, Christopher, 238
Dowland, John, 186

257

INDEX

dream visions, 159–60, 163
drum, 162
DuBartas, 99
Duffin, Ross, 3, 138
DuRocher, Richard, 80, 221–22, 226

Elizabeth I, 24, 184
Elyot, Sir Thomas, 142
emblems, 6–8, 45, 50, 75, 107, 137–38, 145, 159–60, 188–89
Enterline, Lynn, 18, 47
epithalamiums, 151
Erasmus, 131
etymology, 79, 97–99

Fable of Ovid Treting of Narcissus, The, 86
Faucit, Helena, 58–59
Feltham, Owen, 238
Field, Christopher, 187–88
figuration, 213–20, 229, 241–42
Fish, Stanley, 228
Fludd, Robert, 81, 92–96, 98
    "Temple of Music," 93–95
fly, 33
Folkerth, Wes, 3
Fox-Good, Jacquelyn, 177
Frye, Northrop, 182, 199, 203

Gaffurio, Franchino, 89, 91, 103, 107, 111
Galilei, Vincenzo, 231
Gascoigne, George, 18–19, 43, 72, 238–39
gender roles, 77–78. *See also* women
ghosts, 160, 181, 189–98
Gibbons, Orlando, 185, 187
Golding, Arthur, 81, 83–88, 126, 173
Gosson, Stephen, 30, 101, 214
    Playes Confuted, 146
    Schoole of Abuse, The, 21–27, 32, 91, 132, 146, 229, 231–32, 234–35
Gouk, Penelope, 96, 169
Greene, Robert (*Pandosto*), 198–99
Gresham College, 96–103, 184–85, 188
grief, 41–43, 45, 47
Guillory, John, 239

Hake, Edward, 25
Hanslick, Eduard, 53
harmony, 88–103, 129, 164, 213
    political uses of, 142–43, 144–57
harp, 6–8, 21, 229
Hazlitt, William, 50, 53–54, 55, 57
heresy, 190, 198
hermeticism, 188
hexachords, 188

hieroglyphics, 26–27, 87
Hoffmann, E. T. A., 55
Hollander, John, 3, 124, 146–47
Homer, 21
Hooker, Richard, 26
hornpipe, 155, 211–12
horns, 32
Howard, Jean, 28, 141
humanist education, 130–31, 134–35

iconoclasm, 180–83, 186, 190, 202
iconography, 74, 194, 214, 216, 222–24, 226
idolatry, 12, 180–83, 205. *See also* Reformism
    John Bull and, 184–90
    theater and, 190–98
Ireland, 6–8

James, Heather, 31, 145, 160
James I, 6–8
Jameson, Anna, 56–57
Jewishness, 156
Johnson, Ben, 175
Johnson, Robert, 177
Johnson, Samuel, 239
Jones, Inigo, 220
Jonson, Ben, 219–20
Judd, Cristle Collins, 103

Kendrick, Christopher, 241
Kepler, Johannes, 94
King, Rosalind, 151
Kircher, Athanasius, 94, 119
kithara (cithara), 231

Lake, Arthur, 26
Lamb, Mary Ellen, 183
language, Renaissance theories of, 10
Laudianism and anti-Laudianism, 215, 218, 234
Lavinius, Peter, 81, 84
Lawes, Henry, 232–33, 236, 240–41
Leggatt, Alexander, 133–34
Lindley, David, 140, 169, 209–10, 240
Lodge, Thomas, 91–92
Lupton, Julia Reinhard, 194, 199
lute, 77–78, 93, 103, 230
Luther, Martin, 18–19, 24, 35–36, 43
lyre, 230

Macrobius, 89, 162
madness, 47–51, 159
magic, 12, 164–65, 167–70, 172–73, 181–82, 193–94, 205
Marlowe, Christopher, 238–39

marriage, 133, 141, 151
Martz, Louis, 229
masques
  antitheatricalism and, 216–20, 234
  music and, 228–42
  Ovid and, 221–28
  wedding, 141, 174–76
mathematics, 2, 16–17, 79, 91, 99, 106–13, 115–19
McClary, Susan, 17, 20, 48, 54
McGuire, Maryann, 218
melancholy, 139, 160–61, 163
Mersenne, Marin, 94
Metz, G. Harold, 28
Milton, 141
  "Ad Patrem," 230–31
  "L'Allegro," 239
  A Maske, 12, 214–42
  Arcades, 234, 239
  Areopagitica, 213–215, 235–37, 242
  "At A Solemn Music," 233–34
  Elegy 6, 230
  Lycidas, 234
  "On the Harmony of the Spheres," 213–14, 236–37
  "On the Morning of Christ's Nativity," 201, 239
  Paradise Lost, 216, 238–40
  "The Passion," 229–30
Minear, Erin, 149, 151
misogyny, 59
Moritz, Karl Philipp, 56
Morley, Thomas, 82, 104–13, 114, 115, 116, 131
Mountfort, Susan, 51–52, 63
music
  absolute music, 53–56
  acoustic theories of, 93, 169
  allegory and, 6–8, 11, 80–89, 93, 99–101, 137–41, 147, 163–64
  Boethian definition of, 79, 156
  composition practices, 187–89
  defenses of, 20–21, 26–27, 98–99
  femininity and, 27–28, 31, 46–47, 60–61, 78
  heavenly music (*musica mundana*), 163, 174, 188–89, 213–14, 233–34, 236–37, 241
  materiality of, 157–64
  modern theories of, 16–17, 105
  musical sympathy, 36–37
  nature and, 8–10
  notation of, 22–23, 109–11
  philology and, 79, 97–99, 103
  poetry, relationship to, 3–5, 8, 20–21, 121, 229–31
  physical production of, 30, 75–76
  Reformist criticism of, 23–28, 91–92, 165, 183, 186, 203, 232
  teaching of, 78–80, 96–119, 126, 131–32, 142–43
  visual representation of, 63–64, 73–74, 79, 89, 91, 93–95, 106–8, 111–12, 116–19
musica ficta, 188
musica speculativa, 8, 23, 88–113, 142–44, 148, 154–55. *See also* music: allegory and; Pythagoras
musical instruments. *See individual instruments*
musical scale, 109–10, 113–15

natural philosophy, 97
Neoplatonism, 11, 141, 143, 152–53, 157, 159–60, 162–64, 174–79, 182–83, 199
Newton, Isaac, 96
nightingale, 18–19, 42, 71–73, 221, 227
Noble, Richmond, 3
noise, 10, 15, 149, 170–71, 198–99, 212
Norbrook, David, 215
North, Thomas, 13

Orgel, Stephen, 182, 219
Ovid
  allegory in, 12–15, 80–88, 92–93, 99–101, 128–29, 136–37, 152, 154, 223–25
  Amores, 127–28, 238
  Ars Amatoria, 130–31, 133
  Heroides, 130–32
    Ariadne, 176–77
  Metamorphoses, 12, 37
    Actaeon, 38–39, 123, 135–36
    Apollo, 129, 225
    Arachne, 200–201
    Autolycus and Philammon, 124, 183, 202–9
    Canens and Picus, 172–73
    Charybdis, 228
    Chione, 203
    Circe, 165, 172–73, 222–24
    Daphne, 217, 225
    Deucalion and Pyrrha, 100–101
    Echo, 221–22
    Hecuba, 40–41, 45, 50, 66, 74–75
    Io, 38, 129
    Jove and Europa, 127–28, 200
    Medea, 165, 173–74
    Mercury, 202–3
    Neptune, 200
    Niobe, 45, 76

Ovid (*continued*)
　Metamorphoses (*continued*)
　　Orpheus, 34–35, 39–40, 69–71, 100, 171–74, 176–78, 219
　　Phaëthon, 197
　　Philomela, 18–19, 34–35, 38–39, 42, 50, 66, 69, 71–73, 221–22, 227–28, 238–40
　　Polyxena, 41
　　Pygmalion, 183, 194–98, 210
　　Pythagoras, 82–83, 125–26
　　Scylla, 222–28
　Milton and, 214–16, 221–28
　moralizing interpretations of (*see* Ovid: allegory in)
　Reformist attacks on, 221–25
　sensuous qualities of poetry, 85–88
　sympathy and, 36–43
Ovide Moralisé, 81
Oxford University, 188

Pafford, J. H. P., 205
paganism, 197
Palisca, Claude, 79, 88
Parthenia, 185, 187–88
pastoral, 198–212
Paul, Jean (*Hesperus*), 56
Paul, Saint, 191
Peacham, Henry, 6–8, 145
Peend, Thomas, 76
Petrarchan poetry, 68–69, 123
Petty, William, 96–97, 102
Phillippy, Patricia, 131
Pilkington, Francis, 110
Pillow, Kirk, 49
pipe, 92–93
Platonism, 94
Pollack, Janet, 185, 188
polyphony, 24–25, 27–28, 216, 229, 232–35
Praetorius, 79
prayer, 196–97
Prince Edward, 187
Prince Henry, 187
Princess Elizabeth, 187
promiscuity
　of music, 19, 82, 157
　of women, 27–28, 31, 228
Protestantism. *See* Reformism
Prynne, William, 27, 46, 214, 217–18, 228, 238
psalms, 25, 209, 211
Ptolemy, 107
Puritanism. *See* Reformism
Puttenham, George, 4, 121, 124, 151, 155–56

Pythagoras, 82–83, 91–93, 99–102, 163, 213, 236–37
　discovery of music, 88–91

Quint, David, 160

rape
　of Lavinia, 19, 31, 38, 42
　of Lucrece, 67–76
　of Philomela, 227
Ravenscroft, Thomas, 106
Reformism, 180–81, 196, 211–12, 214–16, 229, 232–42. *See also* antitheatricalism; music: Reformist criticism of
rhetoric, 43, 121–22
　teaching of, 41, 84
Robinson, Thomas, 103
Romano, Giulio, 190
Romanticism
　interpretation of Ophelia, 48–51
　theories of music, 51–65
Rosicrucianism, 94
Ross, Lawrence, 148
Rothstein, Edward, 16
Rousseau, 56
Rowley, Samuel, 186–87

sacred and profane art, 198–212
Sandys, George, 81, 84, 87–88
Seng, Peter, 62, 207
sexuality, 151–52, 194–96
　female, 48, 58–64
　in music, 202–9
Shakespeare
　As You Like It, 82, 134–41
　Cymbeline, 157–60, 162
　Hamlet, 11, 44, 45–51, 65, 69, 82, 166
　　Ophelia, 51–65
　Henry IV, Part Two, 153
　King John, 153
　Julius Caesar, 146–48
　Love's Labour's Lost, 82, 119–22
　A Midsummer Night's Dream, 13–15
　Much Ado About Nothing, 162
　Othello, 148–52
　Pericles, 157, 160–64
　Richard II, 152–53
　The Merchant of Venice, 1–2, 154–57
　The Merry Wives of Windsor, 212
　The Rape of Lucrece, 11, 45–46, 50–51, 65–76, 239
　The Taming of the Shrew, 77–78, 82, 126–30, 196
　The Tempest, 157, 164–79, 180, 183

Titus Andronicus, 11, 19–20, 28–36, 48, 68, 82, 136
Troilus and Cressida, 144–46
Twelfth Night, 82, 122–26
The Winter's Tale, 12, 124, 180–83, 189–98, 212, 240
Showalter, Elaine, 47–48, 52
Sidney, Philip, 124
Simmons, Jean, 60
Smith, Bruce, 3, 14
songs, 58–63, 124, 140, 149, 202–9. *See also* ballads
sound, 19–20, 29–31, 50–51, 93, 169
　meaning and, 8–10
　musica speculative and, 103–13
　musical performance and, 113–19
　natural, 167–70
　visual allegory and, 8
Spenser, 172, 231
St. Omer's Cathedral, 185, 189
stage directions, musical, 28–29, 32
statues, 181–82, 190–98, 205
Sternfeld, F. W., 60
stone and stoniness, 40–41, 45–46
Strachey, Edward, 55–56
Striggio, 111
Stubbes, Philip, 22, 27
subjectivity, 47–48, 54, 155–56, 162, 177, 210–12
sublimity, 49, 54, 57–58
superstition, 12, 181, 191, 193
Swetnam, Joseph, 27
sympathy, 36–41, 45

Taverner, John, 27, 81, 137, 154, 184–88
　Gresham College music lectures, 96–103
Teskey, Gordon, 77, 126
theater. *See* antitheatricalism; idolatry: theater and

Thomas, Alfred, 205
travel (experience), 139
Triest, Johann Karl Friedrich, 57
Troy, representations of, 74–75, 144–45, 172
trumpet, 20, 29, 162
Tye, Christopher, 187

Venus, 194, 197
viol, 230
Virgil
　Aeneid, 94, 159, 171
　Eclogues, 134, 234
voice and voicelessness, 12, 19–20, 32, 34–36, 37, 63, 240

Wagner, Richard, 11, 167
warbling, 18, 71, 238–41
Ward, John, 184–85
Welsford, Enid, 218
Whitney, Geffrey, 107
Willis, Paul, 141
Wilson, John, 204
Wilson, Thomas, 84
wind instruments, 234
Wingate, Charles, 51–52
Winkler, Amanda, 60
women, 11. *See also* music: femininity and
　gender roles, 77–78, 131
　promiscuity of, 27–28, 31, 228
　sexuality, 48, 58–64
　and speech, 27–28, 45–51, 65–76
　as students of music, 82
Wood, Anthony, 184
Wright, Louis B., 203
Wright, Thomas, 139, 161–62

Zajko, Vanda, 128
Zarlino, Gioseffo, 89, 107